Theodicies in Conflict

Recent Titles in
Contributions to the Study of Religion
Series Editor: Henry W. Bowden

Theodicies in Conflict

A DILEMMA IN PURITAN ETHICS AND NINETEENTH-CENTURY AMERICAN LITERATURE

Richard Forrer

CONTRIBUTIONS TO THE STUDY OF RELIGION, NUMBER 17

GREENWOOD PRESS

NEW YORK · WESTPORT, CONNECTICUT · LONDON

Library of Congress Cataloging-in-Publication Data

Forrer, Richard.
   Theodicies in conflict.

   (Contributions to the study of religion, ISSN
0196-7053 ; no. 17)
   Bibliography: p.
   Includes index.
   1. American literature—19th century—History and
criticism.   2. Theodicy in literature.   3. Puritans—
United States.   4. Christian ethics—United States—
History.   5. Religion and literature.   I. Title.
II. Series.
PS217.T48F67   1986   810'.9'382   85-27220
ISBN 0-313-25191-6 (lib. bdg. : alk. paper)

Library of Congress Catalog Card Number: 85-27220
ISBN: 0-313-25191-6
ISSN: 0196-7053

First published in 1986

Greenwood Press, Inc.
88 Post Road West
Westport, Connecticut 06881

Printed in the United States of America

The paper used in this book complies with the
Permanent Paper Standard issued by the National
Information Standards Organization (Z39.48-1984).

10 9 8 7 6 5 4 3 2 1

Copyright Acknowledgments

Grateful acknowledgment is given for permission to quote from *Significa* by Irving Wallace, David Wallechinsky, and Amy Wallace (New York: E. P. Dutton, Inc., 1983). Portions of chapter 1, "A Dilemma in Puritan Ethics," appeared in different form as Richard Forrer's "The Puritan Religious Dilemma: The Ethical Dimensions of God's Sovereignty," in *Journal of the American Academy of Religion,* vol. XLIV (December 1976), pp. 613–28 and is reprinted by permission. Portions of chapter 7, "James Fenimore Cooper's Leatherstocking Novels: A Hybrid Theodicy," appeared in different form as Richard Forrer's "The Recovery of the Puritan Theodicy in Cooper's Leatherstocking Novels," in *Journal of the American Studies Association of Texas,* vol. XII (1981), Copyright © American Studies Association of Texas and is reprinted by permission.

For Jim and Jennifer

Contents

Foreword

Throughout the history of human intellectual systems many thinkers have tried to reconcile ideas about divine justice with the existence of evil. Their conclusions have succeeded in explaining, at least temporarily, relationships between heaven and human action. But answers become dated because social conditions change and because different perspectives raise new questions. This study analyzes several classic positions on the question of theodicy, thereby setting the context for understanding how American culture developed during some of its more formative stages.

The Puritans brought to the New World an ideology that resolved tension between divine sovereignty and human will by making moral responsibility subordinate to God's majesty. Later thinkers found this relationship unacceptable because they perceived God as less awesome and their world as less amoral. Mercantile society and confidence in rationalism called for a new metaphysics, one more compatible with democratic life than that afforded by the old orthodox pronouncements. Richard Forrer makes these opposing sensibilities plain. He expounds the reasoning behind each of the antithetical viewpoints and shows why egalitarian influences came to exert increased emphasis in American strivings for a moral order. In so doing, he provides a useful capsule of intellectual development from the Mathers and Edwards to Mayhew, Chauncy, and Channing.

But that is only the beginning of Forrer's accomplishment. After these two strains of American theology reached an impasse, they did not die from mutual attrition or lack of creative discussion. They penetrated the larger world of American ideas, particularly the sphere of imaginative literature where powerful thinkers considered them again in light of new contexts. Forrer's most important achievement is to stress this continuity and to discuss emergent American literature in light of these traditional theological conundrums. The best creative writers in American fiction continued to ask Puritan questions, and the works of Cooper, Hawthorne, Emerson, and Melville are better understood with that perspective in mind. These authors were not theologians in disguise but, as Forrer shows, serious explorers of meaning on the growing edge of American experience. Further, by defining humanity within both alternatives of the theological stalemate, these literary figures probed for solutions to the conceptual problem while constructing a new genre of belles lettres. The strength of this book is not that it makes literature secondary to philosophical concerns, but rather that it shows how such enduring preoccupations about human responsibility and evil lie at the core of early American literature.

This careful study provides clear exposition of an early current in American thought. It accomplishes a much larger task as well: by delineating the general problem of early democracy, it maps out a helpful context for literary analysis in this country. Forrer takes early models of the cosmos and shows how those ways of explaining and relating to the world were challenged within the Puritan tradition itself. Then he explains how fictional writers tapped the imaginative potential in that heritage in order to interpret human experience in new ways and to comprehend both the potential and limits of democratic society. As Americans moved west, their ideas and behavior changed in dynamic ways. Literary figures of that time were custodians of American culture while they developed its sensitivities. Their work expressed, in Forrer's words, "the new feelings, thoughts, and conflicts that were gradually welling up from the moils of social, political, and religious change taking place in nineteenth-century America." This book helps us see how that was so.

H. W. Bowden

Acknowledgments

At various stages in the preparation of this book, I have received the generous assistance and helpful criticism of many colleagues, friends, and students. I wish especially to mention the critical responses of Paul Boller, James Moseley, James Duke, Claudia Camp, Ronald Flowers, and Sally Stewart. These people helped to make this a better book. Special thanks are due my good friend and colleague James Rurak, who has been unfailing in his encouragement, probing questions, and stimulating insights. To him I dedicate this book.

Several people assisted my research and helped to prepare this manuscript: Mathew Swora, Cathy Cralle, Robert Davis, Ryan Hazen, Nancy Bailey, John Regan, John Dungan. The computer expertise of N. S. Ranganath and Larry Grummer deserves special mention; both rendered meticulous assistance. Nancy Brown's sure eye for syntax made this a more readable manuscript; her constant support was invaluable.

This book has its origins in classes I had with Giles Gunn. I wish to thank him for his support, criticism, and understanding during my graduate years.

I wish to thank Kenneth Lawrence, chairman of the Religion-Studies Department at Texas Christian University, for reducing my teaching responsibilities during the early stages of writing. His patience and understanding, as both a friend and a colleague, have been a constant source of encouragement.

This project was supported by several grants from the Texas Christian University Research Foundation and funds provided by the Graduate Studies and Research Division of the University.

A final word of thanks must be extended to my friends and colleagues on the Religion-Studies faculty who have provided a congenial atmosphere for testing and working out the ideas that shape this book.

Theodicies in Conflict

Introduction

American Puritanism has profoundly shaped the development of American culture, but defining the nature of this influence is still a subject of much controversy. Perhaps one of the more controversial, or at least more variegated, areas in Puritan studies is that which treats the relationship between Puritanism and the emergence of the American literary tradition. Many such studies define Puritan themes or imagery in American writings, others explore how the Puritan outlook influenced the subject matter or literary structure itself, while others show how Puritanism created particular kinds of paradigms for understanding human experience which subsequently are embodied in literary works, shaping the modes of experience they dramatize.

Another possible approach, the one employed in this study, is to demonstrate how Puritanism gives rise to particular models of the cosmos which established culturally prescribed ways for relating to the world, how these models are challenged within the Puritan tradition itself, and then how these models are subsequently appropriated by such writers as William Dunlap, James Fenimore Cooper, Nathaniel Hawthorne, Ralph Waldo Emerson, and Herman Melville as a means for comprehending and evaluating the social, moral, and religious conflicts generated by American democratic structures and the westward expansion of American society from 1800 to 1860.

Puritan writers most fully articulated these models of the cosmos in their treatment of the problem of theodicy, a problem which increasingly vexed not only orthodox Puritan theologicans during the seventeenth and eighteenth centuries but also the more liberal theologians of the late 1700s and early 1800s. It is this increasingly insistent, sometimes harried, sometimes frantic response to the problem of theodicy as well as the problematical tensions it eventually created which can help us better understand several important works of American literature written between 1798 and 1860.

Tracing its development will establish the context for a literary analysis which shows how some American writers incorporated Puritan cultural premises within their fictive worlds as critical tools for comprehending and evaluating their own contemporary world—how some of the fictive worlds they created released the imaginative potential within their Puritan heritage for viewing and appropriating human experience in new ways.

The first part of this book defines a dilemma endemic to Puritan ethics— the dilemma of how to reconcile belief in God's sovereignty with a meaningful notion of moral striving. It describes how this initial dilemma gave rise to a theological debate—a debate which reaches back at least to the tension between the Davidic kingship and the prophets[1]—regarding the adequacy of two contrary theodicies for interpreting human experience. In the American Protestant tradition, these theodicies provided diametrically opposed alternatives for articulating the religious meanings of the continuing encounter with the changing American environment.[2]

The two theodicies which are the focus of this debate, the Puritan theodicy and the rationalistic theodicy, expressed contrasting visions of God and His relationship to humankind. The Puritan theodicy advocated a sovereign God who orchestrates all happenings, creating a symphonic whole in which everything that happens, for good or ill, has its necessary and rightful place in His redemptive plan for the universe. Everything happens as it does because it expresses God's justice and mercy; even His arbitrary election of some to eternal salvation and others, the vast majority of humankind, to eternal damnation expresses divine justice and mercy. The seemingly arbitrary and amoral aspects of human experience are presented as having an underlying logic which God dictates, but which is beyond human comprehension. The Puritan theodicy thus based its model of reality on the mysterious and incomprehensible redemptive purposes of a sovereign deity.

The rationalistic theodicy, on the other hand, portrayed a rational and benevolent democratic deity who refuses to abuse His power over His creation, who voluntarily acts within established ethical limits in His responses to humankind, who honors people's claims to equitable treatment as an inalienable right, who grants people the freedom to determine their own religious destinies, who is a paternalistic deity helping everyone to achieve salvation. In short, the rationalistic theodicy based its model of reality on a God whose traits are the matching opposites of those the Puritans attributed to Him.

Hence these two theodicies are predicated on opposing religious modes of experiencing the world which determine their respective understandings

of the world and of what constitutes appropriate moral and religious behavior. Each provides a metaphysic which describes a cosmic moral order
and each demonstrates how the style of life dictated by this metaphysic is
the logical outcome of the described moral structure of reality.

This kind of synthesizing activity exemplifies what Clifford Geertz understands to be the essential function any religion performs for any culture.[3] Religion, he argues, provides both a general model of reality or "world
view"—its conception of the world, the self, and the relations between
them—and a normative model for behavior or "ethos"—the aesthetic and
moral life style it recommends people should live in such a world. Geertz
argues that religious symbols, especially when combined with religious rituals, make a group's ethos rationally and morally acceptable by showing
how the style of life it endorses is fully conformable to the cosmic order
which the world view depicts, while the world view itself is rendered credible by presenting its image of cosmic order as ideally synchronized with
such a life style. The world view defines a distinctive way of thinking about
the world, while the ethos prescribes "a preferred mode of experiencing"—or feeling about and reacting to—the cosmic order described by the
world view.[4]

However, any synthesis of world view and ethos, according to Geertz,
defines not only what is desirable in the world it describes but also what
is undesirable. The reality of evil is acknowledged when religious rituals
employing sacred symbols dramatize the conflict between good and evil, a
conflict that often seems inexplicably weighted in favor of evil. The existence of evil as manifested in seemingly arbitrary and inexplicable events
suggests that the world is chaotic, without a rational or moral order, and
that no reliable basis exists for making sound moral judgments.

A society thus moves "from a troubled perception of disorder" toward
the formulation of an image of an ordered world, an image that dramatizes how the ambiguous interrelationships between good and evil are the
logical or rational outcome of the moral structure of reality.[5] A successful
fusion of world view and ethos "will account for, and even celebrate the
perceived ambiguities, puzzles, and paradoxes in human experience."[6]
Without such a synthesis of world view and ethos, Geertz concludes, or
when such a synthesis no longer remains authoritative for people, their
experience loses all form and order and they experience the world as an
inexplicable and threatening reality.[7]

The Puritan tradition did not experience such a crisis until the latter half
of the seventeenth century. The founding Puritans had synthesized a world
view and ethos through allegiance to their vision of a religious Utopia.
They believed that God had formed a special covenant with them which
promised them unique privileges and rewards if they carried out the sacred
errand of building the New Jerusalem in the American wilderness, and

which also stipulated that He would punish them, destroy their society if necessary, if the Puritans failed to complete their special "errand into the wilderness."

No more than a generation later, and throughout the seventeenth century, Puritan preachers increasingly complained—in what Robert Pope calls the "myth of declension"[8]—that Puritan society was becoming immoral, irreligious, and materialistic, that it was betraying its allegiance to the religious Utopia envisioned by the founding Puritans, and that God would therefore destroy it unless the people reaffirmed the founders' covenant with God to build the New Jerusalem in the American wilderness. But rather than being destroyed, New England was developing into a bustling commercial society, and the ways of becoming successful in this commercial society violated the kinds of obligations by which the Puritans measured loyalty to the covenant.

It seemed to many second- and third-generation Puritans that God was discarding the "errand into the wilderness" which He Himself had inspired. If this were so, they argued, then God was also nullifying the system of rewards and punishments established by the covenant and thereby divesting all moral striving of any reliable basis. How could they define any moral order shaping human affairs, they asked, if God had altered His response to the behavior He Himself had prescribed for them within the framework of the covenant? In short, many were questioning whether the synthesis of world view and ethos which the covenant theology described deserved allegiance in an environment that no longer seemed to confirm or require such a world view or ethos.

Side by side, however, with the founders' affirmation of a God who abides (within the framework of the covenant) by a predictable system of rewards and punishments is the affirmation of a sovereign deity who disregards all human expectations and canons of justice. The paradox of the Puritans' belief in the covenant theology is that it seems they accepted a sovereign God as a primary source of order so long as they believed that they were successfully making the American wilderness conform to their vision of God's city on earth. But when it became apparent that faithful adherence to the founders' vision of a New Jerusalem in the American wilderness could not guarantee the success of their errand, that the covenant theology itself no longer articulated their experience of the contemporary world, then such an awesome God became morally problematical to them as they sought both an adequate world view for explaining the changes taking place around them and an appropriate ethos that would enable them to survive within such an environment.

Here, then, was a basic dilemma in Puritan ethics during the latter part of the seventeenth and early part of the eighteenth century: to demonstrate how the notion of a sovereign God, whose inscrutability and power could not be defined or comprehended either in terms of human ethical standards or in terms of the covenant theology, could provide a reliable foundation for morality within the framework of a commercial society. The issue at stake here, as theologians recognized, was whether they could cast the orthodox notion of a sovereign God into a theodicy which provides a rationally acceptable explanation for the seemingly arbitrary and amoral aspects of human experience, and, in so doing, make ethically acceptable those aspects of God that made Him seem arbitrary and amoral.

To be sure, many Puritan preachers—through church sermons, election sermons, histories of New England, collections of divine providences, biographies, and autobiographies—responded to this development by reaffirming the founders' covenant with God. They argued that its synthesis of world view and ethos still constituted the normative understanding of Puritan experience. But such important Puritan spokesmen as Urian Oakes, Increase Mather, Cotton Mather, Samuel Willard, and Jonathan Edwards sought to articulate their experience of the changing American environment in terms of a world view and ethos that were compatible with their belief in a sovereign God. This fusion of world view and ethos constituted the Puritan theodicy.

However, such factors as the more democratic cultural climate of the latter 1700s and early 1800s, the emergence of deism, and an increasing skepticism in religious matters prompted many to reject the Puritan theodicy and its synthesis of world view and ethos. Such representative liberal theologians as Jonathan Mayhew, Charles Chauncy, and William Ellery Channing argued that the sovereign God of Puritan orthodoxy is an amoral deity, an unjust tyrant, whose arbitrary disposition of human destinies denies people any reliable foundation for the moral life. Such seeming capriciousness on God's part represented to these theologians not only an unwarranted abuse of divine power but also the same gross disrespect for human life against which they struggled in earthly authorities. Their orientation toward the increasingly democratic ethos of American culture led them to reject the Puritan theodicy as ethically unacceptable and to replace it with a theodicy which was its opposite, a theodicy which expressed the rationalistic and egalitarian moral values shaping the emerging American Republic.

The rationalistic theodicy thus redefined God's sovereignty and the self's relationship to that sovereignty in a way which reconciled it with democratic values. People could now imagine that their egalitarian dictates actually mirrored the universal moral order; they could relate to the world and God as though both confirmed the strictest human canons of justice. Liberal theologians thus believed that they had created a successful fusion of the rationalistic world view and ethos which preserved the possibility of believing in a sovereign but humane God within an egalitarian society.[9]

By the early 1800s, then, Americans had formulated in these two theodicies, the Puritan and the rationalistic, two antithetical ways of experiencing the world, opposing models which articulated alternative religious meanings for the Puritans' encounter with a changing American environment. During the first half of the nineteenth century, theologians were still using these models to reflect on the moral and religious implications of American democracy. But the debate about the respective merits of these two theodicies had reached a theological stalemate. Liberal theologians would consider nothing less than a sweeping repudiation of the Puritan theodicy as portraying an amoral universe; conservative theologians castigated the liberal theologians for describing a world that mirrored the human conscience rather than the "Wholly Other" whose mysterious and unpredictable ways made Him, not humankind, the center of the universe. No significant advance in the debate seemed possible until the adequacy of these theodicies for explaining the moral ambiguities of human experience could be tested in the unfolding and rapidly changing reality of American life itself.

Such a testing was in fact forced upon the adherents of the rationalistic theodicy by the westward expansion of society. Although this theodicy seemed to be an appropriate expression of human experience in an increasingly democratic and relatively developed society, the social and personal conflicts created by experiences on the ever-expanding frontier posed moral and religious problems that seemed unanswerable within the framework of such a theodicy. Many turned once again to the Puritan theodicy in an effort to understand and evaluate the social, moral, and religious conflicts which were generated by this new democratic "errand into the wilderness."[10] The result was an experienced conflict between two opposing modes for understanding and responding to the world without any apparent means for reconciling them. Hence the predicament internal to Puritan ethics, and the ways in which theologians dealt with it, became endemic elements shaping the unresolved theological dilemma within early American democracy.

At the same time, when it seemed evident that new strategies would have to be developed for breaking this theological impasse, we find such early- and mid-nineteenth-century authors as William Dunlap, James Fenimore Cooper, Nathaniel Hawthorne, Ralph Waldo Emerson, and Herman Melville exploring various efforts to create from the complexities of American experience a successful fusion of world view and ethos. These authors variously appropriated for dramatic purposes the religious ways of experiencing the world—how the self feels and thinks and acts when it accepts the religious premises—which theologians had formulated in the Puritan and rationalistic theodicies. They in fact explore in some of their major writings the adequacy of both the Puritan and rationalistic theodicies as explanations of human affairs; a few explore the possibility of synthesizing both theodicies into a more comprehensive understanding of human experience. Though these writers may not have deliberately set out to resolve the theological debate about two contrasting theodicies, still Puritan and liberal theologians and these writers seem preoccupied with the problem of synthesizing a world view and ethos. Furthermore, they formulate this problem in precisely the same terms—those of the Puritan and rationalistic theodicies.

Indeed, the thesis of this book is that the writers it analyzes were themselves participants, whether consciously or not, in a theological debate endemic to the formation of early American culture; that they, furthermore, reconceptualized the debate in ways that allowed people to redefine their humanity by living *within* the unsettled dilemma; and that in so doing they expanded the debate to the point of creating a new horizon for understanding its religious, moral, and social implications, thereby providing potential resources for moving beyond the theological stalemate. They were not theologians in disguise. Rather, they were writers whose explorations of the psychological, moral, and religious consequences of the contrasting religious premises shaping the theological debate established the foundation for a new literary tradition. Thus did these premises become critical tools in the efforts of these writers to make sense of and to evaluate the conflicts resulting from the democratic structures and the expansion of American society between 1800 and 1860.

It will be equally important to determine how the religious premises these writers employed function within their works—how they shape the content, form, and structure of the world of any particular work. Their use of these religious premises helps explain, for example, the metaphysical qualities which such critics as Richard Chase, Lionel Trilling, Richard Poirier, and A. D. Van Nostrand attribute to many American writings.[11] Certainly those works examined here are more concerned with the self's relation to the universe than to society. The self in these works is typically defined in terms of a cosmic order. The self adopts a style of life which fully conforms to that order by fusing a world view and ethos in a way that gives life coherence and meaning. The dramatic narrative and the process of synthesizing a world view and ethos go hand in hand: the narrative gives rise to an ethos and world view; the process of integrating the two gives structure and meaning to the narrative.

Another influence of the religious premises shaping these works can be summarized this way: all of these works focus on the self's confrontation with the reality of evil. Such a claim might perhaps be made about many works from any literary tradition. But a fundamental difference lies in the fact that in the American works examined here the self characteristically experiences and confronts evil on religious grounds, not as a social phenomenon but as a metaphysical reality, as a structuring principle of human existence. The self resolves its confrontation with evil by seeking to demonstrate how its mode of experiencing the world gives rise to a world view and ethos and to a synthesis of the two which makes evil a rationally comprehensible and morally acceptable component of human experience. This again is the metaphysical drama of the self implied in the Puritan and rationalistic theodicies.

Focusing upon this drama of the self also helps to explain why there are so many solitary or "marginal" figures in these works. Their isolation is not simply a matter of fleeing from society; it also results in part from their efforts to find—or to create or define—a space wherein they can seek answers to religious questions in ways that society denies them. It might be said, in many cases at least, that such figures seek out experiences beyond the pale of conventionally accepted behavior in order to establish a new framework for solving the problem of evil. Being on the margin of society means in these works that the self defines itself in terms of realities or experiences that defy traditional moral and religious categories. This ambiguous situation provides a testing ground for exploring the possibilities and limitations of the religious premises shaping the Puritan and rationalistic theodicies.

What we discover in these fictions is that being on the margin of society often gives rise to a mode of vision which has a potential for synthesizing these religious premises that is lacking in traditional theological resources. But achieving this fusion remains a problem because this synthesizing mode of vision is evoked, and also constantly challenged, by the ambiguities of experience. The barriers to realizing such a synthesis are no less important for understanding these works than the attempt to achieve it. Hence these works dramatize the problematical nature of the self's efforts to create a successful fusion of world view and ethos in the kind of world that confronts the self.

The attempt here to interpret particular literary works in terms of the theological debate outlined above is not intended to make their literary values a secondary concern. Little can be said about the historical significance of a literary work unless we first understand the uniqueness of the experience it renders, the logic of the world within which that experience occurs, and how the author makes us participate in that experience so that the values it discloses seem compelling to us. Such formal concerns will be addressed in the analysis of each work. But these concerns will also be related to the fact that these literary works re-present different modes of experiencing the world which make a particular world view and ethos, when fused together, seem a plausible way to integrate the self with the cosmos. In so doing, they explore the kinds of possibilities for human existence which emerge within the world envisioned by the premises which shape both the Puritan and rationalistic theodicies.

It is in this sense that these religious premises become organizing principles of literary form in most of the works studied here. To describe structurally how this is, in fact, the case can help us in part define their authors as distinctively American writers.[12] Certainly the attempt explored in these works to create and to fuse a world view and ethos is, as Clifford Geertz reminds us, a universal religious phenomenon; it is in no way unique to these works. What is distinctive about these works is that they formulated this effort in the same terms as did their theological predecessors.

This book does not try to establish that this resemblance amongst divergent American writings defines a historical continuity, even though it seems reasonable to assume that the wide-ranging consistency of such resemblances points toward some kind of historical continuity. Rather, the value of this kind of study is that it suggests how some of the acknowledged classics of the American literary tradition have explored and evaluated those religious meanings attributed to the "American experience" which are based on the religious premises inherited from the Puritan legacy. It demonstrates how the authors selected for study have sought to complicate or even modify habitual Protestant modes of experiencing the world by creating fictive constructs that test the limitations of those modes and their possibilities for releasing new interpretations of human experience. These authors are, in the best sense, both religious critics of Protestant culture and cultural critics of Protestant religion.

Indeed, such writers as William Dunlap, James Fenimore Cooper, Nathaniel Hawthorne, Ralph Waldo Emerson, and Herman Melville ultimately reformulated the Puritan legacy, whether consciously or unconsciously, in ways that gradually expanded it beyond the confines of conventional theological discourse. They repossessed this theological inheritance as a usable critical resource for exploring and evaluating the moral and religious problems of early nineteenth-century culture. And by thus repossessing this religious legacy through narrative constructs, these writers contributed to the making of a new literary tradition, itself a great legacy which provides valuable resources for helping us reappropriate our various religious inheritances within a pluralistic society.

PART ONE

A THEOLOGICAL LEGACY

1

A Dilemma in Puritan Ethics

THE PURITAN WORLD VIEW AND ETHOS

The Puritans were a hard-nosed people; they had to be since they daily
lived, as it were, eyeball to eyeball with a hard-nosed God. Here was a
sovereign God who, as supreme Lord over all creation, spared or destroyed human lives and consigned people to eternal salvation or damnation without regard for their individual merit; a stern God who, as Roger
Williams puts it, often required of even His own people, the elect, that
they "[lie] down in the Dust that God may tread upon them, and be exalted";[1] an incomprehensible God whose "works"—to quote Increase
Mather—"sometimes seem to run counter with his word: so that there is
a dark and amazing intricacie in the ways of providence";[2] a punitive God
who, in Cotton Mather's portrayal, gave evil dominance over the world as
a means both to punish humankind and to thwart the good they sought
to accomplish in their daily activities. This vision of God allowed no room
for spiritual squeamishness, though Cotton Mather, that staunchest of Puritans, does let himself lament that God's way of structuring human existence is "enough to make one *sick of the world*."[3]

Nor did this vision of God give much leeway for questioning His treatment of humankind. There is in fact no Job-like voice of protest against
God in American Puritanism. The Puritan was taught that the ways of
God, though often mysterious, were nevertheless unquestionably right because He *is* God; that the inequities of human experience expressed either
God's exaltation of some persons over others or God's just punishment of
sinners; that one's situation in life, no matter how undesirable or unmerited, was one of the millions of small lynchpins God created in order to

hold the world together in the precise way necessary for realizing His ultimate purposes.[4] As John Calvin puts it: "The will of God is the supreme
rule of righteousness, so that everything which he wills must be held to be
righteous by the mere fact of his willing it. Therefore, when it is asked
why the Lord did so, we must answer, Because he pleased."[5]

And yet at times the Puritan precariously bordered upon questioning the
ways of God. For example, Thomas Shepard, who held the Puritan belief
that God sometimes punishes the sins of parents by taking the lives of their
children, chastised himself at length after the death of his first child for his
weakness of faith and insufficient fear of God which he believed justly
provoked God to punish him.[6] After the death of his third child, however,
Shepard was less self-condemning in his laconic comment that the child's
death "was no small affliction and heartbreaking to me that I should provoke the Lord to strike at my innocent children for my sake."[7] This statement, with its emphasis upon the word "innocent," eloquently suggests an
underlying but muted sense of injustice.

Even a conventional and pious Puritan like Anne Bradstreet momentarily found herself verging on a complaint against God. In a poem which
describes her response to watching her house burn to the ground, she reaffirms her belief in a just God: "I blest his Name that gave and took,/
That layd my goods now in the dvst:/ Yea so it was, and so 'twas jvst./ It
was his own: it was not mine;/ Far be it that I should repine./ He might
of All justly bereft,/ But yet sufficient for us left." As she daily passes the
charred ruins, however, she realizes that she has lost not only a house and
her possessions, but also their former capacity to evoke the fond memories
associated with them. It is this latter loss which prompts her moving lament: "In silence ever shalt thou lye;/ Adieu, Adieu; All's vanity." This is
the pivotal point of the poem; in their ambiguity, these words can suggest
either a characteristically Puritan affirmation of life's evanescence or an
empty sense of loss. If they suggest the latter, as they seem to do, she stifles
her grievance by reminding herself that all earthly possessions are "mouldring
dvst" and by counseling herself to raise her "thoughts above the skye/
That dunghill mists may flie."

Her vision of heaven as a house which Christ has bought for her with
his blood leads her to disavow all remaining attachment to her destroyed
possessions, since in heaven "Ther's wealth enovgh, I need no more;/ Farewell my Pelf, farewell my Store./ The world no longer let me Love,/ My
hope and Treasure lyes Above."[8] In typical Puritan fashion, Anne Bradstreet concludes that the capacity of the world to deceive people, even
within the intimacy of family life, makes it necessary to rely fully upon
God as the only trustworthy reality in an otherwise unreliable world.[9] The
poem dramatizes the Puritan vision of a world unresponsive to human
ethical expectations—a deceptive, precarious, and unreliable world in which
the Christian's faith and good deeds in no way guarantee a better or safer

life. Bradstreet deeply feels the sense of injury and loss such a world inflicts upon her; but rather than make this the basis for protesting against God, she uses God as the basis for protesting against her own feelings, against the self which defines itself in terms of past possessions, relationships, and memories.

One factor among many contributing to this lack of complaint against God in early Puritan literature was perhaps the distinction which Puritans made between the covenant of works and the covenant of grace. Although the distinction between these two covenants defined two contrasting conceptions of morality as well as the basic differences between the elect and the unregenerate, it also defined the kind of treatment Christians could expect from God. They would not be given preferential treatment in this life in exchange for their faith; indeed God might increase their temporal sufferings while letting the unregenerate fare much better. This understanding of God is at the very heart of the distinction between the covenant of works and the covenant of grace.

The origins of these two ideas need not be restated here.[10] It is sufficient to note that Reformed thinkers in Germany and England—Zwingli, Cocceius, Oecolampadius, Bullinger, Bucer, Tyndale—as well as Calvin in Geneva, were simultaneously developing the idea of the covenant of grace during the early 1500s,[11] that this idea "became fixed in English theology" during the brief reign of Edward VI,[12] and that by 1585 the notion of a covenant of works made between God and Adam had considerable vogue on the Continent until, by the early decades of the 1600s, it had become a widely accepted tenet of Puritan thought.[13] Such English theologians as William Ames, William Perkins, and John Preston further elaborated these two convenants for English Puritanism. Hence, by 1630, when the Puritans sailed aboard the *Arbella* to the American wilderness, Puritan thought had developed the notion of covenant into two opposing conceptions of morality, one based on works or human merit, the other on faith or divine grace. This dichotomization of human experience decisively shaped the American Puritan's way of thinking about human experience.

John Preston's influential volume of eighteen sermons, *The New Covenant, or the Saints Portion* (1629), was the primary English work American Puritans read on the covenant of grace until the publication in 1651 of Peter Bulkely's *The Gospel-Covenant; or, The Covenant of Grace Opened.* This work provided a more systematic and clearer treatment of the covenant of grace than was found in Preston's lumbering book. It became so popular among colonial Puritans that it went through several editions during the late 1600s and early 1700s. It demonstrates how the Puritans sought to define, by means of the distinction between the covenant of grace and the covenant of works, a meaningful notion of morality that was compatible with their notion of a sovereign God.

Bulkely argues that the covenant of grace cannot be properly understood without a prior understanding of the covenant of works. "The Covenant of workes was made with man in the state of Innocency before his fall; . . . before the fall, there was no impossibilitie, but man was able to have fulfilled the Law, and therefore God might justly require such obedience of him . . . he might have had life by the Covenant of workes" (p. 106).[14] Since God made the covenant of works "with all men, all men being in Adams loins, and he standing as a publique person in the roome of all his children" (p. 108), Adam's fall not only annulled the covenant of works for all people but also corrupted them, thereby making it impossible for them to fulfill the law. "We are dead . . . in sinne, and our workes are dead workes" which "cannot bring life unto them that doe them; nor can wee quicken our own soules" (p. 329). Hence people can regain the life originally promised them in the covenant of works only if God Himself grants them a new opportunity for obedience on different terms.

This He had done in the covenant of grace. According to this covenant, Christ's perfect obedience and sacrificial death rendered the just payment God requires for Adam's disobedience. Christ thus became the mediator who reunited God once again with humankind. What this covenant requires is not perfect obedience to the law but faith in Christ as the sole giver of life; such faith is the necessary prerequisite for salvation. Nevertheless, the covenant of grace, no less than the covenant of works, requires complete obedience to God's commandments, but the nature of this requirement is radically different in each covenant. In the covenant of works, people must justify themselves before God by performing obedient works without divine assistance; in the covenant of grace, the spirit of Jesus Christ enables people to perform such works "not as part of our righteousnesse, but that thereby we should glorifie God, and manifest it that we are made righteous by Christ" (p. 60). Although these works cannot make a person acceptable to God, He still rewards such works by accepting the person solely because of his faith. "In the Covenant of workes," then, "a man is left to himselfe, to stand by his own strength; But in the Covenant of grace God undertakes for us, to keep us through faith," the sole condition of the covenant of grace.

However, this condition places no limits upon the freedom of God's grace, Bulkely argues, "Because faith is not of our selves, but it is the gift of God; and, secondly, Because faith doth not come to God boastingly, to claime life by the workes of righteousnesse, which wee have done; but comes to him with an emptie hand to receive what grace and mercy is willing to give; such condition as this, doth no more derogate from the freeness of grace, than doth the beggars receiving of the almes given him, derogate from the kindnesse of him that gave it" (p. 382).[15] God in His sovereign mercy accepts people solely because of the faith He confers upon them. Nor do the sins of those within the covenant nullify God's acceptance; for despite their many lapses, if they remain firm in their faith, repent their sins, and continue to do good works, God will forgive them and reward them with eternal life. Reliance on the covenant of works gives people no such assurance about their destiny, only doubt, suspicion, and fear. "But the Covenant of grace rested in, and trusted unto . . . reconciles the heart unto God . . . and makes of two one, working peace and love" (pp. 99, 348).

Unlike the covenant of works, however, the covenant of grace is not available to all people but only to those who "are given unto Christ by the Father" (p. 108)—though they, no less than the unsaved, deserve eternal damnation. The covenant of grace is therefore based not on God's justice as was the covenant of works but rather on divine grace. That God especially designed these covenants to serve such contrary principles, Bulkely asserts, is substantiated by the fact that "in the Covenant of workes, God reveals himself as a just God, rewarding good, and punishing evil, condemning sin; but in the Covenant of grace, he shews himself a God gracious and merciful, forgiving iniquity" (pp. 82–83). Everyone in the covenant of works is treated equitably; people who commit the same sin receive the same punishment regardless of their station in life.

The covenant of grace, however, embodies a kind of injustice created by God's merciful but unequal treatment of His people. God has mercy on whomever He chooses without regard for either the person's station or his personal merit, often choosing the vilest person over a worthier one. In addition, God confers more advantages upon some recipients of grace than upon others. But this inequity of treatment should cause no one to question the dispensation of God, since God is free to bestow His mercy in whatever way pleases Him. Indeed, true faith seeks no more than it receives and "makes us look at the Lords government as a mercifull government, bringing peace and blessing unto those that are under it" (p. 347). The covenant of works thus expresses a conventional notion of morality based upon a legalistic concept of justice, while the covenant of grace presents a redefinition of the moral life based upon the mercy of a sovereign deity who never justifies His ways to humankind.

A more homely but more trenchant expression of the kind of life God requires of those within the covenant of grace is found in Roger Williams' *Experiments of Spiritual Life and Health* (1652), a lengthy letter to his wife in which he seeks to restore her dwindling faith after a long illness that nearly took her life. He reminds her, in typical Puritan fashion, that she must not seek her solace in the pleasures and comforts of this world, since they are too brief and uncertain and will only further exacerbate her anxiety and perplexity. Rather, the only trustworthy object for her faith is God. Therefore the truly religious person will accord "upright *submission* . . . to all that he believes to be the *will* and *pleasure* of his Heavenly *Father*" (p. 60).[16] Such submission requires not only complete obedience to God's commandments, attendance at public worship, participation in the sacraments, and making "it our *worke* and *trade*, to aime at *glorifying* our Maker in doing good to men," but also an unquestioning acceptance of all personal afflictions and miseries as God's means of purging one's inner self of its sins (p. 92). True Christians even "conceive a kinde of pleasure" in suffering at the hands of God. When God requires it, they will "[lie] down in the Dust that God may tread upon them, and be exalted" (pp. 88, 81)—and perhaps this belief that a true Christian takes delight in suffering at the hands of God helps in part to explain the lack in early Puritan writings of protest against the ways of God.

Williams here articulates the Puritan notion of humiliation and its implication that there can be no genuine "*strength of Spirituall life*" unless people are fully willing to be destroyed by God should He require it to realize His mysterious purposes (p. 87). The supreme manifestation of such self-denial occurs "when the *glory* of the *Lord* and the salvation of *God's* people is so great, and so dear in our eyes, that we can wish . . . that we not onely lose our *temporall*, but our eternal *state* and *welfare*" (p. 99). For Williams, a concern to gain salvation cannot have priority over one's commitment to God, nor over one's devotion to "Truth" either; for as he elsewhere states, "having bought Truth deare, we must not sell it cheape, not the least graine of it for the whole World, no not for the saving of Soules, though our own most precious."[17] Both God and Truth are to be desired solely for what they are, not for any advantage they can confer upon people.

Indeed Christians, according to Williams, cannot expect to gain either kinder treatment from God or worldly rewards for their faithful obedience. Nor does the fact that Christ's atoning death has already appeased God's wrath towards his people mean that God exempts them from suffering "the fearful strokes of his displeasure." God may in fact require Christians to suffer more than those who reject God, in order to help purify His chosen people and also to "vindicate *Gods* name and *Justice* before an unrighteous *world*, and beare him witnesse of his *immortality*, even towards his owne *children*" (p. 108). Even Christ, he reminds his wife, had to bear "the impartial flames of Gods justice on that green and innocent tree . . . when he stood surety in the room of *sinners* to make *satisfaction* for their transgressions" (pp. 108–9). The regenerate have no claims on God; they should expect a fate no better than that suffered by Christ. The expectation that God will not mistreat obedient Christians may conform to human notions of justice, but when applied to God, Williams asserts, it only leads people to misconceive the true nature of divine justice.[18] In Williams' words, this expectation is one of "the *colours* and *pretences* which we poor sinners invent to our selves, to hide from our eyes, the *greatnesse* and *dreadfulnesse* and terrours of [divine justice]" (p. 106). For Williams, human canons of justice are therefore inadequate for either conceptualizing or rendering judgment against divine justice which is designed not to palliate people but to punish and purge their spiritual corruption.

What is important here for Williams, as for Puritan theologians in general, is not the actual adversity itself which befalls any individual, but rather the redemptive function this adversity serves for either that person or others. Hence what appears to be cruel, arbitrary, or unjust from a human perspective is, from God's perspective, the way divine grace mysteriously carries out its redemptive purposes. The Puritans thus explained the injustices and sufferings of human existence, not in the psychological or social terms, but as elements made necessary by the very structure of the cosmic order itself.

The covenant of grace thus provided what the Puritans considered a fully adequate explanation for the injustices and inequities of human experience as well as definitive answers to the kinds of questions about God's justice that are implicit in the Puritan notion of God's sovereignty. So long as mercy, not justice, is the ultimate religious category, they asserted, then all events, no matter how arbitrary or accidental they may seem, have a rationale that explains them in redemptive terms. This rationale may not be ethically acceptable when evaluated by human canons of justice; but were divine justice to act in accordance with the dictates of human notions of justice, there would then be no room, they contended, for the mercy which God bestows on sinners who in no way merit that mercy.

Though this view of the world has the effect of making an individual uncertain about his or her religious destiny, it also places God, not the self, at the center of existence—and this is precisely what Puritan theologians said was most desirable about this world view. Human notions of justice, they argued, give the self pre-eminence over God and for this reason are unreliable guides for defining our expectations of life. Only the covenant of grace can serve as such a guide.

The covenant of grace also defined the style of life recommended by the Puritan world view. The self is to sacrifice itself for the glory of God, unquestioningly accept all suffering and tribulations as necessary to the fulfillment of God's redemptive purposes, do good works without expecting any benefits or rewards, have faith in Jesus Christ and the mysterious workings of divine providence, and submit itself to both scriptual teachings and the preaching, sacraments, and discipline provided by the church. This ethos is shown to be fully conformable to the cosmic order which the Puritan world view describes, while the world view itself becomes credible because its image of cosmic order is presented as ideally suited to accommodate such a style of life. From the Puritan perspective, then, the covenant of grace represented a successful fusion of world view and ethos.

But Puritan thought was more ambiguous about this fusion of world view and ethos than is indicated in the covenant of grace. This fusion described a way of life which has as its basic premise the notion that no amount of moral striving can determine one's religious destiny since God is unresponsive to such striving. Yet, in their understanding of their relationship to the American wilderness, the Puritans modified this synthesis in a way which seems to make God responsive to human moral effort. The difference here is important, for it shows not only how the Puritans sometimes tried to moderate the radical ethical implications of their notion of a sovereign deity, but also how they themselves sought out a moral order in the world more reliable than the one described in the covenant of grace.

GOD'S CONTROVERSY WITH NEW ENGLAND

Perry Miller has demonstrated that the founding Puritans—at least those who sailed with John Winthrop aboard the *Arbella* in 1630—believed that God had formed a covenant with them wherein He agreed to become their God and accord them special privileges if they would perform the sacred errand of building the New Jerusalem in the American wilderness.[19] The "worke wee have in hand," heard the Puritan voyagers in a sermon he preached aboard the *Arbella*, "is by mutuall consent through a special overruleing providence . . . to seeke out a place of Cohabitation and Consortshipp vnder a due forme of Government both ciuill and ecclesiasticall . . . therfore wee must not content our selues with vsual ordinary means. . . . That which the most in thiere Churches maineteine as a truth in profession onely, wee must bring into familiar and constant practice. . . . Thus stands the cause between God and vs, wee are entered into Covenant with him for this worke."[20]

Winthrop gave the early Puritan migration a religious rationale by envisioning the American wilderness as a haven that God had especially set aside for the Puritans to finish the work of the Reformation. The success of this "errand into the wilderness" was mandatory for Winthrop since the Puritans would be the focus of the world's attention. As Winthrop put it in his now famous words, "wee must Consider that wee shall be as a Citty vppon a Hill, the eies of all people are vppon us.[21]

Acceptance of the covenant with God to make the American wilderness into a heavenly city was, for Winthrop, to become "God's New Israel."[22] He envisioned the Puritans sailing for the American wilderness as being like the Israelites of old entering the land of Canaan; they were about to take possession of a promised land where they could choose either life or death in accordance with the terms set forth in the covenant. God "hath taken vs to be his after a most strickt and peculiar manner which will make him the more Jealous of our love and obedience soe he tells the people of Israell, you onely have I knowne of all the families of the Earthe therefore will I punishe you for your Transgressions."[23]

Winthrop's sermon demonstrates how the notion of a covenant with God encouraged the Puritans to use the Old Testament as the touchstone for understanding their experience—to see in the Old Testament a pre-figuration of their own encounter with the American wilderness.[24] Ancient Israelite history thus became a template for identifying similar, if not identical, patterns of experience in the Puritans' encounter with the American wilderness. This procedure enabled the Puritans to extract guidelines from the Old Testament for understanding, sometimes even predicting, God's treatment of His modern-day Israel. It was a mode of interpretation which not only presented the Puritans as significant actors in the universal drama of divine redemption; it also presented history as inexorably shaped by a moral logic which manifests itself in the patterns of human experience that constantly recur in, and thereby link, the ancient and modern worlds. The Puritan founders of New England thus transformed an undeveloped wilderness into an orderly moral universe by means of their typology and covenant theology.

To these early Puritans, God's covenant with them to build the New Jerusalem in the American wilderness was an inequivocal expression of divine providence and the American wilderness an unproblematical setting for realizing God's providential plans.[25] Certainly the founders of the Massachusetts Bay Colony viewed the wilderness as a passive partner in their mission. Winthrop's sermon aboard the *Arbella*, for example, lacks any forebodings that the unknown land they were about to settle might be an impediment to their enterprise. He envisions the virgin continent as a *tabula rasa* upon which the Puritans can successfully imprint their religious vision of society;[26] but there is a cautionary note in his warning that, if the Puritans disobey the articles of the covenant, God will destroy them, making them "a story and a by-word through the world."[27]

In the first decades of settlement, many Puritan writers remained optimistic about the success of their religious mission. They depicted the Puritans of 1630–1650 as successfully transforming the wilderness into a city which, in John Higginson's words, "would dazzle the Eyes of Angels, daunt the Hearts of Devils, ravish and chain fast the Affections of all the Saints."[28] Thomas Shepard described New England during the time the mother country was in the throes of civil war as being serene after the initial difficulties of the 1630s, while Winthrop interpreted the misfortunes of persons antagonistic to the Puritan state from 1630–1649 as divine judgments which proved that "the presence and power of God [is] in his ordinances, and his blessing [is] upon his people, while they endeavor to walk before him with uprightness."[29] Edward Johnson further elaborates this image of an upright people successfully building the New Jerusalem with God's assistance in his history of Massachusetts, *Wonder-Working Providence of Sions Saviour* (1654). The Puritans, in Johnson's view, had worked so diligently to achieve the privileged destiny God desires for them that nothing could hinder their attaining it; Christ would not let the work of the New England churches be undone.

> Doth Christ build Churches? who can them deface?
> He purchast them, none can his right deny:
> Not all the world, ten thousand worlds; his grace
> Caus'd him once them at greater price to buy.
> Nor marvell then if Kings and Kingdomes he
> Destroy'd, when they do cause his folke to flee.
>
> Christ is come down possession for to take
> Of his deer purchase; who can hinder him:
> Not all the Armies earthly men can make:
> Millions of spirits, although Divels grim:
> Can Pope or Turke with all their mortall power,
> Stay Christ from his inheritance one hour?[30]

Prior to 1650, then, such Puritan writers as William Bradford, John Winthrop, Thomas Shepard, and Edward Johnson depict a people who, with God's assistance, are in the process of successfully transforming the wilderness into a society that will "justifie the Lords Expectations upon this ground."[31]

The God of the Puritan covenant was responsive to moral and religious striving, and to this extent could be defined by human standards of justice. He was sufficiently reliable in the eyes of the early Puritans that during the early decades of settlement they envisioned God's covenant with them as an unequivocal expression of divine providence. Certainly the wilderness was physically challenging, frequently imposing serious loss of life and crops upon the Puritan community. But because they experienced what they believed to be God's support and guidance throughout their hardships in seeking to build the New Jerusalem, the early Puritans theologically considered the American wilderness to be an unproblematical setting for realizing God's providential plans. Hence the founders' encounter with the undeveloped wilderness posed no serious difficulties regarding allegiance to their covenant with God.

Nevertheless, there were many difficulties that jeopardized the Puritan project. Indian attacks, inclement weather, and sickness greatly reduced the Puritan population; the Antinomian controversy, Roger Williams, and the Quakers created internal dissensions; and the economic pressures to move further westward in search of tillable land threatened the cohesiveness of the tightly knit Puritan community. An episode which William Bradford lamented—the westward migration in 1644 of several families from a small Plymouth church—was reenacted again and again as the early Puritans and their descendants pursued the wilderness promise of a better life elsewhere.[32]

Bradford, Winthrop, and others used both legal and ecclesiastical means to prevent settlers from migrating westward, and the initial success of such efforts led Thomas Shepard to say as late as 1648 that God was still working through His people to ensure the success of their sacred mission.[33]

Hence the only adequate response to English criticism of the Puritan "errand into the wilderness," he told the New Englanders, was to maintain a steadfast reliance on the grace of God. He assured them that although "we be a people of many weaknesses and wants," God will "yet owne us, and rather correct us in mercy, then cast us off in displeasure, and scatter us in this Wilderness."[34]

Prior to 1660, then, Puritan writings tended to emphasize a beneficent and merciful God who was helping the founding Puritans complete the Reformation in the churches of New England.[35] This portrayal of God's protective beneficence may also help in part to explain the lack of complaint against God in early Puritan literature.

After 1660, however, Puritan writers gradually moved away from this vision of God as they sought to come to terms with what A. N. Kaul wittily calls the "God-Cod" conflict.[36] Puritan preachers took to task an emerging commercial society which, in its dispersal of people and its secular concerns, was radically at odds with the founders' original religious model—though it has been maintained that Puritanism in general, especially in its notions of calling and wealth, "had no quarrel with either commerce or mobility."[37] They found the new commercialism to be an acid eating away the religious values and practices of Puritan society. An increasing number of sermons, especially election sermons, described a society corrupted by debauchery, drinking, unfair business practices, unruly children who flouted parental authority, hypocrisy, dissension in the churches, and blasphemy. But what most incriminated Puritan society in the eyes of these preachers was the apostasy and lack of religious zeal which they perceived in the general populace.

Robert G. Pope argues, however, that there was no such waning of religion during the latter part of the seventeenth century, but rather a sharp increase in church membership after 1676.[38] He views the Puritan jeremiads as having contributed to, if not created, "a myth of declension," a misconception which resulted from the perplexity second- and third-generation preachers experienced as they sought to make sense of "the changing world around them."[39] Pope's interpretation has not gone unchallenged.[40] But whether Pope is correct or not, the shape of Puritan society was changing. And surely it is just as important to understand the kind of response Puritan preachers made to these changes from a theological perspective that did not easily accommodate process, change, and diversity as it is to determine the accuracy of their perceptions.

Throughout the 1660s and 1670s, Puritan preachers continued to deliver their jeremiads in which they relentlessly pressed what Michael Wigglesworth calls "God's controversy with New England" (1622). They typically interpreted such events as droughts, loss of crops, loss of life and property during skirmishes with the Indians—and especially King Philip's War in 1675–1676, when dozens of English towns were destroyed "and colonial armies had been . . . all but obliterated"[41]—as God's wrathful punishment of a people about to derail their sacred mission through their failure to obey the terms of God's covenant with the founding fathers.[42] Their repeated warnings of imminent disaster echo God's admonition in Wigglesworth's poem: "For thinke not, O Backsliders, in your heart,/ That I shall still your evill manners beare:/ Your sinns me press as sheaves do load a cart,/ And therefore I will plague you for this geare/ Except you seriously, and soon, repent,/ Ile not delay your pain and heavy punishment."[43]

Some later preachers stressed that Puritan society was not yet beyond repair. In his election sermon of 1668, for example, William Stoughton told his audience that God was placing the Puritans on probation and recalling them "to justifie the Lords expectations upon this ground."[44] According to Stoughton, this period of probation was the last of the "advantages and Priviledges" that God would confer on His people. Should the Puritans ignore it and thereby thwart "his Covenant-interest in us," then "Ruine upon Ruine, Destruction upon Destruction would come, until one stone were not left upon another."[45] Sixteen years later William Hubbard, using a typological interpretation, set forth a modified notion of probation. New England, he argued, had become a wilderness where the Puritans, like the ancient Israelites, must wander until purged of their worldliness when they could once again begin taking possession of the promised land. "God in his infinite wisdom did train [the Israelites] up to encounter with Marches and Journeyings in the wilderness, and then acquainted them with the difficulties of a long War, that they might learn obedience by what they underwent."[46] God was placing His people on a probation which would entail a painful but necessary process of purification through suffering and death.

This urgent sense of God's wrathful controversy with New England reached its climactic expression in the famous "reforming synod" of 1679 after nearly two decades of Indian wars, smallpox epidemics, and serious losses of life, property, and crops. "It is not for nothing," stated the synod's report, "that the merciful God, who doth not willingly afflict nor grieve the Children of men, hath done all these things unto us; yea and sometimes with a Cloud hath covered himself, that our Prayer should not pass through."[47] The report catalogued the people's many sins as sufficient explanation for why "Clouds of wrath are hanging over [New England's] Churches,"[48] and warned them that God would finally destroy their society and make this holocaust a salutary warning to future generations unless they reformed their ways and renewed the founders' original covenant with God, since Scripture presented this as the only successful way to regain divine favor.[49]

Five years later, Increase Mather, who had called the reforming synod into being, once again reaffirmed its basic contentions in his *Doctrine of*

Divine Providence. Like the synod and the many preachers who predicted the destruction of a wayward society, he suggests that many factors yet mitigate against such an apocalyptic end of their New Jerusalem. He urges New Englanders to take up their neglected religious duties with new fervor. A people thus bent on reforming themselves, Mather contends, will once again win God's favor. "Search the Scripture, and you will not find one instance of a People set for Reformation, but God delivered them out of the hands of those that sought their ruin."[50] Moreover, since God has brought a scattered people to the American wilderness, has made room for them by destroying the Indians with decimating plagues, and has established churches everywhere in New England, He will not be quick to destroy His burgeoning New Jerusalem. Moreover, "some of the first Generation are yet with us, the Kindness of whose youth when they followed him into a wilderness, into a land which was not sown, God still remembers and will remember. Search the Records of Ancient times, and you will never find, that when God has Created a new Heaven and a new earth, all was layd utterly waste and desolate, whilest any of those whom God honoured to be the first foundation were living."[51] Like many of the jeremiads, as well as the report of the reforming synod, Mather here reminds his readers of what he considered the heroic achievements of the founding fathers.

Indeed, second- and third-generation preachers increasingly invoked the image of a heroic age of zealous faith when the founding fathers lived in complete harmony with God's will and enjoyed His protective beneficence.[52] Michael Wigglesworth, for example, in the first ten stanzas of his poetic jeremiad, "God's Controversy with New-England," recalled the heroic faith and deeds of the migrating Puritans by lamenting what he considered a declension of faith in the first- and second-generation Puritans born in the American wilderness. "Are these the men that erst at my command/ Forsook their ancient seats and native soile,/ To follow me into a desart land,/ Contemning all the travell and the toile,/ Whose love was such to purest ordinances/ As made them set at nought their fair inheritances?"[53] These early heroes of the faith had known the munificence of God's blessing because they were faithful to their covenant with God. "Is this the people blest with bounteous store,/ By land and sea full richly clad and fed,/ Whom plenty's self stands waiting still before,/ And poureth out their cups well tempered?/ For whose dear sake an howling wilderness/ I lately turned into a fruitful paradeis?"[54]

This idealization of the past continued into the 1700s, perhaps achieving its most memorable expression in a sermon Thomas Prince delivered to mark the centennial of the arrival of John Winthrop and the small band of Puritans which accompanied him. After briefly detailing the hardships they endured, first in England, then in New England, and after portraying how God beneficently protected them during their journey to the American wilderness and throughout the difficulties they experienced in the first decades of settlement, he praises their religious virtues. To this he adds: "And to the great glory of God be it spoken—there never was perhaps before seen such a body of pious people together on the face of the earth."[55] It is an image of an idyllic past of heroic faith; by 1730, it had become a cultural myth of a paradise being lost.

Like so many of his predecessors, Prince called the people to repossess this heroic past, to recover the single-minded devotion of the early saints which, according to this version of Puritan history, invoked God's protection against the various threats to realizing their sacred errand. It was a strategy Puritan preachers repeatedly used—almost in an incantatory fashion—as they attempted to reverse the profound changes taking place around them.

People were becoming less responsive, however, to these calls to use the past as a template for shaping and understanding their present experience. They saw that the pursuit of worldly preoccupations rather than the pursuit of the covenant obligations was increasingly becoming the path to success. Many therefore concluded that the system of divine rewards and punishments described in the founders' covenant with God no longer provided an adequate religious explanation for their contemporary experience.[56]

The once unproblematical covenant now gave rise to disturbing questions about the nature of God. Why had God concealed from them the intractable nature of the wilderness? Why had God bound them to a covenant inalterably opposed to the creation of a commercial society, while He rewarded those whose worldly preoccupations were creating such a society? In short, why was God making violation of the covenant the true measure of success?[57] Not only did the covenant itself no longer seem trustworthy as a guide for predicting God's response to His New Israel; God Himself seemed untrustworthy.[58] He had betrayed the Puritans by supporting the growth of a worldly society; He had led them to the American wilderness only to undermine the very enterprise He Himself had inspired.

THE DILEMMA

However, side by side with the affirmation of a God who abides by a predictable system of rewards and punishments was the affirmation of a sovereign deity who cannot be defined by human moral expectations. The Puritan notion of God's sovereignty affirmed that God, precisely because He is the sovereign Creator, determines human destinies without regard to anyone's moral striving, no matter how sincere or meritorious that striving might be. The persistent sinner will attain salvation if it is predestined by God; conversely, no amount of virtuous living can prevent eternal damnation if that be a part of God's providential plan for the universe. People simply cannot make God fashion a destiny for them that accords with their personal, moral, and religious desires.

Such a God, at least from a human perspective, often realizes His redemptive purposes in ways that violate human canons of justice. At its most extreme this understanding of God meant for the Puritan, as Puritan preachers frequently and solemnly observed in their sermons, that when the eternal salvation of one person requires the suffering, death, or eternal damnation of another (or others), God will either design or concur with the temporal conditions necessary for effecting this drama of salvation in order to glorify His sovereignty over humankind. Questions inevitably arose about the goodness and justice of such a deity as well as about the desirability of moral striving when God is said to be unresponsive to it.

Such questions became increasingly urgent during the latter half of the seventeenth century as new problems arose which forced Puritan theologians and preachers to re-examine the terms of their covenant with God. Many of their writings presuppose an awareness that people were seriously questioning whether the fusion of world view and ethos represented by the covenant theology was adequate for expressing their contemporary experience of the changing American environment. Because their encounter with the wilderness was undermining this inherited synthesis of world view and ethos, many Puritans experienced the world as an inexplicable and threatening reality. As a seeming consequence, Puritan writings from 1650 to 1690—despite the recurring reaffirmation of the covenant theology—increasingly portrayed a sovereign God who overturns human expectations and religious certitudes.[59]

As early as 1654, for example, Edward Johnson tried to explain the Puritans' emerging sense of uncertainty by saying that "the Lord [had been] pleased to hide from the Eyes of His people the difficulties they [were] to encounter withall in a new Plantation, [so] that they might not thereby be hindered from taking the worke in hand."[60] He had lured the founders to the American wilderness by making it appear less formidable than it really was in order to carry out purposes beyond their ken. This is not Winthrop's plain-spoken God of the covenant; rather, this God is capable of misleading His people in order not only to realize His purposes but also to express His autonomous control of the world.

God's sovereignty is similarly emphasized in Michael Wigglesworth's popular poem, "The Day of Doom" (1662), which portrays a God who preempts all complaints about His withholding grace from those who seek it. "Am I alone of what's my own, no Master or no Lord?/ Or if I am, how can you claim what I to some afford?/ Will you demand Grace at my hand, and challenge what is mine?/ Will you teach me whom to set free, and thus my Grace confine?"[61] A later and more striking statement of God's autonomy is that of Edward Taylor, who, in his preface to "God's

Determinations," describes an almighty Creator: "Whose Little finger at his pleasure Can/ Out mete ten thousand worlds with halfe a Span:/ Whose Might Almighty can be half a looks/ Root up the rocks and rock the hills by th' roots./ Can take this mighty World up in his hande,/ And shake it like a Squitchen or a Wand."[62] This God, according to William Hubbard, sets the Indians at enmity with His people, and despite the fact that He moves both sides to needless cruelty and bloodshed, He "is not bound to render the world an Account" of the "holy Ends" He is seeking to achieve by these means.[63] All attempts to judge this God in human terms can only backfire at the expense of human dignity. As Taylor graphically puts it: "Were th'Heavens sick? must wee their Doctors bee/ And Physick them with pills, our sin?/ To make them purge and vomit; see:/ And Excrements outfling?/ We've griev'd them by such Physick that they shed/ Their excrements upon our lofty heads."[64] In these poems, Taylor describes a sovereign God who is responsible to no ethical constraints, a reality which from a human perspective precariously borders on the demonic.

Yet, as Thomas Johnson notes, Taylor often renders in his later poetry an explicit tension between such a sovereign God and a God who is "Meat, Med'cine, Sweetness, sparkling Beautys, to/Enamour Souls with Flaming Flakes of love"[65] —an imagistic tension which perhaps reflects the Puritans' growing sense that the times were out of joint. It must be remembered that Taylor wrote these poems during the 1680s when there was not only angry dissension among people in the Massachusetts Bay Colony, but also ennervating doubt whether their holy experiment could survive England's increasing control of their land and government. As a result of such circumstances the Puritans, during the 1690s, sought a new understanding of their relationship to the wilderness and to God.[66]

Hence, during a period when their sacred mission seemed on the verge of collapse and many no longer believed that the covenant theology provided an adequate explanation for their experience, the Puritans frequently reaffirmed the notion of a sovereign deity who is beyond all ethical and rational categories. For a few He seemed so far beyond human reach that they ventured to intimate that God had disappeared.[67]

The latter half of the seventeenth century, then, was a period of growing theological disorientation for the Puritans. They found it increasingly difficult to reconcile their present experience with the synthesis of world view and ethos which the founders had articulated in their covenant with God. If God had in fact been working through history to help the founders impose their religious vision on the American wilderness, if through His protective beneficence God had led them to believe they would successfully complete their "errand into the wilderness," how, they asked, were they to characterize a God who allowed the New Englanders to create a society which seemingly contravened His own original purposes? Either the covenant theology would have to be stretched considerably or else another metaphysic would have to be formulated in order to explain this phenomenon, because a new ethos—a new style of life—was emerging in Puritan society which was incompatible with the metaphysical world view that characterized the covenant theology.

It was inevitable that during this time, when their understanding of themselves as God's New Israel became problematical for many Puritans, people would not only raise serious moral questions about the nature of God, but also demand answers other than the traditional affirmation that God works out His purposes in mysterious ways.[68] People had no difficulty in demonstrating that the notion of a sovereign God who is not bound by any ethical constraints suggests a reality which, from a human perspective, precariously borders on the demonic, an implication which continually plagued the Augustinian-Calvinistic advocates of predestination. Nor was it difficult for people to show how a deity who disregards moral striving—or, at least, who rejects it as the basis for gaining salvation—seemingly renders all moral commitments futile, if not altogether unnecessary.

Theologians therefore had to treat not only the problem of proving that the Puritan vision of God's sovereignty did not ultimately entail a capricious, even demonic God, but also the problem of having to demonstrate why a God-centered morality is desirable in a universe which is experienced as unresponsive to moral striving. Indeed, if the world is not shaped by a universal moral order that confirms man's highest ethical standards— if the nature of divine justice is such that its treatment of the morally good differs little, if any, from its treatment of the vilest sinners, thereby making such ethical distinctions seem pointless—what then, it was asked, is the basis for affirming the necessity of any morality?

In order to answer such questions, Puritan theologians had to elaborate their understanding of human moral effort in a way that required them to walk a fine line. On the one hand, the Puritan sought to convince the unregenerate that moral behavior was not a reliable pathway to the religious life; on the other hand, this conviction had to be evoked without leading the unregenerate to conclude that they could therefore ignore morality until God, if He had ordained it, converted them to the religious life. On the one hand, the Puritan described a world where God determines whether a person will be of the elect or of the damned not by the moral quality of the person's life but by His arbitrary fiat; on the other hand, he affirmed the necessity for morality in a world that seemed unresponsive to moral striving. On the one hand, the Puritan wanted to attribute all happenings to God's sovereign control over His creation; on the other hand, he asserted that this vision of God did not ultimately entail a capricious, much less demonic, deity, that this vision of God would in fact make ethical sense of the seemingly demonic aspects of life. It was a very fine line indeed that Puritans had to walk if they were to adhere to all these assertions.

Here, then, was a basic dilemma in Puritan ethics during the latter part of the seventeenth and early part of the eighteenth century: to show how the notion of a sovereign God, whose inscrutability and power could not be defined or comprehended in terms of human ethical standards, could nevertheless account for the demonic aspects of life in a way that would provide a reliable foundation for morality in a commercial society.[69] Or an alternative way of stating this dilemma is that Puritan theologians found it increasingly necessary to demonstrate that the synthesis of world view and ethos formulated in the covenant of grace was a symbolic system still adequate for expressing the Puritan encounter with the American wilderness.

By 1684, this dilemma, along with the social, commercial, and political forces then emerging, had become sufficiently problematical to provoke even such a stalwart Puritan as Increase Mather to consider the possibility that the Puritan faith could lose its viability in a society increasingly hostile to it if Puritan preachers could not resolve its own internal dilemma. Such spokesmen as Urian Oakes, Increase Mather, Cotton Mather, Samuel Willard, and Jonathan Edwards combined the various strands in the Puritan vision of God into a theodicy which they believed reconciled a sovereign God beyond all ethical categorization with a meaningful notion of moral commitment. The necessity to resolve this internal dilemma along these lines increasingly preoccupied Puritan theologians as the various pressures to form a notion of an ethically comprehensible God increased in a changing cultural climate.

It was such continuing efforts by Puritan theologians to overcome this dilemma that established Puritanism as one of the important participants in a larger theological debate that gradually emerged as American society became democratically oriented, a debate which, though it assumed many guises and took place at many different levels, essentially focused on the reconcilability of belief in a sovereign God with the belief that moral striving is meaningful and necessary, perhaps even redemptive. The problem progressively became whether the theodicy Puritan theologians developed in response to their own dilemma could provide a comprehensive explanation of human experience that would also be ethically acceptable to an emerging democratic society.

2

The Puritan Theodicy

A SOVEREIGN DEITY

The origins of this dilemma in part lie in the difficulties which the Puritans encountered as they sought to impose their vision of a religious Utopia upon the American wilderness. To resolve this dilemma, theologians, during the latter 1600s and early 1700s, forged the many-stranded Puritan vision of God into a theodicy which they believed fully explained the seemingly arbitrary and amoral aspects of human experience. They wanted to show not only that this theodicy successfully synthesized the Puritan world view and ethos, but also that its vision of the moral complexities of human experience was a reliable moral guide amidst the felt discontinuities between their contemporary and past experiences of the American environment. No new synthesis of world view and ethos, they contended, was necessary.

Foremost among these efforts are Urian Oakes' sermon "The Sovereign Efficacy of Divine Providence" (1667), two works by Increase Mather, *Remarkable Providences* (1684) and *Doctrine of Divine Providence* (1684), Cotton Mather's *Bonifacius: An Essay upon the Good* (1710), Samuel Willard's two sermons "Morality not to be Relied on for Life" (1700) and "The Law Established by the Gospel" (1700), as well as his *Compleat Body of Divinity* (1727), and several of Jonathan Edwards' works, most notably his *Treatise Concerning Religious Affections* (1746) and *The Nature of True Virtue* (1755). These works, together with the jeremiads, expressed the various ways theologians used the Puritan theodicy to define a moral structure in human experience which could accommodate the Puritan vision of a sovereign God.

In his election sermon "The Sovereign Efficacy of Divine Providence," delivered during a period when droughts, epidemics, and skirmishes with Indians had seriously depleted the Puritan population, Urian Oakes reasserts the Puritan notion that God "makes and disposes the Lot, or Chance of every man, whatever it is."[1] Oakes admits that from a human perspective such a God often appears unethical in His treatment of humankind. "All Casualties in the World," including such a "sad event" as either an accidental murder or the death of innocent bystanders in a natural catastrophe, make God seem capricious, even demonic.[2] However, the human perspective on such events is severely limited because it seeks to explain them solely in terms of natural or "second causes." For the most part God permits humankind to work out the individual destinies He has predetermined for them through the orderly proceedings of natural causation. So necessary is this divine concurrence in the operation of natural causes "that There can be no real Effect produced by the Creature without it."[3]

But not all events can be explained as resulting from second causes. There are times when God, seeing that second causes are insufficient for realizing His purposes, directly intervenes in people's lives as a first or primary cause. From the perspective of second causes, such divine interventions have the appearance of being incomprehensibly arbitrary; from God's perspective, they are absolutely necessary for realizing His redemptive purposes.[4] "Chance is something that falls out beside the Scope, Intention, and foresight of Man, the Reason and cause whereof may be hid from him; and so it excludes the Counsel of Men; but it doth not exclude the Counsel and Providence of *God*; but is ordered and governed thereby."[5]

One of the many examples Oakes provides to illustrate this argument is that of a fast runner who trips and loses the race he expected to win. His tripping may seem an accident; but if he has become too proud of his swiftness, believing that he can win any race, it can then be viewed as an event which God himself precipitates, not only to humble the runner's pride but also to teach him that none of his capacities or skills can guarantee the success of any enterprise he undertakes. God "may blast our Undertakings" at any moment as a means of punishing our sinful aspirations, or simply because "it makes sometimes for the glory of God, to disappoint Men of greatest Abilities," to show "that He gives, or denies Success, according to His own good pleasure." Not even those within the covenant of grace are exempt from having God overturn their plans or projects. But in such instances God is demonstrating His "*mercy* . . . to his People . . . for it is best for them, in some Cases, to be defeated and disappointed," perhaps as a testing of faith, as a chastisement for sin, or as a purging of worldly desires.[6] Everyone, even the most exemplary Christian, must be prepared to be severely disappointed or even ruined by God should it suit His purposes. "Herein," declares Oakes, "the absolute Soveraignity and Dominion of God appears."[7]

God further manifests His sovereignty in the strategies He devises for helping the elect achieve salvation. The tragedies, inequities, and sufferings a person experiences can be God's means of working his salvation, or, if not his salvation, the salvation of others who either witness or hear of his tragic career. Puritan writings resort to this explanation for such events as crippling diseases, serious financial losses, brilliant careers unexpectedly overturned, and the premature deaths of children or spouses when they cannot be explained as being either a punishment for sin or a testing of faith.[8] God thus uses people as tools for accomplishing His redemptive purposes, no matter what agony it causes them.

It is human depravity itself, Oakes asserts, which inevitably places God in the position of having to effect people's salvation through such circuitous strategies that disregard all human canons of justice. Since Adam's fall people have been totally corrupt, seeking in everything they do to make the world spiral about themselves for their own self-glorification. So irretrievably inclined are people to self-worship that ultimately God can focus their attention and keep it focused upon Himself only by making the universe uncontrollable, unpredictable, deceptive, and precarious, so precarious that each moment can bring an unexpected disaster which suddenly ruins or ends a person's life, no matter how exemplary it is, thereby nullifying all his efforts. Oakes' concluding advice therefore is: "Labour to be prepared and provided for Disappointments."[9]

God's abrogation of human ethical standards is, in Oakes' view, fully justifiable precisely because of its redemptive effects. No other method of governance, he concludes, is better suited for bringing the maximum number of persons to salvation in a world where their sinful nature constantly works against it. In such a world, neither salvation nor the process leading to salvation can be adequately explained by any human notion of justice. Nevertheless, even though the universe might not conform to their ethical categories, the Puritans, according to Oakes, can find consolation in the fact that all events in their lives, even the most insignificant or bizarre, contribute to the gradual evolution of God's providential plan for humankind.

INCREASE MATHER: THE DOCTRINE OF DIVINE PROVIDENCE

Another such effort to provide a comprehensive explanation for all human experience, this time based on the Puritan notion of divine providence, is Increase Mather's *Remarkable Providences Illustrative of the Earlier Days of American Colonisation*, a work which provides an unsystematic interpretation of the Puritan past. In 1681, the ministers of the Massachusetts Bay Colony commissioned Mather to compile a collection of "remarkable providences" in order to give both their generation and succeeding generations a clear picture of God's providential dealings with the early settlers.[10] Mather creates the image of a heroic past when God protected the Puritan founders against all threats to their sacred errand. *Remarkable Providences* is, in fact, a collection of dozens of isolated episodes from the Puritan past which he uses to celebrate not only that past but also the wisdom and justice of God. So consistently does Mather insist that his examples illustrate the nature of divine justice that this work can be viewed as part of the early Puritan effort to formulate a theodicy based on the Puritan notion of a sovereign God.

A few examples randomly drawn from Mather's list of divine providences will suffice to characterize his emphasis upon divine justice. Migrating Puritans who remain firm in their faith miraculously manage, through divine intervention, to survive disastrous storms at sea that destroy the unfaithful. A man shot through the head by an Indian survives this wound ("It would fill a volume," Mather writes, "to give an account of all the memorable preservations in the time of the later war with the Indians").[11] Lightning strikes a chimney; among those seated around the fireplace, the only person killed is a notorious blasphemer whose tongue is scorched though the rest of his body appears unharmed. An autopsy performed upon a non-believer after a heart attack discloses that his heart has turned to stone. A drunkard suffocates in his own vomit. A man who shoves a minister from the pulpit in order to preach his own sermon is struck dumb for life. Corpses disclose their murderers. Quakers and other enemies of the church are mysteriously killed or plagued with demons.[12]

Remarkable Providences thus portrays a world which for Mather displays a clear commensurability between a sin and its punishment. Mather's son Cotton later stresses this commensurability when he cautions overzealous Puritans against interpreting any event as God's punishment unless "some convincing circumstance and character . . . something in the time of it, or in its resemblance to the fault for which it comes, or in the confession of the person chastised" strongly indicates God's punitive agency.[13] God's treatment of people, according to Increase and Cotton Mather, is therefore neither arbitrary nor demonic but expresses a morally justifiable ordering of events which they are able—and obliged—to discern through careful observation of the events themselves.[14] Mather's *Remarkable Providences*, like his son's additional collection of divine providences in *Magnalia Christi Americana* (1702), were intended to provide correct models of interpretation which people could use to interpret their experiences. The Mathers were demonstrating in these works how Christians could use a theodicy based upon the Puritan notion of a sovereign God to make sense of any happening in their daily lives.

Whereas Increase Mather's *Remarkable Providences* is an exercise in practical theology, his *Doctrine of Divine Providence* is a theoretical elaboration of divine justice in terms of the Puritan notion of God's sovereignty. Mather's concern in the sermons that constitute this work is not to justify the ways of God to his congregation; rather, it is to demonstrate that the moral complexities of human experience can be adequately explained only by the notion "that there is an over ruling hand of providence in what cometh to pass, in the world" (p. 3).[15]

Mather begins his argument for the necessity of believing in divine providence by suggesting that the world is like a wheel which, without a hand to guide it, "will presently Turn out of the way and fall to the ground; so if there were not a divine hand to manage the wheel of Providence, all things would run into confusion, and the World would come to ruin in one day" (p. 22). This image of the wheel becomes Mather's controlling metaphor. He describes every part of the world as having its own separate "wheel of divine providence. . . . There are as many wheels as there are quarters of the world. There is a wheel for the North and a wheel for the South, a wheel for the East and a wheel for the West. A wheel for *Asia*, and a wheel for *Africa*; a wheel for *Europe*, and a wheel for *America* too" (p. 9). Human experience, according to Mather, can be conceived as a complex series of interrelated wheels; all "the Changes and vicissitudes which are amongst things here below" can be seen as manifesting the turning of these wheels (p. 16). Even the most insignificant events are "like the small wheel of a clock which sets all the rest agoing"—each wheel, of course, being fully controlled by the hand of divine providence (p. 30).

Mather does not mean by this image to suggest the deistic notion of a God who, once having set His creation in motion, never again interferes with its orderly workings. To the contrary, Mather's God, reflecting the Puritan notion of God as primary cause, periodically intervenes in human affairs. Some wheels He slows down, others He speeds up, thereby readjusting His creation from time to time in order to ensure that it fulfills His own purposes. The wheels are the natural realm of second causes which explain ordinary events, or what Mather calls the "work of ordinary Providence" (p. 45). But such extraordinary happenings as accidents, chance events, things that occur at just the right time, and people or natural objects acting contrary to their nature and inclinations can be adequately explained only as issuing from the direct intervention of divine providence.

Moreover, Mather asserts, the rewards and punishments which people receive express a fairly rigorous moral order.[16] They are the surest evidence for the existence of a divine providence whose justice, though sometimes surpassing human comprehension, nevertheless largely remains rationally comprehensible since God generally tailors rewards or punishments to suit the nature and degree of people's good or sinful actions. Mather observes, for example, that every punishment for sin suitably reveals the sin itself. People sometimes suffer the very evil they have designed or perpetrated against others, "so that there is a . . . suffering in the same kind; the sinner is paid off in his own Coyn" (p. 62).

Sometimes the punishments people suffer have "some Resemblance and Analogy with their sins" (p. 65). Carnal sins are often accompanied by bodily miseries or diseases; "Spiritual sins are usually punished with Spiritual Plagues" (p. 67). At other times God's judgments are in accordance with the objects or instruments that occasion the sin. People might desire, for example, particular material possessions or prestigious positions. "Either God will punish them by takeing away that which their hearts are inordenately set upon, or else He will cause that Idol to become a scourge and plague" (p. 69).

God's providence can also suit the punishment to the place or the time of the sin. A judgment may occur at the very same place a person committed a sin, as it did for King Ahab, or at the very same time of year when the sin was committed, as it did for the Jews whose Temple the Romans destroyed during Passover, the time of year when they crucified Jesus Christ.

God also punishes sins of omission no less than He punishes sins of commission. Those Christians who neglect such religious duties as prayer, participation in baptism and the Lord's Supper, public worship, obedience to the Ten Commandments, and raising children in the Christian faith will provoke God's wrath. The death of children can be viewed in this light. "It may be some of you have neglected Family dutyes; you have not prayed for and with your Children as you ought to have done. Or you have neglected to build God's house and therefore he does break and pull down your houses" by taking the life of a child (p. 97).

Nor does repentance for a sin necessarily deter a suitable punishment. To illustrate this point, Mather cites the case of a duelist who repented having killed an opponent and later "became a pattern of Mortification and Holiness." Nevertheless he died by bleeding to death as an appropriate punishment for the kind of death he had inflicted upon his opponent. So stringent is God's justice that "tho' it be most true that God pardons Sin to those that truly repent of it; Nevertheless he useth so to order things by his providence, as that the mark of his displeasure shall appear" (p. 81). But just as God punishes people in ways that suit their sins, so He also seeks to proportion "*rewards of mercy according* to what the works of men *have been*. As he dispenseth Judgements according to evil works, so mercies according to good works; only with this difference that in the one there is merit but not in the other. When God punisheth men they receive the due desert of their deeds, but when he bestows blessings; that's meer mercy" (p. 75).

God has constructed such a moral universe, Mather argues, not only to demonstrate to people through His judgments and mercies that He exists and controls everything through His sovereign providence, but also to help people identify their sins through the nature of their afflictions. Yet people must exercise caution at this point; any affliction can be either a punishment for sin, a testing of faith, or a medicinal purging of sin. Mather counsels his readers to evaluate their experience in terms of each explanation before drawing any conclusions.

The Puritans were thus required to scrutinize every aspect of their experience in the light of alternative explanations; even after such strenuous self-examination, they still could not conclude decisively that it gave them a correct understanding of their experience. The Puritan theodicy, as Mather elaborates it, neither provides certitude nor encourages complacency in the religious life. Rather, it evokes a deepening sense of life's moral complexities while also encouraging distrust of the capacity of human reason to comprehend those complexities.

Moreover, God, according to Mather, futher complicates people's efforts to understand their experience by not always consistently punishing sin. The wicked often prosper; but Mather assures his readers that God has good reasons for letting some sinners gain worldly advantages. One such reason for not punishing some sinners is that God thereby enables us to "conclude that there is a judgment to come, a *day of wrath* which the wicked are reserved for" (p. 28). Or God will let the prosperity of the wicked increase "so that they may have the greater downfal at last, and that the Power and justice of God in punishing them, may be the more glorious and illustrious." Because their prosperity entices them to commit an increasing number of sins, their misery will likewise be increased, for they "will have the more sin to answer for before him that sitteth upon the throne forever" (p. 29).

But sometimes the wicked prosper their entire lives, suffering no punishments whatsoever, while "the righteous see nothing but miserable days in this world," often dying ignominiously. Such extreme circumstances, which seemingly defy the very dictates of divine justice itself, pose an incomprehensible mystery which Mather describes in one of his most candid passages: "*Sometimes there is a seeming contradiction in divine providence. . . .* The providences of God seem to Interfere with one another sometimes. One providence seems to look this way, another providence seems to look that way, quite contrary one to another. . . . the works of God sometimes seem to run counter with his word: so that there is a dark and amazing intricacie in the ways of providence. This is *a wheel within a wheel.* Not only wise but good men have sometimes been put to a nonplus here" (p. 43). One's only recourse in the face of such an insoluble mystery is first to view each providence in its own context, then in the context of other providences, until finally, when the complexities outstrip human comprehension, one must confess one's limitations.

Mather, like Urian Oakes, describes human experience as being a quilted pattern of complexly interlinked and counterbalancing designs in which even the most accidental happenings are not arbitrary but fully determined by a divine logic that is ultimately beyond human comprehension. "There's no tracing of the Lord in the paths of his Providence. . . . There is no such track of providence, as that men shall thereby be able fully to understand by what Rules the Holy and Wise God ordereth all events Prosperous and adverse which come to pass in the world" (p. 42). Although people cannot immediately understand the judgments of God, these judgments nevertheless "are (and shall at last appear to be) Just, and Equal, and Good" (Preface). Eternal damnation itself will ultimately be seen as an expression of divine justice. Even from a human perspective, Mather asserts, it is clear that anyone who relies solely on his own moral efforts has no right to say that God is unjust in consigning him to eternal damnation, since God clearly requires not only obedience to His moral law but also the "fruits of Faith, and Repentance, and Holiness in life and conversation" (p. 104).

Mather appeals to the distinction between the covenant of works and the covenant of grace when he further asserts that any effort to be moral which is not infused with divine grace only sets people at odds with God. When people understand their relationship with God only in ethical terms, they cannot understand, much less submit themselves to, the divine imperative that they seek out every opportunity to glorify God, even when it requires their own ruin. "I confess that tho a man should have nothing for his pains yet if he might be so happy as to promote the glory of God in an active way, that alone is happiness enough. No Creature is capable of an higher dignity then this is, to be made use of as an instrument of Gods glory" (p. 144). No one, according to this perspective, becomes truly moral until he completely submits himself to the will of a sovereign God and relinquishes all demands that God's treatment of him conform to human ethical expectations.

Mather's later sermons, however, expressed his awareness that this vision of a sovereign God poses moral problems that cannot be ignored. For example, if the premature deaths of infants, children, and young adults are to be attributed to God, does this not raise serious questions about God's goodness? In 1697, Mather addressed himself to this problem before the Harvard student body in a sermon which seeks to make sense of the accidental drowning of two Harvard students whose behavior had always been exemplary. From a human perspective, says Mather, these premature deaths seem to be the arbitrary act of an unaccountably cruel God; but from a divine perspective these deaths serve God's redemptive purposes by testing the faith of Christians and by reminding sinners that God has created a precarious and unpredictable universe in which they cannot rely upon themselves for salvation. In this way God not only keeps Christians constantly watchful over the state of their souls, but perhaps also promotes the conversion of hardened sinners. Near the close of his sermon Mather voices the hope for the Harvard student body "that the Lord would sanctify what has hapned to awaken you unto serious thoughts about Death and Eternity. Who knows but that God may make these sudden Deaths, an occasion of promising the Salvation, & Eternal Life of some amongst you." [17] Mather thus echoes Urian Oakes' argument that God, in His "mere Pleasure and Providence," ordains all tragic and chance happenings in order to realize redemptive purposes which He cannot achieve in any other way, and that these redemptive consequences justify His seemingly harsh treatment of humankind.

Another moral problem inherent in the Puritan notion of God's sovereignty regards the necessity for moral and religious striving. As many sermons during this period indicate, people were frequently arguing that belief in a God who saves or damns them without regard for their moral behavior makes any commitment to moral values seem futile, if not altogether unnecessary. Mather posed this problem through the eyes of unconverted sinners in his sermon "Predestination and Human Exertions" (1710). "Ask them why they don't reform their Lives, why don't you Turn over a new leaf, and amend your ways and your doings, they will answer, God does not give me Grace. I can't Convert myself, and God does not Convert me. Thus do they insinuate as if God were in fault, and the blame of their Unconversion to be imputed unto him." [18] To be sure, Mather continues, no effort to do good can compel God to confer His grace; nor can it be denied that God often converts sinners despite their hardness of heart. "Nay, sometimes when Sinners have been in the height of their Resistance and Rebellion, to shew the exceeding Riches of his Grace, God has then Converted them." [19] But this is no good reason for persisting in sin, since "God is not bound to give Sinners Grace: He is an absolute Sovereign, and may give Grace or deny Grace to whom he pleaseth." [20]

Moreover, "Sinners can do more towards their own conversion then they do or will do" by avoiding those things that are a hindrance to conversion and by doing those things (such as keeping godly company, reading godly books, and thinking about serious spiritual matters) which have "a tendency to promote Conversion." [21]

Since people have it within their power to work toward conversion, Mather argues, no one, not even those who believe that God denies them His grace, has any excuse for abandoning all moral and religious striving. [22] To do so might preclude any possibilities for conversion, whereas conversion might possibly result from the unstinting effort to improve one's self. Should a lifetime of such effort fail to bring the desired experience of God's grace, the sinner still has one last recourse. On judgment day, when he must account for himself, he can call God into account by saying (and Mather's sermon closes with these words): "Lord, Thou knowest I did all that possibly I could do, for the obtaining [of] Grace, and for all that, Thou didst withhold it from me." [23] By implying that his listeners could bank on the outside chance that their good behavior might still evoke God's grace in the hereafter, Mather sought to preserve a tenuous relationship between moral striving and salvation in a world which seemed indifferent to serious moral commitments.[24]

COTTON MATHER: THE PURITAN UNDERSTANDING OF MORALITY

Adherence to moral values in a world indifferent to them was no less problematical for the faithful than it was for the unregenerate. At least this was Cotton Mather's contention in his frequently misunderstood work, *Bonifacius: An Essay Upon the Good*. This work advocates doing good works; indeed, the largest part of it is devoted to describing a "vast variety of new ways to do good" that will make Christians the "most useful men in the world" (pp. 20, 15).[25] However, these projects for doing good cannot be understood apart from Mather's effort to demonstrate that the morality of Christians gives them no advantage over sinners (except to make them more "useful"). Christians and sinners alike, says Mather, must share the incertitudes of a world governed by a sovereign deity who shapes people's lives without regard for their desires, good deeds, faithfulness, or ethical conceptions of justice. God permits Satan to arouse "vile *ideas*" and "calumnies" in others which will "clog all the good [Christians] propose to do." Even "if the Devil were asleep there is malignity enough in the hearts of *wicked men* themselves, to render a man that will *do good*, very distasteful and uneasy to them" (p. 147). Moreover, the world, Satan, and even God frequently make the efforts of Christians to do good the occasion for their ruin.

Mather gives the Christian facing such a world no leeway for self-pity. He reminds his readers that Christ himself was vilified and put to death for his good works, and that a Christian's conformity to Christ is imperfect until he, too, is *"despised and rejected of men"* (p. 147). True Christian humility is "a consent to be made *nothing*"—a complete yielding of one's self to being victimized by an evil world for seeking to do good (p. 143). "If you hear the hopes of disaffected men, to see you *come to nothing, hear* it with as much satisfaction as they can *hope* it. Embrace . . . *annihilations* . . . be insensible of any *merits* in your performances. Lie in the dust, and be willing that both God and man should lay you there" (pp. 144, 149).

Nor does Mather give Christians any hope that God will lessen the power of evil to nullify their efforts to do good. To the contrary, God has given this power to the forces of evil as a means to punish a sinful world.

If men always upon *intentions* and *inventions* to *do good*, were so generally beloved and esteemed as they might be, they would be *instruments* of doing more *good*, than the justice of Heaven, can yet allow to be done for *such* a world. *The World is not worthy* of them, nor of that *good* that is endeavored by them. To deprive the world of that *good*, they must be left unto a strange *aversion* for those men that would fain do it. This cripples them, fetters them, defeats their excellent purposes! (P. 145)[26]

That God has structured human existence in this way is "enough," Mather admits, "To make one *sick of the world*; but it "should not make thee sick of *essays to do good in the world*" (p. 10). Why should it not? Mather's answer to this question sets forth the basic reasons which Puritan orthodoxy provides for the necessity of being moral in a universe that remains antagonistic to humankind's best moral efforts.

First and foremost, says Mather, Christians must remember that God has conferred upon them the grace which enables them to do the good works unregenerate sinners cannot do. This divinely bestowed capacity for doing good, according to the first of three "evangelical *principles*" that Mather describes, requires obedience to God's moral law.

Though our Saviour has furnished us, with a perfect and spotless *righteousness*, when His obedience to the Law, is placed into our account; yet it is a sin for us at all to fall short in our own obedience to the Law. . . . [But] We are not under the Law as a *covenant of works*. Our own exactness in doing of good works, is not now the *condition* of our *entering into life*. Woe unto us if it *were*! But still, the *Covenant of Grace* holds us to it, as our *duty*; and if we are in the *Covenant of Grace*, we shall make it our *study*, to do those *good works* which once were the terms of our *entering into life*. (Pp. 28–29)

The second evangelical principle which Mather enunciates states that obedience to "the law of *good works*, which we *enjoy* . . . in the Ten Commandments" in no way makes Christians acceptable or righteous in God's eyes (p. 28). Only their faith in Christ makes Christians acceptable to God; "yet good works are demanded of us, to *justify* our *faith*; to *demonstrate* that it is indeed that *precious faith*." One of the surest signs of true faith is a life of unstinting efforts to do good in the face of all adversities. The Christian must maintain himself at this peak of striving, else he will be barred from heaven: "A *workless faith* is a *worthless* faith" (p. 29). Mather here sustains what David Levin calls "that dizzy world of circular argument and begged questions in which Puritans struggled to distinguish faith from works without becoming either antinomians or (to use a word from *Bonifacius*) merit mongers."[27]

Mather continues to walk this fine line when he articulates his third evangelical principle. It affirms that good works are to be evaluated not in terms of their goodness or consequences, but solely in terms of their adequacy as expressions of faith in God. Christians are to express their gratitude for salvation by doing good deeds; to do good out of gratitude to God is to glorify God, the "great End" of human existence (p. 19). "None but a good man, is really a living man; and the more good any man does,

the more he really *lives. All the rest is death*; or belongs to it" (p. 7).
Consequently, what the Christian gains by being virtuous is not worldly
success or happiness as the world understands it, but rather the sheer pleasure of doing good because God expects it.

The practice of virtue thus evokes in the Christian "a sort of *holy Epicurism*" that is its own reward (p. 151).[28] To expect any reward other
than this for being moral, according to Mather, is to be unrealistic, since
God has made true morality a sure path to suffering or even personal ruin
in order to prove that the world is untrustworthy and, as a consequence,
to evoke in people a faith that acknowledges Him as the only trustworthy
reality in such a world.

Bonifacius thus clearly advocates the Puritan theodicy which gives uncompromising expression to the notion of a sovereign God who frequently
disregards all ethical expectations for the sake of realizing His redemptive
purposes.

Though one would not immediately associate the names of Cotton Mather
and Sören Kierkegaard, *Bonifacius*, like many of the earlier Puritan writings already discussed, explored the problem of God in a way which prefigured the religious concerns Kierkegaard later expressed in his interpretation of the Abraham story.[29] According to Kierkegaard, God's command
to Abraham to sacrifice his son, Isaac, expressed a "teleological suspension
of the ethical." By this Kierkegaard means that God purposely directed
Abraham to suspend the injunction not to kill as a means of testing Abraham's faith. Abraham's holiness, as Geoffry Clive observes, rests "on a
paradox, namely, his preparedness to stand above the Law out of respect
for the Lawgiver. . . . He makes himself an exception to the universal
. . . by obeying an esoteric supernatural voice enjoining murder."[30] A
God who thus exacts unethical behavior as proof of a person's faith—who
thereby undermines the ethical by making it a source of temptation to
disobey Him—is, according to Kierkegaard, exercising an unchallengeable
sovereignty that transcends all ethical and rational categories.

Many Puritan writers similarly affirmed the unethical prerogatives of
God's sovereignty, though none said that God would require unethical
actions of people as proof of their faith, or, for that matter, for any reason.
Certainly in *Bonifacius* Mather made explicit a key notion which is implicit in the Puritan theodicy, namely, that a divine teleological suspension
of the ethical best explains a world which contravenes all ethical conceptions of justice. A world in which God divests the moral life of all guarantees requires that people become moral and religious solely because God
is what He is, not because He confers rewards on their goodness and faithfulness.

Mather could advocate such an extreme non-utilitarian view of morality
precisely because he affirmed a sovereign deity whose providential beneficence controls everything. God, who sees the complex web of interrela-

tionships among all people, will transform their actions into those consequences, good or bad, which can best accomplish His own mysterious
purposes.[31] People must simply be and act as God's moral law commands
them to be and act.

The Puritans arduously, almost obsessively, sought an answer for the
problem of evil which would confirm their belief that God, far from being
monstrous in His autonomous control of the world, is the only reality that
makes goodness possible in a corrupt and corrupting world. But the Puritan, as Mather's analysis indicates, also refused to blink away the obvious
discrepancies, injustices, and evils of a world wherein—as Jonathan Edwards put it—"the cause of the just is not vindicated."[32]

In such a world, the necessity for being moral, according to the Puritan
theology, was based solely on God's command that people glorify Him
through their moral behavior. If people as a consequence are ruined, then
remaining moral in the face of such treatment redounds all the more to
the glory of God. Puritan theologians, in short, refused to compromise
their understanding of the morally problematical nature of human existence: both God and human experience were exceedingly complex. The
Puritans did their best to represent faithfully both kinds of complexities,
even at the expense, finally, of leaving God ethically incomprehensible and
unacceptable to many.

Mather's understanding of morality in *Bonifacius* gives little support, if
any, to the view that this work was the harbinger of the utilitarian moralism that was beginning to emerge in early eighteenth-century America.
Mather's staunch denials that people gain either merit or salvation through
their good actions, and his equally staunch affirmations that being truly
virtuous inevitably imposes extreme suffering upon the individual, did little to encourage a simplistic or legalistic attitude toward the moral life.
And Mather's stern vision of the Christian's lifelong struggle against "a
most vehement visible malice permitted by God to resist mankind" left no
room whatsoever for any naive faith in the power of goodness to overcome evil (p. 146).

Yet there are two aspects of Mather's position which partially justify
some of the criticisms levelled against *Bonifacius* ever since Benjamin
Franklin published his Silence Dogood essays. The first is that Mather required the Christian at all times to do the right deed with the right intention regardless of the consequences. Mather never considered the possible
bad consequences of a good action either for the Christian or for others;[33]
all he could bring himself to say was that good deeds will most likely, but
not inevitably, have good consequences. This emphasis upon the act and
its motivation derived from Mather's belief that God's overruling providence orchestrates the consequences of all human actions.

Another problematical aspect of *Bonifacius* is Mather's contention that
people must always do what the moral law prescribes. This emphasis pre-

cariously bordered on legalistic moralism. Mather's position did not make room for circumstances that might justify committing a "wrong" deed if it could have better consequences than a virtuous action. Nor did it allow for the possibility that what is right in one set of circumstances might be wrong in others. Nothing in Mather's position encouraged a person to complicate his moral consciousness along these lines, precisely because to undertake such considerations was, for Mather, to usurp the prerogatives of God. The true moral consciousness, according to Mather, does not seek to shape life according to its own perceptions and expectations, but rather lets God shape and direct these expectations and perceptions in accordance with His own redemptive purposes. *Bonifacius* thus represented an uncompromising statement of the Puritan belief that anything less than full conformity to the sovereign will of God is a spurious morality.

SAMUEL WILLARD: A TRADITION REAFFIRMED

The Mathers' concern to define the relationship between morality and belief in a sovereign God was shared by many of their contemporaries, most notably Samuel Willard, one of the Bay Colony's major theologians. Willard undertook a systematic reassessment of Puritan orthodoxy "in the light of the new situation of Massachusetts during the painful transition from colony to province,"[34] a reassessment which in part reflected his effort to overturn an emerging moralism that was being disseminated by works like Giles Firmin's *The Real Christian*, first published in 1670. In Willard's view, Firmin's position subverted both the moral and the religious life.

Firmin directly challenged the Puritan tradition by rejecting its notion of a sovereign God who demands that people exalt His glory above all things, including their own happiness and salvation.[35] The basis for his challenge was that he could find in the Bible "not one duty that God requires of his creatures, which is contrary to his creatures happiness. . . . Never did God declare against self, or call a man to deny himself in that which hinders his own salvation and happiness" (pp. 141, 209). According to Firmin, God refuses either to impose His will upon people or to compel them to act contrary to their free will; God realizes that people "must cease to be . . . rational creature[s] in so doing" (p. 172)—a claim which ignores the entire prophetic tradition of the Old Testament. The only means at God's disposal for effecting people's salvation is to persuade them rationally that salvation is preferable to damnation. "What the Sovereign God might have done with his Creature, I deny not; but it hath pleased him graciously to deal with man as a rational creature, giving him commandments. . . . He gives arguments suitable to them. . . . He is pleased to invite us, allure us to obedience, by promises of great reward" (pp. 122, 307).

The process of conversion, as Firmin describes it, is one in which God,

Christ, and Satan must function as cosmological salesmen who seek to sell their respective products—redemption and sin—by advertising them in ways that make them appealing to people.[36] God must then wait while a person "deliberates, ponders, [and] observes" the proffered items, finally choosing the one he considers the better buy (p. 244). If God successfully presents Himself in His most attractive light, people will see the benefits of redemption and naturally choose it because it serves their self-interest to do so.[37] The "real Christian," in Firmin's view, is one who demands from God sufficient rational grounds for choosing salvation, and only after receiving them chooses Christ over Satan.[38] Salvation here no longer constitutes a means to glorify God; it has become a bartering process which constricts God's sovereignty, since God must appeal to people solely on their own terms and accept their final decision.

Firmin's God therefore fully conforms to human ethical and rational expectations. "All God's wayes are Rational; what is irrational, or contrary to sound reason, cannot be imputed to his wayes" (p. 298). This respect for human ethical demands prevents God from ever suspending the ethical for the purpose of realizing His own desires. In *The Real Christian*, then, Firmin humanized the divine sovereignty and, by implication, gave prominence, if not normative status, to those moral values compatible with a notion of God who places ethical limits on the use of His power.

It was just this idea—that God tamely uses rational and moral means to persuade people to become moral and religious—which prompted Willard to assert that the problem posed by moralism "is of a great Moment as almost any thing that I know of."[39] The problem for Willard was that any conception of the moral life based on an ethical notion of God denied divine grace any role in making the moral life possible. It denied the Puritan belief in a sovereign deity who confers on some and withholds from others the possibility of being moral regardless of their personal merits or demerits. Willard devoted several of his public lectures on the Christian faith (which were posthumously published in 1727 as *A Compleat Body of Divinity*) to reaffirming the concept of a sovereign deity who providentially governs all things in accordance with His own purposes without justifying His ways to humankind.

Everything that happens, says Willard, expresses the "Arbitrary Government of God, who acts as a great Monarch, who gives not an account of His matters to the Children of Men, but holds the Creature in a full Subordination to His absolute pleasure."[40] God's providential government is not completely arbitrary, for He co-operates with the natural realm of second causes.[41] Willard appeals to the Puritan doctrine of God's concurrence with the orderly workings of natural causation as early as his first published sermon (1673), where he defines God as "the first mover[;] he is as it were the first wheel of the great clock of the world, or the spring of this watch. Second beings have an operation, but it hath an absolute dependence upon his co-operation."[42] God normally works through the "ordinary" means of natural causation until their inadequacy for achieving His purposes leads Him to use "extraordinary" means which are inexplicable in terms of natural law.[43] Willard thus reasserts the Puritan view of God's providential governance of human affairs; nothing happens or exists unless God allows or causes it to happen or exist.[44] The "whole world," as Willard metaphorically puts it, "is a sucking infant depending on the breasts of divine providence."[45]

To reaffirm God's sovereignty was, for Willard, to reaffirm the primacy of divine grace.[46] Like his predecessors, Willard unswervingly adhered to the Reformed notion that "the sovereignty of divine grace, which can neither be prevented nor obliged by any thing in or for us, is a pillar-truth of the Christian religion."[47] People's lives are ultimately to be assessed as being either within or outside the pale of God's saving grace—that is to say, the covenant of grace. Those who refuse to own the covenant of grace, or who live solely in accordance with the covenant of works, are natural men living in a state of apostasy in the wilderness of the world, exiled from God's healing grace. Only those who own the covenant of grace can finally be saved.[48]

But owning the covenant only makes this a possibility, not an actuality. The "covenant promise" of salvation requires that people first fulfill specific conditions. "Simply and precisely because the covenant of grace is a covenant is it essential for there to be specified conditions that must be met in order for the promise to be binding: 'hence this performance' of the conditional terms on man's part is 'the very way to enjoy the performance of the promise' on God's part."[49] These conditions are faith, repentance, and a life of Christian charity. Only when these conditions are met does God make good His promise.

Willard cautions his readers, however, against thinking that faith, repentance, and good works either merit or earn divine favor. Anyone who thinks this way about the religious life is still a natural man who believes, in accordance with the covenant of works, that he can gain salvation through his moral efforts. To be sure, the morality of the natural man helps him to be "useful for the publick benefit"; but no matter how faithfully he is thereby seeking to obey God's will, such efforts cannot lead him to salvation.[50] The reason for this, as Bulkely and earlier covenant theologians had noted, is that Adam's fall annulled the covenant of works. It is now impossible, Willard asserts, for people to expiate the curse of disobedience through any amount of good works.

As a consequence, the covenant of works is superseded by the covenant of grace in which people become acceptable to God solely through faith.[51] Those who are thus accepted by God know that they can do nothing to merit their salvation. Faith "makes us to do nothing at all with any opinion of meriting by it: we will do nothing so as to expect that for the sake

of our doing, we shall obtain any thing from God. . . . We renounce all
our own Righteousness in the bottom, that so we may be built upon [the
righteousness] of Christ."[52]

The choice to live a life of faith was itself experienced as a mysterious
gift inexplicable in ethical terms, since the world was experienced as being
indifferent to all moral striving. Only divine grace provided an adequate
explanation for a person's deliberate choice to adopt the ethos recommended by the Puritan world view, and living this life style made the Puritans' description of the world seem accurate. World view and ethos thus
mutually corroborated each other, their point of intersection being the experience of divine grace.

Despite this emphasis on the pivotal importance of divine grace, Willard, like earlier Puritan theologians, maintains that the covenant of grace
re-establishes the necessity for God's moral law. God holds the law before
the people, "making them to see the face of their Souls and of their lives
in it, as in a glass." What they see is an image of their own righteousness
falling far short of "legal perfection."[53] The moral law, like the ceremonial
part of the law, thus discloses to people *their absolute need of an Expia-
tory Sacrifice to take away the guilt of sin from them*," thereby demonstrating the necessity for accepting Jesus Christ as their savior.[54] Obedience to the moral law is also necessary because, in His covenant with
Adam before the fall, "God gave [the law] to man to be an everlasting
Rule to direct him in all things."[55] Adam's fall nullified both the covenant
of works and humankind's capacity to fulfill the law, but not the commandments themselves or humankind's duty to obey them. Both the commandments and obedience to them therefore remain basic to the covenant
of grace.

In the covenant of grace, however, the Christian's faith in Christ enables
him to obey the law and, through his faith and continual repentance, to
develop a life of true virtue that "proceeds from [Christ] to us."[56] God
accepts only this kind of morality which, as Willard puts it, makes it "ser-
viceable to our salvation."[57] The "moral man" who seeks through his own
efforts to gain salvation "hath no claim to the spiritual and saving priviledges of this Covenant, nor doth he desire it, counting that he can do well
enough without it . . . he is really under the Law, and therefore must
stand or fall according to the sentence of it."[58]

True morality thus constitutes only that obedience to God's moral laws
which seeks to glorify God. For Willard, as for the Mathers and Puritan
thought in general, the covenant of grace redefines morality in a way which
distinguishes true virtue from those conventional notions of virtue that
pertain only to "outward behavior."[59]

However, Willard's analysis of the moral life does not express the characteristic Puritan mistrust of the conscience. The conscience, as Willard
defines it, is an innate part of human nature which recognizes the justice,

goodness, and obligatory nature of the moral law and accepts the duty of obeying it.[60] It is that activity of the human understanding which "exerts itself with respect to the law of God, and makes a judgment of it," telling people how God expects them to pursue their goals.[61] Willard admits that the conscience can sometimes be mistaken; but nothing, he maintains, can destroy its capacity to disclose a person to himself as God sees him. The fully awakened conscience is that self-knowledge which corresponds with God's knowledge of one's true self. In thus giving the conscience a more prominent role in the covenant of grace, Willard anticipated the direction liberal theologians would later take in developing their visions of God's moral nature.

Prior to his death in 1707, Willard's work constituted the high water mark in the Puritan effort to elaborate both a theodicy and a theocentric definition of morality thoroughly consistent with the Puritan notion of God's sovereignty. But there is little that differentiates his synthesis of the Puritan world view and ethos from that found in the writings of Urian Oakes, Increase Mather, and Cotton Mather. They did not reinterpret the Puritan world view in the light of contemporary social changes, but rather finally reaffirmed it. Like Anne Bradstreet, Roger Williams, Michael Wigglesworth, and Edward Taylor, they described a dangerous and precarious world in which the only trustworthy reality is God; an enticing world which traps people into believing that its allurements are to be given precedence over God; a morally complex and confusing world which, in its frequent imposition of a harsher destiny upon the elect than upon the unregenerate, its indifference to moral striving, and its random dislocation of human lives, provokes and defies human comprehension. It danced before the Puritan imagination like a potential Medusa's head that could be safely viewed only by the backward glance into Perseus' mirror.

This world view, consciously or unconsciously, affected their literary style. The convoluted arguments and the labyrinth of language which frequently characterize Puritan writings seem an effort to mirror the morally convoluted labyrinths of the world portrayed in the Puritan outlook. In an almost incantatory fashion, these writings invoked a world of bypaths that could easily lead people astray, a world of disparate happenings which, from a human perspective, discloses no apparent moral logic underlying them. It is a chaotic world which God continuously remolds as it fragments itself. This presentation of a confusing and chaotic world also invoked particular responses to such a world: a sense that the world is far more complex than it appears on the surface, a sense of wariness about ever being able to comprehend fully this morally ambiguous world, a sense of distrust regarding the reliability of this world, and a sense of incertitude and vigilance regarding one's status in such a world. Puritan theologians emphasized their rational approach to human experience; but their style of argument had a dramatic element in it which made their audience think and feel in terms of a world that frequently defies people's rational and ethical expectations.

Such a world requires that the self constantly call itself into question, even within the covenant of grace. The unregenerate self, because of its self-deceiving belief that it can guarantee its life through its own efforts, is by nature one which refuses to doubt their efficacy. Such efforts create a false sense of security which the individual must criticize so as to avoid the pitfalls of self-deception. But even the regenerate self which believes it is infused with divine grace cannot forego this process of self-questioning, for it must vigilantly examine whether it is deceiving itself about being a member of the elect. According to the Puritan outlook, the only true test that demonstrated, insofar as such matters could be demonstrated in this life, that the self was not so deceived was its active willingness to sacrifice itself—its desires, its expectations, even its life—for the glory of God. Morality, in this view, is neither doing good deeds because they are praiseworthy or because they make one feel good, nor being virtuous in order to attain happiness, nor doing good as society envisions it; rather, true morality consists solely in performing those actions which God requires regardless of the consequences to one's self.

The Puritan theodicy thus described a world view which made the style of life it endorsed seem the necessary condition for life within the world it portrayed; the ethos it recommended made the world view it described seem an actual state of affairs ideally arranged to accommodate such a style of life.

It is this same synthesis of world view and ethos which Jonathan Edwards further elaborated in his treatment of the Puritan theodicy. Edwards in fact developed the Puritan ethos into a systematic moral vision of all human experience, thereby making a culturally prescribed religious mode of experiencing the world the normative foundation for defining true morality in all social contexts. His writings, especially the *Treatise Concerning Religious Affections* and *The Nature of True Virtue*, are a monument to the Puritan effort to demonstrate how the values which the Puritan world view endorses are the necessary conditions of life in a precarious and untrustworthy world.

3

Jonathan Edwards: Morality and a Sovereign God

GOD'S SOVEREIGNTY AND GOD'S MORAL GOVERNMENT

No theologian in American Puritanism, not even Samuel Willard in his compendious *Compleat Body of Divinity*, rivals Jonathan Edwards in his comprehensive and systematic explication of the Puritan world view and ethos. In parading the entire range of Puritan dogma through his writings, Edwards testifies to the vitality of a Puritan piety which glorified the sovereign God of the Puritan theodicy. Almost every aspect of his theology affirms the Puritan theodicy with its particular fusion of world view and ethos; his writings are the showcase for viewing how the Puritan theodicy functioned as a means to resolve the ethical dilemma posed by belief in a sovereign deity.[1]

Neither the religious life nor the moral life, in Edwards' view, can be understood apart from the Puritan affirmation of a sovereign God who shapes human destinies according to His pleasure. "The sovereignty of God is his absolute, independent right of disposing of all creatures according to his own pleasure" (W, 2:850).[2] There is nothing people can do to frustrate, baffle, or undermine God's providential designs; conversely, what "man determines, never comes to pass, unless God determines it" (W, 2:534). God actively opposed all human schemes for gaining a sense of security because they encourage a rebellious self-reliance which blinds people to their helpless status before a sovereign God. Edwards vividly renders this helplessness in his now infamous image of people as loathsome spiders that God dangles over the pit of hell by a single thread.[3] Each moment their destruction is imminent. All that preserves them from destruction "is the mere arbitrary will, and unconvenanted, unobliged forbearance of an incensed God" (W, 2:9).[4]

Those who die unregenerate will face an eternity of being crushed beneath "the infinite weight" of God's "almighty merciless vengeance" (W, 2:11). "And though [God] will know that you cannot bear the weight of omnipotence treading upon you, yet he will not regard that, but he will crush you under his feet without mercy; he will crush out your blood, and make it fly, and it shall be sprinkled on his garments, so as to stain all his raiment" (W, 2:10). No appeal to dignity of person or human rights can mitigate this irremediable suffering, since God intends it to be a warning to the unregenerate which might effect their conversion and salvation (W, 2:11).[5] Edwards' rendering of the human predicament is designed to help his audience imaginatively see and feel their complete dependence upon the grace of a sovereign God whose very sovereignty places Him beyond all ethical categories.[6]

Edwards reaffirms the necessity for such dependence on God in his "Dissertation Concerning the End for Which the World was Created." He contends that God created the world solely to express His own regard for Himself, to delight in the expression of His divine perfections in nature and human affairs. This, not any special regard for humankind, is the end for which God created the world. Humankind's purpose in this scheme of things is to praise and glorify God's holy attributes with an unsurpassable joy in its special privilege of having been granted the gift of life. Nevertheless God's regard for Himself in creating the world involves His helping humankind become virtuous. "God in seeking his glory, seeks the good of his creatures" (W, 1:104). He confers happiness or goodness on people solely to serve His own pleasure. People must therefore acknowledge their complete dependence upon God's self-regard, and joyfully accept the fact that their happiness and goodness are not the supreme goal of creation, but rather serve only to reflect God's glory, itself the ultimate end of human beings and all creation.

That God uses the eternal suffering of sinners to glorify His justice and majesty neither impeaches "the glory of any of [God's] attributes" nor provides any basis for maligning God's sovereign use of His power. Nothing that God does can be wrong (W, 2:850). "It is impossible for an infinitely wise and good being to do otherwise, than to choose what he sees on the whole to be best" (W, 2:537). Furthermore, the Book of Job, according to Edwards, demonstrates that people have no right to expect God to explain why He shapes human destinies as He does. "It is fit that God should dwell in thick darkness, or in a light to which no man can approach" if only because, by making people aware of the infinite distance between human understanding and God's comprehension, it reminds them of their finite status before an infinite God (W, 2:108).[7]

Like his Puritan forebears, Edwards does not try to resolve the dilemma of Puritan ethics by abandoning the notion of a God whose "sovereign pleasure" in arbitrarily determining human destinies is unresponsive to human ethical expectations. Rather, he seeks to demonstrate that God expresses His sovereignty in ways that are most appropriate to the human condition of total depravity, especially in His manipulation of evil.

Evil exists by God's permission, according to Edwards, in order that God can use evil to glorify both His justice and His capacity to create good. Evil is an evil thing in itself, Edwards admits, but when viewed from the perspective of "the universality of things," evil often has good consequences (W, 2:528). As Edwards puts it: "If God sees that good will come of [evil], and more good than otherwise, so that when the whole series of events is viewed by God, and all things balanced, the sum total of good with the evil is more than without it, all being subtracted that needs be subtracted, and added that is to be added; if the sum total of good thus considered, be greatest, greater than the sum in any other case, then it will follow that God, if he be a wise and holy being, must will it" (W, 2:542). God thus decrees sinful actions not as sin but "for the sake of the good that he causes to arise from the sinfulness thereof" (W, 2:527). Edwards denies, however, that this notion makes God "the author of sin." In his view, it only implies "that God has decreed that he will permit all the sin that ever comes to pass, and that upon his permitting it, it will certainly come to pass" (W, 2:533).

God therefore relies upon evil as one necessary means among many to achieve His redemptive purposes in a world otherwise recalcitrant to their realization. The Puritan theodicy, as Edwards elaborates it, makes evil no less morally desirable than good itself, for rather than obscuring God's redemptive nature, evil discloses it.

There would be no manifestation of God's grace of true goodness, if there was no sin to be pardoned, no misery to be saved from. . . . We little consider how much the sense of good is heightened by the sense of evil both moral and natural. And as it is necessary that there should be evil, because the display of the glory of God could not but be imperfect and incomplete without it, so evil is necessary, in order to the highest happiness of the creature, and the completeness of that communication of God, for which he made the world; because the creature's happiness consists in the knowledge of God, and sense of his love.

Then too, as Edwards adds, our "sense of good" would be "comparatively dull and flat, without the knowledge of evil" (W, 2:528).

Edwards carefully emphasizes how the Puritan theodicy defines good and evil not in terms of isolated experiences, but in terms of how all human experiences—through God's coordination of them—harmonize with one another in order to make the best of all possible worlds. Increase Mather used the image of interlocking wheels to illustrate this point; Edwards uses the image of converging rivers.

God's providence may not unfitly be compared to a large and long river, having innumerable branches, beginning in different regions, and at a great distance one from another, and all conspiring to one common issue. After their very diverse and apparent contrary courses, they all collect together, the nearer they come to their common end, and at length discharge themselves at one mouth into the same ocean. The different streams of this river are apt to appear like mere confusion to us, because of our limited sight, whereby we cannot see the whole at once. A man who sees but one or two streams at a time, cannot tell what their course tends to. Their course seems very crooked, and different streams seem to run for a while different and contrary ways: and if we view things at a distance, there seem to be innumerable obstacles and impediments in the way, as rocks and mountains, and the like; to hinder their ever uniting, and coming to the ocean; but yet if we trace them, they all unite at last, all come to the same issue, disgorging themselves in one into the same great ocean. Not one of all the streams fail. (W, 1:617).

Such an overview, according to Edwards, presents a mosaic the beauty of which, as Roland Delattre observes, "provides the measure of good and evil throughout the whole graded system of being."[8] Particular events which appear from a limited human perspective to be irreconcilable with God's perfections are thus seen from His perspective as contributing to His ordering of the totality of existence into a beautiful pattern that is realizing His purposes. Such a God often appears capricious, cruel, and even demonic in His treatment of humankind.

But God's ethical nature, according to Edwards, clearly manifests itself in a divine moral government which, as Edwards describes it, embodies a "regular, equal disposing of rewards and punishments of men according to their moral estate." The existence of this moral government, however, cannot be demonstrated through human affairs which manifest no such "distributive justice and judicial equity" on God's part. (W, 2:513).[9] Its existence can be proven only through the scriptural revelation that God has prepared a future life of eternal happiness for those who remain obedient to His moral government and a life of eternal suffering for those who ignore it. Through this moral government God allots a certain measure of sin to every individual; when this allotted measure is used up, each person then dies to face an eternal punishment commensurate with his or her own sins.

This "connexion between the measure of men's sins, and the measure of punishment" illustrates for Edwards the equitableness of divine justice; and, when placed in conjunction with the idea of apportioned sins, it also explains many of the apparent injustices of this world (W, 2:122). For according to Edwards, one reason God lets the wicked prosper is because they must live out the greater measure of sin assigned them; the greater measure of sin, which their prosperity enables them to complete, will also bring a greater punishment upon them in the afterlife. The worldly advantages which sinners seemingly undeservedly enjoy are therefore the well-deserved means to eternal punishment. Here is a theodicy which affirms a sovereign God and yet, in Edwards' view, also establishes a reliable foundation for the moral life.

Given this view of the world, Edwards believed he could answer the moral objections of both the unregenerate and the saved to their respective lots in life. On the one hand, the universe which he describes preempts the arguments of the unregenerate that they need not try to be moral or religious until they experience divine grace. A moral government which assures eternal punishment for a life of sin is itself a sufficiently compelling reason for seeking to live in conformity with God's will. On the other hand, Christians who question the trustworthiness of a God who imposes injustices and tribulation upon them despite their complete devotion to Him must remember that God's moral government remains a fully reliable object for their trust and hope.[10] God would not be so cruel, Edwards asserts, as to awaken in people the capacity for loving and desiring to be with their Creator for all eternity, "and yet to so order it, that such desire should be disappointed; so that [their] loving [their] Creator, should in some sense make [them] the more miserable" (W, 2:515). Nevertheless, he reminds the elect that full conformity to God's will guarantees them no rewards whatsoever in this life. He also reminds the unregenerate that their efforts to conform to God's will, no matter how persistent or well-intentioned they are, cannot effect their salvation.

Because of these caveats, Edwards' effort to hold in tension the notions of God's moral government and God's "sovereign and arbitrary grace" raises the same questions that recurringly plagued the Puritan notions of the covenant of works and the covenant of grace (W, 2:548). They are questions about the nature of both the moral and religious life as well as about the nature of their relationship.[11] If the very effort to do good deeds—to conform to God's will—does not define the genuine moral life, how then is true morality to be distinguished from false morality? Why does the moral striving of the unregenerate, no matter how exemplary, not constitute genuine morality? If Christians suffer a worse life than the unregenerate, how can they be sure they are actually members of the elect? If true Christians are predestined to eternal salvation, why then should they be moral, especially if they must suffer more than sinners? Increase Mather, Cotton Mather, and Samuel Willard had no difficulty in reaffirming the orthodox answers to such questions.

However, the Great Awakening and the heated discussions that were its aftermath complicated Edwards' consideration of these questions, first in his *Treatise Concerning Religious Affections*, which sets forth the criteria for defining true religion, and later in *The Nature of True Virtue*, which elaborates the criteria for distinguishing genuine from spurious morality. These two systematic works comprise the most comprehensive formulation within American Puritanism of the religious and ethical implications of the

Puritan theodicy. They further elaborate how the ethos recommended by the Puritan world view is the only appropriate response to the world it describes, and how the concept of grace fuses the Puritan world view and ethos.

THE RELIGIOUS LIFE: *TREATISE CONCERNING RELIGIOUS AFFECTIONS*

The Great Awakening was often characterized by such forms of behavior as revelatory visions, moaning and yelling, and seizures; people in the congregations, even preachers, occasionally tore off their clothes,[12] behavior that certainly did not conform to the traditional pattern of Puritan conversion experiences.[13] But there were many evangelical preachers like Gilbert Tennent and James Davenport who believed that emotional outbursts like these manifested a "feeling Experience" of the holy spirit, or a "new Birth"; they further maintained that no one, not even an appointed minister, is truly religious until he has experienced "the new Birth."[14]

However, critics of the Great Awakening such as Charles Chauncy and Jonathan Mayhew argued that the excessive forms of emotional behavior encouraged by many evangelical preachers were not religious experiences, but rather subverted true religion since they neither conformed to the traditional pattern of conversion experiences nor appealed to people's rational and moral faculties, only to their passions.[15] Edwards stood firmly against the critics because he believed the Great Awakening to be the outpouring of the Holy Spirit.[16] The large number of conversions, first in Northhampton and then in surrounding towns in the early 1740s, marked for him the inauguration of the Kingdom of God in America.[17]

But Edwards developed his position in a way that challenged the supporters of the Great Awakening no less than its critics. This double-edged stance is especially evident in his *Treatise Concerning Religious Affections*. This work undercuts not only those critics who attacked the Great Awakening as being nothing more than a cloddish form of "enthusiasm," but also those supporters of the Great Awakening who identified the workings of the Holy Spirit with the specific forms of religious behavior which the critics condemned.[18] Both camps, he argued, were wrongly focusing their attention upon epiphenomena that have nothing to do with true religiosity.[19]

Edwards advanced this discussion by analyzing the role of the affections in religious experience. The affections, as Edwards defines them, are not emotions of all kinds but only those which express the deepest impulses or "inclinations"—the love or hatred of a particular idea, object or person—which give a person's life its basic orientation or direction. He further distinguishes the affections from the passions. The passions are those inclinations which overwhelm the mind, wrest away its power for making rational choices, and propel the person into irrational behavior. The affections are a union of inclinations and mind which strives to achieve the clarity of understanding which makes rational choices possible. Edwards used this distinction between the affections and passions to challenge both the revivalists, who contended that religion is primarily a matter of the passions, and the critics of the Great Awakening, who defined religion as primarily a matter of the intellect.[20] Neither the passions nor the intellect—nor even all affections—said Edwards, define the essence of genuine religion. Rather, true religion "in great part, consists in holy affections" which express an inclination to love and glorify God in all our thoughts and actions (p. 107). An unswerving commitment to God in thought, word, and deed constitutes the "holy love" which Edwards calls "the essence of all true religion" (p. 107).[21]

Edwards further elaborated this definition of religion in the *Treatise* by defining those signs which he believed constituted the clearest assurance that people were witnessing the genuine work of the Holy Spirit. As William Clebsch observes: "The religious question was not *whether* salvation was actual but how sainthood stamped itself on the soul and how its being stamped there could be accurately known."[22] A brief consideration of these signs is necessary for understanding not only Edwards' view of true religion but also his view of true virtue, since for him both are virtually identical. The signs of genuine religiosity which Edwards set forth in the *Treatise* are the working presuppositions for his analysis of the moral life in *The Nature of True Virtue*. In both works, Edwards fused the Puritan world view and ethos into a theodicy which, in his view, provided a sufficient rational justification for pursuing the moral life in a universe that seemed indifferent to moral behavior.

A person knows that he is a recipient of saving grace, Edwards contends, when he exhibits twelve signs—not eight, ten, or even eleven, but all twelve. The first sign is a person's transformation into a new being. Such a transformation of the self occurs because God confers upon the religious person a sixth sense which He withholds from the unregenerate person. This sixth sense is a supernatural mode of perception, a direct vision of God which redirects the religious person's inclinations solely toward God, thereby reintegrating the self. Through this sixth sense God confers the capacity to exercise the will, the understanding, and the affections as God requires, while the "natural man," untouched by God's saving grace, remains doomed to eternal damnation.[23] The first sign consequently reinforces the doctrine of predestination.

The next two signs are the Christian's perception of both God's moral excellence and beauty through the sixth sense. The truly religious person apprehends God's holiness as something that is good and beautiful in itself, as deserving unconditional love, and worships God solely for this reason without regard for any personal benefits.[24] Edwards' fourth sign is a "spiritual, supernatural understanding," a "spiritual light" which infuses the mind, enabling it to see and "taste" "God's moral perfection" (pp. 270, 271, 273). The religious person thus acquires the fifth sign, an immediate certainty of the truth of religious doctrines (i.e., Puritan doctrines). Edwards adds the caveat, however, that such certitude is an inadequate sign unless it further leads the believer voluntarily to acknowledge God's moral excellence, glory and sovereignty, and to excoriate one's own pride and self-elevation—a most important sign to Edwards, as he acknowledges in his "Personal Narrative."

Moreover, such certitude should be accompanied by a permanent change in the person which expresses not only a recognition of but also a loving inclination of the heart toward God's moral beauty. Edwards uses this seventh sign as the occasion to analyze the process of conversion. For Edwards, conversion is not a specific experience which saves people but a lifelong process of turning to God, a continuous moral renovation of human nature.[25] All sinful inclinations remain, but their power is destroyed because they no longer stand at the center of the new self which progresses toward an unachievable perfection.

The last five signs specify the kind of moral renovation which characterizes true conversion. Truly religious persons, according to Edwards, will strive to be Christlike by embodying and relishing the Christian virtues of love, meekness, and quietness of spirit, and also by exercising tenderness and compassion toward others. Two additional tests for such persons are that they give their religious life symmetry by maintaining a balance among their various religious affections, and if they increasingly desire to bridge what they increasingly experience to be an unbridgeable gap between themselves and God. But the most important sign of genuine religious affections—the twelfth—is Christian practice. Christians must manifest "practical, or effective exercises" of grace in both their public and private lives (p. 432).[26]

Edwards cautions his reader, however, against mistaking this emphasis upon Christian deeds for a legal moralism that advocates the merit of human works.[27] No deed, no matter how righteous it is, makes a person acceptable in God's sight. Even in the case of the elect, God ultimately looks not to their deeds but rather to the quality of the soul shaping their deeds. Since it is difficult for people to discern this spiritual quality underlying human actions, they easily accept as truly virtuous the hypocrite who deliberately acts in ways that make him appear to be a Christian. To help people avoid such deceptions Edwards seeks in *The Nature of True Virtue* to demonstrate why the moral qualities, behavior, and perceptions of the unregenerate can never be normative for defining true morality. This work could be the concluding section of the *Treatise* because it systematically explores the moral implications of the sixth sense and the spiritual understanding it makes possible.

Edwards further attempts to prove that the notion of a sovereign God, who by and large remains incomprehensible in ethical terms, can nevertheless provide a reliable foundation for morality. The *Treatise* and *True Virtue* together constitute at one level the most systematic effort made by any American theologian to resolve this ethical dilemma within the framework of the Puritan theodicy.

THE MORAL LIFE: *THE NATURE OF TRUE VIRTUE*

Edwards begins his analysis of the moral life by providing a definition of true virtue which emphasizes neither particular kinds of actions nor the consequences of human actions, but rather the quality of a person's relationship to universal being. "True virtue most essentially consists in *benevolence to being in general*. Or perhaps, to speak more accurately, it is that consent, propensity and union of heart to being in general, which is immediately exercised in a general good will" (p. 3).[28] But this consent to being in general must also include one's consent to "benevolent being" or God (p. 9). Edwards finally defines true virtue as "primarily and most essentially . . . a supreme love to God; and that where this is wanting, there can be no true virtue" (p. 18). No benevolence toward other beings constitutes true virtue if it fails to express "union of heart to general existence and . . . love to God" (p. 78). "A truly virtuous mind . . . seeks the glory of God, and makes this his supreme, governing, and ultimate end" by being fully agreeable to God's designs (p. 25). Edwards uses this definition to demonstrate why the morality of the natural man should not be mistaken for true virtue.

One reason why the two should not be confused, Edwards argues, is that true virtue is based upon primary beauty while the morality of the natural man is based upon secondary beauty. Primary beauty is "consent, agreement, or union of being to being" (p. 27), that "cordial agreement" or union of mind and heart with God's purposes which is "peculiar to spiritual beings" (pp. 31, 28). Secondary beauty "consists in a mutual consent and agreement of different things, in form, manner, quantity, and visible end or design; called by the various names of regularity, order, uniformity, symmetry proportion, harmony . . . such is the sweet mutual consent and agreement of the various notes of a melodious tune" (p. 28). It is a natural union or "agreement of parts" which does not involve the will, disposition, or affection of the heart. Such an agreement is found not only in natural and material objects but also in such immaterial realities as wisdom, the ordering of a society, and the virtue of justice; each mirrors a harmonious correspondence between various parts naturally united in their tendency to achieve one general purpose. However, "a taste of this kind of beauty is entirely a different thing from a taste of true virtue. Who will affirm, that a disposition to approve of the harmony of good music, or the beauty of a square or equilateral triangle, is the same with true holiness, or a truly virtuous disposition of mind? It is a relish of uniformity and proportion that determines the mind to approve these things . . . and be pleased with equal uniformity and proportion among spiritual things which are equally discerned" (p. 40).

Nevertheless, because God has "constituted the external world in analogy to the spiritual world," secondary beauty can be appropriately viewed as an "image of the true, spiritual beauty" (p. 30). Hence, even though a "taste" for secondary beauty does not in itself partake of true virtue, it does foreshadow spiritual possibilities which the natural man lacks but may gain through the agency of divine grace.

Another reason why the morality of natural man should not be confused with true virtue, Edwards contends, is that the former is based upon the selfish regard either for whatever is pleasing to one's self or for one's own private interest. Many forms of behavior which appear to be virtuous, such as people loving those who love them or being grateful to those who help them, are frequently motivated only by a concern for how they can benefit themselves. The approval or disapproval of various actions can also derive from self-love. The desire to be praised, for example, can lead people publicly to disapprove of particular vices which privately they condone. Edwards further adds that the approval of various virtues and disapproval of various vices might be nothing more than a function of habit, the moral reflex, so to speak, which society has taught and expects from people. *True Virtue* expresses the Puritan belief that even peoples' best actions all too often only camouflage their natural depravity.

Like his Puritan forebears, Edwards extended this distrust of moral behavior to the conscience itself. The human conscience, according to Edwards, consists of two elements. The first is the consciousness of being either consistent or inconsistent with ourselves when we blame or praise others. By imaginatively placing ourselves in the stead of others, we can judge whether our condemning or lauding a person's action is consistent with what we would expect for ourselves in the same circumstances. But Edwards maintains that this effort is itself self-serving because it reflects a desire to treat others as we want them to treat us—a desire based on the natural man's recognition that the way we treat others will most likely evoke similar treatment from them.

The second element in the conscience, for Edwards, is a sense of proper proportion between an evil deed and its punishment or a good deed and the gratitude it evokes. This sense of desert enables the conscience to laud true virtue and condemn the lack of it, to praise and blame what true virtue praises and blames, and even to see the justice and beauty of yielding one's life to God. "The natural conscience, if the understanding be properly enlightened, and stupifying prejudices are removed, concurs with the law of God, is of equal extent with it, and joins its voice with it in every article" (p. 68).

However, such concurrence of the natural conscience with God's law, as in a person's strict adherence to a legalistic moralism, is often mistakenly identified as true virtue. Were the conscience in fact really the source of true virtue, Edwards argues, then it would lead to mass spiritual reformation of both individuals and society. But the course of history, Edwards observes, clearly shows that the conscience has no such redemptive consequences. In characteristically Puritan fashion, then, Edwards rejects the conscience as a normative source for defining true virtue.

Nor do those natural instincts which lead people to act in ways that make them appear virtuous provide the norms for identifying true virtue. Parental affections, for example, are said by Edwards to be naturally rooted in self-love; they express a private benevolence that extends only to the smaller system of the family within the larger system that is being in general. Parental affections therefore neither express nor give rise to benevolence toward being in general. Edwards likewise argues that pity, the natural instinct people feel toward others who are in distress, is not an expression of true virtue. Though pity expresses an instinctual grief for the torments others suffer, it is frequently extended to those whose happiness or prosperity might otherwise evoke indifference, or grief, or even the malevolent desire that calamity fall upon them in their happiness. People mistake these and other natural instincts for true virtue because they embody "the negation or absence of true moral evil" (p. 91), because there are truly virtuous affections that have the same name (e.g., compassion, love, pity, gratitude, love of justice), because both can have identical effects, and because within their private spheres many natural affections, such as those between husband and wife or parent and child, are beautiful. But when viewed from the perspective of their relationship to being in general, it then becomes evident that the natural instincts are rooted in self-love rather than in benevolence toward being itself.

Ultimately, however, the natural instincts and affections do become truly virtuous for Edwards when God bestows upon people a spiritual sense (i.e., the new sixth sense). They are then transformed into holy affections because they are fully determined by both benevolence toward being in general and love for God. Hence, "there may be a virtuous love of parents to children, and between other near relatives, a virtuous love of our town, or country, or nation," a truly virtuous pity which not only grieves for the sufferings of all sentient life but also rejoices in the happiness of others, and "also a virtuous love of justice, arising from pure benevolence to being in general" (p. 96).

Even the conscience when touched by grace becomes a "sanctified conscience" which expresses "a virtuous sense of desert different from what

is natural or common" (p. 96). The conscience of the natural man supports a notion of justice based on the individual's desire that people receive
good or evil in proportion to the good or evil things they do; the sanctified
conscience, which views being in general from God's perspective, attains a
notion of justice based not upon personal desires but upon the necessary
nature of things which is indifferent to personal desires. Only the sanctified
conscience is able to live in full conformity with this necessity in its relationships with others and God, for it can "see that consent to being in
general, and supreme respect to the Being of beings, is most just; and that
every thing which is inconsistent with it, and interferes with it, or flows
from the want of it, is unjust and deserves the opposition of universal
existence" (pp. 69–70).[29] In Edwards' view, then, both the truly moral
and the truly religious life are rooted in an identical spiritual consciousness
which distinguishes them from a spurious morality and a spurious religiosity.

But Edwards does more than define the differences between true and
false morality. *True Virtue* is also an attempt to demonstrate how the Puritan theodicy makes true virtue, as he defines it, necessary in a world fully
determined by a sovereign deity who frequently violates human canons of
justice in His treatment of people. The only appropriate response to such
a sovereign deity, according to Edwards—and here he articulates the Puritan doctrine of humiliation—is for people to "humbly and calmly lie in
the dust before [Him]," to "abase [themselves] and exalt God alone," even
when He requires their ruin, death, or damnation to realize His redemptive
purposes.[30] To serve and glorify God in this way is, in Edwards' view, the
only way people can be "useful" to God. Edwards thus sets forth the Puritan view that any argument for the necessity of moral behavior which is
based upon the supposed benefits it is said to confer upon the self, such as
divine rewards or personal happiness, betrays people through its false view
of the nature of reality.

Human experience, according to this perspective, reflects no such reliable connection between morality and these supposed benefits. Rather, the
necessity for being moral derives solely from God's requiring it to glorify
Himself, though being moral might very well entail much suffering, perhaps even ruin one's life. Doing a good deed that is unbeneficial to one's
self simply because God requires it is, in this view, as important as, if not
more important than, either the deed itself or its consequences. But the
capacity for such obedient action is solely the gift of divine grace. True
virtue is therefore the surest sign of salvation.

Here, then, was a model for behavior commensurate with the Puritan
world view which emphasizes a sovereign deity. Morality or true virtue,
as defined by the Puritan theodicy, is not so much a way of living (though
the basic Christian virtues must be practiced) as it is an orientation toward
God which fully subordinates the self to God's redemptive purposes, even

sacrifices the self, if required, in order to help realize those purposes. People must fully conform their lives to the will of God, not because they will thereby attain any security, guarantees, or rewards, but because it is the way a sovereign God requires people to serve and glorify Him. This vision of the moral life repudiates the self that seeks through its own efforts to create the destiny it desires for itself; it affirms that self which fully surrenders itself to God's purposes, no matter how inimical they are to the self, and through this act of self-surrender celebrates and even delights in those purposes. Goodness or true virtue, in this view, ultimately has nothing to do either with the self accomplishing something good for itself or others or with the self's efforts to realize its best possibilities. Rather, true virtue is giving one's full consent to God's will in all things without questioning His purposes, no matter how unjust or inhumane they may seem from a human perspective.

Those who realize such virtue are the elect, and their becoming truly moral is made possible only through the agency of divine grace operating within them. Nothing good a person does can make him or her truly virtuous. Still, Puritan preachers maintained that everyone must strive to be virtuous, for, even though doing so places God under no obligation to people, it may nevertheless occasion the kind of conversion experience which signifies that one is a member of the elect. To live otherwise might be the very sign of one's eternal damnation. Hence the Puritans believed that the model for the life of true virtue which they advocated demonstrated the necessity for being moral in a world seemingly unresponsive to moral striving.

The Puritan theodicy thus described a world view which made the style of life it recommended seem the necessary condition for life within the world it portrayed; the ethos it recommended made the world view it described seem an actual state of affairs ideally arranged to accommodate such a style of life. It was a circular process of reinforcement: the authoritative experiences that were part of the ethos justified, even compelled, belief in the model of reality, and the authoritative image of an inevitable logic which is said to characterize human existence justified, even compelled, acceptance of the model for human behavior.

Edwards made it clear that the point of intersection between the Puritan world view and ethos is the experience of divine grace.[31] The Puritan world view seemingly arose from experiencing the world as providing no moral or religious guarantees, from long-term experience of thwarted desires and expectations, and from the inexplicable fact that both the law and gospel enabled some to take "delight" in such an uncontrollable world of religious and moral uncertainty. The choice of the life style which the Puritan world view endorsed was experienced as a mysterious gift in the face of the realization that most people choose to live in ways that glorify the self. This mode of experiencing the world was anticipated and confirmed by a particular reading of the Bible, a reading which gave rise to the distinction between the covenant of works and the covenant of grace. The former explained people's attempts to guarantee their lives through their own efforts as resulting from human depravity, while the latter explained the choice to rely solely on God as resulting from divine grace. From this distinction came such directives for living amidst uncertainties as unquestioning acceptance of God's sovereignty, faith in Christ and the mysterious workings of divine providence, church attendance and participation in the sacraments, obedience to the law as defined by the Old Testament, doing good works without seeking any rewards or benefits, and complete submission to God's will, no matter how much suffering it entails.

Thus the means of grace—the Scriptures, through both their law and gospel, and the church, through its preaching, sacraments, and discipline—provided important structures of orientation within a world of religious and moral uncertainties. Like his predecessors, Edwards believed that the Puritan theodicy, through its concept of grace, fused the Puritan world view and ethos in a way that successfully reconciled a God beyond ethical categories with a meaningful notion of moral striving.

Edwards was, of course, also trying to show the inadequacies of conventional notions of the moral life in a world experienced as being indifferent to all moral striving. Conventional morality defined moral behavior in terms of the quality of actions, the intentions shaping them, or their consequences, whereas Edwards rooted the moral life solely in the experience of grace. Conventional morality maintained that human beings were fully capable of being good and self-sacrificing, but Edwards argued that human striving, no matter how self-sacrificing it might appear by conventional standards, could never be truly moral until God Himself conferred that capacity upon a person. Conventional morality said that being moral is necessary because it upholds social order, humanizes relationships between people, and benefits a person in the long run, whereas Edwards, who rejected these pragmatic arguments, contended that being moral is necessary simply because it is the way God expects people to glorify His majesty and sovereignty. The moral life benefits the individual only insofar as his continuous attempts to glorify God constitute a source of pleasure and satisfaction for him, even when they require his ruin. Because Edwards thus defined the Puritan ethos as the only style of life acceptable to God, he finally presented this culturally preferred religious mode of experiencing the world as the very foundation for defining true morality on a universal scale.

Edwards' argument for morality could have little appeal to those outside the select religious coterie of the already saved, since, in this view, no moral striving can contribute to one's salvation until God, according to His own good pleasure, infuses it with His grace. "All that remained," as James Jones rightly observes, "was for [Charles] Chauncy to suggest a new definition of the divine good pleasure: that it pleased God to save all men, that God had more pleasure in redeeming men than in damning them." [32] This repudiation of the Puritan theodicy would have far-reaching implications, not the least of which would be a redefinition of world view and ethos that was quite antithetical to those articulated in the Puritan theodicy. Thus it is that the difficulties Puritan theologians experienced in elaborating a Puritan theodicy ultimately flowered into a larger theological discussion about whether the Puritan theodicy provides an accurate model for symbolizing the moral and religious implications of the American experiment in democracy.

4

The Rationalistic Theodicy

JONATHAN MAYHEW: GOD'S LIMITED SOVEREIGNTY

The role that religion played between 1750 and 1800—from the aftermath of the Great Awakening through the American Revolution to the advent of a westward-growing democratic society—was an exceedingly complex one, as can be seen in even a few of the diverse interpretations of this period. Sidney Mead, for example, describes this period as a time when religious conservatives, religious liberals, and deists formed an alliance to work for the separation of church and state.[1] Alan Heimert characterizes it as a period when the evangelical clergy, in response to the collapse of "the communities and the social assumptions inherited from the seventeenth century," offered "the American people new commitments, political as well as ethical."[2] Perry Miller, in tracing the Puritan influence on this period, demonstrates how various writers increasingly relied upon a modified Puritan jeremiad in order to justify resistance to and finally rebellion against England,[3] while William McLoughlin, going one step further, portrays religion during this period as one of the major forces that were shaping an American cultural cohesion.[4]

In his analysis of the ideological origins of the American Revolution, Bernard Bailyn contends that throughout these decades people increasingly fused the struggles for civil and religious liberty until, after the Revolution, this mutual reinforcement culminated in the disestablishment of religion.[5] Martin Marty also emphasizes the movement during this period toward religious disestablishment but argues that, rather than being a radical change that provoked much resentment, it was an innovation already anticipated in four colonies and one which people, both proestablishment and pro-dissent, accepted "with a sigh of relief, in a spirit of tidying up, and with only whimpers of reaction."[6] Following the lead of John Adams, Edwin Gaustad maintains that Americans during this period underwent a mental revolution which prepared them to accept complete religious freedom—a freedom which came not "at one stroke in 1783, or 1789, or 1791," but rather "sometimes sputtering and hesitating, oftentimes with enthusiastic dispatch, it eventually came everywhere."[7]

In more recent studies, Sydney Ahlstrom describes this period not only as one of political and social transformation, but also as a "turbulent epoch" that "introduced modes of thought which in subtle ways contributed to theological transformation,"[8] while Catherine Albanese, in seeking to define this theological transformation, concludes that this period gave rise to "a new sacral myth of origins."[9] Robert Bellah and Conrad Cherry see in this period the origins of American "civil religion."[10] And William May, who defines various stages in the development of the American Enlightenment, views these decades as a time of "competition between the familiar Moderate Enlightenment and the slowly dawning Revolutionary Enlightenment, and of both with inherited Protestant culture," a competition that "ends with the defeat or perhaps the assimilation of the Enlightenment in the formative period of nineteenth-century culture."[11]

All of these interpretations focus our attention upon a transition from an old to a new cultural order between 1750 and 1800. Although it is not the intent of this study to explore such cultural change, it is noteworthy that most of these historians variously suggest how transformations in theological thought mirror the social and political transformation of the age. Only Ahlstrom asserts that it is difficult to make any "theological-political correlations" during this period.[12] Certainly the changes taking place in religious thought between 1750 and 1800 were in part responses to a changing American environment, though over the generations historians have been disputing just how much social change actually took place because of the Revolution.[13]

Still, without denying the validity of this correlation between social structure and religious change—a correlation which Mary Douglas, Peter Berger, Clifford Geertz, and Victor Turner have been developing in the fields of social and cultural anthropology[14]—these changes in American religious thought also reflect an inner dynamic most clearly expressed by an emerging theological debate. The Puritan theodicy was essentially a "tribal" justification for its own particular mode of experiencing the world.[15] But when another way of experiencing the world gradually emerged—one which " 'interiorized' the significance of natural law and rendered it more man-centered, stressing human rights rather than cosmic order, the individual rather than the state, liberty rather than obedience"[16]—it redefined the boundaries of the "tribe" and, in so doing, created a new tribal justification for its own view of both the world and an appropriate ethos within such a world.[17]

This is, in part, the significance of the notable development of a rationalistic theodicy, itself the polar opposite of the Puritan theodicy, during the cultural transition from an old to a new cultural order between 1750 and 1800.[18] Whereas the Puritan theodicy maintained that God's sovereignty and human notions of justice were mutually incompatible, the rationalistic theodicy, as initially formulated by Jonathan Mayhew and Charles Chauncy, linked the notion of divine sovereignty with moral and political notions of human justice. The first significant public appeal to the rationalistic theodicy on the American scene occurs in Jonathan Mayhew's "Discourse Concerning Unlimited Submission and Nonresistance to the Higher Powers" (1750), though it was clearly prefigured by the rationalistic notion of God set forth in European deism and in Giles Firmin's *The Real Christian*. Mayhew's pamphlet was reprinted several times throughout the colonies between 1750 and 1775; publicly acknowledged as a classic in its own right, it expressed political and religious sentiments that touched responsive chords in a large segment of the colonial populace.[19]

Like many sermons during this period, Mayhew's *Discourse* reflects a preoccupation with political matters, especially the problem of political power.[20] Arbitrary actions by both the British government and unsympathetic royalist governors as well as the aggressive tactics of the Anglican church in the colonies contributed to a growing concern among colonists to re-examine the relationship between rulers and their subjects.[21] The theory of the divine right of kings had been challenged by the Cromwellian revolution and by those like John Milton who justified the revolution in both political and religious terms. Despite such dissenting criticism, England ruled the American colonies in accordance with the divine right theory.[22] Americans by and large did not question this theory. Following the lead of Calvinistic orthodoxy which had supported it,[23] they "continued to assume, as had their predecessors for generations before, that a healthy society was a hierarchical society. . . . [that] external differences among men, reflecting the principle of hierarchical order, were necessary and proper, and would remain; they were intrinsic to the nature of things."[24]

Still, there were circumstances which gradually eroded this support, though "nowhere, at any time in the colonial years," Bailyn asserts, "were the implications of these circumstances articulated or justified."[25] The Puritans had established a church polity that was independent not only of the Anglican church but also of the English throne; loyalty to the congregational church did not require taking a loyalty oath to the king. Puritanism has in fact been seen as the seedbed of many tendencies that contributed to the outbreak of the American Revolution.[26] Life in the wilderness, as has been frequently observed, was inimical to the preservation of elaborate social distinctions. The Great Awakening challenged the traditional notions of both religious authority and social distinctions by making personal religious experience the ultimate authority for defining and justifying the self's autonomy from all forms of authority, political or religious.[27] Both colonial politics and the religious controversies that followed the Great Awakening were characterized by factions which, in their petty quibbles to advance their own interests at the expense of the general welfare, tended to erode public respect for both political and religious institutions. Moreover, three thousand miles of ocean separated the colonies from England, giving them relative freedom to determine their own destinies without direct—or quick—interference from British authorities. Then, too, the undeveloped western frontier, which troubled Thomas Jefferson's utopian vision of a small, self-contained agrarian society,[28] existed as both an imaginative and real possibility that would ultimately give religion a new shape within the American environment.[29]

Such circumstances eventually encouraged an attitude of independence toward British authority. By 1750, when Mayhew delivered his *Discourse* justifying civil disobedience, many colonists were ready to give it a sympathetic hearing, and the event which precipitated his address assured such a hearing. A few weeks prior to the anniversary of the beheading of Charles I, Anglican preachers began to denounce the Puritans as regicides and to advocate passive obedience to royal authority. Angered by these affirmations of divine right theory, Mayhew delivered three sermons on the subject. The final sermon was the *Discourse*, which he preached on the anniversary day itself. In this sermon Mayhew directly attacks the theory of the divine right of kings; in so doing he also challenges the notion of God advocated by the Puritan theodicy.

Mayhew's argument largely rests on an exegesis of Romans 13:1-8, a passage in which St. Paul argues that subjects owe their rulers unlimited fealty. According to St. Paul, resisting rulers who are ordained by God is to resist God Himself, "and they that resist shall receive to themselves damnation" (Rom. 13:2). Exponents of the divine right theory believed this passage indisputably supported their contention that Scripture itself "makes all resistance to princes a crime, in any case whatever" (p. 222).[30] Mayhew, however, seeks to demonstrate that St. Paul advocates not unquestioning submission to all rulers, no matter how tyrannical they are, but rather submission only to "good" rulers. The Pauline passage, according to Mayhew's interpretation, defines a good ruler as one who makes "the general welfare" of society the sole end of all his administrative actions (p. 221). God ordains rulers to pursue this end, and so long as their governments, whatever their form, serve the general welfare of society, "disobedience to civil rulers in the due exercise of their authority is not merely a *Political sin but an heinous offense against God and religion*" (p. 220).

But disobedience to "tyrants and public oppressors" who "destroy the public welfare" is permissible because they "are not entitled to obedience from their subjects by virtue of anything here laid down by the inspired Apostle" (p. 231). The scriptural authority for this assertion, Mayhew declares, is that Paul himself, by claiming that citizens, no less than rulers, are "obliged to secure and promote [the social welfare] as far as in us lies," implies that they must resist tyrannical rulers (p. 232). Nor can tyrants legitimate their abuse of power by appealing to the authority of law. For the implication of Paul's argument, as Mayhew presents it, is that citizens are obligated to obey only those laws which "are not inconsistent with the ordinances and commands of God, the supreme lawgiver, or with any other higher antecedent obligations" (p. 225). To obey a law that contravenes God's commands is to disobey God; to resist a king who tyrannically exacts such obedience is to obey God. Such resistance is a religious duty rather than an offense against God.

Mayhew declares that the situation which the Puritans faced under Charles I required their rejection of him as their ruler. He had violated both the social welfare and divine law by forcing citizens to support laws inconsistent with God's commands. Charles I "had, in fact, *unkinged* himself" by "assuming a power above the laws in direct contradiction to his coronation oath, and governing the greatest part of his time in the most arbitrary oppressive manner" (pp. 242, 240). The uprising against Charles I was therefore neither a revolution nor a rebellion but "a most righteous and glorious stand made in defense of the natural and legal rights of the people against the unnatural and illegal encroachments of arbitrary power" (p. 241). No ruler has any right, much less divine sanction, to ruin a society as Charles I was doing through "attempting to overturn law and equity and the constitution, and to exercise a wanton licentious *sovereignty* over the properties, consciences, and lives of all the people" (pp. 241–42).

Mayhew, shifting from scriptural exegesis as the basis for his argument, now appeals to his rationalistic vision of God. Not even God as "the supreme Governor of the world," Mayhew asserts, has the right to exercise His sovereignty in such "an absolutely arbitrary and despotic manner. The power of this Almighty King . . . is limited by law, not, indeed, by *acts of Parliament* but by the eternal *laws* of truth, wisdom, and equity, and the everlasting tables of right reason—tables that cannot be *repealed*, or *thrown down* and broken like those of Moses" (p. 242). Mayhew here replaces the Puritan vision of God, which he says "inconsiderately" portrays Him as a tyrannical sovereign, with a God whose sovereign power is constrained within rationally prescribed ethical limits. He notes that unscrupulous rulers can construe their being ordained by a God who frequently engages in a teleological suspension of the ethical as a divine sanction "to do what they please" with impunity (p. 233). But when divine sovereignty is itself conceived as limited by inviolable universal laws, then no ruler can justify any abrogation of the laws which limit his power. Mayhew's *Discourse* thus suggests that by 1750 the contours of a rationalistic theodicy were emerging on the American scene—a theodicy which, because Mayhew demonstrated the compatibility between its political implications and democratic values, became a shaping force on the political scene during the 1760s and 1770s.[31]

Of course, the rationalistic theodicy was not Mayhew's creation. Its concept of God was closely akin to the deist's notion of a rational God whose orderly regulation of the world expresses not only a lawful natural order but also a reliable moral order through which God discloses Himself to human reason.[32] But the theodicy which Mayhew presents in his *Discourse* (which was written one-third of a century before deism became a significant religious force on the American scene) can be viewed not so much as an extension of English deism, but more as a means through which the growing number of people dissatisfied with their Puritan heritage could express their rejection of the Puritan notion of God and understanding of morality. It provided a concept of God which expressed this emerging dissent. Had it done only this, however, it could hardly have presented itself as a serious alternative to the Puritan theodicy which was still widely accepted in New England.[33]

The rationalistic theodicy also set forth a new vision of the world. It described a democratic cosmos that is the opposite of the universe described by the Puritan theodicy. It transformed democratic values into a mode of experiencing the world diametrically opposed to that which Puritan orthodoxy articulated, and it recommended a style of life that bears no resemblance to the Puritan ethos. Liberal theologians used their discussions of the problem of theodicy as the occasion to articulate a new world view and ethos, and to synthesize the two in a way that opened new possibilities for interpreting human experience. Mayhew's *Discourse* indicates that as early as the 1740s, when the theological climate was undergoing rapid changes, the battle lines were already being drawn for a theological debate regarding the adequacy of the Puritan theodicy for helping Americans formulate the religious meanings of their contemporary encounter with the American environment. The issues at stake in this debate during the latter part of the eighteenth century are perhaps nowhere more clearly articulated than in Charles Chauncy's work, *The Mystery hid from Ages and Generations, made manifest by the Gospel-Revelation: or, The Salvation of All Men the Grand Thing Aimed at in the Scheme of God* (1784).

CHARLES CHAUNCY: UNIVERSAL SALVATION

In this work, Chauncy—a stern critic of Edwards' defense of the Great Awakening—develops a vision of God that is quite contrary to that advocated by his Puritan heritage.[34] The book in fact constitutes an extensive

polemic against the orthodox notions of total depravity, limited atonement, and eternal damnation. Simply put, Chauncy's thesis is that an "infinitely benevolent" God desires the salvation of all humankind, and that
"if such a Being as we justly conceive God to be, is *really willing, sincerely
desirous* that all men should be saved, *they certainly shall be saved*" (pp. 1,
163).[35] Chauncy supports this rejection of the Puritan notion of limited
atonement by appealing to the Bible. The Scriptures, he argues, define a
scheme which God has designed for saving the entire human race, "not-
withstanding the *lapse of the one man Adam . . .* " (p. v). The book largely
consists of Chauncy's exegesis of many scriptural passages which he claims
either express or support the idea of universal salvation, but 1 Corinthians
15:24-29, he maintains, is the passage which decisively proves that God
will finally save all humankind (pp. 198ff.). The details of Chauncy's scriptural exegesis cannot be examined here; but it is important to note that he
rests the validity of his argument upon his exegetical work, which includes
his using the idea of universal salvation to interpret many biblical passages
"in a sense that is *highly honourable* to *God,* and *Christ,* and universally
joyful to men" (p. 249). Chauncy presents God in that light which best
glorifies and honors His "supremely and absolutely perfect benevolence"
(p. 3).

Nothing better glorifies divine benevolence, according to Chauncy, than
God's scheme of universal salvation. At the very heart of this scheme is
Jesus Christ, for it is Christ's obedience—"and eminently his obedience to
death"—which has led God "to make happiness attainable by any of the
race of Adam" (p. 19). "Christ died, not for a select number of men only,
but for mankind *universally,* and *without exception* or *limitation*" (p. 20).
Since God took "such an extraordinary step" as sacrificing His own Son
for the welfare of the human race and refuses, in any vindictive way, to
place limits on the atoning power of Christ's death, there can be no doubt,
Chauncy asserts, that God will exercise all possible means for effecting the
salvation of all humankind (p. 40).

Chauncy adds, however, that the notion of universal salvation does not
mean that everyone will achieve salvation in this life. Those who die without ever reforming their sinful ways will be miserable after death in proportion to their moral depravity. But this "misery will be inflicted with a
salutary view"; for the afterlife is "a state of discipline, [which God has]
designed for the amendment of the sufferers themselves, as well as the
good of others, and wisely adapted as a means to this end, they may well
be recovered and formed to a meetness for immortality and honor" (p. 11).
Chauncy thus portrays a benevolent deity who, through both moral and
rational means appropriate to humankind's nature, "will, sooner or later,
in THIS STATE OR ANOTHER, reduce [all people] under a willing and
obedient subjection to his moral government" (pp. 170–71).

Such a view of divine benevolence redefines God's sovereignty in a way which no longer dishonors God. "I doubt not," Chauncy writes of the orthodox Puritan view of divine sovereignty, "it has been a perplexing difficulty to most persons (I am sure, it has been such to me), how to reconcile the doctrine, which dooms so great a number of the human race to eternal flames, with the essential, absolutely perfect, goodness of the Deity" (p. 14). Nor can he reconcile his view of God with the notion of eternal damnation which, if true, could be enforced only by a monstrously vindictive God. The scheme of universal salvation, in Chauncy's view, is itself sufficient rebuttal to this notion since it discloses a benevolent deity who equitably punishes people only to the extent required by their sins, who suitably adapts the punishment of sin to both its nature and its seriousness, and who moreover designs the punishment to help effect the individual's final salvation. The distinction between the elect and the reprobate has almost vanished.

So has the way of perceiving the world as being absolutely dependent upon a sovereign God who controls everything in ways that are frequently detrimental to humankind. Everything that God does, according to Chauncy, is morally and rationally consistent with his infinite mercy, benevolence, and justice. "It is impossible that should come from God, which is *unworthy of him* nor would any external evidence be sufficient to justify a man in believing him to be the author of that, which in its own nature, is *unreasonable* and *absurd*" (p. 361). This statement precariously borders on a willful blindness to any event or personal experience which might call into question his belief in a God who exercises His supremacy over people in ways that honor both their ethical expectations and the integrity and autonomy of the human personality.

Although liberal theologians could morally accept only this vision of God, staunch conservatives such as Samuel Mather rejected it as unscriptural. Most of the objections which Mather raised in response to an earlier and much shorter version of *The Salvation of All Men* treated exegetical matters. One of his objections, namely, that Chauncy's view of the afterlife is not scriptural but merely restates the Roman Catholic view of purgatory, is ironic given Chauncy's own attack upon what he calls the "enormous falsehoods" (the idea of purgatory being one of these) taught by the Roman Catholic Church (p. 362).[36] Chauncy never addressed himself to this charge. He did, however, devote several pages to answering Mather's contention that, because the notion of universal salvation maintains that all divine punishments of sin will inevitably come to an end, it thereby encourages people to persist in their sinful ways. Mather insisted that the doctrine of eternal damnation is necessary because divine justice requires such a fate for impenitent sinners and because, without it, wrongdoing only becomes more attractive to people.[37] To the contrary, Chauncy rebutted, the notion of universal salvation restricts human sinfulness even more than the doctrine of eternal damnation. The latter notion is so incredible to many people, he asserted, that they reject it, while the former notion, which views divine punishments both in this life and the hereafter as intended for humankind's good, presents a more plausible understanding of punishment which prompts people to give the afterlife serious attention. Moreover, if God has predestined everyone to salvation, this undercuts any reason whatsoever for becoming immoral; people might as well become moral now, since God will sooner or later persuade them to become moral anyway.[38] When stated this way, Chauncy's argument does not support the conclusion that "in regard to his position on this most central Puritan question [of God's sovereignty], Chauncy died well within the faith of his fathers."[39] To be sure, Chauncy never rejected the Puritan notion of God's sovereignty over His creation, but he did redefine that sovereignty as being exercised by God in ways that make Him morally acceptable by human standards.

Chauncy's God is, in fact, a model for the morally impeccable use of sovereign power. His treatment of people is never tyrannical despite His having predestined all humankind to salvation. Though God will permit no one to resist His sovereign decree, He, like Giles Firmin's God, relies solely upon moral and rational persuasion, not coercion, in order finally to elicit obedient subjection to His will. What Mayhew says of sovereign power at a political level is essentially what Chauncy says of divine power at a universal level. That is to say, Mayhew's notion that a good ruler is one who promotes the social welfare can be seen in Chauncy's notion that God benevolently exercises His sovereign power solely for the welfare of all people, namely, their redemption. For Chauncy, the scheme of universal salvation has the advantage over Puritan orthodoxy of being "*more honourable* to the *infinitely perfect Being*, and more conducive to the *real advantage* of mankind" (p. 363).

Moreover Chauncy believed that the scheme of universal salvation solved the problem of evil. "*Evils* and *sufferings*, whether *present* or *future*, in this *world* or *another*, are a *disciplinary mean* wisely and powerfully adapted to promote the *good* of the *patients themselves*, as well as others; they stand connected with *this end* in the plan of God, and will, in the last result of its operation, certainly bring it into *fact*. Instead therefore of being a *contradiction* to, they very obviously coincide with, *wise* and *reasonable benevolence*: Yea, they are a wonderful illustration of it" (pp. 366–67). Even the unmerited injustices of this world, or what Chauncy calls "that *inverted conduct* of Providence" (p. 224), are the means God has designed for preparing people "in the wisest and best-adapted manner, for that NEW and GRAND DISPENSATION, which is yet to take place" (p. 225). Chauncy thus justifies the evils, suffering, and injustices of human existence as indispensable means to God's realizing His benevolent scheme of universal salvation.

Ultimately, *The Salvation of All Men* can be viewed as Chauncy's systematic effort to repudiate the Puritan notion of the divine teleological suspension of the ethical as a morally acceptable religious explanation of human experience. The God whom Chauncy describes is a democratic sovereign whose chief concern is to violate none of the rights which he has conferred upon people, among them being the right to salvation. This is no longer the awesome Puritan deity whose actions frequently contravene all human expectations, but a divine egalitarian who is obligated to fulfill humankind's claims upon Him; His sovereignty now constitutes the moral foundation for democratic ideals.

Chauncy's notion "that the divine benevolence necessarily entailed universal salvation, . . . that Christian regeneration was the appropriation of a God-given right never really withheld," [40] no doubt mirrors the prevailing mood of a period when the "original theocratic impulse to found a City upon a Hill to the greater glory of God [was being] displaced by the more secular desire to build a nation in the wilderness which testified instead to the inalienable rights of man." [41] This notion also expresses the essence of the "enlightened" or "reasonable" Christianity to which this emphasis on human rights was giving rise during the American Enlightenment. [42] Democratic ideals, according to this view, required an egalitarian God; and by redefining divine sovereignty in terms of the democratic notion of equal human rights, Chauncy believed that he had resolved all the moral problems which plagued the Puritan concept of God's sovereignty.

The contrast between the rationalistic theodicy which Chauncy articulated and the Puritan theodicy could not be more complete. The world described by the rationalistic theodicy is a democratic cosmos wherein each individual can lay claim to certain moral and religious guarantees, and presiding over this cosmos is an egalitarian God who protects each individual's inalienable right to the benefits of these guarantees. Not only has everyone an equal opportunity to gain salvation through living a moral life; each person, according to Chauncy, will ultimately be persuaded by God to make such a choice. It is a cosmos of fair play and equitability before the universal laws of God which is easily comprehended and explained by democratic canons of justice.

The rationalistic theodicy thus enabled people to think and feel in terms of the egalitarian values which are the moral foundation of American democracy. [43] In a very real sense, it embodied the democratic sensibility seeking both to formulate its own mode of experiencing the world and to justify its contention that this way of experiencing the world is morally preferable to that described by the Puritan theodicy. Hence the rationalistic theodicy fully harmonized with—even religiously sanctioned—the moral, social, and political values shaping the American Revolution and the newly emerging American Republic.

That American democracy was giving rise to a religious vision of God more compatible with its controlling egalitarian moral ideals is further demonstrated by a work like J. Hector St. John de Crèvecoeur's *Letters from an American Farmer* (1783). In this extremely popular work, Crève-coeur transforms the Puritan covenant theology in a way which redefines the relationship between God and the moral life in terms that were endorsed by such representatives of enlightened thought as George Washington and Benjamin Franklin.[44]

CRÈVECOEUR: THE AGRARIAN COVENANT

The *Letters from an American Farmer*, twelve in all, present contradictory images of the American wilderness. On the one hand, Crèvecoeur describes the wilderness as being characterized by both the predatory struggle of animals for survival—animals prey on each other, the stronger animals assert their power over the weaker ones in a show of prowess—and the predatory struggle between people which issues in atrocities that reveal a deeply ingrained human depravity. He decries the vicious litigiousness which he sees prevailing among Americans, the uncouth, lawless, and often barbarous ways of the first wave of settlers who cleared the wilderness, the tragic decimation of Indian tribes through disease, alcohol, and military conquest, and the brutal maltreatment of black slaves on southern plantations. Crèvecoeur's outrage against people's inhumanity to their fellow beings most clearly surfaces during his encounter with a slave who, because he had killed the plantation overseer, is suspended in a cage to die the slow, painful death of being eaten alive by birds and insects. This scene prompts two of his most radical comments in the letters. "Is there then no superintending power who conducts the moral operations of the world, as well as the physical? The same sublime hand which guides the planets round the sun with so much exactness, which preserves the arrangement of the whole with such exalted wisdom and paternal care, and prevents the vast system from falling into confusion; doth it abandon mankind to all the errors, the follies, and the miseries, which their most frantic rage, and their most dangerous vices and passions can produce?" (p. 161).[45]

Not satisfied with this explanation, Crèvecoeur further suggests that "the perverseness of human nature," especially when reinforced and implemented by those who have power over others, "often thwarts the tendency of the most forcible causes, and prevents their subsequent salutary effects, though ordained for the good of man by the governor of the universe" (p. 163). This radical suggestion that God is Himself impotent in the face of human evil to carry out His own redemptive plans for people remains buried in Crèvecoeur's narrative because it conflicts with his own rationalistic vision of God and the agrarian covenant he believes shapes life in America.

For side by side with this image of the dark underside of the pre-Revolutionary American wilderness is a contrasting image of the wilderness which prefigures the Adamic myth R. W. B. Lewis treats in *The American Adam*. Crèvecoeur envisions the wilderness at many points in his narrative as an idyllic Garden of Eden wherein Americans have "a divinely granted second chance" to begin history anew.[46] He portrays European immigrants, especially those who are industrious, frugal, and sober in their efforts to settle the American wilderness, as feeling "the effects of a sort of resurrection" into new beings who are liberated from the various constraints imposed upon them in their European homelands (p. 54).[47] The American wilderness, according to Crèvecoeur, erases European history and enables Americans to create a new history based on an agrarian society of uncorrupted institutions, laws, and customs.

All that is required to realize this new Edenic asylum for migrating Europeans is that they establish a right relationship with the land. For presiding over the entrance to this fresh garden of the New World is a beneficent deity—"our great parent" as Crèvecoeur calls him—who extends this promise of the agrarian covenant like "a sort of premature Statue of Liberty welcoming the poor and the oppressed":[48] "Welcome to my shores, distressed European; bless the hour in which thou didst see my verdant fields, my fair navigable rivers, and my green mountains!—If thou wilt be honest, sober, and industrious, I have greater rewards to confer on thee— ease and independence. . . . Go thou and work and till; thou shalt prosper, provided thou be just, grateful, and industrious" (pp. 63–64).[49] Despite his occasional descriptions of an amoral universe and human depravity, and despite the disturbing questions raised by these descriptions, Crèvecoeur nevertheless basically develops, in the first eleven letters, this alternative image of the American wilderness as a predictable moral universe which inevitably rewards virtuous, sober, and industrious tillers of the land and punishes unvirtuous wastrels who refuse to work the land. He suggests that the farmer's direct contact with the soil fulfills all of his physical, moral, and spiritual needs, and also makes him a model of virtue.

He reinforces this suggestion throughout the middle letters by elaborating his belief that those whose lives and fortunes are inextricably linked with the unpredictable ways of the sea do not—and cannot—develop the stable traits of the farmer.[50] Fishermen, whalers, and shipowners will develop customs, prejudices, and moral practices which make them wholly unlike those "who live by cultivating the earth" (p. 121). Only the farmer can be assured of gaining a peaceful, prosperous, and secure existence, while all others, placing themselves at the mercy of uncontrollable circumstances, attain such an existence only quite by chance.

Crèvecoeur's prime example of how strict adherence to the agrarian covenant inevitably leads to financial success and independence is himself. The 371-acre farm which he owns provides him a financially secure, leisurely, and peaceful existence—what he calls a "substantial system of felicity" (p. 18)—and he parades it in all of its aspects before the reader in order to prove that America "is no place of punishment" (p. 62). His own life, he repeatedly argues, is but the inexorable result of God's faithfulness to His promise that in America "sobriety and industry [will] never fail to meet with the most ample [financial] rewards" (p. 83). The irony that he inherited his farm from his father who had already lavishly provisioned it with orchards, livestock, and tillable meadows entirely escapes Crève-coeur.

In contrast to the wealth Crèvecoeur amasses, Andrew the Hebridean, whom Crèvecoeur holds up as a model for how a poor man easily pro-gresses (over a period of four years) to financial security and freedom "by the gradual operation of sobriety, honesty, and emigration," attains only a modicum of wealth (p. 64). But Crèvecoeur had earlier cautioned his reader that, in endorsing the agrarian covenant, he did "not mean that every one who comes will grow rich in a little time; no, but he may pro-cure an easy, decent maintenance, by his industry. Instead of starving he will be fed, instead of being idle he will have employment; and these are riches enough for such men as come over here" (p. 53). What is important to Crèvecoeur is not the amount of wealth accrued but rather his belief that wealth, freedom, and security are the inevitable outcome of being a virtuous farmer and that God Himself guarantees this result.

But the American Revolution nearly collapses Crèvecoeur's belief in such a reliable moral order.[51] During the Revolution, his neighborhood, as he describes it in the twelfth letter—his jeremiad-like response to the Ameri-can Revolution—has become a battleground for the warring factions. Every day he expects new outbreaks of fighting that might arbitrarily destroy farms which the owners, like himself, believe they have earned as their just reward for living a life of virtue, sobriety, and industry. His initial re-sponse to such "indiscriminate blows" is a feeling of betrayal (p. 202). "Why has the master of the world permitted so much indiscriminate evil throughout every part of this poor planet, at all times, and among all kinds of people? It ought surely to be the punishment of the wicked only. . . . Oh virtue! is this all the reward thou hast to confer on thy votaries? Either thou art only a chimera, or thou art a timid useless being" (pp. 203, 206). But rather than accept the explanations implied in these comments about his chaotic situation—that he is in fact not a virtuous person, or that God no longer abides by the terms of the agrarian covenant, or that God is amoral or even demonic—Crèvecoeur settles for the explanation that "evil" men are besieging America in an attempt to replace its peaceful agrarian society with a "fictitious" one that does not conform to his vision of God (p. 209).

This belief, as well as his desire to remain neutral in the contest between Great Britain and the American colonies, leads Crèvecoeur to devise a scheme for protecting his family. He proposes to remove himself and his family to a remote Indian village untroubled by the war. He concedes that his family will need to perform a few activities that are dictated by the Indians' way of life. But by and large his plan is to create a miniature replica of his farm which will pattern his family's life after the old agrarian model.[52] His family will ride this tribal haven piggyback, as it were, until the Revolution burns itself out, and then return home where Crèvecoeur believes he will regain his farm as a "reward" that God will confer upon him for the misfortunes he has stoically endured and his virtuous loyalty to the values of the agrarian covenant. Ultimately, Crèvecoeur's scheme is his means for proving, at least in his own case, that God still upholds the agrarian covenant and its predictable system of rewards and punishments.

Like the Puritans when facing their own theological dilemma, Crèvecoeur presents a complicated religious vision that expresses contradictory ideas of the American wilderness and God. Unable to live within the tension created by these opposing views, Crèvecoeur resolves it simply by ignoring the darker side of life that he depicts in the *Letters*. Though he has striking evidence for human depravity, he still affirms the automatic development of virtue in those who assiduously work the soil; though his experience, by challenging his belief that a person's moral nature determines his destiny, raises disturbing questions about the nature of God, he nevertheless clings to his belief in a morally reliable deity. Like such representatives of the American Enlightenment as Benjamin Franklin and Thomas Jefferson, Crèvecoeur conceptualizes a God who, in conformity with the rationalistic, democratic, and agrarian values of late eighteenth-century New England, ethically binds Himself to enforcing a predictable moral system of rewards and punishments.

Crèvecoeur's formulation of the democratic mode of experiencing the world finally issues in a theodicy which makes America a showplace for the kind of legal contract God is said to propose for helping humankind become virtuous, a contract which legitimates the demands both parties can make upon each other in carrying out their stipulated obligations. The *Letters* thus demonstrate how the period between 1750 and 1800, in giving "priority to political issues," gave rise "to governmental or legalistic ways of conceiving traditional theological questions."[53]

By the last decades of the 1700s, then, Americans had formulated two conflicting theodicies, the Puritan and the rationalistic, through which they gave expression to alternative religious meanings for their encounter with the American environment and the changes this environment underwent during nearly two centuries of historical experience. Puritan theologians had explored the problem of theodicy in the context of seeking to explain their experience of a wilderness that unexpectedly facilitated the growth of a successful commercial society rather than the New Jerusalem envisioned by the founding fathers. They sought to create a synthesis of world view and ethos which would provide a sense of order and orientation in a world that was increasingly experienced as being no longer explicable in terms of their covenant theology. Their essential problem was that of re-conciling a sovereign God with the moral and religious expectations generated by the Puritan notion of a morally reliable covenant established with God.

Liberal theologians rejected the Puritan theodicy. But their explorations of the problem of theodicy also took place within the broader cultural context of the American Revolution and the establishment of the American Republic. They created a new world view and corresponding ethos which were compatible with the new democratic "city on a hill"—a city many believed was sanctioned by God—and fused them in a way that justified its mode of experiencing the world. Their essential problem was that of redefining God's sovereignty in terms of democratic moral values.

Hence, what initially began as a dilemma internal to Puritan ethics eventually flowered into a larger theological debate about the moral and religious implications of American democracy. Though the cultural context for discussing the problem of theodicy had changed considerably, what remained constant throughout these discussions is that theologians treated this problem as one of defining and fusing a world view and ethos in a way that would justify a particular mode of experiencing the world. The debate thus reflects at its deepest levels how New England culture, rather than being unified by a common sense of orientation within the changing American environment, gave rise to alternative orientations.

5

Theodicies in Conflict

WILLIAM ELLERY CHANNING: A REFORMULATED RATIONALISTIC THEODICY

By the first three decades of the nineteenth century, the theological battle lines had been firmly drawn between the advocates of the Puritan and rationalistic theodicies. This polarization dominated New England theology during the first half of the century and is clearly manifested by the works of such theologians as William Ellery Channing, Nathaniel William Taylor, and Edward Beecher. Their reliance on the theological conventions established by the debate merely reinforced the impasse which had emerged as early as 1785.

William Ellery Channing, a leading exponent of Unitarian Christianity, gave Enlightenment ideals their clearest theological expression in the early decades of the nineteenth century, though he is also a transition figure from eighteenth- to nineteenth-century standards. It is clear that "in his arguments with orthodoxy he was carrying on . . . the defense of rational and moral religion begun in New England by Charles Chauncy and Lemuel Briant"; but, as Henry May notes, he also assimilated the Enlightenment with the "new environment" of "nineteenth-century piety and reforming morality" through his pietistic extension of Chauncy's own initial formulation of the democratic implications of American moralism and rationalism.[1] Nevertheless, despite this synthesizing aspect of his thought, Channing failed to recast the theological debate into new terms that could advance the discussion beyond its current stalemate.

Channing defended his repudiation of Puritan orthodoxy in his famous "Moral Argument Against Calvinism" (1820). This sermon, which bases

its argument on democratic ideals and a radically generous assessment of
human nature, sets forth the major objections to Puritan doctrine which
liberal writings tediously repeated throughout the following four decades.
Channings's primary objection, of course, is that the God of Puritan orthodoxy is an unjust and cruel tyrant. He calls Him a deity of "infinite
malignity and oppression" who, heedless of the suffering He causes, uses
people as mere tools and playthings within His divine dispensation solely
to glorify His sovereignty over humankind (p. 466).[2] Christians "have too
often felt as if [God] were raised, by his greatness and sovereignty, above
the principles of morality, above those eternal laws of equity and rectitude
to which all other beings are subjected" (p. 376).

But Channing perceived that his age was ready to discard this notion of
God's sovereignty. He would have agreed, at least in spirit, with the later
declaration of Methodist theologian R. S. Foster in a work which echoes
Channing's "Moral Argument Against Calvinism," "that if such doctrines
[about God's sovereignty] were true, the final judgment would turn into a
protest rally where 'heaven and hell would equally revolt at . . . [God's
plan], and all rational beings conspire to execrate the almighty monster.' "[3] Though Channing's repudiation of the Puritans' reliance on their
notion of God's sovereignty for explaining human experience in terms of
a divine teleological suspension of the ethical often rose to artistic elo-
quence, Foster's expression of this repudiation, which voices the very heart
and soul of the democratic theological liberal imagination, has a disarming
simplicity and candor that makes its argument all the more persuasive.

In Calvinism, all things are resolved into sovereignty. No difficulty so great, but
the sovereignty of God explains it. No absurdity, or contradiction, or blasphemy
so appalling, but [that God's sovereignty] is its defense. . . . That God is sovereign, no one disputes. That he has a right to rule, and does rule in heaven and
earth, is not even questioned. But we protest, in the name of reason and religion,
and for the honor of God, against appealing to his sovereignty for the purpose of
propagating slanders against his character—against so understanding and constru-
ing it, as to bring it in conflict with his justice and other attributes of his nature.
He has no rights inconsistent with his own glorious nature—he has no sovereignty
that can act adversely to his glorious perfections. He is a sovereign. But he is a
sovereign God not a sovereign devil. He is not an irresponsible, blind, capricious
sovereignty. His rights and his rule are not resolvable into mere arbitrary acts of
will. He rules in righteousness, and wisdom, and truth. And what conflicts with
these, God claims no right to—he has no right to; to say to the contrary would be
to dishonor him. The sovereignty of God, therefore, never should be quoted in
support of, or excuse for, what is manifestly contrary to these. . . . Does he es-
teem such a defense—a defense which demonizes his character to illustrate his
sovereignty? No, no, it is a mistake! God's sovereignty explains no principle that
is manifestly wrong—sanctions no fact that is inconsistent with justice. 'The Judge
of the whole earth will do right'; he cannot do wrong. His sovereignty gives him
no such power.[4]

Such uncompromising rejection of hierarchical authority—whether governmental, ecclesiastical, or divine—which exempted itself from all rational and moral limitations on the use of its power was a primary thrust in the formation of such important denominational bodies as the Methodists, the Baptists, the Presbyterians, and the Disciples of Christ.[5]

Channing was rightly convinced that what Henry May and others have described as the confident social egalitarianism of his age (an egalitarianism which piqued, sometimes repulsed, many European observers) would lead to the demise of the Puritan world view and ethos.[6] As Channing puts it, Puritan orthodoxy "has to contend with foes more formidable than theologians, with foes, from whom it cannot shield itself in mystery and metaphysical subtilties, we mean with the progress of the human mind, and with the progress of the spirit of the Gospel."[7] This theme of spiritual (as well as material and political) progress was to be increasingly sounded in both orthodox and liberal thought.[8]

Channing also objected to the orthodox conception of the moral life. He adamantly rejected the Puritan doctrine of humiliation. It offended human dignity, he maintained, desecrated the liberating powers of human reason, ignored the humanizing impulses of the conscience, and violated the individual's right to determine what kind of deity merits his worship. Moreover, Puritan orthodoxy, in his view, denied people any moral agency. The only basis he saw for the moral life in Puritan doctrine was its appeal to people's fear of eternal damnation at the hands of an arbitrary tyrant. Such a deity, he maintained—and it was the common liberal charge—"if made our pattern, would convert us into monsters" (p. 467), a conclusion which Herman Melville would later dramatize in Ahab's tragic career. A universe shaped by the erratic and arbitrary actions of a divine tyrant could only support arguments for immoral behavior. It is an argument which Puritan theologians repeatedly sought to refute, but Channing found their rebuttals inadequate, even dehumanizing if adopted as the basis for defining true virtue. He therefore concluded that nothing is more important from the Unitarian perspective than developing a concept of God that provides the strongest possible incentive for becoming moral.

Channing envisions God as one whose "almighty power is entirely submitted to his perceptions of rectitude; and this is the ground of our piety. . . . We venerate not the loftiness of God's throne, but the equity and goodness in which it is established" (p. 376). Both the disdain of worshiping naked power and the requirement that God treat people equitably are dictates of the conscience which Channing believes God has instilled in people. He calls the conscience both "the voice of God" and "the Divinity within us" which enable people to "understand through sympathy God's perception of the right, the good, the holy, the just" (pp. 293–94). Because He has implanted egalitarian ideals in the conscience of humankind, God makes Himself ethically accountable to people's moral expectations. As Channing puts it in "The Moral Argument Against Calvinism," it is through the conscience that God "authorize[s] [people] to expect from their Creator the most benevolent and equitable government. . . . Our Creator has . . . waived his own claims on our veneration and obedience, any farther than He discovers himself to us in characters of benevolence, equity, and righteousness. He rests his authority on the perfect coincidence of his will and government with those great and fundamental principles of morality written on our souls" (pp. 463, 465). God thus obligates people to judge Him according to the moral demands of their consciences; "to decline [this duty]," Channing warns, "is to violate the primary law of nature" (p. 465). In Willard's view, the fully awakened conscience only passively mirrors God's own knowledge of the self. In Channing's view, however, the conscience becomes not only a miniature replica of the universal moral order through which God administers human affairs, but also the ultimate judge which compels God to act in accordance with its own final judgments. This, of course, is the kind of contention which prompted orthodox critics to declare that liberal theology was based not on love of God but on love of self.[9]

Because Channing portrayed a God who fully submits Himself to the judgments of the human conscience, he naturally repudiated the orthodox doctrine of original sin. The doctrine teaches "that God brings us into life wholly depraved so that under the innocent features of our childhood is hidden a nature averse to all good and propense to all evil, a nature which exposes us to God's displeasure and wrath, even before we have acquired power to understand our duties or to reflect upon our actions" (p. 377). All sin therefore merits endless punishment despite an irreparable condition inherited from Adam and Eve. Such a "false and dishonorable" view of God not only casts a chilling pall over any desire to become virtuous, but also subverts any belief in God's paternal goodness and justice—even leads people to the conclusion that God is malevolent (p. 378).

In his personal correspondence, Channing describes what he considers the spiritually unhinging logic of belief in the doctrine of innate depravity; and, in a tone that echoes Crèvecoeur's earlier lament to his paternal God, offers the Unitarian vision of God as the only healing remedy for this "mournful" effect.

If [the doctrine of original sin] be believed, I think there is ground for a despondence bordering on insanity. If I, and my beloved friends, and my whole race, have come from the hands of our Creator wholly depraved, irresistibly propense to all evil, and averse to all good,—if only a portion are chosen to escape from this miserable state, and if the rest are to be consigned by the Being who gave us our depraved and wretched nature to endless torments in inextinguishable flames,— then I do think that nothing remains but to mourn in anguish of heart; then existence is a curse, and the Creator is———.

O, my merciful Father! I cannot speak of thee in the language which this system would suggest. No! thou hast been too kind to me to deserve this reproach from my lips. Thou hast created me to be happy; thou callest me to virtue and piety, because in these consists my felicity; and thou wilt demand nothing from me but what thou givest the ability to perform.[10]

Channing never denied that people were easily corrupted, that they abused, enslaved, and murdered others to achieve their own selfish ends; but he would not grant that God had conferred upon people an innate depravity which inevitably disposed them to commit such evils in order to provoke God's wrath and eternal punishment.

Perhaps most repugnant to his moral sensibility was the orthodox belief in infant damnation. "Now, according to the plainest principles of morality, we maintain that a natural constitution of the mind, unfailingly disposing it to evil, and to evil alone, would absolve it from guilt; that to give existence under this condition would argue unspeakable cruelty; and that to punish the sin of this unhappily constituted child with endless ruin would be a wrong unparalleled by the most merciless despotism" (p. 377). Channing likewise objects to what he views as the Calvinist portrayal of God's willingness to lure those predestined to damnation toward a false promise of salvation. Like later liberal theologians, he was morally outraged by a God who calls sinners to repent knowing that they cannot, yet increases their eternal punishment for their refusal to obey His call. Perhaps no one expressed this point as imploringly as R. S. Foster.

Could Satanic cruelty display greater malevolence than is here supposed? Every mercy, every call, every seeming good, is so arranged as necessarily to sink the poor, miserable victim deeper into the quenchless flames of eternal damnation. Thou glorious God of the universe, whose very nature is love, what a representation of thy character!—holding out to thy hapless, miserable creatures, an empty semblance of good, which it is *impossible*, in the nature of things, for them to attain. . . . Dreadful! dreadful! dreadful! Thou great Spirit of the heavens, art thou such a monster as this![11]

Like Foster, Channing maintains that such orthodox beliefs cannot be a true representation of God's character because they are incompatible with His goodness and equity.

Nor can this objection be answered, according to Channing, by the orthodox assertions that such inconsistencies between God and our common notions of justice and goodness only manifest the limits of human understanding and that God is an infinite, incomprehensible, and mysterious being who cannot be judged by the canons of human reason and morality. To be sure, Channing admits, "God is *incomprehensible*. . . . But He is not therefore unintelligible" (p. 463). Human reason and moral perception cannot penetrate the secret counsels of God. Nevertheless they are God-given faculties through which God has chosen to communicate Himself to people. Therefore their "testimony against Calvinism is worthy of trust" (p. 467).

Channing's argument for God's intelligibility assumes that all divine attributes such as His goodness, benevolence, mercy, and justice "are essentially the same in God and man, though differing in degree, in Purity, and in extent of operation" (p. 464). Despite their flawed human expression, these attributes undergo no change in an infinite and perfect being. "If they did, we should lose the Supreme Being through his very infinity. Our ideas of him would fade away into mere sounds" (p. 294). Channing here expresses his unorthodox belief that "the idea of God, sublime and awful as it is, is the idea of our own spiritual nature, purified and enlarged to infinity" (p. 293); God is the perfect person. Indeed, in Channing's view, human dignity and spiritual potential are based upon the essential likeness of the human mind to God. This similarity makes the mind a source of divine revelation. "That unbounded spiritual energy which we call God is conceived by us only through consciousness, through the knowledge of ourselves" (p. 293). The human mind furthermore contains "traces of infinity" in those "spiritual faculties" which desire "unlimited expansion" (p. 294). Humankind thus accurately mirrors the image of God. By thus fully humanizing God, Channing believed that he had resolved the dilemma in Puritan ethics which he maintained arose simply because the Puritans conceptualized God as a Wholly Other who bears no resemblance to human beings.

Channing redefines God for Unitarianism as "an all-communicating Parent" who is "the perfection of virtue," who is infinitely kind, just, benevolent, and "good to every individual, as well as to the general system" (pp. 296, 376).

We ascribe to him not only the name but the dispositions and principles of a father. We believe that He has a father's concern for his creatures, a father's desire for their improvement, a father's equity in proportioning his commands to their powers, a father's joy in their progress, a father's readiness to receive the penitent, and a father's justice for the incorrigible. We look upon this world as a place of education in which He is training men by prosperity and adversity, by aids and obstructions, by conflicts of reason and passion, by motives to duty and temptations to sin, by a various discipline suited to free and moral beings for union with himself and for a sublime and ever-growing virtue in heaven. (P. 377)

Because God seeks through his justice and mercy to help people achieve happiness, these two attributes are in perfect harmony, the more so since both express God's attentiveness to every person's moral character.[12] "God's mercy, as we understand it, desires strongly the happiness of the guilty— but only through their penitence. It has a regard to character as truly as his justice. It defers punishment, and suffers long, that the sinner may return to his duty, but leaves the impenitent and unyielding to the fearful retribution threatened in God's word" (pp. 376–77). The God Channing portrays is an impeccably moral and benevolent parent who takes everyone aspiring to salvation by the hand and, without exposing them to more trials and suffering than they can endure, patiently and kindly guides them through the process of achieving salvation.

Channing thus envisions the world as a large houshold over which a parental God presides as a gracious host who sees to it that his guests are hospitably treated in accord with a meticulous code of gentleman-like conduct.[13] Such a "purifying, comforting, and honorable" view of God's sovereignty, he asserts, is "more friendly to practical piety and pure morals than the opposite [i.e., Puritan] doctrines, because it gives clearer and nobler views of duty and stronger motives to its performance" (pp. 377, 383). Hence, in response to what he considered an amoral notion of God's sovereignty, Channing elaborated a morally consistent world view which could serve as the basis for a coherent moral life.

In one of his most memorable sermons, "Likeness to God" (1828), Channing provides further encouragement to moral striving through his unorthodox contention that people can achieve moral perfection—or in Channing's words, "unfold the divine likeness" in themselves—unaided by divine grace (p. 297). Human beings, he affirms, are nothing if not morally free agents. All virtue "has its foundation in the moral nature of man . . . and in the power of forming his temper and life according to conscience, . . . no dispositions infused into us without our own moral activity are of the nature of virtue, and therefore we reject the doctrine of irresistible divine influence on the human mind, moulding it into goodness as marble is hewn into a statue" (p. 380). For this reason, he concludes, true virtue as defined by orthodoxy—as a possibility conferred upon the individual only by divine grace—can never be "the object of moral approbation," since it is "a forced and vehement virtue" rather than the outgrowth of the moral laws of human nature (pp. 380, 297).

Freed from the grip of a tyrannical God, people can and will make the kinds of moral choices that guarantee their eternal salvation. Virtue and reason, he believed, would inevitably triumph over human temptations and the corruptions of society, even over the glaring inequities of race, gender, and slavery. As Channing puts it, in a letter lamenting the rifts with friends caused by his abolitionist sermons: "It is enough to know that this human world, of which we form a portion, lives, suffers, and is moving onward, under the eye and care of the Infinite Father. Before his pure, omnipotent goodness, all oppressions must fall; and under his reign our highest aspirations, prayers, and hopes for suffering humanity must, sooner or later, receive an accomplishment, beyond the power of prophecy to utter or of thought to comprehend" (p. 819). Channing thus believed that he had solved the problem of evil with his notion (a notion that was to become the foundation of liberal progressivism) that God is gradually raising people through their sufferings and miseries to yet unimaginable spiritual heights. To doubt such spiritual progress was, in Channing's view, to doubt the beneficence, goodness, and moral consistency of God Himself.

The liberal ethos (or the model for behavior) which Channing sets forth, and further elaborates in his twelve discourses entitled *The Perfect Life*, is antithetical to the Puritan understanding of true virtue. Gone is the Puritan doctrine of humiliation, its belief that virtue, even that rooted in divine grace, does not increase the individual's merit in God's eyes, and the affirmation that God sometimes makes people's virtuous efforts a source of ill will or harm to themselves. The Puritan world view prompted Channing and other liberal theologians to ask questions which Puritan theologians believed they had answered. If God is in fact unresponsive to all moral striving, why then seek to do good for others? Why should people try to improve themselves by pursuing humanizing goals? Why should people be concerned about the consequences of their actions? Moreover, if only the regenerate or the elect are capable of true morality, is there then nothing good or valuable about the moral desires and efforts of the unregenerate? Why even encourage the unregenerate to be moral if only divine grace makes true virtue possible? And if becoming truly moral is ultimately a function of being elected to eternal salvation, why should people not wait until they have a conversion experience before striving to live a moral life? Why be moral at all if God turns people's best efforts to their disadvantage?

Liberal theologians believed they had bypassed such questions through their portrayal of a God who voluntarily places ethical constraints upon His actions, and who responds to people in ways that are commensurate with the moral quality of their lives. They describe a universal moral order wherein those who violate its dictates God punishes and those who conform to them He rewards with salvation. God is obligated, according to this view, to confer salvation on the self which seeks to guarantee its destiny through its own moral and religious efforts.

The rationalistic theodicy thus described a predictable system of rewards and punishments—a world view of religious and moral guarantees—that made the style of life it recommended seem the only humanizing way to live within the world it depicted. The ethos it recommended made this world view seem the actual structure of reality to which this style of life was the only appropriate response. This synthesis of world view and ethos demonstrated to the satisfaction of liberal theologians that being virtuous in a world responsive to moral striving was not only necessary but the only sensible option rational people would choose for themselves.

It is clear from the writings of such liberal theologians as Mayhew, Chauncy, and Channing that their outlook on life emerged from experiencing the world as providing all people inalienable rights to justice and salvation, and that this experience defined for them the point of intersection between the rationalistic world view and ethos. Equal access to these inalienable rights is required and legitimated, according to these theologians, by the ethical dictates of the most inward self, whose dignity and self-respect God Himself would not violate when exercising His sovereign power. They saw these ethical dictates to be not only divinely instilled principles which were to regulate both human behavior and God's responses to His human creation, but also a divine confirmation that people could take "delight" in their freedom to obligate God to themselves without fearing to presume on divine prerogatives. The liberal ethos thus essentially constitutes a humanitarian moralism which emphasizes human dignity, divinely bestowed inalienable rights, God's equity and probity in His treatment of humankind, and people's God-given capacity to achieve both moral perfection and salvation through their own efforts.

Though this moralism could give rise to the spiritual and social optimism, even spiritual euphoria, which characterizes, say, the early writings of Ralph Waldo Emerson, it could also become the legalistic moralism of contemporary orthodoxy which self-righteously rationalized the existence of slavery. Such a rationalization is perhaps nowhere more memorably expressed than by a reviewer in the *Boston Courier*, a politically and religiously conservative paper which excoriated both the feminist and abolitionist movements during the 1840s and 1850s.[14]

And one would think that the people might reasonably see the wisdom of leaving this whole matter to be moulded, in the progress of events, by an all-wise Providence, since it evidently is not to be controlled by the short-sighted incapacity of man. To a fanatic, of course, such an argument would be quite unavailing, who has no faith in Providence, nor in that gradual operation of its silent agencies, through which it finally educes good out of evil, perhaps only in the long course of centuries, by means not foreseen, and avoiding sudden convulsions and dangerous disarrangements in the natural or the moral affairs of the world.[15]

"At its worst," as Henry May observes, "American moralism could justify anything";[16] and Boston, according to Channing, exemplified a legalistic moralism at its worst.[17]

Channing's transformation of basic Enlightenment ideals into a fully humanized notion of God "pointed the liberal direction which Protestant thinkers in America would pursue for over a century."[18] It helped to unite religion with the emerging humanitarian and reform movements; it also paved the way for the later development of that religious progressivism which would idealize not only humanity and society but even America itself in God's image.[19] And certainly the development of American Transcendentalism owes much to Channing.[20] The remarkable similarity between his ideas and those which Emerson expresses in *Nature* and the *Divinity School Address* suggests the impact Unitarianism made upon

Emerson.[21] But he, like all his fellow Transcendentalists, finally repudiated it. As Perry Miller observes, they "had to move through a Unitarian stage in order therefore to become Transcendentalists by rejecting it!"[22] Unitarianism, then, as defined by Channing, helped to transpose the issues expressed in the theological debate regarding the adequacy of the Puritan and rationalistic theodicies as explanations of human experience into the idiom of New England Transcendentalism.

NATHANIEL WILLIAM TAYLOR: A REFORMULATED PURITAN THEODICY

These issues were also passed on to the age of American Transcendentalism through the modified form of Edwardian theology known as "Taylorism." Nathaniel William Taylor, who essentially identified himself with the theological position of Jonathan Edwards (though he rejected Edwards' doctrine of the will),[23] nevertheless revised the thrust of Edwards' theology by seeking to redefine the basic doctrines of New England orthodoxy in terms of God's moral government. Whereas Edwards in his defense of the Puritan theodicy had maintained a balance between God's absolute sovereignty and His moral government, Taylor, in an effort "to formulate an acceptable compromise" between the Unitarians and anti-Unitarians, fully subordinated God's sovereignty to His moral government.[24] In his important sermon *Concio ad Clerum* (1828), the acknowledged manifesto of Taylorism, Taylor develops this "compromise" in a way which he believes refutes the liberal contention that the orthodox understanding of God's sovereignty makes Him responsible for sin and evil.

Sin and evil, Taylor argues, arise solely from human "moral depravity," a person's *"free choice of some object rather than God as his chief good— or a free preference of the world and worldly good, to the will and glory of God."*[25] He accepts the liberal view that there can be no moral life without this freedom of choice; yet, he also affirms the orthodox view that people inevitably choose the world rather than God. Taylor explains this paradox by saying that all people "are depraved by nature," that people, like a sick tree that bears bad fruit in any soil, *"will sin and only sin in all the appropriate circumstances of their being."*[26] But God cannot be held accountable for sin because people are born morally depraved; to envision God as the author of sin would make its punishment ethically absurd. "On this point, I need only ask—does God create in men a sinful nature, and damn them for the very nature he creates? Believe this, who can?"[27] Still, Taylor realizes he must answer why it is that people are born with sinful propensities.

Despite innate depravity, Taylor asserts, no one can presume to criticize God for creating this kind of world rather than another kind. Such presumption assumes "that God could have adopted a moral system, and prevented all sin, or at least, the present degree of sin." But no human mind has the capacity to ascertain the truth of this assumption;[28] nor does it have the capacity to determine whether God's grace, had He created a different world, would be as readily available in such a world as it is in the present one. Our ignorance in these matters, Taylor concludes (as did Chauncy and Channing), requires that we account for the "facts" of life in a way that "does most reverence to God."[29]

For Taylor, there is only one such explanation: the present world is the best of all possible worlds. God may be unable to prevent the emergence of evil in a world where people are free to sin; He will, however, "secure under the present system of things, the greatest degree of holiness and the least degree of sin, which *it is possible to him in the nature of things to secure.*"[30] God thus uses evil to "accomplish the highest good," a "greater good than he can secure by placing [people] in any other condition or circumstances."[31] Taylor further suggests that the existence of evil is necessary to the attainment of salvation. "For we know of no creature of God, whose holiness is secured without that influence which results either directly or indirectly, from the existence of sin and its punishment."[32] God is a "benevolent moral Governer" who, unable to check the evil tendencies of His creation, makes them work for people's benefit.[33] The fact that evil serves to implement God's providential moral government is, in Taylor's view, not only ample justification for God's permitting evil to exist but also indisputable proof that God has established a universal moral order that is a reliable object for people's trust.

Taylor's portrayal of a sovereign deity whose benevolent efforts on people's behalf are limited by "the nature of things" reformulates the Puritan theodicy in a way which seeks to reconcile God's sovereignty with the notion of human depravity. It was for Taylor the only possible way within the framework of Christian monotheism to explain a brutal and brutalizing world in ethical terms. Nevertheless, his reformulation of the Puritan theodicy failed to advance the theological debate. As it were, he only reshuffled the used deck of Puritan doctrines beneath the table and then tried to palm it off as a new and better deck. The Unitarians could not accept Taylor's affirmation of human depravity, while the traditionalists rejected his limitation of God's sovereignty. So long as the debate continued within its established theological conventions, there seemed to be no way, without placing severe strains upon the monotheistic bent of the Christian tradition, to reconcile the orthodox and liberal theodicies. And when at least one eminent theologian, Edward Beecher, offered a radical solution for this hiatus in his now obscure work, *The Conflict of Ages; or The Great Debate on the Moral Relations of God and Man* (1854), the result was a theological stillbirth.

EDWARD BEECHER: A RECONCILIATION OF THEODICIES?

Beecher was preoccupied with the problem of evil. In 1827, he described in his notebook what he considered the essence of the problem: "Evil exists. If it does prove malevolence in God we are lost, or else must love a partial being. We cannot analyze the thing."[34] Analyze he did, however. He admits that for years the problem of evil so bedeviled him that he felt as though he "had been groping in some vast cathedral, in the gloom of midnight, vainly striving to comprehend its parts and relations" (p. 191).[35] This struggle finally led to his experiencing "an entire eclipse of the character of God" (p. 187). When he did arrive at an acceptable solution, he believed, as he proposes to demonstrate in *The Conflict of Ages*, that he could describe a coherent world view that would provide a reliable foundation for the moral life.

Beecher maintains that the greatest conflict shaping the history of the church, from the third century A.D. to the middle of the nineteenth century, has been that regarding "the moral renovation of man." His primary concern, however, is to formulate and ultimately to solve this conflict in terms of the seemingly irreconcilable debate about the Puritan and rationalistic theodicies within the American theological tradition. On the one side have been those like Taylor and earlier orthodox theologians who advocated "the doctrine of a supernatural regeneration rendered necessary by the native and original depravity of man, and effected according to the eternal purposes of a divine and mysterious sovereignty" (p. 2). On the other side are those like Channing and his earlier liberal forebears who opposed this doctrine because its vision of a God who punishes people for an innate depravity which He confers upon them and which they cannot alter conflicts "with the fundamental principles of honor and right" (p. 3).

The orthodox and democratic sensibilities are here in direct collision. The result is "that experience in which the principles of honor and right, and also the facts concerning the depravity and ruin of man, are both retained" without perceiving "any apparent mode of reconciliation" for the conflict between them (pp. 184, 188). The logical resolution to this conflict, he observes, is the conclusion that a universe in which the "more violent manifestations of [children's] depravity seem to be the unfoldings of a corrupt nature, given to them by God before any knowledge, choice or consent, of their own," is a "malevolent" one (p. 190).

Beecher refuses to accept this conclusion, however, since it leads people to a skeptical despair that borders on "insanity."[36] Yet, like Taylor, he also maintains that both affirmations—that of innate depravity and that of an honorable and just God—are necessary for the effectual moral renovation of humankind. He thus proposes that the primary task of Christianity (the task he sets for himself in *The Conflict of Ages*) is to reconcile the orthodox view of human depravity that goes "to the bottom of the human malady" with the liberal notion of an honorable and just God whom people can love "without doing violence" to their ethical sensibilities (p. 208).

These two views, according to Beecher, have seemed irreconcilable because of a single wrong assumption that shapes all Christian thought. It is "the simple and plausible assumption THAT MEN AS THEY COME INTO THIS WORLD ARE NEW-CREATED BEINGS. That they are NEW-BORN beings, is plain enough; that they are, therefore, NEW-CREATED beings, is certainly a mere assumption" (pp. 211–12). If people are newly created beings, an honorable God would be obligated to give them "original constitutions, healthy and well-balanced, and tending decidedly and effectually toward good." God would also be obligated to place them "in such circumstances that there shall be an overbalance of influences and tendencies on the side of holiness, and not of sin. Such are the conceded demands of the principles of equity and of honor" (p. 214). So long, then, as Christian thought assumes that people are newly created, it can provide no adequate justification for the manner in which God disadvantages and abuses people in this world.

The only way to eliminate this problem, according to Beecher, is to replace the assumption that people are newly created beings in this world with the assumption that people lived in a prior state of existence which fully satisfied the demands of honor and right. If people then subsequently "revolted and corrupted themselves, and forfeited their rights, and were introduced into this world under a dispensation of sovereignty, disclosing both justice and mercy,—then [the] conflict . . . can be at once and entirely removed" (p. 222). Human depravity therefore results not from Adam's original sin but from a previous existence in which people were "the unreasonable and inexcusable author[s] of [their] own corruption and ruin" (p. 227). Hence "the laws of honor and right, towards new-created minds, are not observed in this world, because men are born under a forfeiture of them, and are 'by nature children of wrath' " (pp. 487–88).

Because of this state of affairs, God has benevolently made this world "a moral hospital of the universe" wherein "the diseased of past ages" are exposed to God's healing mercies (p. 232). It constitutes a system of miseries and tribulations which, if people accept them as the trials and discipline necessary for their renovation, will enable them to achieve salvation. Beecher concludes that because such a "remedial system" provides people the opportunity to end their revolt against God it fully justifies both the adverse circumstances they experience in this world and God's consequent punishment of those who freely deny the assistance He offers for helping them achieve salvation.

The notion of pre-existence, according to Beecher, has several advantages. It reconciles the Puritan and rationalistic theodicies in a way that preserves the essential outlines of the Puritan understanding of human experience, ascribes nothing to God that is "at war with the highest principles of honor and right" (p. 230), retains the dignity of humankind's free agency, and solves the problem of evil. But by basing this synthesis upon a concept which runs contrary to the fundamental religious premises of western religious thought,[37] Beecher forecloses the possibility that anyone, conservative or liberal, would give his enterprise serious consideration. *The Conflict of Ages* thus clearly reflects the impasse which the debate, itself stretching back to early Christian times, had reached by 1850.

THE AMERICAN DEBATE

In America, this debate assumes its own distinctive form through the complexity of religious responses to the changing American environment. Four distinct stages can in fact be discerned in the evolution of this debate. The first stage constituted the Puritans' initial attitude toward the yet undeveloped wilderness. They believed the wilderness to be a passive reality that would easily accommodate itself to their utopian vision of the New Jerusalem. Ironically, it emphasized both the rational deity of the covenant, who establishes and abides by a predictable system of rewards and punishments regarding the Puritan errand into the wilderness, and a mysterious, unpredictable, sovereign God whose treatment of humankind violates human canons of justice. These two emphases were held in an uneasy tension within first- and second-generation theological writings. Theologians simply let the occasion determine which concept of God they would appeal to. There was no effort to synthesize these contradictory conceptions of God.

Stage two was dominated by a troubling sense of the problematical nature of the American wilderness. The efforts to create the New Jerusalem were giving way to the gradual commercialization of society which was successfully establishing a new system of rewards and punishments—i.e., it was redefining success in more secular terms—without suffering the repercussions promised in the covenant with God for failing to realize its utopian vision. These social changes called into question the synthesis of world view and ethos set forth in the covenant theology. For many, the moral and religious expectations generated by the covenant theology no longer seemed appropriate to their contemporary world. Puritan theologians had a twofold response to the resulting sense of disorientation: they reaffirmed the necessity for strict adherence to the covenant obligations while at the same time increasingly emphasizing God's sovereignty in a way that rendered it irreconcilable with the covenant theology. The uneasy tension between the emphases on a mysterious and sovereign God and on the far more rational and predictable deity of the covenant now became a problematical rift in Puritan thought.

The third stage, though initiated prior to the American Revolution, nevertheless basically characterizes the five decades following the Revolution. It marks a crucial theological adaptation to the gradual "democratization of mind" during this period.[38] Liberal theologians who repudiated the Puritan theodicy articulated an alternative theodicy which redefines God's sovereignty in terms of egalitarian ideals and provides a religious justification for the democratic mode of experiencing the world. The tension in early Puritan thought between two contrasting images of God was thus resolved with the development of two theodicies which express diametrically opposed syntheses of world view and ethos. In these two theodicies, the debate gave rise to a set of constants, two culturally prescribed modes for viewing and experiencing the world which American Protestant culture developed from 1630 to 1830 in response to new religious situations.

However, as Edward Beecher had recognized as late as 1854, the debate was only moving in useless circles, like a Mississippi riverboat with its paddle wheels moving in opposing directions.[39] Rather than seeking to formulate a creative synthesis of the two theodicies that might advance the debate beyond its current impasse, theologians simply reaffirmed them as either/or alternatives. They remained the two basic models for theological reflection as theologians continued to wrestle with the problem of defining a world view and ethos which, when successfully conjoined, would mirror the complexities of a people's encounter with a constantly changing American environment.

This problem had deep cultural roots. Such important nineteenth-century authors as William Dunlap, James Fenimore Cooper, Nathaniel Hawthorne, Ralph Waldo Emerson, and Herman Melville also explored various efforts to create from the complexities of American experience a successful fusion of world view and ethos. These writers—some consciously, others unconsciously—transformed this implied metaphysical drama of the self in both the Puritan and liberal treatments of the problem of theodicy into explicit narrative forms. This in part helps to explain the metaphysical qualities of such American classics as the Leatherstocking novels, *The Scarlet Letter*, and *Moby-Dick*. In such works the narrative form and the process of synthesizing a world view and ethos go hand in hand; the narrative gives rise to an ethos and world view while the process of integrating the two gives structure and meaning to the narrative.

Certainly the attempt to create and to fuse a world view and ethos is, as Clifford Geertz reminds us, a universal religious phenomenon; it is in no way unique to these works, or, for that matter, to the prior debate. What makes these literary works distinctive is that the authors, like their theological predecessors, formulated the process of synthesizing a world view and ethos in the terms established by the debate regarding the Puritan and rationalistic theodicies. No attempt is made here to establish any historical continuity based on this resemblance amongst divergent American writings, even though it seems reasonable to assume that the wide-ranging consistency of such resemblances points toward some kind of continuity. Rather, the argument set forth is that the religious assumptions shaping the debate variously functioned as the organizing principles of the literary works chosen here for analysis; that such works, for example, as the Leatherstocking novels, *The Scarlet Letter*, and *Moby-Dick* dramatize both the contrary world views and modes of experiencing the world—how the self feels, thinks, and acts within the world view—prescribed by the Puritan and rationalistic theodicies; and that these works, when viewed from this perspective, mark the fourth stage of the debate from 1820 to 1860.

That is to say, in these works the authors did not merely describe inherited religious world views and modes of experience but also evaluated their adequacy for expressing the new feelings, thoughts, and conflicts that were gradually welling up from the moil of social, political, and religious change taking place in nineteenth-century America. To paraphrase Gordon Kaufman's rendering of the unique religious situation now facing humankind, these authors were trying to show that the dual symbols of divine sovereignty inherited from the debate were no longer adequate, at least separately, for grasping the new religious situation facing nineteenth-century Americans, that they concealed rather than illuminated the true nature of their predicament.[40] In various ways, they sought to demonstrate for their contemporaries that the changes taking place in their historical situation required "changes in [their] religious symbolism and in the frames of reference within which [they made their] value judgments and moral choices."[41] In some cases, but most notably that of Melville, this effort involved a radical reconsideration of "some of the most fundamental axioms of western religious symbolism and faith."[42] And in all cases it called for at least a complication or even modification of the accepted religious modes of experiencing and viewing the world. The questions which the Puritans repeatedly asked as they treated the problem of theodicy become the questions these authors ask in their works, thereby demonstrating, as one critic observes of the pre–Civil War period, that Puritanism still had the power to force the best creative writers of the time "to continue to ask its questions."[43]

Indeed, such authors as Dunlap, Cooper, Hawthorne, Emerson, and Melville, when viewed collectively, ultimately reformulated the Puritan legacy in ways that gradually expanded it beyond the confines of conventional theological discourse. They repossessed this theological inheritance as a usable critical resource for exploring and evaluating the moral and religious problems of early nineteenth-century American culture. And by thus repossessing this religious legacy through narrative constructs, these writers contributed to the making of a new literary tradition, itself a great legacy.

PART TWO

A LITERARY LEGACY

6

William Dunlap and James Fenimore Cooper: A Problematical American Revolution

Many studies have demonstrated how such major American writers as James Fenimore Cooper, Nathaniel Hawthorne, Ralph Waldo Emerson, and Herman Melville were consciously bent on using their craft either to adapt European literary forms to American materials or to recast these native materials into new literary forms. But their writings frequently reflect as much a struggle to discover an adequate metaphysical framework for interpreting the moral and religious ambiguities of American democracy as they do the struggle to shape their chosen materials into an adequate literary form.[1] "The task of the American writer," as Robert Spiller observes, "was . . . more than merely the finding of the most suitable literary form; it was that of probing the effects of democratic theory on inherited and transplanted values."[2]

Both kinds of struggle frequently go hand in hand in their works. Narrative strategies were required that could accommodate the quest for a metaphysical framework able to incorporate the moral and religious tensions of American democracy, while the metaphysical framework had to evolve dramatically from the narrative structure itself. This search for an adequate metaphysics in part involved an exploration of those syntheses of world view and ethos which constituted the Protestant gestalt shaping American culture from 1630 to 1820, syntheses which had been defined and made publicly accessible by the theological debate regarding the adequacy of the Puritan and rationalistic theodicies for explaining human experience.

The fact that these authors variously explored the Puritan and rationalistic theodicies in many of their works suggests that, by the early nineteenth century, these theodicies expressed culturally prescribed ways of experiencing and viewing the world. But as several works by these authors indicate, these inherited syntheses of world view and ethos were becoming problematical within the rapidly changing environment of early nineteenth-century America.[3] To be sure, their works are first and last literary constructs and are to be examined as such. But there can be no doubt that, at least in the works selected here for study, the authors were testing the adequacy of these theodicies for interpreting their contemporary experiences. When viewed in this light, these particular works can be collectively defined as creative efforts to re-evaluate the fundamental moral and religious values shaping American Protestant culture.

WILLIAM DUNLAP: THE MORALITY OF THE AMERICAN REVOLUTION

Any reassessment of a cultural tradition rests in part upon the recognition of the problematical nature of its shaping ideals. Such recognition came slowly in the newly formed Republic, if only because many Americans believed that God had ordained the Revolution and therewith sanctioned its ideals. This idea is succinctly expressed in James Fenimore Cooper's *The Pilot* (1824) by a young defender of the colonial cause when, in a discussion of the morality of the American Revolution, she asks her Tory guardian: "In what behalf would a just Providence sooner exercise its merciful power, than to protect the daring children of an oppressed country, while contending against tyranny and countless wrongs?"[4]

During the two decades following the Revolution, Americans were riding a wave of egalitarian euphoria that was to continue rippling through the early nineteenth century. They frequently portrayed the Republic as the bastion of justice, liberty, and virtue, as a repossessed city on a hill whose democratic virtues would purge the corruptions of Europe and eventually transform the entire world in its own image.[5] Even an Englishman, who had been made an honorary citizen of the United States, wrote that "the last step in human progress is to be made in America."[6] Looking toward this new society it believed was dawning in late eighteenth-century America, the young Republic as yet gave no particular thought to the anarchistic implications of its democratic principles nor to how these principles themselves might come into irreconcilable conflict.

But there was also an experienced conflict between the efforts to realize this utopian democratic society and adherence to traditional institutions and values. "The 1780's in America," writes Henry May, "can be seen as a time of uneasy equilibrium, of innovation and conservative adaptation everywhere mixed, of enthusiasm and fear both muted by the necessities of a compromise."[7] The events of the 1790s, in both Europe and America, further exacerbated this cultural conflict until, near the century's close, the literary scene gave slight indications of an emerging awareness of the problematical nature of democratic values. William Dunlap's play, *André* (1798), for example, which "is now considered one of the best surviving American dramas of the eighteenth century,"[8] explored both the moral complexities of the American Revolution and the tragic implications of its shaping ideals.[9] In so doing, Dunlap raised serious moral questions about the synthesis of world view and ethos described in the rationalistic theodicy.

André eventually became a very popular play because of its rousing patriotism in its support of the American Revolution, but initially neither Dunlap's contemporary audiences nor critics were very receptive to the play,[10] since Dunlap presents André, the famed British spy, in a sympathetic light.[11] André had gained international reputation as a courageous and honorable British officer before he was discovered in disguise behind the American lines. A military tribunal consequently convicted him of being a spy and sentenced him to death by hanging, the means of death accorded to common criminals.

The play opens at this point. Bland, an American officer whose life André had saved while the former was a British prisoner of war, is visiting him in jail. After hearing André confess that he conspired with Benedict Arnold to help bring about the downfall of the colonies, Bland justifies André's activities as being part of his patriotic duty. André refuses to exonerate himself. Not only did he act against his own conscience, he tells Bland, but he also sought undying fame through his traitorous activities. "Thy country for my death incurs no blame" (p. 59).[12] His only request is that Bland try to have his form of execution commuted from hanging to the firing squad, "a soldier's death" (p. 59). Bland refuses to do anything less than try to save André's life. But if he fails—"If worth like thine must thus be sacrificed/To policy so cruel and unjust" (p. 59)—he vows that he will join the British army in order to avenge his friend's death.

In the remainder of the play, Dunlap explores the issue whether justice is best served by André's release or execution. The figure in the play who must finally resolve this problem is George Washington. As supreme commander of the colonial forces, he alone has the power to revoke the military tribunal's sentence. Throughout the play Washington is presented as a model of rationality, temperance, and virtue who thoughtfully considers but finally rejects the various reasons offered for sparing André's life.[13]

It is the long-range effect of André's death, not his personal predicament, which determines Washington's response to Bland's request that he release André. Bland argues that his own patriotic service to the colonies merits the granting of this request and, moreover, that André's release is the only appropriate way to reward both his goodness and courage in saving his (i.e., Bland's) life when nothing required him to do so. Not even wartime conditions, Bland asserts, justify the unjust treatment of a virtuous person. Washington admits that Bland's moral arguments are persuasive. But he contends that as supreme commander of the American forces

he must subsume such moral considerations to his obligation to advance
the general welfare of the colonies, even of the world.

> I know the virtues of this man and love them.
> But the destiny of millions, millions
> Yet unborn, depends upon the rigor
> Of this moment. The haughty Briton laughs
> To scorn our armies and our councils.
> Mercy, Humanity, call loudly, that we make
> Our new despised power be felt, vindictive.
> Millions demand the death of this young man.
> My injur'd country, he his forfeit life
> Must yield, to shield thy lacerated breast
> From torture. (P. 62)

After Washington refuses his request, Bland treasonously tears the cockade
from his helmet, declares his refusal to serve a "country that forgets to
reverence virtue" (p. 62), and leaves Washington to contemplate this trea-
sonous action.

Nor does Washington waver in the face of the British threat to execute
his old friend, Bland's father, should André be put to death. He tells the
British officer bearing this message that André's execution is certain, since
it will serve the "good" of the colonial cause as will also the death of
Bland's father if it "Can further fire [our] country to resistance" against
England (pp. 64, 65). This situation affords the occasion for much patriotic bombast after Washington reads a note from Bland's father which
curtly states: "Do *your* duty" (p. 65).

Although this message from his friend enables Washington to remain
firm when Bland's mother requests André's release, André's fiancée, Honoria, almost changes Washington's mind. Honoria, whose father had falsely
led André to believe that she had rejected him for another suitor, crosses
the Atlantic to be with André. When she hears of André's plight, she visits
Washington and tearfully implores him to let her and André return to
England. For the first time Washington questions his decision. But when
their conversation is disrupted by the news that an American officer of
good reputation has been ignominiously hanged by "lawless" British scouts,
Washington irrevocably seals André's fate. The entrance of the messenger
bearing this news, which parallels the traditional use of the *deus ex machina*, thus provides the occasion for accepting an easy patriotic, even legalistic, solution for a difficult moral dilemma.

Counterbalancing these developments is André's inner struggle to accept
his imminent death.[14] Although he had unflinchingly faced death several
times on the battlefield, he now finds that "his cool,/ His sure approach,
requires a fortitude/ Which naught but conscious rectitude can/ give" (p. 57).
Debarred from an honorable death, André strives to meet his unwanted
fate with something more than the sense of disgrace it evokes in him. He

blames no one but himself for his plight; he desires only to die a soldier's death before a firing squad rather than a felon's death on the gallows. Upon learning that Washington upholds the tribunal's sentence of death by hanging, André muses: "Is there no way to escape that infamy? What then is infamy—no matter—no matter" (p. 65).

The solution to his problem appears, he believes, when he learns that the British will execute Bland's father if he himself is put to death. He promises Bland that he will send a message to the British general requesting the release of his father. "If, at this moment,/ when the pangs of death already touch me,/ Firmly my mind against injustice strives,/ And the last impulse to my vital powers/ Is given by anxious wishes to redeem/ My fellow-men from pain; surely my end,/ Howe'er accomplish'd, is not infamous" (p. 66). To struggle against injustice despite his own situation is, for André, the only way to make his otherwise dishonorable death an honorable one. After learning that his request has gained the release of Bland's father, André "cheerfully" goes to his death, while Bland, having lost his composure, is led away from the place of execution so that his "wild" looks and gestures will not disrupt André's "manly calmness" (p. 74).

André is thus a half-allegorical, half-dramatic treatment of circumstances which call into question the notion that human virtue can guarantee a morally commensurate destiny. Crèvecoeur confronts the same problem in his twelfth letter; but rather than seeking to complicate his understanding of the moral life, he plans a secluded retreat where he believes he can recreate the circumstances that will reaffirm his agrarian notion that being virtuous guarantees particular rewards. Dunlap's play, however, affirms that this agrarian notion of virtue cannot explain the full range of human experience. André's career, as even Washington admits, demonstrates that there is no necessary connection between a person's merit and his destiny. By suggesting a world view more closely aligned with that of the Puritan theodicy, Dunlap questions the world view which shapes both the rationalistic theodicy and Crèvecoeur's notion of the agrarian covenant. Furthermore, in André's attempt to work for the benefit of another without reward, regardless of his own adverse circumstances, Dunlap echoes Cotton Mather's notion that virtue constitutes those efforts to do good through which people seek not to benefit themselves but only to glorify God, though André himself expresses no such religious understanding of his action. Dunlap is seemingly using André's career as a dramatic means for exploring the viability of the Puritan understanding of virtue when divested of its supernatural sanctions in a world which seems indifferent to human goodness.[15]

But Washington's dilemma, in which he experiences a conflict between the agrarian notion that virtue will be rewarded and the notion (popularized by Mayhew) that a good ruler serves the general welfare, suggests the necessity for a broader reassessment of both agrarian and Revolutionary ideals. To decide André's fate in accordance with either principle requires that he violate the other. Washington thus suspends his allegiance to the agrarian notion of virtue in order to benefit the general welfare of the colonies, thereby dramatizing the tragic potential of one of the American Revolution's basic ideals. Such a conflict within the moral foundation of American democracy suggests the necessity for developing a more complex moral vision having a dual focus which can resolve, or at least accommodate, such dilemmas. Later writers further affirmed that formulating such a dual vision, even a comprehensive synthesis of the Puritan and rationalistic theodicies, was a religious problem endemic to early nineteenth-century American culture.

JAMES FENIMORE COOPER: THE MORALITY OF THE AMERICAN REVOLUTION RECONSIDERED

In *The Spy* (1821) and *Wyandotté* (1843), James Fenimore Cooper also explored the problematical nature of the American Revolution.[16] Three of Cooper's first five novels were in fact set during the Revolution. It provided a morally complex background for exploring such contemporary issues as national independence, individual freedom, and political identity—problems which he analyzed in such nonfictional works as *Notions of the Americans* (1828) and *The American Democrat* (1838). So important was the Revolution to Cooper's evaluation of American society that he contemplated writing a sixth Leatherstocking novel set during this period;[17] and according to his own description of the three Littlepage novels—*Satanstoe* (1845), *The Chainbearer* (1845), and *The Redskins* (1846)—he traced the development of a single family from the colonial period through the Revolution to the formation of the Republic in order to examine the social and economic impact of the Revolution.[18] In *The Spy* and *Wyandotté*, two of his most complicated fictions, Cooper turned to the war for independence not only to uncover the moral roots of his contemporary society but also to dramatize the cultural and spiritual ambiguities of American democracy, ambiguities which Hawthorne, Emerson, and Melville further explored. Like them, he reassessed basic American ideals in terms of the moral tensions they generated. Throughout his career Cooper pursued this task by seeking to determine which world view best explains these conflicts and what ethos best suits the world described by this understanding of the world. In both novels, but most especially in *The Spy*—a work which was successfully adapted for the stage by several playwrights[19]—Cooper moved toward the conclusion that the polarities created by the Revolution can be accommodated only by a dual moral perspective that transcends conventional norms. Here, as in the Leatherstocking novels, Cooper demonstrated his preoccupation with discovering a reliable basis for moral commitment in a world of opposing values.

The stage for examining this problem in *The Spy* is the "neutral ground" around New York City.[20] Most of the action takes place in an unsettled valley situated midway between the British and American forces where various loyalties inevitably come into conflict. The wilderness, as Edwin Fussell suggests, becomes a "poetic space" in Cooper's fiction for rendering the kinds of conflicts experienced within the boundary between the two worlds of civilization and nature.[21] Cooper also uses this strategy in the Leatherstocking novels, while other novelists, such as Hawthorne and Melville, develop it further within their works until it finally becomes for later authors a "perfunctory or implicit" literary convention.[22] In *The Spy*, the wilderness functions as a buffer zone between the British and American forces which attracts those who are unwilling to become involved in the war. But because both armies are seeking control of this region, the families who have tentatively taken up residence there are exposed to unexpected raids from both sides. Like Crèvecoeur, these temporary settlers find themselves in the heart of an arbitrary reality that ignores all moral distinctions, since "the law was momentarily extinct in that particular district, and justice was administered subject to the bias of personal interests and the passions of the strongest."[23]

Cooper thus creates a "neutral" area where both the American and British perspectives have validity, where each erratically enforces its own dictates. Stephen Railton has noted that such conflicts between competing values, beliefs, and loyalties abound in Cooper's works. "Ideas set forth in them directly refute each other. Antithetical judgments are made upon the very same subjects. Within particular novels, two conflicting sets of values often compete not for the reader's sympathy only, but, one feels, for the author's."[24] But at least in *The Spy* and *Wyandotté*, as well as in the Leatherstocking novels, Cooper seeks to discover within this kind of morally chaotic situation a moral foundation for a double vision which can reconcile such conflicting perspectives.

In *The Spy*, the English perspective is represented by the Wharton family. Mr. Wharton, a former English officer, has moved his family to this neutral territory in order to avoid making any commitment that might endanger their lives, though his son, Henry, remains a captain in the British Army. Henry subsequently visits his family, is captured by an American force, and placed in the care of Peyton Dunwoodie who loves—and is loved by—Fran, one of Mr. Wharton's daughters. Their various loyalties are thereby brought into conflict. As an officer, Dunwoodie's obligations to his country must take precedence over his personal loyalties to Fran and the Wharton family, while Fran, after Dunwoodie refuses her request to release her brother, affirms her familial allegiances by severing her relationship with Dunwoodie, though she continues to love him.

Cooper praises both Fran's adherence to familial ties and Dunwoodie's selfless commitment to the American cause. Nevertheless, in this early work, as in the later Effingham novels, Cooper emphasizes the importance, even the inviolability, of family loyalties. The Wharton family is what might be called, in Cooper's fiction, an "ideal" family, a family which, in its adherence to conventional morality, gives loyalty to its own members priority over all extrafamilial obligations. Moreover, their neutrality also helps to counteract the brutalizing conditions of war. For while they recognize the seemingly irreconcilable conflict between both sides in the war, they still keep pathways of communication open between them. The Wharton family serves as a kind of conduit for discussions between the representatives of the American and English positions.

And when loyalties to family and country, as manifested in the relationship between Dunwoodie and Fran, become divisive, Cooper provides a facile resolution for the conflict. Contrary to her threat, Fran marries Dunwoodie even while soldiers under his command still hold Henry captive. Meanwhile, Dunwoodie has received from Harper (who we later learn is George Washington) a promise, which Dunwoodie communicates to Henry, that Henry's life will not be endangered. Despite this assurance, Henry escapes. Angered by this news, Dunwoodie disregards his wife's pleas on Henry's behalf and makes preparations to pursue him. At the last moment, however, Dunwoodie receives a communiqué from Washington ordering him to carry out another assignment unrelated to capturing Henry. Like Dunlap in *André*, Cooper here resolves a difficult moral dilemma by means of a messenger who dramatically functions as a *deus ex machina*. But such a simplistic solution is overshadowed by the figure of Harvey Birch, whose tragic career in *The Spy* further complicates Cooper's treatment of conflicting moral allegiance.

Harvey Birch is ostensibly a peddler who sells his wares behind both British and American lines. In reality, he is an American spy who works closely with Washington. However, in order to serve the American cause more effectively, Birch creates a public image of being a British spy. So successful is this ruse of being a traitor that a military court has condemned him to be hanged or shot on sight. American soldiers capture him four times. Each time he barely misses being hanged because Washington, we are made to understand, secretly effects his escape. These escapes only further jeopardize his life since the American forces redouble their efforts to capture him. Moreover, they beat his aging father (who subsequently dies) and burn his house. With his reputation ruined and his life constantly imperiled, Birch never marries because of the stigma and danger his name would confer upon his family.

Even after the war Birch is not exonerated. Washington refuses to clear his name for fear of the repercussions to others, presumably others (perhaps some Britishers) who were also members of the American spy network. Birch consequently changes his name after the war and, without regret for having thus served the American cause, moves to a small rural village where no one knows him and dies there in obscurity and poverty. This ending to the novel seems an implicit criticism of a moral position which, despite its obligations to many others who had been part of the American spy system, permits Birch to die publicly unrecognized for his heroic exploits.

It might also be argued that in Birch's career Cooper is celebrating a vision of morality that closely resembles that set forth in the Puritan tradition. In contrast to the Willoughbys and Dunwoodie, Birch tragically sacrifices everything dear to him—his father, his home, his future—out of an unswerving, selfless loyalty to democratic ideals which he believes were ordained by God. Birch represents a moral position which requires him, heedless of his own destiny, willingly to accept whatever humiliation, degradation, or harm results from his commitment to realizing a new democratic social order that will benefit others. By dramatizing in Birch's career how the American Revolution gives rise to and legitimates such a quasi-Puritan redefinition of morality, Cooper implies that the very origins of the Republic have bequeathed to future generations the problem of creating a dual moral vision which can synthesize, or at least accommodate, the seemingly irreconcilable obligations to conventional morality and to that religious duty which suspends traditional norms in the name of higher ideals.

In *The Spy*, then, the Revolution functions less as a historical event than as a metaphor for the tensions and struggles which the characters must face within a complicated network of affairs. Indeed, the Revolution provided Cooper a metaphor for a complicated world view and moral vision that could not be accommodated by his chosen aesthetic structure.[25] *The Spy* represents the first attempt by an American novelist to come to terms with the moral and religious implications of the American environment in a way that raises serious questions about the prevailing notion that the American experiment in democracy embodied an unambiguous revelation of God's redemptive purposes. It is the beginning of a long literary inquest into what Harry Levin calls "the American nightmare"[26]—those murky areas of the past which could provide some analogy for the darker aspects of early nineteenth-century American culture. Spiller rightly observes that "with this novel American fiction was fairly launched."[27] Certainly *The Spy* identifies a major problem that was to preoccupy such writers as Cooper, Hawthorne, Emerson, and Melville.

That problem is whether a reliable foundation for the moral life still exists within those situations which disconfirm the traditionally accepted framework for making value judgments and moral choices. In *Wyandotté*, as in *The Spy*, Cooper examines this problem through a literary strategy which contrasts the efforts to remain neutral during the American Revolution with a more complicated response to this chaotic period. The Willoughbys, a British family sympathetic to both the American and British causes, seek to avoid any entangling commitments to either side by moving to a wilderness region located midway between the contending armies, where they intend to remain until the Revolution ends. In order to protect themselves against unexpected raids by the British, Americans, or their Indian allies, the Willoughbys build a fortress-like haven which they stock with goods, guns, and ammunition. By means of this armed neutrality they seek to guarantee their safety in the lawless wilderness.

A quite different stance is embodied by Wyandotté, who represents the Indian perspective on the Revolution. Rejected by his own tribe, Wyandotté is forced to live as an outcast on the fringes of three cultures—the Indian, the British, and the American—where he shifts his allegiances as the situation requires.[28] Wyandotté had served under Mr. Willoughby, a former British officer who once severely flogged him. Despite this bitter memory, he gives his loyalty to the Willoughby family while also serving as a spy for both the American and British forces. But Mr. Willoughby's repeated threats to flog him should he betray their family finally prompt Wyandotté, in accordance with his own notion of justice, to murder Mr. Willoughby. Willoughby's death is the heart of the novel. For even though Edgar Allan Poe calls it "a species of poetical justice,"[29] it demonstrates how even a personal relationship between Indian and white is tragically marred by seemingly irreconcilable cultural animosities. It poses the larger problem whether it is possible to adjudicate conflicting cultural norms by means of any universal standards—a problem that is central to the intervening Leatherstocking novels.

Yet, despite his killing Mr. Willoughby (the murder remains unsolved until the end of the novel), Wyandotté later risks his life to help protect the defenseless Willoughby family when they are attacked by a combined force of colonial soldiers and Indians. This heroic action is motivated by his unflinching devotion to Mrs. Willoughby for having nursed him through a nearly fatal illness. These actions, along with his implied efforts to gain acceptance by various Indian tribes, disclose his intense struggle to retain a personal integrity, perhaps even to redefine it, in the face of the conflicting moral demands imposed upon him by the British, the Americans, and his own Indian heritage—a struggle which, in Poe's view, made Wyandotté the most interesting Indian in Cooper's fiction.

Ultimately, however, unlike Harvey Birch who faces a similar situation, Wyandotté proves to be a wily moral chameleon. He is a disconnected pastiche of allegiances; which allegiance he chooses to follow at any given time is dictated solely by his circumstances. This willingness to compromise all of his commitments points toward an amoral resolution of the kinds of moral conflicts the wilderness represents in Cooper's fiction.[30] The novel, as one critic observes, verges on being "a darker, more ambiguous version of *The Pioneers*,"[31] but Cooper, unwilling to pursue Wyandotté's stance to its logical conclusion, has him first confess the murder and then convert to Christianity in repentance for his misdeeds. Though his journals make it clear that Cooper did not become a serious student of the Bible or Christianity until 1848,[32] *Wyandotté* (1843) seems to bear out Robert Spiller's contention that, beginning with this novel, "Cooper entered a new experimental phase of his career, a phase of moral and religious didacticism which had been specifically indicated in his earlier career only by the Puritan novel *The Wept of Wish-ton-Wish* in 1829."[33]

Nevertheless, despite his didactic conclusion to *Wyandotté*, in both this novel and *The Spy* Cooper explores the moral and spiritual ambiguities of the American Revolution and the democratic ideals it sponsored. In these novels, Cooper moves beyond Crèvecoeur's myopic treatment of the Revolution by using this anarchical period as a dramatic resource for examining the possible foundations of a moral perspective that could reconcile conflicting values. Both of these works—and perhaps especially *Wyandotté*, which Spiller calls the "least pleasant" of Cooper's thirty-two novels—"helped to prepare the way for a more realistic treatment of American society and its problems" by such authors as Hawthorne, Melville, and Mark Twain.[34] Like Dunlap, Cooper presents the American Revolution as a tragic affirmation of ideals which were not viewed by the general populace as having any problematical implications. Both stress how the effort to realize the democratic ideals endorsed by the rationalistic theodicy finally discloses a world that resembles the world depicted by the Puritan theodicy; and both dramatize how adherence to these ideals can require a style of life or ethos incompatible with that recommended by the rationalistic theodicy.

The major religious question their works pose is not whether to accept or reject either theodicy, but whether it is possible to synthesize them into a more comprehensive explanation of human experience. These writers were suggesting that Americans had inherited this problem from their revolutionary origins (although it was also a legacy of the Puritan tradition), and they reassessed American ideals in light of this problem.

But the social context for carrying out this reassessment differed considerably in each case. Dunlap was still addressing a basically colonial mindset, though it was increasingly fraught with tensions, while Cooper's youthful imagination was decisively formed by the first fifteen years of the nineteenth century, when "a really new society was painfully being born."[35] "Change was a striking feature of American life throughout the first three centuries," Stow Persons observes, "but change was never so extensive or so significant as during the democratic era of the first half of the nineteenth century."[36] From 1800 to 1815, writes Henry May, "Americans were conscious that they were living in a new period, but the nature of this period was not yet clear. All the forces of change which were to produce nineteenth-century culture were gathering strength, but their effects were as yet unmanifest."[37] It was a time when, as Robert Spiller puts it, "American culture had sent down its first firm roots into the new soil, but what fruits it might bear were still uncertain." American culture was experiencing the pangs of "stumbling self-discovery," but, as many critics have argued, Cooper viewed these cultural growing pains as "forces of disintegration in the political and social structure of his country" which were crumbling the very moral foundations of American democracy.[38]

This was not an unreasonable response to the centrifugal forces which seemed to be stretching the traditional roles of American institutions to their breaking points. During the period between 1800 and 1815, Americans were experiencing a sudden growth in population, an increasing contrast between traditional forms of authority and privilege and a show of egalitarian feeling among lower classes that often offended European travelers, and an irreversible, though as yet limited, migration of pioneers westward as far as the Ohio River.[39] Moreover, religion and politics were undergoing innovative changes both in "method and organization."[40] "Beyond these all-important realms, and also in the center of both," May observes,

the real movement was taking place in the elusive realm of feeling. What was expressed in the crude assertions [of Republican manners] Europeans found so hard to take was an ardent and emotional insistence on social equality. Egalitarian feelings, in America, often ran far ahead of fact, but yet in the long run affected many kinds of reality. This was a kind of egalitarianism quite different from that proclaimed in Europe by the Revolutionary Enlightenment, arising less out of frustration and resentment and more out of confidence.

At the end of this period. . . . Frontier expansion, mass immigration, the continental market, and even manufacturing were set free to create nineteenth-century America, with all its chaos, turbulence, unsolved problems, and gathering power. Eventually, these forces were to be expressed in fresh and appropriate cultural symbols.

Before 1815, however, new realities and new feelings had not found adequate expression. Familiar modes and ideas derived from the old European world, including most of those associated with Enlightenment, were obviously becoming less useful and appropriate in America. If they hung on for a while in attenuated form, it was because no substitutes were yet available.[41]

If cultural symbols include the form of religious symbolization articulated by the Puritan and rationalistic theodicies, then it is clear that Dunlap and Cooper were questioning whether the fusion of world view and ethos each articulated was adequate for expressing the "new realities and new feelings" generated by the rapidly changing environment of the American Republic from 1776 to 1815.

Through the career of Natty Bumppo, Cooper further explored whether the westward expansion of American democracy was itself generating any such adequate forms of religious symbolization, whether democratic cultural symbols were emerging which could accommodate the religious pluralism that was increasingly shaping life on the American frontier in many important ways.[42] Cooper groped toward a cultural synthesis that could accommodate the kind of changes, conflicts, and feelings that characterized an egalitarian frontier that was beginning to shed any commitment to inherited religious responses to the constantly changing American environment. The Leatherstocking novels, sandwiched between *The Spy* and *Wyandotté*, thus suggest how Cooper, despite his lingering aristocratic sentiments,[43] was seeking to formulate a complicated moral vision that would transcend the Puritan and liberal understandings of the world and the moral life.

7

James Fenimore Cooper's Leatherstocking Novels: A Hybrid Theodicy

THE WESTWARD MOVEMENT AND THE PROBLEM OF THEODICY

It was Cooper who first recognized the moral challenge which the westward movement posed for both the literary and religious imagination. Even the great American historian Frances Parkman, who published his classic account of the westward migration, *The Oregon Trail*, in 1849, and soon thereafter wrote his voluminous history of the colonial American wilderness, had a myopic vision of this internal migration. Parkman it was who, in his 1852 review of Cooper's collected works, declared that "Cooper is the most original, the most thoroughly national" of American authors and touted Leatherstocking as a uniquely American creation that would assure Cooper's international recognition.[1]

Still, like Mark Twain in his savage onslaught upon "Fenimore Cooper's Literary Offenses," Parkman derided Cooper's portrayal of noble Indians, maintaining that the treacherous Magua, not the honest, generous, and faithful Uncas, most closely resembles "a genuine Indian."[2] More importantly, he believed—as did the Puritans on a more limited scale—that the wilderness simply had to give way to what he considered would be the utopian fruition of Protestant culture. He did not blink at the devastation of Indian culture required by the westward expansion of Protestant Christianity. "Civilization has a destroying as well as a creating power. It is exterminating the buffalo and the Indian, over whose fate too many lamentations, real or affected, have been sounded for us to renew them here. It must, moreover, eventually sweep from before it a class of men, its own precursors and pioneers, so remarkable both in their virtues and their faults, that few will see their extinction without regret. Of these men Leather-stocking is the representative."[3] Here is the Protestant sensibility at its cavalier worst, ignoring the tragic cultural conflicts and moral dilemmas generated by America's "westward course of empire," as it condoned the destruction of nature and the Indians as a necessary convenience for trans-planting what, in Parkman's view, was a superior culture.[4]

Cooper is the antithesis of Parkman. In his famous Leatherstocking nov-els—*The Pioneers* (1823), *The Last of the Mohicans* (1826), *The Prairie* (1827), *The Pathfinder* (1840), and *The Deerslayer* (1841)—which consti-tute the first systematic effort in American letters to explore America's westward expansion, Cooper presents this migratory process as a tragic drama of irreconcilable moral, religious, and racial conflicts. The stage for this drama is the yet virgin wilderness or prairie, except in *The Pioneers*, which portrays a settled territory regulated by law.[5] The wilderness in these novels is a place of social and moral anarchy where the Indian and white cultures collide, each side asserting and justifying its claims on its own terms.[6] Central to Cooper's dramatization of this seemingly irreconcilable conflict between two ways of life is whether the frontier itself can give rise to the kind of religious vision which reconciles their opposing cultural val-ues.

That Cooper attributed great importance to this problem is evident in the fact that it preoccupies Leatherstocking, or Natty Bumppo, throughout most of his career. Natty lives on the borderline between the Indian and white cultures. Their convergence in him creates tensions which are de-fined in terms of the polarities between civilization and nature, the individ-ual conscience and social laws,[7] authority and freedom, and anarchy and the conservation of tradition—polarities which are essential to an under-standing of most of Cooper's work. These tensions characterize what for Natty is a traumatic and finally disillusioning transition from a colonial to a republican society.

Natty's dilemma is prefigured by *The Spy* in its portrayal of Harvey Birch's tragic career during the throes of revolution. Like Birch, Natty is a solitary figure in that boundary situation wherein the traditionally ac-cepted frames of reference for helping people to make value judgments and moral decisions are no longer relevant. In Birch's career, Cooper drama-tized the kind of moral integrity which, although undefinable and unac-ceptable in terms of conventional morality, nevertheless embodies an un-flinching commitment to the realization of democratic ideals. But the tragic price he pays for remaining loyal to these ideals raises serious questions about the value of such a commitment. Natty too must decide for or against democratic ideals; but adopting them within the "neutral territory" of the wilderness requires that he develop an unorthodox moral stance which violates all conventional notions of morality. Since Cooper wrote *The Spy* before the Leatherstocking novels and *Wyandotté* afterwards, it is clear that marginal figures like Natty assumed increasing importance in his effort to discover a reliable foundation for a moral perspective that could reconcile conflicting values in a pluralistic environment.

Natty's initial problem in this regard is to make sense of the tragic combat between the Indian and white cultures, of white civilization's inexorable westward march which decimated both the Indian population and the virgin forests. The world of the Leatherstocking novels seems to evoke and abet human rapaciousness, greed, and racial enmities. Carnage prevails, almost as though this world were doomed to destroy itself, to become a physical wasteland. Even as early as *The Pioneers*, the first of the Leatherstocking novels, Cooper, though initially describing the settlement of the western frontier in positive terms, quickly dramatizes—especially in the famous pigeon-shooting scene—the accompanying spoliation of nature. And the last Leatherstocking novel ends with this pessimistic conclusion about America's westward expansion: "We live in a world of transgressions and selfishness, and no pictures that represent us otherwise can be true; though, happily for human nature, gleamings of that pure Spirit in whose likeness man has been fashioned, are to be seen relieving its deformities, and mitigating, if not excusing, its crimes" (*D*, p. 612).[8] Even where the possibility exists, as between Natty and his friend Chingachgook, for a relationship of mutual trust, respect, and devotion between Indians and whites, such a possibility can do very little, if anything, to change their world for the better. So malleable is his world to the pressures of human evil that Natty is finally compelled to develop a religious explanation of human experience which he believes upholds the justice and goodness of God in creating such a world.

Indeed, the Leatherstocking novels in part constitute Cooper's extended treatment of the problem of theodicy which demonstrates that, long before 1848, Cooper was exploring religious problems integral to early nineteenth-century culture.[9] Throughout his career, Natty enacts the metaphysical drama of the self in the Puritan and rationalistic theodicies. He tries to resolve his confrontation with the reality of evil by seeking, first, to demonstrate how his mode of experiencing the world gives rise to a world view and corresponding ethos and, secondly, to create a synthesis of the two which enables him to explain the existence of evil in rational and moral terms. The dramatic narrative and the process of synthesizing a world view and ethos go hand in hand: the narrative conflicts Natty experiences give rise to an ethos and world view, while his attempt to integrate the two gives structure and meaning to the narrative in each of the Leatherstocking novels.

Cooper probably had no direct knowledge of the preceding theological debate regarding the Puritan and rationalistic theodicies. Yet, in the Leatherstocking novels he certainly casts the moral and religious problems posed by America's westward migration in terms of that debate's established conventions. By showing how these kinds of religious problems emerge in Natty's career, Cooper became the first literary artist to dramatize how the cultural conflicts generated by America's westward growth in the late 1700s and early 1800s ultimately posed the problem of theodicy.

As a youth (from 1730 to 1750), Natty is surrounded by the unspoiled wilderness. After losing his family, he is raised first by Delaware Indians for ten years and later by a Moravian family, the Effinghams.[10] By the time of his exploits in the French and Indian War, Natty has become a solitary hunter who has few friends other than two Delaware Indians, Chingachgook and his son Uncas. In an effort to live an uncorrupted life, a life that fully conforms to his highest religious ideals, Natty has retreated to the forests where, as Cooper puts it, he becomes "a being removed from the every-day inducements to err, which abound in civilized life" (D, p. 8). Each of the Leatherstocking novels portrays his repeated withdrawal from society to find happiness in communing with nature. Even the prospect of living comfortably near the son of the family who helped raise him cannot swerve him from his choice of the wilderness over civilization. When the newlyweds, Oliver Effingham and Elizabeth Temple, offer to use part of their wealth to provide him a settled and secure life, the aging Natty replies: "I know you mean all for the best, but our ways doesn't agree. I love the woods, and ye relish the face of man; . . . The meanest of God's creatures be made for some use, and I'm formed for the wilderness" (Pi, p. 504). Renouncing marriage, social position, financial security, ownership of land—even owning a small place to live in (though he sometimes inhabits a ramshackle hut which the Effinghams provided for his use when he became a hunter)—Natty continues his trek westward as society encroaches upon the wilderness, finally to spend his last years on the open prairie.

A rigorous moral code guides all his conduct. He risks his life in order to rescue friends, keeps all his promises, refuses to lie, cheat, or steal under any circumstances, kills no animals or birds except those he needs for food—he denounces the "wasty ways" of civilization represented, for example, by the famous pigeon-shooting scene in The Pioneers (p. 293)—possesses nothing more than his dogs and his rifle, "Killdeer," and worships God daily. During his youthful days, according to Natty, he nearly succumbed to three temptations that would have violated his personal code of honor. The first temptation occurred when he found a pack of beaver skins that belonged to a Frenchman trapping in English territory. Though the law sanctioned his taking them, Natty says, "I remembered that such laws wasn't made for us hunters, and bethought me that the poor man might have built great expectations for the next winter on the sale of his skins; and I left them where they lay." (Pa, p. 494). Long before he established his reputation as the best shot in the woods, he found a rifle which he knew would make him an expert marksman, but he resisted the temptation to steal it. Natty calls the third temptation "the hardest of them all." He happened upon six Hurons—enemies of the Delawares who had raised him—their guns placed so as to be easily removed. But rather than massacre unarmed enemies, as he knew Chingachgook would have done, he waited until they awakened, followed them, and then in an ambush which jeopardized his life he killed all but one. Here, as throughout his career, Natty has refused to take unfair advantage of anyone, believing that equity of opportunity is required even in warfare. What emerges in the Leatherstocking novels is the portrait of a saintly figure, or what Cooper calls "a sort of type of what Adam might have been supposed to be before the fall, though certainly not without sin" (D, p. 153)—the first "full-fledged fictional Adam" of unsullied integrity who also refuses to take an exploitive attitude toward the forest whose beauty, he believes, should be preserved unmarred.[11]

Indeed, Natty experiences the virgin forest as a holy reality which consistently awakens in him a pietistic reverence for its pristine beauty. He already expresses this religious response to the wilderness during his youthful encounter with the unspoiled beauty of Lake Glimmerglass, "the heart" of the wilderness in the Leatherstocking novels.[12] As he sees the lake for the first time and experiences "the holy calm of nature" that surrounds it, he tells his companion: "This is grand!—'tis solemn!—'tis an edication of itself to look upon! . . . not a tree disturbed even by a red-skin hand, as I can discover, but everything left in the ordering of the Lord to live and die according to his own designs and laws" (D, pp. 47, 34).[13] Natty here resembles an Adamic figure looking upon a freshly created world—"a second paradise" (Pi, p. 321)—in wonder and awe as he experiences himself to be in the very presence of God, a world "fresh and beautiful as it came from [God's] hand" (Pa, p. 105). It is, to borrow the words of David Davis, "the world of genesis, fresh, dazzling, still emanating the divine spirit of its origin."[14] The wilderness is for him an object of majestic beauty which not only fully satisfies people's aesthetic need for beauty, but also provides an unquestionable sanction for their belief in a presiding deity who controls everything in accordance with His own mysterious purposes. He variously calls the wilderness "the garden of the Lord" (Pr, p. 228),[15] "the temple of the Lord" (LM, p. 275), "the open hand of Providence" (Pa, p. 32), and "the great school of Providence" (Pa, p. 492), designations which express his belief that the woods everywhere bear "the impress . . . of the divine hand of their creator" (D, p. 307).

However, as he watches the wilderness being transformed into a democratic society, he also presents a less positive view of God's manifestation in nature. The Prairie, for example—though certainly "from start to finish . . . valedictory in tone"[16]—expresses not only Natty's sad lament that the gradual mutilation of the wilderness is the desecration of a holy reality,[17] but also his apocalyptic vision of nature. He views the vast open expanses of prairie as God's own deliberate wastage of the wilderness. God, he asserts, "has placed this barren belt of prairie, behind the states, to warn men to what their folly may yet bring the land" (*Pr*, p. 19). Having lost all hope for his country, he asks: "What will the Yankee choppers say, when they have cut their path from the eastern to the western waters, and find that a hand, which can lay the 'arth bare at a blow, has been here and swept the country, in very mockery of their wickedness. They will turn on their tracks like a fox that doubles, and then the rank smell of their own footsteps will show them the madness of their waste" (*Pr*, p. 81).[18]

For Natty, the loss of the wilderness means the loss of any positive communication between humankind and God. He considers nature to be the medium through which God directly speaks to him, especially "on a calm, solemn, quiet day, in a forest, when his voice is heard in the creaking of a dead branch, or in the song of a bird" (*Pa*, p. 106). Through nature he experiences an unmediated relationship with God which he achieves nowhere else, an experience he seeks to cultivate throughout his lifetime:[19] "none know how often the hand of God is seen in the wilderness, but them that rove it for a man's life" (*Pi*, p. 324). Natty summarizes his religious quest when, near the end of his life, he describes himself as one "but little gifted in the fables of what you call the Old World, seeing that my time has been mainly passed looking natur' steadily in the face, and in reasoning on what I've seen, rather than on what I've heard in traditions" (*Pr*, pp. 276–77). In his clearest and most succinct statement about his relationship to God in the wilderness, Natty asserts that, while visiting various forts, he endeavored "to worship garrison fashion, but never could raise within me the solemn feelings and true affection that I feel when alone with God in the forest. There I seem to stand face to face with my Master; all around me is fresh and beautiful as it came from his hand; and there is no nicety or doctrine to chill feelin's. No, no; the woods are the true temple, a'ter all, for there the thoughts are free to mount higher even than the clouds" (*Pa*, p. 105). Because it repeatedly evokes and sustains what he considers pure religious feelings, the untouched wilderness becomes for Natty the only object fully commensurate with his need for a trustworthy reality.

Moreover, since he believes that God speaks directly to humankind through nature, he maintains that only through nature can people gain reliable knowledge of God. Natty holds the rationalistic belief of the Enlightenment that nature is a well-ordered reality which, in its orderly workings at all levels of life, discloses divine laws that make God rationally comprehensible. However, according to Natty, these laws can be discerned only through symbolic forms which people must learn how to read. To illustrate this point to a companion, Natty points to a sunset and a mass of nearby clouds and says: "Yonder is the signal given to man to seek his food and natural rest; better and wiser would it be, if he could understand the signs of nature, and take a lesson from the fowls of the air, and the beasts of the fields" (*LM*, p. 156). Nature, in his view, is a book of divine wisdom that has its own language—its own system of natural signs that symbolize spiritual facts—which, when rightly read, provide reliable knowledge of God.

In addition to laying bare the rational structure of God's mind, these laws also reveal God's ethical expectations of humankind. They provide the absolute norms for defining what is right in any circumstance. Everything in nature, Natty asserts, has a "lawful" status, a rightful place and function "according to [God's] own wise ordering" which prescribes what God expects from people (*Pr*, pp. 228, 59).[20] This includes the instinctive behavior of both animals and humans. There are many times in the Leatherstocking novels when Natty accepts such behavior as exemplifying what is natural and therefore right in God's eyes. When, for example, in *The Pathfinder*, Mabel Dunham instinctively begs Natty during an Indian attack to bring her wounded father inside the besieged blockhouse even though opening the door could give entrance to the Indians, Natty says of Mabel's plea: "This is natur', and it is the law of God" (*Pa*, p. 435).[21] He consequently risks his own life (as well as the lives of those within the blockhouse) by opening the door, since to do otherwise, he believes, would be to contravene God's direct command. There are many such instances in Natty's career when, in seeking to obey the dictates of God, he jeopardizes his own life heedless of the consequences to himself.

In thus accepting nature as the full revelation of God's will, Natty accords it a moral authority which, in his view, makes all legal systems superfluous. Allegiance to God, he maintains, requires that he discount any human law which contradicts divine law. "Laws," he says in *The Deerslayer*, "don't all come from the same quarter. God has given us his'n, and some come from the Colony, and others come from the King and parliament. When the Colony's laws, or even the King's laws, run ag'in the laws of God, they get to be onlawful, and ought not be obeyed. I hold to a white man's respecting white laws, so long as they do not cross the track of a law comin' from a higher authority; and for a red man to obey his own red-skin usages, under the same privilege" (*D*, p. 50). Natty recognizes no authority but those dictates of his own conscience which emerge from his communion with God in the wilderness while experiencing awe and wonder at His handiwork in nature. He proclaims the conscience to be the ultimate arbiter of what is right and wrong; and when the King's laws violate its dictates he will repudiate those laws since, as he tells Judith Hutter, the conscience "is king with me" (*D*, p. 452). Natty thus advocates civil disobedience toward any law which, by his obeying it, brings him into conflict with divine law. Were he to affirm no more than this, he would only be echoing a basic presupposition of American thought from

Jonathan Mayhew through Henry David Thoreau to Martin Luther King, Jr., on civil disobedience.

But he further expresses a radical disrespect for all human laws. All laws, he maintains, are the corrupt and corrupting creation of people's worst impulses. The "twisty ways of the law" (*Pi*, p. 321) create social inequalities by establishing property rights which enable some people to obtain large portions of land and the privileges of ownership that they deny to others;[22] the law justifies the destruction of the wilderness in the name of law and order;[23] it deprives him of his past vocation as a hunter,[24] it enslaves people by restricting their God-given freedom,[25] and although it provides protection for those who cannot protect themselves, it still nullifies this advantage by enabling people to use it to protect their own interests and to exploit and repress the underprivileged.[26] He describes the American legal system as having an octopus-like stranglehold on every aspect of human life. The arm of the law, he complains, has become a

busy and a troublesome arm . . . here in this land of America; where, as they say, man is left greatly to the following of his own wishes, compared to other countries; and happier, ay, and more manly and more honest too, is he for the privilege! Why do you know . . . that there are regions where the law is so busy as to say, In this fashion shall you live, in that fashion shall you die, and in such another fashion shall you take leave of the world, to be sent before the judgement-seat of the Lord! A wicked and a troublesome meddling is that, with the business of One who has not made his creatures to be herded like oxen, and driven from field to field as their stupid and selfish keepers may judge of their need and wants. A miserable land must that be, where they fetter the mind as well as the body, and where the creatures of God being born children, are kept so by the wicked inventions of men who would take upon themselves the office of the great Governor of all! (*Pr*, pp. 402–3)[27]

So radical is Natty's attitude toward the law that he considers it humankind's effort to take upon itself what is solely God's prerogative—namely, the right to legislate what people can and cannot do—thereby making human legal systems a principle source of evil in the world.[28]

Moreover, Natty contends that the law, by establishing and protecting property rights—rights which he believes only increase people's lust for more land and encourage their wastage of valuable resources—denies people a right relationship with the wilderness. No one, he asserts, rightfully owns land in the wilderness, unless it be the Indians whose ancient use of the land gives them prior rights to it. But he repudiates all such private ownership, a repudiation which, along with his ascetic moral stance, makes it impossible for him to marry either Mabel Dunham, the only woman he ever courts, or Judith Hutter, who offers him her entire estate around Lake Glimmerglass if he will marry her.[29] People, he maintains, are to establish a natural relationship with the land by communally acting as its trustees.

They are to preserve the land as it exists, using only what is necessary to fulfill their basic needs—"Use, but don't waste" could be his motto regarding the land (*Pi*, p. 273)—and then replace what is used for future generations.

For Natty, being a trustee of the land also entails unrestricted access to all wilderness territory and the freedom to hunt animals whenever needed for food and clothing. But the law—by protecting property boundaries, by allowing massive plots of the wilderness to be destroyed, and by prescribing hunting seasons—destroys this inviolable relationship with nature. Hence Natty looks upon the law as society's attempt to impose upon him (and others) a life style which nullifies what for him are the fundamental prerequisites for living in harmony with nature: an unrestricted life in the wilderness, an uncluttered life that survives on the bare necessities, and a dedication to God which transcends all allegiances to society and its laws. Natty's attitude toward the law expresses his desire, in the face of the inexorable changes taking place on the frontier until his death in 1806, to preserve a past idyllic relationship with the wilderness when he enjoyed unlimited access to the yet undeveloped forests—when nothing governed his actions but his own personal code of survival. This past relationship with nature, he believes, confers upon him certain inalienable rights that no social or legal authority can abrogate.

It is surprising that, given his radically antinomian position, only in *The Pioneers* does Natty come into open conflict with the law. In this novel, the first of the Leatherstocking tales, Cooper portrays the westward movement in 1794 (the fourth year of Cooper's life) as a rapacious, uncontrollable onslaught against an unspoiled wilderness. It poses the spectacle of a second garden of Eden being gradually destroyed in the name of imposing law and order.[30] During the American Revolution the Americans confiscate the property of Major Effingham, whose family raised Natty during his youth, and Judge Marmaduke Temple, a family friend and prototype of the empire builder, buys the land with the intention, we later learn, of returning it to them. But when circumstances finally lead him to believe that the Effinghams are dead (a belief that is disconfirmed only many years later), he seeks to realize his vision of a wilderness transformed into "towns, manufactories, bridges, canals, mines, and all other resources of an old country" by selling plots of land to pioneers and incorporating them into a settlement named after himself (*Pi*, p. 354). His exploitive approach to the land is diametrically opposed to Natty's religious vision of the wilderness. It parallels the expressed attitude of Cooper's father in his only published book, *A Guide in the Wilderness*, that "if fifty thousand acres be settled, so that there is but one man upon a thousand acres, there can be no one convenience of life attainable; neither roads, school, church, meeting, nor any other of those advantages, without which man's life would resemble that of a wild beast."[31]

What the Judge builds he also controls. He alone enacts the laws governing the settlement, and he alone decides a defendant's fate by presiding as the judge who enforces these laws. Some of these laws prohibit the public from hunting on private property and further restrict the killing of animals to prescribed hunting seasons. When Judge Temple learns that Natty has killed a deer prior to the hunting season, he sends the justice of the peace, Hiram Doolittle, to collect the fine from Natty for breaking the law. When Natty tells him that he cannot now pay the fine, Doolittle abuses his authority by trying to enter Natty's hut against his explicit refusal. Natty manhandles him and is subsequently brought before Judge Temple, who further charges him with assaulting an officer of the law. Natty pleads innocent to the charge, "for there's no guilt," he tells the Judge, "in doing what's right; and I'd rather died on the spot, than had [Doolittle] put foot in the hut at that moment" (*Pi*, p. 401). But Natty gives no further explanation since the reason for his assault on Doolittle (as we learn only at the end of the novel) is that he is secretly taking care of Major Effingham, formerly a great military hero but now a senile invalid, in order to protect him against public ridicule.[32] Judge Temple sentences Natty to one hour in the public stocks, fines him one hundred dollars, and requires that he remain imprisoned until the fine is paid.

Natty accepts the fine but not the imprisonment. No one, he asserts, not even Judge Temple, has the authority to violate those inalienable rights which he believes his past relationship to the land has conferred upon him. "I've travelled these mountains," he tells Judge Temple, "when you was no judge, but an infant in your mother's arms; and I feel as if I had a right and a privilege to travel them ag'in afore I die" (*Pi*, p. 408).[33] After promising the Judge that he will pay the fine with money obtained from selling skins, Natty tries to leave the courtroom as though no one will question his right to do so. He is stopped, placed in the stocks, and then put in jail.[34] When Judge Temple subsequently sends his daughter, Elizabeth, to offer two hundred dollars with which to pay the fine, Natty rejects the money; accepting it would mean breaking his promise to repay the fine with his own money. He escapes jail, rejoins Chingachgook to help care for Major Effingham, and plans to fulfill his promise to the Judge as soon as possible.

At the heart of this novel is the conflict between the Judge, who represents the conventional value system of society, and Natty, who symbolizes the values of the solitary individual in the wilderness.[35] Though Cooper ambiguously endorses both prototypes, the Judge's behavior at many points in the novel leaves little doubt in the reader's mind about Natty's moral superiority. The moral distance between the two is perhaps nowhere more obvious than during the wanton slaughter of thousands of pigeons, most of which are left to rot. After professing agreement with Natty's condemnation of this needless waste the Judge himself begins shooting the birds after Natty leaves the scene in disgust. Natty, of course, moves further westward with pioneers following closely on his heels.

Judge Temple's conventional morality cannot come to terms with the kinds of conflict on the frontier which require more than a legal resolution. He realizes, when Natty migrates westward ostensibly in defeat, "that there are still more profound and complex ambiguities that even the settlement of this issue [the conflict between the claims of the individual and society] cannot solve."[36] Yet, even though Natty has moved westward, he "escapes from the Judge only to be subsumed under the Judge's project for settling the continent."[37]

Cooper leaves these ambiguities unresolved. Dramatist rather than didactic moralist at this point in his life, Cooper dramatizes through Natty's career the conflict between the values of a settled society and the unrestricted freedom of life in the wilderness. Natty places what he believes are the divinely ordained dictates of both his past relationship to the wilderness and his sense of honor above those of the law. He even becomes an outlaw in order to honor these dictates which for him are the only acceptable touchstone for determining what is right or wrong. He consistently denies society's legal definitions of how he should act, since only in this way can he remain true to his religious vision of what he ought to be.

Indeed, Natty—along with Harvey Birch—heads a long line of American fictive heroes who believe that their moral or religious commitments legitimately place them beyond the claims of conventional morality. True morality cannot be based upon obedience to socially established laws, in Natty's view, because they are corrupting, and therefore untrustworthy, sources for moral norms. The dangers inherent in this perspective are readily apparent in the career of Ishmael Bush, whose own ideas about the law, "though drawn from very different premises" Cooper notes, are "in singular accordance with those" that Natty espouses (Pr, p. 64).

Like Natty, Ishmael Bush asserts that human laws need not be obeyed because, like Natty, he believes that they violate people's natural relationship with nature by wrongfully according property rights that establish social inequities. Moreover, he too believes that his allegiance to divine law (as it is manifested in the Old Testament) justifies suspending his allegiance to all human laws. So close are Natty's and Ishmael's views on the law that Cooper, perhaps by conscious design, never lets Natty learn that Ishmael—upon discovering that his son was murdered by his wife's brother, Abiram White—tries and executes the murderer in accordance with Old Testament law. Natty's knowledge of these illegal proceedings might have forced Cooper to moderate Natty's perspective by having him, as he nowhere does, explicitly affirm the necessity for law.[38] Natty might have rejected Ishmael's action on religious grounds. He believes that all punishments for human misdeeds must be established and carried out solely by God, who will do so during a final judgment day, "the great day when the whites shall meet the red-skins in judgment, and justice shall be the law, and not power" (*Pi*, p. 505).[39] A confrontation between Natty and Ishmael about the trial would have been dramatic. But it would also have relieved the moral tension which gives *The Prairie* its dramatic interest. Whatever his response might have been, whatever their similarities of viewpoint, we know that Natty, unlike Ishmael Bush, never attempts to be an arbiter or instrument of divine justice, nor in any way seeks to implement or vindicate his own desires in the name of divine law.

Still, despite the moral integrity Natty achieves through his own unswerving loyalty to God, he is nevertheless aware of the problematical nature of such religious commitment. No less than the law, moral and religious values, according to Natty, are also important sources of evil. People's adherence to diverse and often contradictory values inevitably generates the kinds of cultural and racial conflict exemplified in the tragic struggle between Indians and whites. In an effort to make sense of such religious diversity and conflict, Natty develops his notion of "gifts" in the last two Leatherstocking novels, *The Pathfinder* and *The Deerslayer*. This notion shows Natty, who has basically developed rationalistic attitudes toward the wilderness in the first three novels, now revising these attitudes in terms of the Puritan theodicy.

NATTY BUMPPO'S DOUBLE VISION

The differences between people and cultures, Natty argues, arise from the assorted natural "gifts" that characterize humankind. These gifts are not part of human nature itself, but are divinely bestowed capabilities which people develop in accordance with their race, sex, social status, and profession. Natty therefore differentiates people in terms of their natural gifts: "town gifts," "settlement gifts," "preaching gifts," "gifts of the wood," and among the latter Natty includes his own expert skill with a rifle (*D*, p. 489). These gifts are divine imperatives: in bestowing them, God expects each person to be true to his or her own special gifts. Because of this obligation, Natty asserts that "it's sinful"—that "it's flying in the face of Providence"—"to withstand nat'ral gifts" (*D*, p. 32; *Pa*, p. 184). These gifts "fortify natur' as it might be, and excuse a thousand acts and idees. Still the creatur' is the same at the bottom; just as a man who is clad in regimentals is the same as the man who is clad in skins. The garments make a change in the eye, and some change in the conduct perhaps; but none in the man. Herein lies the apology for gifts; seein' that you expect different conduct from one in silks and satins from one in homespun; though the Lord, who didn't make the dresses, but who made the creatur's themselves, looks only at his own work" (*D*, p. 489).

Each race also has its own unique gifts. Like every individual, each race is therefore obligated by God to develop its own "lawful gifts." To covet the gifts of other individuals or races is sinful. It is "lawful work," he asserts, for Indians to scalp the dead, but it would "unhumanize" an Indian to practice "town gifts," while a white person would be unhumanized by trying to adopt gifts that are unique to Indians (*D*, pp. 49, 89). People are not to be blamed for following their particular gifts, since they are only living as God requires them to live.[40]

When he is reminded that it is precisely this adherence to natural gifts which reinforces the barriers and enmities separating one race from another, Natty appeals to divine wisdom. Gifts, he replies, "were bestowed by the Lord for wise ends, though neither you nor me can follow them in all their windings" (*Pa*, p. 89).[41] Not that he desires the cultural barriers generated by people's diverse gifts, as his own relationship with Chingachgook and Uncas demonstrates.[42] But his own experience on the frontier, beginning with his first combat to the death with an Indian in *The Deerslayer*, has led him to conclude that racial conflict is part of the natural order of things. The often-noted backward progression in the Leatherstocking novels from Natty's old age to his youth may represent a movement from "a fairly conventional American account of the Westward Movement to a far more imaginative, complex, and critical view" of the irrevocable loss of a wilderness paradise;[43] it may signal, in D. H. Lawrence's words, "a gradual sloughing of the old skin, towards a new youth," a formulation of "the myth of America";[44] or it might describe "a movement from historicity to mythos," from "historical time" to "mythic time."[45] But it also dramatizes how this Adamic paradise was the scene of a tragic duel between two contrasting cultures.

The episode in which Natty, facing a hostile Mingo on the edge of Lake Glimmerglass, kills him, certainly portrays a young man's ritualistic initiation into manhood; but it also personalizes, both for Natty and the reader, the seemingly irreconcilable struggle for the American wilderness.[46] In a broader sense, it represents his initiation into a moral consciousness of the tragic racial conflict which his culture has generated and for which it provides no means of resolution other than racial domination or extinction.

Natty can reconcile this conflict only through his notion of gifts. This notion affirms that diverse moral and religious values exist as part of God's overarching mysterious design that for its realization requires, even predetermines, their incompatibility and the resulting racial enmities.[47] This version of a divine teleological suspension of the ethical enables Natty to honor the diverse gifts shaping both the Indian and white cultures. But he also admits that it makes God rationally and ethically incomprehensible in human terms.

Furthermore, Natty's God seemingly makes it inevitable that some people will oppose Him, since fulfilling their obligations to live in accordance with their natural gifts sometimes demands that they violate scriptural injunctions. In *The Deerslayer*, for example, he notes that using his natural gifts to survive in the wilderness sometimes requires a vengeful response that violates the scriptural command that when struck on one cheek he should turn the other. He therefore alters this biblical teaching into one that is less radical: "I don't understand by this any more than that it's best to do this, if *possible*. Revenge is an Injin gift, and forgiveness a white man's. That's all. Overlook all you can is what's meant; and not revenge all you can" (D, p. 93). Another such conflict arises later when he skirmishes with Indians during a period of war. After Natty kills an Indian who tries to murder him, Hetty Hutter upbraids him for breaking the biblical commandment not to kill others. He justifies his action as a necessity of war; "many things," he tells her, "are lawful in war, which would be unlawful in peace." But when she further says that good must always be returned for evil in all circumstances, Natty replies: "Ah, Hetty, that may do among the missionaries, but 'twould make an onsartain life in the woods. The Panther [the Indian Natty had killed] craved my blood. . . . 'Twould have been ag'in natur' not to raise a hand in such a trial, and 'twould have done discredit to my training and gifts" (D, p. 543).[48]

Natty thus describes a conflict within divine law itself. The effort to realize divinely bestowed gifts sometimes requires people to violate scriptural injunctions defining how they ought to act. It is a conflict which Natty finally resolves by affirming that people are to rely on the dictates of their natural gifts, even if by so doing they disobey the will of God as defined by Scripture. Warfare between cultures, racial animosities, the necessity for disregarding scriptural precepts—all are said to be induced by God Himself as the means He uses to shape human lives in ways that accomplish His own hidden purposes.

Natty's notion of gifts thus clearly complicates his rationalistic vision of nature as an unproblematical source of religious and moral norms. Although this notion is an attempt to hold his religious absolutism in tandem with a moral relativism that accepts the validity of divergent and often conflicting cultural values, it presents a double image of the wilderness which reflects the problematical nature of American culture from a religious perspective. Though the virgin wilderness, as in *The Deerslayer*, often resembles an idyllic Garden of Eden—or what Cooper called a "second paradise"—it is also a deadly garden of hostile warfare throughout the Leatherstocking novels (as well as in *The Spy* and *Wyandotté*). For all its splendor and plenitude, the wilderness is, as Cooper puts it, a "lawless region" (D, p. 516). Natty himself describes the prairie as "a region where a strong arm is far better than the right, and where the white law is as little known as needed" (Pr, p. 235). The wilderness is both a moral haven for Natty—*the* place where he can maintain his uncorrupted moral integrity—and a hellish reality which makes survival a brutal and brutalizing process. Its majestic beauty discloses to Natty both the rational and humane God of the rationalistic theodicy and the Puritan God who frequently engages in a teleological suspension of the ethical in order to carry out His mysterious purposes. The wilderness thus gives rise to both his natural and Puritan theologies, brings them into conflict, and provides no means for resolving this contradiction.[49]

Hence the dramatic interest of the Leatherstocking novels does not reside solely in Natty's many dangerous adventures as a hunter, scout, and guide. There is also Natty's intellectual adventure of seeking to develop a world view which both reflects and explains the harsh realities he encounters in the wilderness during America's westward expansion. What had once been, in Natty's view, an undisturbed garden of Eden has now increasingly become the arena for bloody warfare. He seeks to understand the conflict between the Indian and white cultures and the gradual loss of the virginal wilderness in terms of his natural theology. But he discovers that its rationalistic premises—that God directly reveals His creativity, benevolence, and moral demands through both human instinct and the orderly workings of nature—cannot account for racial enmities and the cruelty, rapaciousness, and greed he encounters everywhere on the frontier.

As a consequence Natty also portrays a God who imposes on humankind a tangled skein of gifts which inevitably generates open hostilities between differing cultures, a God who confers natural gifts that are the source of dictates which often contradict scriptural imperatives. Unable to explain the existence of evil by means of his rationalistic assumptions, he describes a world wherein the obedience God exacts of people gives rise to various forms of evil which God ultimately uses to realize His own redemptive purposes. Like the Puritan world view, Natty's understanding of the world is predicated upon a divine teleological suspension of the ethical.

However, such a world does not prompt Natty to raise any disturbing ethical questions about a sovereign deity who radically differs from the beneficent God nature discloses to him. Nor does he protest against such a God as being unjust or demonic or make such a chaotic world the occasion for legitimizing amoral behavior. To the contrary, Natty affirms that in the face of such grim realities people must maintain an unflinching moral integrity, an integrity which is the hallmark of Natty's career. This probity is most strikingly exemplified in *The Deerslayer* when he keeps a promise to the Hurons that means almost certain death. The Hutters' house which sits on stilts in the middle of Lake Glimmerglass is surrounded by the Hurons who hold Natty captive. When Natty offers to negotiate the Hutters' surrender, the Hurons, knowing of his reputation for keeping his word, release him after he promises to return within twenty-four hours. When he is unable to convince the Hutters that they should surrender, he returns to the Hurons because, as he puts it, he has made a "pledge," and "a bargain is a bargain, though it be made with a vagabond" (*D*, pp. 427, 438). But Natty also considers his promise to the Hurons a "solemn bargain" between himself and God, who, he believes, requires that he keep all promises regardless of the consequences to himself (*D*, p. 450). To break the promise would be to taint the uncorrupted integrity he seeks to maintain in his allegiance to God.

Natty in fact consistently endangers his life in order to carry out his obligations to others, for he considers these obligations to be as inviolable as his obligations to God.[50] Devoted to his friends Chingachgook and Uncas, he frequently lays his life on the line in order to save them.[51] Cooper tells us that such hazards incurred on behalf of his friends became "necessary to the enjoyment of his existence" (*LM*, p. 290). He might well have added that the strong allegiance they express seems, in part, to function as a surrogate for the family ties that are missing from Natty's monkish existence in the wilderness.

Natty is no less selfless in his commitment to those who are under his care than he is in his commitment to his friends. When, for example, Cora Munro in *The Last of the Mohicans* is captured by the sinister Indian renegade, Magua, who intends to make her his wife, Natty offers to exchange himself for Cora, knowing that it could mean his death at Magua's hands. Then, too, he takes it upon himself to care for his ailing foster father, Major Effingham, and to escape from jail in order to help safeguard the major in the cave where he is concealed, though doing so makes his own life precarious.

Natty exemplifies an uncompromising obedience to divine law. He is "a truly religious American hero" who, throughout his career, suspends any allegiance to conventional morality in order to remain faithful to the dictates of God regardless of the consequences to himself.[52] Such a life style, Natty argues, is necessary because God Himself requires it as a way of serving His glory and secret purposes, even though He often realizes those purposes by means of a teleological suspension of the ethical. Natty becomes the personification of those highest ideals Cooper tested and finally affirmed through Natty's incorruptibly humane survival in the brutal and brutalizing world of the Leatherstocking novels—though the Effingham novels affirm antithetical values.[53] He is a "paragon of probity, stability, self-discipline, simplicity, faith, energy, courage, integrity, prudence, sincerity, truthfulness, freshness of sensibility, and, overall, of a 'beautiful and unerring sense of justice.' He is America as America ought to be. . . . Leatherstocking is a paradigm of the ideal democratic ethos in the Era of Good Feeling and Age of Jackson, the new man of the New World."[54] Cooper delivers his own final encomium in *Home as Found* when the old commodore, a long-time resident around Lake Glimmerglass, says of Natty: "He was a great man! They may talk of their Jeffersons and Jacksons, but I set down Washington and Natty Bumppo as the two only really great men of my time."[55]

So exemplary is Natty's moral integrity that the reader of the Leatherstocking novels hardly remembers the flaws in his character. Railton perhaps goes too far when he says that "Natty's virtues—purity of motive, courage of heart, virtuosity in action, fidelity to his gifts—define a fundamentally juvenile sensibility."[56] But certainly Natty is provincial, superstitious, illiterate, ignorant (and boasts of it at times),[57] tediously verbose, prideful, envious, and a racial bigot who proclaims white culture to be superior to Indian culture.[58] Cooper himself describes Natty's "lingering pride of color" as a major "weak spot" in his character.[59] And perhaps his racial prejudice no less than his principled adherence to his bachelorhood in the wilderness prompts his refusal to marry the squaw of an Indian warrior he has killed. Hunting, though carried out within the precincts of an untouched idyllic paradise, awakens in him a craving for property which violates the Adamic relationship he has established with the wilderness.[60] He even envies Harry Hutter's self-proclaimed ownership of Lake Glimmerglass, though both his attitude toward the law and his notion that people are to be trustees of the land repudiate any such desire for owning property.[61] And his intense pride in his superior marksmanship leads him, against his own hunting code, to kill a hawk in a shooting match with Chingachgook (though he spends a few pages explaining why he should not have killed the bird),[62] to goad and anger some Hurons in a canoe race by jauntily waving Killdeer in the air,[63] and to prove to Mabel Dunham, in a moment of jealousy, that he deliberately lost a shooting match with Jasper Western.[64] Cooper thus repeatedly reminds us of Natty's humanity in a way that he hopes represents "a reasonable picture of human nature, without offering to the spectator a 'monster of goodness' " (D, p. 8).

Despite Cooper's disclaimer, however, the dominant figure people remember is the Leatherstocking who selflessly risks his life for friends and acquaintances, who unswervingly adheres to a rigorous code of honor, who gives up all conventional ways of living by retreating to the wilderness in order to preserve the uncorrupted integrity of his allegiance to God. This is the Leatherstocking who, according to Middleton's (and Cooper's) final assessment of him in The Prairie, "united the better, instead of the worst qualities, of the [white and Indian] people" and who developed a double consciousness that mirrors this blending of cultures.[65]

Indeed, Natty insists that people cannot perceive the world correctly unless they develop a double consciousness which is commensurate with the cultural and moral complexities of human experience. Such a consciousness, for Natty, is a spanning activity, since he believes that in creating a world which evokes a plethora of human possibilities, values, and beliefs, God thereby creates gaps for the human imagination to leap. Bridging these gaps, in Natty's view, is an imperative God imposes upon the human imagination. Only in this way, Natty contends, can people understand the various modes of experiencing the world which God induces in people by means of the diverse gifts He confers upon them. Achieving such a perspective on human experience enables people to acknowledge the complex workings of a God who can be neither defined nor comprehended in terms of the values, beliefs, or human possibilities that characterize any particular culture.

Natty himself obeys this imperative by standing at the borderline between the Indian and white cultures, one leg in each, perceiving life in terms of their unique gifts, values, customs, and modes of thought.[66] He develops an imaginative capacity for seeing, feeling, and thinking about the world in ways that differ radically from his own perspective, a capacity which enables him to accept others in terms of their own gifts as well as to survive in a world of religious, racial, and cultural animosities.[67] To survive in the wilderness requires an act of the imagination which suspends the conventional moral codes of Protestant culture. He warns the enterprising but naive Captain Duncan Heyward that if he tries to predict Indian behavior in terms of the norms and sagacity of his white culture, the Indians will easily deceive or kill him.[68]

Natty thus resolves cultural conflicts not by omitting one of the sides contributing to the conflict, but through an imaginative mode of binocular perception that makes communication possible between diverse peoples. He believes that God has created a world of opposing values which generate enmity between people in order to evoke a double vision which, because it enables people to understand alien ways of being, thereby humanizes them. Such a double vision, in Natty's view, is the moral foundation of that ethos which he believes makes "a true man" (*Pr*, p. 323). This aspect of Cooper's fiction prompted Edwin Fussell's comment that "evidently the best American transcendence results from a reconciliation of opposites."[69] More importantly, Natty believes that it is the existence of evil which functions as the catalyst that drives the imagination toward this act of self-transcendence in the otherwise dehumanizing world of the Leatherstocking novels. Spiritual transcendence is, for him, rooted in the encounter with the reality of evil.[70] Here, then, is a theodicy—an American theodicy—which exonerates God by showing how a world of tragic moral, religious, and racial conflicts is the condition for the possibility of becoming a moral being.

In Natty's career, Cooper dramatizes how the conflicts evoked by the westward movement established a new context for exploring the problem of theodicy. The Leatherstocking novels suggest that the expansion of a democratic society and the ensuing hostilities between the Indian and white cultures required a synthesis of the Puritan and rationalistic theodicies which could explain such tragic conflicts.

Such a synthesis, though a tenuous one, is the foundation for Natty's double vision.[71] His acceptance of the Puritan theodicy is clearly manifested in his affirmations that a sovereign but personal God shapes human lives in mysterious ways that are beyond human comprehension and control,[72] that his first loyalty is to the obligations this God imposes upon him, that God brings people into conflict through the divergent gifts He bestows upon them, and that the demonic aspects of human experience are best explained in terms of a divine teleological suspension of the ethical. He thus affirms the Puritan vision of a God who often shapes human destinies in ways that disregard all human ethical expectations, a God who requires evil and human conflict as part of His well-orchestrated plan for realizing His redemptive purposes, a God who creates such a dangerous and precarious world in order to convince people that they must rely upon Him as the only trustworthy reality. But Natty also advocates the rationalistic theodicy through his understanding of nature as a primary source of moral and religious norms, his belief that the orderly workings of the universe reveal a rational moral order established by God, and his affirmation that people must move beyond a kind of tribal parochialism in moral matters—that people must view their own values in the light of the universal standards revealed by God through nature.[73]

Natty's situation, profoundly shaped as it is by the clash between his rationalistic attitudes and the complexities of the wilderness, prompts him to modify his rationalism (or what others have called his "natural religion" or "natural theism") in accordance with the Puritan theodicy as he seeks a solution for the problem of evil.[74] By thus creating a hybrid theodicy which holds the Puritan and rationalistic theodicies in tandem, Natty creates a more comprehensive, though logically inconsistent, explanation for the kinds of moral and religious conflicts which he experiences during the initial period of America's rapid westward expansion.

Natty's synthesizing activity in response to the conflicts he experiences on the frontier between competing value systems demonstrates how America's westward expansion emerged as a major testing ground for the adequacy of the religious explanations for human experience inherited from the Puritan and rationalistic theodicies. Indeed, the Leatherstocking novels initiate what can be viewed as a fourth stage in the debate regarding these theodicies. The westward movement led many to question whether the rationalistic synthesis of world view and ethos was an adequate formulation of contemporary experience. Although the rationalistic theodicy seemed to be an appropriate expression of the democratic mode of experience, the social, cultural, and personal conflicts generated by the rapidly expanding frontier posed moral and religious dilemmas that seemed unanswerable within the framework of its rationalistic assumptions. It explained the existence of evil and unjust suffering as either a disciplinary measure God uses for helping people attain salvation, or the price people must pay for their freedom of choice, or as God's means to achieving a greater good than He could otherwise attain. The strength of these religious explanations soon paled, however, before such realities as recalcitrant racial enmities, the brutal and predatory side of both nature and human nature, the rampant destruction of the American wilderness, and the experience of contrary moral and religious values that brought the westward migrants into racial, social, and religious conflicts seemingly irreconcilable by rational mediation.

It is noteworthy that the Leatherstocking novels dramatize an important irony in the debate about the Puritan and rationalistic theodicies: namely, that the "errand into the wilderness" spawned by the commercial and increasingly egalitarian society which had given rise to the latter theodicy now required the former for understanding the social, moral, and religious conflicts this new "errand" fostered. Not only had the Puritan theodicy envisioned a brutal, inhumane, and unjust world; it also formulated a mode of experience that more closely corresponded with Cooper's (and many other nineteenth-century American writers') experience of an increasingly problematical environment. Natty thus stands at the portal of American literature as the first figure who, in response to the changing American environment, seeks to develop a complex double vision which accommodates both the Puritan and rationalistic theodicies in a way that explains and reconciles the existence of the conflicting values of America's religious pluralism.

A PROBLEMATICAL RELIGIOUS VISION

Cooper's own attitude toward the theodicy Natty defends remains ambiguous—a stance which, beginning in 1843, Cooper gradually resolved by appealing to the orthodox affirmations of God's sovereignty and wisdom in shaping human affairs, the day of final judgment, and the legalistic necessity to obey His laws as defined in the Old Testament.[75] Such critics as Howard Mumford Jones, Robert Spiller, and others have amply demonstrated that after 1843 Cooper became increasingly disillusioned by what he considered the moral disintegration of American institutions and traditions, and that in many of the novels he wrote between 1843 and 1850, beginning with *Wyandotté*, he developed a moral and religious didacticism which sought to resolve social problems and moral conflicts in terms of the orthodox beliefs of the Episcopal Church.[76] In the novel *Oak Openings* (1848), for example, Cooper accepts and glorifies the westward movement as part of God's providential plan for the spread of Protestant Christianity. He now resolves the social, racial, and religious problems the frontier poses in the Leatherstocking novels by having the Indians convert to Christianity.

But within the Leatherstocking novels, Cooper's artistry reflects the kind of religious complexity that will not settle for a simplistic rendering of, or solution for, the kinds of social, moral and religious conflicts that were at the heart of his experience of the contemporary American environment.

He presents the hybrid theodicy Natty develops as both a creative and a defective explanation for human experience.

However, one major inadequacy of Natty's effort, as Cooper portrays it, is that it suggests the necessity for limiting the appeal to nature as the primary source of moral and religious norms.[77] Not only the selfish and predatory impulses of human nature make this necessary, but also the fact that nature is so contradictory that it can be used to justify virtually anything. Furthermore, Natty fails to reconcile the moral relativity implied by his notion of gifts with his absolutistic commitment to God. His concept of a Last Judgment in which God judges people according to their adherence to their natural gifts, moreover, does not seem to endorse the universal standards he believes God discloses through nature. Nor does Natty ever seek to explore, much less answer, the theological and moral questions raised by his concept of a God who deliberately creates a world wherein obedience to His divine law inevitably brings people into conflict. Then, too, whether his effort to reconcile these theodicies provides an adequate explanation for the existence of evil is questionable. For if evil exists to evoke the kind of human possibility which Natty represents, the question remains why Natty is the only figure in the fictional world of the Leatherstocking novels who imaginatively realizes the kind of double vision which he believes constitutes true self-transcendence. The world in which Natty lives seems effectively to repress its realization.

Nevertheless, despite these problems and despite the seemingly almost insurmountable obstacles to religious transcendence created by the moral universe of the Leatherstocking novels, Cooper implies that Natty's belief in the theodicy he formulates ultimately makes possible both his unswerving moral integrity and his capacity to survive in an American environment hostile to such moral commitment. By thus dramatizing these humanizing consequences of Natty's religious vision, Cooper clearly seems to be suggesting that, in a world which prompts people to live in accordance with their worst impulses, such a vision, despite its problematical nature, remains a desirable alternative for religious belief.

Ultimately, then, the Leatherstocking novels dramatized how the westward movement gave rise to the problem of theodicy. The solution Cooper presents through Natty's career requires new modes of moral and religious perception, but lacking were the literary means to fully develop this solution. Still, Cooper reformulated the major issues shaping the debate regarding the Puritan and rationalistic theodicies in terms of the cultural context of early nineteenth-century America. Such writers as Nathaniel Hawthorne, Ralph Waldo Emerson, and Herman Melville would continue this task, but no one has better claim to being its literary progenitor than Cooper.

8

Nathaniel Hawthorne's *The Scarlet Letter*: Another Hybrid Theodicy

The consciousness of my situation does not always make me sad. Sometimes I look upon the world with a quiet interest, because it cannot concern me personally, and a loving one for the same reason, because nothing selfish can interfere with the sense of brotherhood. Soon to be all spirit, I have already a spiritual sense of human nature, and see deeply into the hearts of mankind, discovering what is hidden from the wisest. . . . I think better of the world than formerly, more generously of its virtues, more mercifully of its faults, with a higher estimate of its present happiness, and brighter hopes of its destiny. My mind has put forth a second crop of blossoms, as the trees do in the Indian summer. No winter will destroy their beauty, for they are fanned by the breeze and freshened by the shower that breathes and falls in the gardens of paradise![1]

THE PROBLEM OF THEODICY IN *THE SCARLET LETTER*

These words which conclude "The Journal of A Solitary Man" are the last written observations of a young man who knows he is about to die from a lingering illness, observations which prompt his friend Oberon, who is reflecting on various excerpts from the now dead man's journal, to comment: "Has not so chastened a spirit found true communion with the pure in Heaven?"[2] The quoted excerpt from the young man's journal, receiving as it does the blessing of Oberon (a name Hawthorne used when a student at Bowdoin),[3] is perhaps the clearest statement in Hawthorne's fiction of the highest spiritual ideal he envisioned for humankind: a selfless generosity which exemplifies both a sympathetic sense of brotherhood with, and a loving benevolence toward, all people.

What is noticeably striking about Hawthorne's fiction, however, is that very few of his characters realize this spiritual possibility: only the small boy in "The Gentle Boy," the dying man in "The Journal of A Solitary Man," and Ernest in "The Great Stone Face." Nothing in these three stories suggests that many others can ever achieve this possibility, nor is there any suggestion that some form of divine agency evokes it. To be sure, its source in the case of the small boy is a humane religious vision and a fund of "unappropriated love" that the world does not know how to appropriate.[4] But in the second case its source is the experience of facing death, and in the last case something as undramatic as the periodic contemplation over a lifetime of a mountain that resembles the features of a benevolent face. The realization of this spiritual ideal is not, in Hawthorne's fiction, inextricably linked with commitment to particular religious values.

Nor is this ideal manifested through prelapsarian innocence. Hawthorne includes morally innocent paragons in his fiction—for example, Rappaccini's daughter, Phoebe Pyncheon, Priscilla, and Hilda—in order to test whether such Adamic figures are as morally interesting as those who, as R. W. B. Lewis puts it, have "stumbled into the time-burdened world of Jonathan Edwards" and experienced the reality of evil.[5] Certainly Hawthorne seeks through the prelapsarian perspective of Phoebe, Priscilla, and Hilda to provide a happy resolution for the moral ambiguities of the tragedies they face, but because their innocence remains intact despite their engagements with evil they lack any convincing moral or spiritual depth. Hence "these characters," as David Levin observes, "will not bear the moral weight that Hawthorne assigns them. They all solve the intellectual or moral problems of their mates by consistently refusing to consider them."[6] Such willful blindness creates a hermetically sealed sensibility which cannot sympathetically respond to human adversity and suffering; and in Hilda's case this willful innocence is itself a source of sanctimonious cruelty. The world portrayed in Hawthorne's fiction, rather than humanizing his characters, seems either to stunt them or to evoke and abet their demonic possibilities.

Indeed, in his most memorable stories, Hawthorne explores the human potential for evil and self-destruction. Readers can easily recall such characters as Ethan Brand and Roderick Elliston who variously wrestle with the knowledge of their own evil impulses; Roger Chillingworth, Aylmer, and Reuben Bourne whose differing schemes ultimately lead them, whether consciously or unconsciously, to destroy others; Rappaccini who, refusing to acknowledge his demonic impulses, callously isolates and destroys his daughter in the name of scientific experimentation;[7] Arthur Dimmesdale who eventually destroys himself through his refusal to share with Hester Prynne the public ignominy she suffers for their adulterous relationship; Young Goodman Brown who, because he becomes disillusioned by and obsessed with his vision of human sin, distrusts and alienates himself from those he had loved and trusted; Hollingsworth whose idealistic scheme for prison reform conceals a massive self-serving egotism; Hepzibah and Clif-

ford Pyncheon whose wasted lives embody the ongoing destructive consequences of building the family mansion on land misappropriated by a much
earlier generation of Pyncheons; and Richard Digby, Reverend Hooper,
and Hester Prynne whose reclusive lives, shaped by their obsession with
the universality of human sin, become living deaths. Such characters seem
driven to destroy themselves. It is as though evil impulses erupt and assume a dictatorship over the human spirit with the force of an inevitable
doom, compelling the individual, consciously or unconsciously, to act out
their dictates.[8]

In Hawthorne's fiction, these actions irreparably deface the human spirit
and relationships. "It is a truth," observes the narrator of *The House of
the Seven Gables* (a "truth" also affirmed by the narrator of *The Scarlet
Letter*), "that no great mistake, whether acted or endured, in our mortal
sphere, is ever really set right."[9] Human corruptibility and egotism in
Hawthorne's characters seem to blot out any possible remedy for the injuries they inflict upon either themselves or others.

But this emphasis upon human corruptness which characterizes much
critical writing on Hawthorne can misguide our understanding of Hawthorne's fictional world. For it is not just human sin that makes moral and
spiritual reparation impossible: the world confronting Hawthorne's characters itself has no healing properties. This is to say, we cannot neglect
how the world of Hawthorne's fiction grasps—or more accurately, mis-
leads—many of his characters in subtle ways that evoke their demonic
possibilities. A good example of such an instance is the famous forest scene
in *The Scarlet Letter*. Hester Prynne has sought out Arthur Dimmesdale
to speak with him alone for the first time in seven years. There, in the virgin
forest, Hester reasserts her female sexuality and convinces Dimmesdale to
flee with her to England where they plan to obliterate the past and start
life anew. Both believe they have regained their humanity within the untouched recesses of nature, a wilderness which seems to evoke and sustain
their strong desire to seek out a new life through denial of the past. The
narrator, however, unequivocally asserts that the forest setting has misled
them to think of freedom in these terms, that their agreement to depart
quickly for England is in fact tantamount to a pact with Satan which has
released their demonic urges. The wilderness (as is frequently the case in
the Leatherstocking novels) is here a no less important source or abetter
of evil than society or human nature.

What emerges in this novel is the image of a world wherein even an
untainted wilderness animates people to choose corrupting strategies for
remedying the injuries they have experienced or inflicted on others. "Even
nature, which, in this novel, is thematically set against the sanctions of
society, cannot be taken simply. The forest is a haunt of evil as well as of
good."[10]

Nothing seemingly remains in this world, not even the healing properties of nature which the Romantic tradition affirmed, to support any redemptive possibilities for Hawthorne's characters. Those few characters mentioned earlier who do realize such possibilities seem to do so not with any logical inevitability, but rather in spite of those inner and outer forces which entrap Hawthorne's characters within destructive processes that are beyond their control.[11]

Certainly it can be argued that in many of his works Hawthorne dramatizes a tragic view of the world nearly identical with that of the Sophoclean tragedies—a flawed world wherein people, fated willy-nilly to live out particular careers, are deceived by the gods themselves into fulfilling their destinies no matter how unjust, inhumane, or undesirable those might be[12]—and that Hawthorne seeks to explore the dramatic potential of viewing modern experience from the perspective of Greek tragedy. There is much in Hawthorne's fiction to support this contention.[13] But such a characterization of Hawthorne's world, though accurate, could blind us to the dramatic purposes such a fictional world serves within any particular work.

Consider, for example, how Hawthorne's narrator in *The House of the Seven Gables* approaches the problematical aspects of Clifford Pyncheon's career. He is a man who, as the omniscient narrator puts it, has, throughout his entire life, "been learning how to be wretched, as one learns a foreign tongue"; and who, now that pain is the reality he most fully knows, must inflict physical pain upon himself while experiencing pleasure in order to make the latter real to him. The narrator himself provides a candid and unqualified theological explanation for Clifford's wasted life. "Clifford saw, it may be, in the mirror of his deeper consciousness, that he was an example and representative of that great class of people whom an inexplicable Providence is continually putting at cross-purposes with the world: breaking what seems its own promise in their nature; withholding their proper food, and setting poison before them for a banquet; and thus— when it might so easily, as one would think, have been adjusted otherwise—making their existence a strangeness, a solitude, and torment."[14] There can be no doubt that the narrator is here affirming a deterministic explanation which is compatible with both Sophoclean tragedy and the Puritan doctrine of predestination; but the imagery in this passage suggests that this narrator, unlike the Puritan, likens such divine interposition, to borrow Paul Ricoeur's fine phrase regarding the divine oracles in *Oedipus at Colonus*, to a "drop of transcendent perfidy" that poisons Clifford's existence.[15] The narrator thus asserts that both the self—"what other dungeon is so dark as one's own heart! What jailer is so inexorable as one's self!"[16]—and divine providence mysteriously conspire to stifle the self's realization of its own best possibilities. However, the narrator of *The Scarlet Letter*, who also gropes with the same religious issues, proposes quite different conclusions about the nature of ultimate reality.

Most analyses of *The Scarlet Letter* which treat the novel's omniscient narrator basically portray him as a consummate artist and story-teller.[17] His major objective, according to this common view, is to render a story from the Puritan past, a story for which he has very few details, either about the events or the people involved. This understanding of the narrator's role has typically emphasized the artistic skills and techniques he uses to weave from such scanty information both an intricate narrative and a complex image of the people—Hester Prynne, Arthur Dimmesdale, Roger Chillingworth, and Pearl—who are the focus of his story. Through his psychological analyses of his characters, as critics have frequently remarked, the narrator further creates a compelling portrait of the Puritans' cultural ethos during their first years in the New England wilderness. While rendering the tragic lives of his major characters, the narrator also depicts how Puritan values shaped social relationships in early Boston. In short, the narrator is viewed as an artistic virtuoso who gives the semblance of life to an otherwise sketchy story from the Puritan past and, in so doing, provides Americans a deeper understanding of their cultural identity.

There is no reason to question this description of the narrator's relationship to his story, so far as it goes. But one can argue that this view of the narrator does not fully describe his role throughout the novel, for it fails to ask what the story itself means to him. The narrator tells the story not only for the sake of telling a good story well, but also for the purpose of making a fictional construct which dramatizes, evaluates, and tentatively answers his own religious questions about human existence. *The Scarlet Letter* is also the story of the narrator's own attempt to grapple with the same religious issues that trouble his central characters.[18] Like them, he is preoccupied with the realities of sin and guilt, evil and suffering, punishment and expiation; like them, he too is forced to ask how—or whether—people can redeem their broken lives; like them, he also seeks a religious explanation for the tragic suffering and wastage of life which they endure for seven years.

But unlike them, he questions the adequacy of the Puritan theodicy as an explanation for human experience, the theodicy from which Hester and Dimmesdale, both orthodox Puritans, derive their explanations for the evil and suffering which engulf their lives. The novel expresses this questioning process at three distinct levels: the narrator's psychological analysis of both the inner lives of the main characters and their tragic relationships,[19] Dimmesdale's use of the Puritan theodicy to make sense of his own sufferings, and the narrator's own critical evalution of the Puritan theodicy in terms of both its psychological consequences and its interpretation of psychological processes. An analysis of these three levels will demonstrate how the narrator not only replaces the Puritan theodicy with a theodicy of his own but also uses the tragic experiences dramatized in the novel to make his theodicy seem a plausible religious explanation of human experience. ·

Indeed, the structure of the novel makes explicit the metaphysical drama of the self implied in the Puritan and rationalistic theodicies, namely, the quest—in this case, the narrator's quest—for a world view and corresponding ethos which—in Clifford Geertz's words—when successfully fused, "will account for, and even celebrate the perceived ambiguities, puzzles, and paradoxes in human experience." This chapter seeks to show how the narrator himself ultimately functions as a character within the story, how his religious views both shape and are shaped by the narrative he creates, and how these religious views are to be understood in relationship to the narrative.[20]

The narrator's quest to synthesize a world view and appropriate ethos in part involves the narrator's imaginative effort to render, in the careers of Hester Prynne and Arthur Dimmesdale, the psychological forces generated by Puritan religious beliefs and, at least in Dimmesdale's case, to dramatize the mode of experiencing the world which the Puritan theodicy prescribed for its adherents. In both cases, a psychological profile of self-destructive forces emerges. Each inhabits an inner world so convulsed and contorted by its unrelieved stresses that it seems to destroy any possibility for religious self-transcendence.

HESTER PRYNNE: A PLAN FOR SALVATION

Hester, for example, deliberately creates a life style that stunts her humanity. She exemplifies a haughty and even compulsive desire to suffer the punishment prescribed by the Puritan community. Even though the authorities require Hester to wear the letter "A" over her breast—the usual punishments of branding and hanging having been waived because her husband is believed to be dead[21]—they do not seek to detain her in the Puritan settlement. But she is compelled with "the force of doom" to remain identified with the place of her adultery: "Her sin, her ignominy, were the roots which she had struck into the soil. . . . The chain that bound her here was of iron links, and galling to her inmost soul, but never could be broken" (pp. 79–80).[22] She is swayed to remain by yet another urge which she represses when she becomes aware of it.

There dwelt, there trode the feet of one with whom she deemed herself connected in union, that, unrecognized on earth, would bring them together before the bar of final judgment, and make that their marriage-altar, for a joint futurity of endless retribution. Over and over again, the tempter of souls had thrust this idea upon Hester's contemplation, and laughed at the passionate and desperate joy with which she seized, and then strove to cast it from her. She barely looked the idea in the face, and hastened to bar it in its dungeon. (P. 80).

She here finds a grim hope through her belief in eternal damnation: if God refuses to pardon their adultery, then she and Dimmesdale, whose affection she unconsciously seeks to nourish through her silence and suffering, can at least share their eternal punishment together. This vision of a mutually shared eternal punishment both expresses and justifies as a masochistic pleasure in suffering, a pleasure which she already derives from remaining in a community which not only condemns but cruelly abuses her.

However, Hester compels herself to believe that her only motive for staying in the Puritan settlement is to work out her salvation through redemptive suffering. "Here, she said to herself, had been the scene of her guilt, and here should be the scene of her earthly punishment; and so, perchance, the torture of her daily shame would at length purge her soul, and work out another purity than that which she had lost; more saintlike, because the result of martyrdom" (p. 80). She imposes upon herself various punishments which she believes will serve as sufficient penance in God's eyes to expiate her sin. Upon leaving prison, she immediately separates herself from the entire community by taking up residence in a ramshackle cottage at the outskirts of the village where the soil is uncultivable.[23] The scrubby trees beside the cottage suggest a skeletal wasteland; it is an appropriate physical analogue or "moral landscape" for both her isolation and the deliberate repression of her creative impulses.[24] No less than Natty she is an isolated figure in the wilderness which, as Fussell observes, becomes for her, as for Natty, the boundary between two seemingly irreconcilable worlds.[25] Though her isolation exemplifies, in one respect, a flight from the condemnatory responses of the Puritan community, it also represents an effort to create a space for herself wherein she seeks to answer her religious questions outside the confines of conventionally accepted thought and behavior.[26] She contemplates suicide and killing Pearl; she maintains a rigid silence among people, except during the interview with Governor Bellingham; she alters her femininity into a bleak figure of frozen sexlessness; she refuses to discipline Pearl, letting her act out her whimsical, and often tyrannical, childish impulses; and she makes herself the moral and spiritual measure when evaluating others and society.

Hester no longer defines herself in terms of traditional moral and religious categories. Rather, she seeks to create a self which establishes and legitimates its own moral and religious categories through its isolation from others.[27] The narrator several times criticizes this strong antinomian thrust in Hester.[28] He rounds out these critical comments by suggesting that, had Pearl never been born, Hester "might have come down to us in history, hand in hand with Ann Hutchinson, as the foundress of a religious sect. She might, in one of her phases, have been a prophetess. She might, and not improbably would, have suffered death from the stern tribunals of the period, for attempting to undermine the foundations of the Puritan establishment" (pp. 163–64). Even Hester at one time imagines herself to be a "destined prophetess" who would reveal a new basis for relationships between men and women" (p. 261). But by the time she returns to Boston after spending several years in Europe, she has come to believe that her past adultery disqualifies her for this role.

She has in fact acted as though her adultery denies her the right to seek out any creative fulfillment for herself. The only creative outlet she allows herself is that which she expresses through her work as an expert seamstress. Even here she severely restricts her creativity, for she makes nothing but crude garments as gifts for the poor, who frequently disparage them. Nevertheless, she does not forego the joy of making lavish clothes for Pearl, such as her crimson velvet tunic. The narrator describes this tunic as being "the scarlet letter in another form; the scarlet letter endowed with life! The mother herself—as if the red ignominy were so deeply scorched into her brain, that all her conceptions assumed its form—had carefully wrought out the similitude; lavishing many hours of morbid ingenuity, to create an analogy between the object of her affection, and the emblem of her guilt and torture" (p. 101). Hester's relationship to her handiwork reflects an ambiguous attitude toward her sense of sin. On the one hand, sewing clothes is a form of penance, the narrator suggests, when she stifles her creativity; on the other hand, when she "allow[s] the gorgeous tendencies of her imagination their full play" in making clothes for Pearl, it expresses her need to transfer the public's attention to Pearl, thereby seeking through her creativity some relief from her own situation (p. 100).

This ambiguity toward her sense of sin is further expressed in her understanding of Pearl. Hester believes that her illicit sexual passions have indelibly stained Pearl's moral purity, and that Pearl has inherited her own evil tendencies which she sees in Pearl's fitful tempers, her frequent repulsion of Hester, her violent animosity toward other children, her adamant refusal to "be made amenable to rules," and her unpredictable moodiness and behavior (p. 89). In addition to viewing Pearl as a mirror image of her own evil impulses, Hester also looks upon Pearl as a demon-like creature appointed by God to carry out His "design of justice and retribution" (p. 179). This is the only interpretation—one which is acceptable within the framework of the Puritan theodicy—that Hester believes adequately explains Pearl's unruly nature and her needling inquisitiveness about why Hester wears the scarlet letter. Hester's morbid preoccupation with her own sin thus leads her to cast Pearl, both as an infant and as a growing child, into a troubling image of demonic and retributive possibilities.

Yet one incident nearly moves Hester to reject this vision of Pearl. Pursuing her "morbid desire" to learn what meaning, if any, Pearl attributes to the scarlet letter, Hester asks the child when seven years old why she thinks her mother wears it (p. 177). Unable to answer the question, Pearl sympathetically grasps Hester's hand and asks her for the answer. This sudden display of sympathy, Hester admits, suggests that the child has "sterling attributes" which could later make her "a noble woman," and she wonders whether Pearl is also an instrument of God's mercy. She realizes that expressing her guilt in a way that is understandable to the child could alter Pearl and their relationship for the better; but she decides against making such a confession, a decision which she rationalizes by telling herself that confessing the truth would be to misuse the child for her own selfish ends and that it would also place an intolerable emotional burden upon Pearl. This refusal to answer Pearl arouses the child's curiosity; she repeatedly badgers her mother to explain why she wears the scarlet letter until Hester, seeing Pearl once again as a demonic creature sent by God to punish her, is pained by her guilt. Here, as elsewhere throughout the novel, Hester unconsciously uses, even provokes, the child's natural curiosity about the letter "A" as a means to further punish herself.

Hester's vision of evil is not, however, restricted to herself and Pearl. Her sense of sin gives rise to her belief that she has a "sympathetic knowledge of the hidden sin in other hearts" (p. 86). Even those whom she had formerly revered—ministers, magistrates, elderly matrons, and adolescent girls—Hester now believes to be hypocritical deceivers whose concealed sins pollute their otherwise unsullied public image. This vision of universal evil, having shattered her faith in human goodness, becomes Hester's obsession. "Such loss of faith," the narrator observes, "is ever one of the saddest results of sin" (p. 87). In his view, Hester's vision of evil has infected and distorted her moral sensibility to such a degree that she has become "half [Satan's] victim" (p. 86); the only "proof that all was not corrupt in this poor victim . . . [is] that Hester Prynne yet struggled to believe that no fellow-mortal was guilty like herself" (p. 87).

It is Pearl who prevents Hester from fully succumbing to her vision of evil. As Hester tells Governor Bellingham, in response to his proposal that Pearl should be raised by a Christian family: "She is my happiness!—she is my torture, nonetheless! Pearl keeps me here in life! Pearl punishes me too! See ye not, she is the scarlet letter, only capable of being loved, and so endowed with a million-fold the power of retribution for my sin!" (p. 112). This ambiguous attitude toward her guilt in her relationship with Pearl expresses a subtle form of self-torture; but her love for Pearl, who symbolizes the scarlet letter for Hester, compensates for the self-destructive impulses the scarlet letter otherwise evokes in her. Loving Pearl awakens in Hester a willingness to struggle against the temptations to become immoral (i.e., to make a pact with Satan), to commit suicide, and even to murder Pearl.[29] Despite the religious masochism she expresses through her relationship with Pearl, this relationship also clearly serves as a humanizing corrective to the harsh punishment which she constantly inflicts upon herself.

The most extreme form this self-imposed punishment takes is the severe repression of her sexual nature, a sacrificial truncation of her life which is already prefigured in her loveless marriage to Roger Chillingworth. "Hester would cease to be a woman," observes Daniel Hoffman, "and be henceforth a living emblem in a morality play: guilt without redemption, suffering without end."[30] For seven years she wears garments made from coarse gray cloth, conceals her luxuriant black hair beneath a cap, and utterly represses all show of emotion in her relationships with others. The result is "a sad transformation" of her physical form which no longer bears any traces of her prior beauty, her passionate nature, or anything else "that Passion would ever dream of clasping in its embrace" (p. 162). Her face is "like a mask; or rather, like the frozen calmness of a dead woman's features" (p. 225).

This dehumanizing denial of her sexuality represents a defiant acceptance of her condemnation by the townspeople, as becomes clear whenever those whom she has helped in their time of need try to thank her for her assistance. Rather than accepting these expressions of gratitude, she silently points to her scarlet letter as though suggesting that her adultery makes her unworthy of their solicitude. "This might be pride," the narrator comments, "but was so like humility, that it produced all the softening influence of the latter quality on the public mind" (pp. 160–61). Indeed, her actions project, whether by conscious or unconscious design, an idealized public image which makes her acceptable to the community.

But what makes this public idealized image most convincing is Hester's ministering to the dying, the sick, the poor, and the troubled without accepting remuneration of any kind. "She was self-ordained a Sister of Mercy; or, we may rather say, the world's heavy hand had so ordained her, when neither the world nor she looked forward to this result" (p. 160). So intensely devoted to helping others does she seem that, for many, "the scarlet letter had the effect of the cross on a nun's bosom. It imparted to the wearer a kind of sacredness, which enabled her to walk securely amid all peril" (p. 161). Hester's reputation is such by the end of seven years that when she talks with the colorfully dressed ship's captain about passages to Europe, the narrator observes that "the matron in town most eminent for rigid morality could not have held such intercourse with less result of scandal than herself" (p. 233). Seven years of isolation, sexual denial, good deeds, personal suffering, and silence regarding her lover's identity have thus elevated Hester to a saintly status which finally leads the magistrates to consider rescinding the requirement that she wear the scarlet letter.

But during the midnight encounter with Dimmesdale on the scaffold, Hester learns that these efforts have also had destructive consequences for others. For upon seeing Dimmesdale standing before her, a figure "on the verge of lunacy," and upon seeing his terror as Chillingworth appears before the scaffold, she then realizes that her silence about Chillingworth's identity has given him the time he needed to discover Dimmesdale's identity and carry out his revenge (p. 165). Seven years earlier, Hester had promised Chillingworth that she would not divulge his identity because she feared that he would retaliate by seeking out and reporting her lover to the authorities. However, on the scaffold, she recognizes—and later, during her meeting with Dimmesdale in the forest, fully realizes—that by concealing her past relationship with Chillingworth she is responsible for Dimmesdale's debilitating suffering; and in recognizing this consequence of her actions, her further responsibility for Chillingworth's hideous transformation into a satanic figure also becomes apparent to her.

This discovery of her unsuspecting role in the ruin of two lives further confirms her vision of evil which she despairingly expresses to Chillingworth as she tells him of her intention to disclose his identity to Dimmesdale. "Do with him as thou wilt! There is no good for him,—no good for me,—no good for thee! There is no good for little Pearl! There is no path to guide us out of this dismal maze of evil, and tumbling, at every step, over the guilt wherewith we have strewn our path" (p. 172). Chillingworth's adamant refusal to forgive both Dimmesdale and herself, even after carrying out his vengeance for nearly seven years, only increases her sense that she is entrapped within a self-perpetuating circle of recrimination and guilt which forecloses all redemptive possibilities. Nothing, she believes, can be salvaged from their ruined lives except the courage to disclose Chillingworth's identity to Dimmesdale.

After she confesses to Dimmesdale, Hester's sense of being doomed to an unredemptive life is momentarily relieved by their agreement to begin a new life in England. She boldly seeks to assume a new identity by removing the scarlet letter. "Let us not look back," she tells Dimmesdale. "The past is gone! Wherefore should we linger upon it now? See! With this symbol, I undo it all, and make it as it had never been" (pp. 200–201). The past does seem to be obliterated as Hester releases her hair from beneath her cap and she once again radiates her youthful beauty; but when Pearl rejoins them, she compels Hester to place the scarlet letter back on her bosom. In thus resuming her former "dreary" self, which Pearl acknowledges to be her real mother, Hester once again feels "a sense of inevitable doom upon her" (p. 210). Yet the euphoria of the moment leads Hester to believe that they can still create a new life dissociated from the past, for she proclaims that during their voyage to England she will toss the scarlet letter overboard and watch it, with their past, sink into oblivion.

The narrator is quick to say, however, that Hester is only deluding herself, that both are irresponsibly fleeing an unpleasant situation rather than resolving it in a life-renewing way. Hester's seven years of isolation and the sense of self-proliferating guilt which fragment and disorient her life have left her with no inhibitions about living what the narrator considers a life of lawless freedom in order to find some relief from her otherwise self-punitive life style. Nothing about her career suggests that religious self-transcendence can be attained through moral striving, self-punishment or

self-recrimination for one's sins, living the isolated life of the religious re-
cluse, or the attempt to create a new life which repudiates the past. Yet,
despite his many criticisms of Hester, the narrator, from beginning to end,
directs our sympathy to Hester and shows her seemingly boundless depths
of courage, endurance, and spiritual fortitude which invest her with a tragic
nobility. There can be no doubt that, as Hyatt Waggoner puts it, "Hester
is the heroine of *The Scarlet Letter*—and . . . the first great tragic heroine
in American fiction."[31]

ARTHUR DIMMESDALE: AN AFFIRMATION OF THE PURITAN THEODICY

Dimmesdale's career, which more clearly exemplifies the Puritan mode
of experiencing the world than Hester's, further underscores the futility of
seeking to redeem past misdeeds through self-punitive measures. Dimmesdale had become a highly respected scholar at Oxford, and his personal
character was such that many believed he would "do as great deeds for
the now feeble New England Church as the early Fathers had achieved for
the infancy of the Christian faith" (p. 119). At the novel's outset, the reader
gains very little insight into Dimmesdale's personality, since the narrator
largely presents him through the eyes of the public, who themselves see
only their idealized image of a minister rather than the man himself. Only
halfway through the novel does the narrator begin to disclose the person
concealed behind the public image.

This process of disclosure, as shall be seen later, is itself of no less concern to the narrator than the various responses of Hester, Dimmesdale,
and the community to their adultery. The narrator initiates this unmasking
process with the revelation that Dimmesdale was Hester's lover. But the
circumstances of this disclosure focus attention not so much on Dimmesdale's adultery as on the act of the discovery itself. Dimmesdale, at the
behest of his congregation, takes up residence with Chillingworth, who, as
Dimmesdale's personal physician, daily supervises his failing health. But
Chillingworth's clinical desire to understand the origins of Dimmesdale's
mysterious illness, as well as his suspicious curiosity about Dimmesdale's
past sins, increasingly obsess him until "a terrible fascination, a kind of
fierce, though still calm, necessity seized the old man within its gripe, and
never set him free again, until he had done all its bidding" (p. 128). The
narrator depicts this obsession through references to Satan and finally
completes this image in his description of Chillingworth's discovery of the
letter on Dimmesdale's breast. "Had a man seen old Roger Chillingworth,
at that moment of ecstasy, he would have had no need to ask how Satan
comports himself, when a precious human soul is lost to heaven, and won
into his kingdom" (p. 137).[32]

This voyeur-like discovery of his secret sin, along with his silent acqui-

escence in the punishment the Puritan community accords Hester—a punishment she endures in part for his sake—make Dimmesdale appear an
odious figure.[33] He does nothing to mitigate her plight or to re-establish
contact with her. He so completely dissociates himself from Hester that
even in their few accidental contacts he refuses to acknowledge her presence, except during the one time she threatens to disclose his identity if
the authorities place Pearl with a Christian family. Nor does her plight
move him to share her disgrace through his own public confession. He
convinces himself that his silence, rather than being self-serving, really serves
the best interests of the community as well as the requirements of divine
justice. He argues, for example, that his "zeal for God's glory and man's
welfare" requires his silence, since to display himself as "black and filthy
in the view of man" would make it impossible for him to achieve good for
others (p. 131). He further contends that his silence is purificatory because
he believes that it imposes upon him a more painful form of suffering than
Hester bears in wearing the scarlet letter. Moreover, the increasing guilt
he feels for not publicly acknowledging his adulterous relationship with
Hester can, in his view, be resolved not through confession but only by
God Himself; therefore, he asserts, he must place his destiny solely in the
hands of God who, "in his justice and wisdom," will either "cure" him of
his inner malaise or use it to "kill" him (p. 136).

These rationalizations for his unwillingness to confess are further bol-
stered by what, from the perspective of Puritan orthodoxy, could only be
considered his strange belief that the person who chooses to conceal his
guilty deeds "must perforce hold [these "hideous" secrets], until the day
when all hidden things shall be revealed. Nor have I read or interpreted
Holy Writ, as to understand that the disclosure of human thoughts and
deeds, then to be made is intended as a part of it. No; these revelations,
unless I greatly err, are meant merely to promote the intellectual satisfaction of all intelligent beings, who will stand waiting, on that day, to see
the dark problem of this life made plain. A knowledge of men's hearts will
be needful to the completest solution of that problem" (pp. 130–31). Believing that he now has a scriptural warrant for remaining silent, he decides not to confess his guilt until the final judgment day when he will do
so "not with reluctance, but with joy unutterable" (p. 131).

Dimmesdale's failure to confess his adultery reflects not only a lack of
moral courage—a flaw which he confesses to Hester while charging her
before the townspeople to disclose his identity—but also a desire to preserve the public's idealized image of him. His congregation considers him
Boston's finest preacher, "a miracle of holiness. They fancied him the mouthpiece of Heaven's messages of wisdom and rebuke, and love" (p. 141).
Dimmesdale subtly and knowingly contributes to this public image when
he enters the pulpit "more than a hundred times" intending to confess his
adultery, but finally only condemns himself in the most general terms as

the vilest of sinners who deserves eternal damnation (p. 142). The congregation, viewing this self-condemnation as further evidence of his saintly character, idealizes Dimmesdale all the more.

Despite his awareness of how he is himself sustaining and strengthening their idealized image of him, he nevertheless gradually comes to believe that this image faithfully mirrors his real self. So deeply ingrained is this belief by the time he meets Hester in the forest that after agreeing to go with her to England his first concern is to bring his professional career in Boston to an honorable conclusion by preaching the obligatory election sermon on the eve of his departure. To perform this duty will, he believes, so favorably impress the people of his congregation that, after his departure, they will remember him as a faithful and honorable public servant. The narrator calls this belief a "sad" form of self-deception which gives evidence of "a subtle disease," namely, his growing incapacity to determine whether the face he wears for others or that which he wears for himself is his true self (p. 214).

The face only he sees is the hypocritical self which he despises. This self-loathing, intensified by his subtle efforts to encourage his congregation's veneration of him as well as by Chillingworth's subtle remarks that increase both his remorse and his despair of pardon, leads Dimmesdale to adopt a masochistic program which surely contributes to his failing health. He flagellates himself, endures physically debilitating fasts, and spends many sleepless nights viewing his face in a mirror.[34] The narrator clearly portrays Dimmesdale's self-inflicted punishment not as a form of religious purification but as pathological behavior which results not so much from the adultery itself as from the despairing self-scrutiny and self-hatred caused by his increasing preoccupation with his hypocrisy and guilt. The new sins which Dimmesdale commits are more deadly, the narrator implies, than the sin they conceal.

Moreover, Dimmesdale's preoccupation with his failure to confess his adultery has other consequences no less harmful to him. The narrator, for example, says that this flaw in Dimmesdale's character so effectively undermines his capacity for making moral discriminations that he can no longer trust his intuitions about others, as is the case in his relationship with Chillingworth. Though Dimmesdale finds Chillingworth to be a repulsive figure, he nevertheless believes that his response discloses something wrong in himself rather than in Chillingworth. The narrator observes that Dimmesdale

would perhaps have seen [Chillingworth's] character more perfectly, if a certain morbidness, to which sick hearts are liable, had not rendered him suspicious of all mankind. Trusting no man as his friend, he could not recognize his enemy when the latter actually appeared. . . . For, as it was impossible [for Dimmesdale] to assign a reason for [his] distrust and abhorrence [of Chillingworth], so Mr.

Dimmesdale, conscious that the poison of one morbid spot was infecting his heart's entire substance, attributed all his presentiments to no other cause. He took himself to task for his bad sympathies in reference to Roger Chillingworth, disregarded the lesson that he should have drawn from them, and did his best to root them out. (Pp. 129, 139)

Dimmesdale's morbidity regarding his adultery also increasingly dissipates his will to live. When Hester encounters him in the forest after seven years of separation, she sees a figure who resembles an upright corpse. The narrator nicely captures Dimmesdale's lifelessness through the halting, listless rhythms in his description of Dimmesdale as Hester secretly observes him in the forest. "There was a listlessness in his gait; as if he saw no reason for taking one step farther, nor felt any desire to do so, but would have been glad of anything to fling himself down at the root of the nearest tree, and lie there passive for evermore. The leaves might bestrew him, and the soil gradually accumulate and form a little hillock over his frame, no matter whether there were life in it or no. Death was too definite an object to be wished for, or avoided" (p. 187). Even when he becomes angry with Hester upon her confession after seven years that Chillingworth was her husband, he lacks the energy to express his anger. Then, paralyzed by his fear that Chillingworth will expose him in retaliation for Hester's divulging his secret, he finally succumbs to his moral lassitude by asking Hester to solve his dilemma for him: "Think for me, Hester! Thou art strong. Resolve for me!" (p. 195). Hester's insistence that he can begin a new life, even assume a new identity, either in the wilderness or in Europe, must be partly viewed in the context of Dimmesdale's moral dissolution. For although she is thereby seeking to assuage her own sense of guilt by extricating him from circumstances which she has helped to create through her past silence, she is also trying to prevent his capitulation without any further struggle. "Preach! Write! Act!" she adjures. "Do anything save lie down and die" (p. 197). Hester's own resolute strength seems to bring Dimmesdale back to life again; for after she agrees to begin life anew with him in England, he literally becomes a revived person.

In contrast to the feeble figure that Hester encountered, the Dimmesdale who returns to Boston "leaped across the plashy places, thrust himself through the clinging underbrush, climbed the ascent, plunged into the hollow, and overcame, in short, all the difficulties of the track with an unweariable activity that astonished him" (p. 215). The imagery here suggests the release of long-suppressed sexual energies which, according to the narrator, are among the immoral impulses that have surfaced in him because of their decision to live together in an unlawful relationship.[35] Dimmesdale experiences these impulses—or what the narrator calls his "profounder self"—upon entering Boston (p. 216). He is quite dumbfounded by his temptations (which he resists) to whisper blasphemous suggestions in an elderly deacon's ear regarding the communion supper, to destroy the faith of the oldest woman in his congregation by confronting her with what he considers an irrefutable argument against the soul's immortality, to arouse the sexual feelings of a young female convert who he knows loves him, to teach some swear words to a group of children, and to exchange bawdy jests with a sailor.

Just when he begins to question his sanity, he encounters or hallucinates the reputed witch, Mistress Hibbins, who offers to introduce him to Satan during a midnight assignation in the forest. Her appearance and offer cause him to question whether he has sold himself to Satan in Hester's guise. This thought, the narrator observes, comes very close to expressing the truth.

He had made a bargain very like it! Tempted by a dream of happiness, he had yielded himself with deliberate choice, as he had never done before, to what he knew was deadly sin. And the infectious poison of that sin had been thus rapidly diffused throughout his moral system. It had stupified all blessed impulses, and awakened into vivid life the whole brotherhood of bad ones. Scorn, bitterness, unprovoked malignity, gratuitous desire of ill, ridicule of whatever was good and holy, all awoke, to tempt, even while they frightened him. And his encounter with old Mistress Hibbins, if it were a real incident, did but show his sympathy and fellowship with wicked mortals and the world of perverted spirits. (P. 221)

Dimmesdale and Hester believe they have established a new and liberating relationship, but the narrator—who precariously borders on portraying Hester as an evil temptress[36]—envisions their future in England as being a tragic recapitulation of sin which he implies can only perpetuate that vicious circle of guilt and self-recrimination already destroying them. However, Dimmesdale overturns their agreement three days later. Apparently motivated by his uncanny knowledge that he is about to die, he publicly confesses his guilt, though his parting words to Hester raise serious moral questions about this confession.

There can be no doubt that Dimmesdale is bent on telling the truth about himself. His election sermon which prophecies "a high and glorious destiny for the newly gathered people of the Lord" has moved his congregation, as he clearly sees, virtually to apotheosize him. But rather than seeking to promote such an idealized image of himself as he has done in the past, he now shatters it. He ascends the scaffold with Hester and Pearl and, after telling the people that he bears the brand of his infamy, he discloses the letter "A" on his chest (p. 247). Dimmesdale never explicitly states that he is Pearl's father. According to his friends his words had not even "remotely implied . . . the slightest connection on his part" with Hester's adultery (p. 257). However, Chillingworth, who tells Dimmesdale several times "Thou has escaped me!" clearly believes that Dimmesdale's action reveals his past relationship with Hester; when Pearl kisses

Dimmesdale she thereby acknowledges him as her father; and the narrator himself states that Dimmesdale's words and actions provide "proofs, clear as mid-day sunshine on the scarlet letter, [which] establish him a false and sin-stained creature of the dust" (p. 257). There is no reason, then, to question the intent of Dimmesdale's action, nor even to question the appropriateness of his confession since the narrator himself has occasionally implied that Dimmesdale has a moral obligation, both to Hester and himself, to make such a public disclosure. Moreover, as Harry Levin observes, Hawthorne wants to make the "Dostoevskian point that every happening must be an accusation to the sinner, who must end by testifying against himself." [37]

What makes Dimmesdale's confession problematical is his own view of it and its relation to his agonized suffering. Seeing that Dimmesdale is dying, Hester seeks from him a reaffirmation of their past love. "Shall we not meet again? . . . Shall we not spend our immortal life together? Surely, we have ransomed one another, with all this woe! Thou lookest far into eternity with those bright dying eyes! Then tell me what thou seest?" Hester has in part endured her suffering because she believed that it served a love which they told themselves, as Dimmesdale himself admits, gave their adultery "a consecration of its own" (p. 194). She still views herself and Dimmesdale in terms of this idealized image of their past relationship. However, Dimmesdale either never shared this view or else has since rejected it; for in his response to her query, he neither reaffirms their past love nor even declares any love for Hester but rather pronounces judgment on their adultery. "Hush, Hester, Hush! . . . The law we broke!—the sin here so awfully revealed!—let these alone be in thy thoughts! I fear! I fear! It may be, that, when we forgot our God,—when we violated our reverence each for the other's soul,—it was thenceforth vain to hope that we could meet hereafter, in an everlasting and pure reunion. God knows; and He is merciful" (p. 254). Hester's feelings upon hearing Dimmesdale say that he considers their adultery an act of desecration can only be surmised. But certainly she must experience these words as a withering rejection of that idealized image of their love which has sustained her through many bleak years of suffering.

Moreover, Dimmesdale seeks to make her further agonize about their adultery by commanding her to make it the focus of her attention, advice which could only mean for Hester the continuation of her punitive life style. What probably comes as the hardest blow to Hester is his suggestion that, barring an act of mercy on God's part, she is now among the eternally damned.

Immediately after this callous response to Hester's long-suffering and unswerving loyalty, Dimmesdale asserts that he has won salvation through his suffering. "[God] hath proved his mercy, most of all, in my afflictions. By giving me this burning torture to bear upon my chest! By sending yonder dark and terrible old man, to keep the torture always at redheat! By bringing me hither, to die this death of triumphant ignominy before the people! Had either of these agonies been wanting, I had been lost for ever! Praised be his name! His will be done! Farewell" (p. 254). As Brooks, Lewis, and Warren put it: "Poor Hester is utterly forgotten. In fact we should add that if the confession is an 'escape' from Chillingworth, it is also, in a deeper fashion, an 'escape' from Hester—from nature, from flesh, from passion, from sexuality, from, in the end, woman, who is the unclean one, the temptress. So even in the heroic moment, there is a deep ambiguity."[38]

Dimmesdale's religious interpretation of his experience, which presents the tragic wastage of lives over the past seven years as a drama God has enacted solely to ensure his redeemed status among the elect, expresses the Puritan vision of a God who frequently ignores human canons of justice for the purpose of realizing His own redemptive designs. Though Dimmesdale is being quite orthodox here, this vision of God nevertheless becomes objectionable, even repugnant, since it provides him a religious justification not only for his long refusal to confess his adultery, but also for a religious egotism that the narrator criticizes throughout the novel.[39]

The most blatant expression of this egotism, in the narrator's view, occurs when Dimmesdale, upon seeing a comet form what he takes to be a red letter "A" in the sky, believes that God is speaking directly to him. The narrator describes this perception as the projection of a diseased mind.

What shall we say, when an individual discovers a revelation, addressed to himself alone, on [the cope of heaven]! In such a case, it could only be the symptom of a highly disordered mental state, when a man, rendered morbidly self-contemplative by long, intense, and secret pain, had extended his egotism over the whole expanse of nature, until the firmament itself should appear no more than a fitting page for his soul's history and fate.

We impute it, therefore, solely to the disease in his own eye and heart, that the minister, looking upward to the zenith, beheld there the appearance of an immense letter,—the letter A,—marked out in lines of dull red light. (P. 154)[40]

The egotism which Dimmesdale expresses here and in his final assertion that he is dying a saved man "does not," as Frederick Crews observes, "subtract from his courage, but it casts doubt on his theory that all the preceding action has been staged by God for the purpose of saving his soul."[41]

THE NARRATOR: A RECONSIDERATION OF THE PURITAN THEODICY

The narrator has designed his narrative so as to raise such a doubt in the reader's mind. As a psychologist of religion, he seeks to dramatize the

Puritan mode of experiencing the world—the Puritan way of perceiving, feeling, thinking about, and responding to the world through its notions of a sovereign God, total depravity, limited atonement, humiliation, and predestination. Both Hester and Dimmesdale adopt punitive life styles as self-imposed penance for their adultery, believing themselves to be undergoing a mandatory period of suffering which God requires of them to expiate their common sin. But such punishment of themselves in the name of their Puritan God only generates an increasingly self-destructive religious masochism. The narrator's dramatization of how the Puritan theodicy evokes such self-destructive psychological responses from Hester and Dimmesdale raises the question whether they are not suffering more from their Puritan mode of experiencing the world than from their adultery, whether their religious actions are not in fact as sinful, if not more so, than their sexual sin.

The narrative thus brings into sharp relief the problematical ethical implications of the Puritan ethos as embodied in the careers of Hester and Dimmesdale. Even though their careers can be viewed as perversions of the Puritan ethos, the narrator nevertheless forces us to ask whether such perversions of the spiritual life result not only from human sin but also from the way in which the Puritan theodicy requires people to view themselves and their relationship to the world.

No less important to the narrator's evaluation of the Puritan theodicy is how the response of the Puritan community shapes Hester's life. By consigning her to wear the letter "A" over her heart for the rest of her life, the authorities thereby impose upon her the painful expiation of repeatedly confessing her sin, as it were, in her daily contacts with others. The Puritan authorities maintain that this stigma is the legally prescribed punishment for adultery that fully implements the will of God. The novel becomes in part a psychological study of Hester's efforts to accommodate herself to this communally prescribed punishment in a society which, because it provides her no other means of atonement for her sin, thereby promotes, or at least tacitly supports, her self-destructiveness. By thus dramatizing how the Puritan community is itself partly responsible for the kind of life Hester lives, how its own response to human sin is a dehumanizing influence of belief in the kind of God described in the Puritan theodicy, the narrator thereby presents the problematical social implications of a society dedicated to living in full conformity with the dictates of this theodicy.

The narrator questions at several levels the moral adequacy of the Puritan theodicy for interpreting human experience. Its world view depicts a world wherein God often realizes His redemptive purposes by using people's personal tragedies and sufferings as a means for working the salvation of others. The narrator, upon viewing the tragic wastage of life in the careers of his characters, casts doubt on the acceptability of this explanation for the evil and suffering they experience in their lives.[42] The Puritan world view describes a world to which the only appropriate response, as the narrator defines it, is a grinding form of self-condemnation, self-torture, and humiliation before God in order to balance the implacable evil tendencies of human depravity. The Puritan ethos prescribes a mode of experiencing the world which the narrator believes can, if fully adopted, seriously damage people's moral sensibilities, rendering them less capable of making appropriate distinctions between good and evil. He maintains that the vision of evil advocated by the Puritan theodicy can lead to an obsession with the reality of evil which isolates people and destroys human relationships. And he further suggests that these consequences in individual lives demonstrate how belief in the Puritan theodicy can and does undermine the humanizing potential of Puritan society. The narrator thus questions the moral adequacy of the Puritan theodicy by showing how both its world view and prescribed ethos only further compound the existence of evil.

But the narrator does not simply question the Puritan theodicy; he also creates a theodicy of his own. This is not to say that the narrator makes no statements that reflect Puritan orthodoxy; he does. A few examples include his assertions that the adultery (which he calls "the rank luxuriance of a guilty passion") and the subsequent birth of Pearl were predetermined by "the inscrutable decree of Providence" (p. 88), that God had enacted His judgment against Hester, that "Providence" is working a judgment against Dimmesdale through his confession (p. 251), and that God, whom he calls 'that ever-wakeful one," sees everything people do, no matter how secretive it is (p. 146). These claims fully accord with the Puritan understanding of divine providence.[43]

But orthodox as such claims might be, their significance is overshadowed by other statements which have quite unorthodox implications. For example, his description of Chillingworth's vindictive ambition to make Dimmesdale confess his adultery to him suggests a chilling vision of the destructive power of human evil. "The clergyman's shy and sensitive reserve had balked this scheme. Roger Chillingworth, however, was inclined to be hardly, if at all, less satisifed with the aspect of affairs, which Providence—using the avenger and his victim for its own purposes, and, perchance, pardoning, where it seemed most to punish—had substituted for his black devices" (p. 138). The narrator's suggestion that God's punishment serves His redemptive purposes expresses Puritan orthodoxy. What is unorthodox about this description of the relationship between Chillingworth and Dimmesdale is its implication that Chillingworth is able to make divine beneficence serve his own evil purposes. That is to say, although the narrator views Dimmesdale's reticence as a beneficent result attributable to God, he also sees it providing Chillingworth a means through which he can vindictively spur Dimmesdale's religious masochism by keeping his conscience "in an irritated state, the tendency of which was, not to cure by wholesome pain, but to disorganize and corrupt his spiritual being" (p. 192).

It could be argued that the narrator is here implying that God intends His merciful actions to evoke Chillingworth's vindictiveness for the purpose of punishing Dimmesdale. That he intends no such implication, however, is perhaps suggested by his citing other instances of how people utilize God's mercy to realize their demonic impulses. One such instance is Hester's vision of Pearl. Contrary to Hester, the narrator maintains that "Providence" is mercifully using Pearl to mitigate the "host of difficulties" which beset Hester (p. 164). She deliberately ignores or denies the good traits in Pearl in order to maintain her view of Pearl as a demonic agent of God's retribution, and thereby transforms what for the narrator is an agent of God's mercy into an instrument of masochistic self-torture.

The narrator adduces yet another example when he describes the "heart of the multitude" in religious terms (p. 65). "When an uninstructed multitude attempts to see with its eyes, it is exceedingly apt to be deceived. When, however, it forms its judgment, as it usually does, on the intuitions of its great and warm heart, the conclusions thus attained are often so profound and so unerring, as to possess the character of truths super-naturally revealed" (p. 126). In the narrator's view, these intuitions to treat others with compassion seemingly have their origins in God, thereby making them a normative guide for action. But he notes that as these intuitions pass through the medium of "the public mind," its unpredictable "despotic" temper—a temper which is seemingly beyond God's control—arbitrarily decides whether to express or suppress them (p. 161).[44] In the latter case the withheld mercy, as Hester's career illustrates, gives the public a diabolical power over the offender. The narrator believes that divine mercy is a reality which God makes available to all people in order to redeem them from the destructive tendencies of their sinful nature; but he also considers it a reality which, rather than being able irresistibly to accomplish its mysterious purposes, is itself frequently, almost inevitably, transformed by human nature into a force for evil. This is decidedly not a Puritan understanding of divine mercy.

Nevertheless, what finally emerges from the narrator's telling of his story is a world view which holds in tandem elements from both the Puritan and rationalistic theodicies. He accepts the rationalistic notion that God is a moral exemplar who fully conforms to people's ethical expectations; for this reason, he repudiates the Puritan notion of God's sovereignty and especially its corollary that God can and does waste human lives in order to effect the salvation of others. But he also rejects the rationalistic belief that people's moral nature is sufficient for effecting their salvation since he accepts the Puritan belief in human depravity. "And be the stern and sad truth spoken, that the breach which guilt has once made into the human soul is never, in this mortal state, repaired. It may be watched and guarded;

so that the enemy shall not force his way again into the citadel, and might even, in his subsequent assaults, select some other avenue, in preference to that where he had formerly succeeded. But there is still the ruined wall, and near it, the stealthy tread of the foe that would win over again his forgotten triumph. . . . So it ever is . . . that an evil deed invests itself with the character of doom" (pp. 199–200, 210). The narrator thus views the destructive processes initiated by human sin and guilt not as a medium through which God punishes people, but rather as an evil power which is a self-perpetuating reality independent of God. Like Edward Beecher in *The Conflict of Ages*, the narrator affirms the necessity for both a doctrine of sin which goes to the heart of the human situation and a notion of God which conforms to humankind's highest ethical principles of justice and honor.[45]

In order to reconcile such beliefs,[46] the narrator finally develops the idea of an ethical deity whose beneficent efforts to help people overcome their sinful impulses are restricted by the destructive power of human sin. Like Nathaniel Taylor, he envisions a God who is limited by "the nature of things"; but unlike Taylor, he understands this limitation to be one that virtually nullifies God's power to carry out His redemptive intentions. Indeed, so limited is God's power that He cannot prevent His mercy from abetting the evil tendencies of human nature. The novel's bleakness—which leads Hyatt Waggoner to conclude that it is "a tragic story containing not much hope for those involved, and perhaps not much for the rest of us"[47]— stems in large part from the narrator's image of human nature as being nearly impervious to the healing effects of divine mercy, and also as being capable of converting that mercy into an instrument of evil. Not only has this deity little control over the outcome of human affairs, His efforts to mitigate evil and suffering often increase them, though sometimes His merciful intentions are realized quite by chance. Whereas the Puritans depict a deity who victimizes people in order to demonstrate His sovereign power over humankind, the narrator's God is Himself victimized by His own beneficent efforts on humankind's behalf.

The narrator's explanation for evil, then, is that it exists not out of some necessity dictated by divine permission or the will of a sovereign God seeking to demonstrate His power, but because human nature sets loose chains of evil consequences which, as they inexorably lengthen themselves throughout human lives, become a self-proliferating reality that virtually cancels the redemptive power of divine mercy. The narrator thus expresses a dualistic vision of the universe wherein the power of evil almost inevitably neutralizes, if not outmatches, the power of God.

At first sight, the narrator seems to affirm a fatalism no less severe and enervating than that which characterizes Hester, Dimmesdale, and Chillingworth. But he balances his sense of doom with a sense of hope lacking in these characters. Even though he believes divine mercy is ineffectual in this world, he still suggests that in the afterlife God's mercy is possibly victorious. In the spiritual world, he asserts, "the old physician and the minister—mutual victims as they have been—may, unawares, have found their earthly stock of hatred and antipathy transmuted into golden love" (pp. 258–59). He also repudiates Hester's notion that she and Dimmesdale might live together in eternal punishment as a perverted religious belief expressing masochistic desires. The former is only a surmise while the latter constitutes no explicit repudiation of the idea of eternal damnation, though the possible destiny which the narrator envisions for Chillingworth implies his belief—and here he echoes both Chauncy and Beecher—that even the most demonic people are not inevitably excluded from divine mercy in the afterlife.

Hence, the narrator, although omniscient, is nevertheless himself a character within the novel who enacts the metaphysical drama of the self implied in the Puritan and rationalistic theodicies. He seeks to create a world view which provides a plausible explanation for the existence of evil and the moral ambiguities of human experience, and a corresponding ethos which responds to them in a creative and life-enhancing manner.

The mediating link between this world view and ethos, for the narrator, is the moral consciousness, not divine grace. The most hopeful element in the narrator's position is his apparent belief that people can become co-workers with God to help Him realize His beneficent purposes. His rendering of the characters in the story implies that people can best accomplish this by genuinely repenting their sins, using what they consider an irreparably ruined life as the new foundation for building a stronger self, and developing a moral consciousness through which they can define themselves in terms of the ambiguous interrelationships between good and evil.

It is in his own narrative career, and most especially in his attitude toward the characters' misdeeds, that he most clearly demonstrates how such a moral consciousness facilitates the expression of divine mercy. After describing Chillingworth's transformation into an "unhumanized mortal," he affirms his own unwillingness to make Chillingworth an object of hatred or vilification: "But, to all these shadowy beings, so long our near acquaintances,—as well Roger Chillingworth as his companions,—we would fain be merciful" (p. 258). This attitude is further manifested in his refusal to describe the "red stigma" on Dimmesdale's breast. To depict it, he asserts, would be an "irreverent" act and, by implication, also a way of making Dimmesdale a more repulsive figure. Ultimately, it could express a pornographic pandering to those baser impulses in both himself and the reader which have been evoked by his unrelenting exposure of human sin. As the narrator puts it: "We have thrown all the light we could acquire upon

[Dimmesdale's red stigma], and would gladly, now that it has done its office, erase its deep print out of our own brain; where long meditation has fixed it in very undesirable distinctness" (pp. 256–57).[48]

Through his artistry the narrator has partly succumbed to the kind of voyeuristic fascination with human sin and guilt that in Chillingworth has become a dehumanizing obsession. By refusing to describe Dimmesdale's stigma, he is, as it were, curbing the Chillingworth in himself and also acknowledging that his own psychological analysis of human sin, like Hester's preoccupation with the secret sins of others, is giving rise to a debilitating misanthropic attitude. He further suggests a kinship with Dimmesdale. The idealized image he has projected of himself as a narrator who is analyzing human sin for the sake of developing a complex moral awareness is, he implies, also a mask which conceals his own baser impulses. His idealized narrative role has potentially become no less corrupting than Dimmesdale's belief in his own idealized image. Thus does the narrator develop a critical attitude toward himself and others while simultaneously expressing an attitude of mercy, a stance which constitutes the artistic analogue for how he believes people can and should become co-workers with a merciful but limited God in His struggle against evil.

This is not to say that he believes the existence of evil inevitably leads people to develop such a moral consciousness. The careers of Hester, Dimmesdale, and Chillingworth show this not to be the case. The world of *The Scarlet Letter* in fact works against people's inevitable growth into such a moral consciousness (just as the world of the Leatherstocking novels seems to work against people's realizing the moral possibility Natty symbolizes). Though only the narrator's stance exemplifies this possibility, it still remains the one redeeming aspect of—and therefore slim justification for—a world shaped by the overwhelming power of evil.

Here, then, is an unorthodox hybrid theodicy through which the narrator seeks to synthesize his rationalistic and Puritan beliefs. The God he portrays is no less problematical than the Puritan God; in some ways He is more problematical. But the narrator suggests through his own narrative posture that living the ethos he recommends enables him to discover and realize his own best possibilities in a world that discourages their realization, that the fusion of world view and ethos in his theodicy generates a mode of experiencing the world which, in his view, defines the life of true virtue.

Nevertheless, his theodicy represents a precarious fusion of rationalistic and Puritan beliefs which he maintains only through an act of the imagination—the creation of the fictional narrative itself. The act of constructing a world view and imaginatively adopting a corresponding ethos through his narrative enables him to live within this tenuous synthesis, and while imaginatively living within this synthesis he defines himself (as well as others) in the face of the moral and psychological complexities he dramatizes in the careers of Hester, Dimmesdale, and Chillingworth. It is, as it were, a vibratory stance, an oscillation within the tension of contrary beliefs that refuses to resolve the contradiction. This provisional way of perceiving and experiencing the world becomes for him the definition of his true humanity.

Such a stance both parallels the double vision Natty Bumppo develops through his attempted synthesis of the rationalistic and Puritan theodicies and foreshadows Ralph Waldo Emerson's gradual development of his own version of such a double vision. The recurrence of this effort to live within a precarious synthesis of rationalistic and Puritan beliefs is itself a noteworthy feature of several major American literary classics written between 1820 and 1860.

9

Ralph Waldo Emerson: A Refocusing of Vision

"NATURE": A RATIONALISTIC THEODICY

Following the lead of Stephen Whicher, recent scholarship on Emerson has further elaborated the rich complexity, vitality, and drama in "Emerson's surprisingly eventful voyage in the world of the mind."[1] It is now generally recognized that his life of thought was not static, but rather a dramatic process of evolution moving in several directions, with each line of movement assuming its own dynamics in relation to the others. Maurice Gonnaud comes close to summarizing the new respect accorded Emerson when he observes: "There is about Emerson's achievement a totality and a consistency which are admirable and at the same time a little frightening."[2]

Yet, as Sherman Paul demonstrated thirty years ago, the consistency of Emerson's writings cannot be that of linear logic.[3] His poetic commitment to circular processes of thought, the repetitious use of metaphors, and his constant recourse to contradictions within each essay and from essay to essay prevented this.[4] By means of such strategies, along with the differing roles he adopted for himself in his essays, Emerson created a peculiarly oscillating world of thought.[5] There is a quality of "doubleness" about Emerson's writings which illustrates his adherence to his own dictum:[6] "He in whom the love of truth predominates will keep himself aloof from dogmatism, and recognize all the opposite negations between which, as walls, his being is swung."[7] Although systematic thinking in the traditional sense characterizes some of his writings, Emerson preferred to describe his notion of a "system" as "dotting a fragmentary curve, recording only what facts he has observed without attempting to arrange them within one outline."[8]

The result is that his thought retains an elusive protean quality which makes it difficult to chart any particular line of development in Emerson's thought. This difficulty is further compounded by the ease with which scholars have been able to collate quotes from the earlier and later writings which create the impression that Emerson retained his youthful idealism throughout his life.[9]

However, Stephen Whicher has successfully demonstrated that Emerson moved from an early rebellious assertion of the self's freedom to an acquiescence in fate during his later years.[10] A central question has become how to evaluate the relationship, the connections, the continuity—if any—between an "earlier" and a "later" Emerson. Such scholars as Whicher, Jonathan Bishop, A. D. Van Nostrand, and Quentin Anderson have variously defined this relationship in terms of personal and social crises, of movement from a radical perspective to one of compromise, of a strategic retreat, or of a shift from idealism to realism. Whicher praises the later Emerson for becoming more cognizant of the reality of evil,[11] while A. D. Van Nostrand sees the later Emerson salvaging his youthful idealism within a deterministic framework;[12] Bishop finds the earlier Emerson to be far more revolutionary than the later Emerson,[13] while Anderson, critical of the "imperial self" which he believes characterized the younger Emerson, contends that his earlier revolutionary perspective is destructive of culture.[14] And more recently Jeffrey Duncan has argued that what appears to be "an irreconcilable about-face" in Emerson's way of saying that "it is the way we see, not what we see, that matters" has "an underlying coherence,"[15] while Lawrence Buell maintains that the later Emerson developed a radically different "persona" in his writings from that which characterizes his earlier works.[16] It has become increasingly clear that Emerson's later writings embody important changes: as Whicher first noted, the Emerson of "Fate" is not the Emerson of "Nature."[17]

"Fate" is in fact no less pivotal for understanding Emerson's religious vision than "Nature," for it culminates an extensive refocusing of vision which Emerson begins as early as "The Method of Nature." This process must certainly be viewed in part as his evolving response to personal crises, social crises, and the new intellectual currents of the day. As "one of the reconcilers of the nineteenth century," Emerson was aware that his mystical idealism would be outmoded in a post-Darwinian world; so he sought to accommodate his idealistic vision of nature to the new scientific model of nature.[18]

But Emerson's refocusing of vision can also be defined in terms of the theological debate about the Puritan and rationalistic theodicies. In "Nature" (1836) he begins with a world view analogous to that which the rationalistic theodicy describes. But in such essays as "The Method of Nature" (1841), "Compensation" (1841), "Spiritual Laws" (1841), "Circles" (1841), "The Poet" (1841), "Experience" (1844), "Character" (1844), and a second essay entitled "Nature" (1844), he gradually moves closer to the world view presented in the Puritan theodicy. In these essays, Emerson modifies his earlier idealism in terms of such basic Puritan ideas as divine providence, predestination, the doctrine of humiliation, and a sovereign God who, in seeking to achieve His redemptive purposes, has recourse to a teleological suspension of the ethical. In "Fate" (1860), he finally attempts to reconcile his earlier idealistic vision of nature and God with Puritan orthodoxy by fashioning a theodicy which enables him to modify his earlier concept of God in a way that still preserves its essential outlines intact. The effort to accomplish this feat without relinquishing most, if not all, of the basic idealistic assumptions of "Nature" becomes a metaphysical drama of reformulating his earlier view of the world and defining a corresponding ethos that would be most suitable to the world he depicts.

"Nature" is Emerson's first effort to make public his transcendental vision of God and nature.[19] There is nothing about nature, as Emerson portrays it in this essay, that is detrimental to humankind. He presents nature in all its aspects as an unproblematical expression of divine beneficence, as performing a kind of priestly role toward humankind on God's behalf. One function of this "ministry" is to enhance people's physical comfort (Wh, p. 25);[20] another is to nourish their inner life. Nature accomplishes this latter function in three ways: it calls people who are emotionally or spiritually depleted to turn to its physical beauty for emotional and spiritual renewal, it enhances human virtue, and it provides, in its universal scheme of physical and spiritual laws, an object of beauty for human contemplation. But according to Emerson, even these simplest of nature's benefits go unheeded by his own generation because poeple see in nature little more than the raw materials for making their life physically comfortable. In the common view, nature is a physical reality that is to be studied solely through the understanding.

Emerson adopts the Neoplatonic Coleridgean distinction between reason and understanding as a means of defining two different approaches to nature. The understanding, as Emerson defines it, is the applied intellect which studies the physical properties of nature by reducing them to mathematical measurements and formulas. Emerson does not deny the usefulness of such mental gymnastics because they make possible the discovery of physical laws, the study of which, in his view, constitutes an inquiry into the spiritual foundation of reality. But he asserts that complete reliance on the understanding hampers, if not precludes, people's spiritual growth beyond the stage of warring savages.

Humankind can easily avoid such a spiritual destiny by establishing the kind of working relationship between reason and the understanding which Emerson describes in the latter half of the essay. He defines reason as that "universal soul within or behind [the] individual life, wherein, as in a firmament, the natures of Justice, Truth, Love, Freedom arise and shine. . . .

it is not mine, or thine, or his, but we are its . . . property and men" (Wh, p. 32). Reason is the permanent, unchanging "Spirit" underlying all existence; its presence in both the human soul and "the NOT ME" of nature makes them essentially identical (Wh, pp. 22, 32). This being the case, people can develop a special mode of perception—a fusion of reason and understanding[21]—which can see the basal Spirit that shapes the physical world. Such a double consciousness is necessary, according to Emerson, not only because "natural facts" are "symbols of particular spiritual facts" (Wh, p. 31), but also because it is the only way to solve "the problem of reconciling the Soul with Nature. . . ."[22] Through this synthesis of reason and understanding, people can perceive in natural facts "the analogy that marries Matter and Mind" (Wh, p. 37)—that is, an analogy which discloses how nature and human existence obey the same spiritual laws. Such analogies based on natural facts become for people, who cannot see the invisible spiritual world, a kind of physical Braille which, when correctly read by reason, enables them to translate the physical world into reliable spiritual knowledge of themselves. Emerson considers this double consciousness the only appropriate response to a world which he envisions as being a polar reality of matter and spirit.

The double consciousness also provides reliable knowledge of God. Emerson bases this claim upon his belief that the "radical correspondence between visible things and human thoughts" which he posits is neither a figment of the imagination nor a sporadic chance occurrence, but rather a structural principle shaping the universe (Wh, p. 33). Natural symbols "preëxist in necessary Ideas in the mind of God, and are what they are by virtue of preceding affections in the world of spirit" (Wh, p. 36). The "necessary Ideas" to which Emerson refers here are the ideas of "Justice and Truth," those "immortal necessary uncreated natures" in the mind of God which are the "absolute" and unconditional ground of all reality (Wh, pp. 46–47). God's own meditation on these ideas, according to Emerson, transforms them into the physical laws which establish right relationships between all natural objects. Natural symbols and the relations that obtain among them therefore make visible the very processes of divine thought: nature is the very mind of God made visually accessible to people. Hence "the axioms of physics translate the laws of ethics" (Wh, p. 35); physical laws "hint or thunder to man the laws of right and wrong and echo the Ten Commandments. . . . The moral law lies at the center of nature and radiates to the circumference." Reason therefore does not focus its attention solely on physical laws themselves—that is the province of the understanding—but looks through them to the quintessentially ethical character of nature. To study this "moral sentiment" of nature increases one's desire and capacity to become virtuous (Wh, p. 39).

But in Emerson's view, nature's disclosure of divine laws ultimately moves beyond the creation of moral beings to promote the yet higher purpose of human redemption. The process of redemption begins when one actually perceives the ideas of "Justice" and "Truth" as they exist in God's mind and how they shape every aspect of His creation. Emerson describes this mode of perception in his image of the transparent eyeball.

In the woods, we return to reason and faith. There I feel that nothing can befall me in life,—no disgrace, no calamity (leaving me my eyes), which nature cannot repair. Standing on the bare ground,—my head bathed by the blithe air and uplifted into infinite space,—all mean egotism vanishes. I become a transparent eye-ball; I am nothing; I see all; the currents of the Universal Being circulate through me; I am part or parcel of God. The name of the nearest friend sounds then foreign and accidental: to be brothers, to be acquaintances, master or servant, is then a trifle and a disturbance. (Wh, p. 24)[23]

He has been literally transformed into the impersonal eye of reason, a form of perception which, because it is "coincident with the axis of things," he believes enables him to perceive the world as God perceives it (Wh, p. 55). Emerson calls this apotheosis of vision in nature the "redemption" or "purification of [the] soul" which, as he puts it, makes us feel that "for the first time, *we exist*" (Wh, pp. 55, 50, 47). The image of the transparent eyeball expresses Emerson's experience of a radical alteration in his conventional sense of self. The old self felt limited by social, moral, and religious constraints; the new self experiences release from all such limitations. The redeemed consciousness is thus simultaneously a mode of perception and a mode of being which give people a sense of virtually unlimited possibility. Emerson rings out this point in three sweeping sentences: "Who can set bounds to the possibilities of man? Once inhale the upper air, being admitted to behold the absolute natures of justice and truth, and we learn that man has access to the entire mind of the Creator, is himself the creator in the infinite. . . . Build therefore your own world" (Wh, pp. 50, 56).

Some critics—Regis Michaud and Stephen Whicher, for example—have suggested that Emerson is here counselling people to create imaginary versions of the world, that he views the world as "nothing more than a fiction of the world,"[24] thereby cutting people "adrift from the belief in any reality external to [themselves]."[25] To further substantiate this claim, critics have pointed to the famous passage which describes his solution to the problem of evil in this early essay. "As fast as you conform your life to the pure idea [i.e., God's idea of truth or justice] in your mind, that [idea] will unfold its great proportions. A correspondent revolution in things will attend the influx of spirit. So fast will disagreeable appearances, swine, spiders, snakes, pests, mad-houses, prisons, enemies, vanish; they are temporary and shall be no more seen" (Wh, p. 56). Emerson is not denying the existence of evil; rather, he is affirming that when one perceives the evils of the world from the impersonal perspective of God, they are seen as the necessary tools God requires for realizing His beneficent purposes. As Duncan puts it, "it is the way we see, not what we see, that matters."[26] When the self views life from God's vantage point, the self no longer experiences worldly evils as a source of personal grievance against God or others. "The soul holds itself off from a too trivial and microscopic study of the universal tablet. It respects the end too much to immerse itself in the means. . . . it accepts from God the phenomemon, as it finds it, as the pure and awful form of religion in the world. It is not hot and passionate at the appearance of what it calls its own good or bad fortune, at the union or opposition of other persons. No man is its enemy. It accepts whatsoever befalls, as part of its lesson" (Wh, p. 48).

Recreating the world through the redeemed consciousness, then, is an activity of the human spirit which involves both seeing the world as God sees it and adopting the kind of life dictated by this perspective. Building one's own world is the effort not to make life conform to the self's desires, but to live a life which, heedless of personal wishes, fully conforms to the ethical dictates God reveals through nature.

The redeemed consciousness, itself a fusion of reason and understanding, discards all conventional distinctions between good and evil by assuming a neutrality toward its own function within the divine scheme. The understanding alone, which makes the self rather than God the focus of its attention, creates a false consciousness which generates Job-like complaints or immoral behavior. Such a self-regarding consciousness, in Emerson's view, can never find an acceptable solution to the problem of evil. But in nature he discovered a beneficent and just deity who evokes the kind of double consciousness which he believed to be a sufficient answer to the problem of evil. Emerson thus articulates what M. H. Abrams, in his treatment of William Wordsworth, calls a "theodicy of the mind in nature."[27]

"Nature" embodies the metaphysical drama of the self in the debate about the Puritan and rationalistic theodicies. Emerson creates a view of the world which makes evil both rationally comprehensible and morally acceptable, and prescribes the kind of ethos which he deems the most appropriate response to the world he describes. It is not necessary to rehearse the extent of such influences on this project as Platonism, Neoplatonism, Thomas Carlyle,[28] Samuel Taylor Coleridge, Emanuel Swedenborg, German idealism, English romanticism, and Unitarian rationalism.[29] Certainly the world view Emerson articulates shows very little Puritan influence, though he prescribes a posture before God which parallels the Puritan doctrine of humiliation. His world view more closely resembles that which William Ellery Channing sets forth in several sermons which Emerson either read or heard;[30] but the impersonal God of "Nature" who makes His thought processes visible in physical forms and natural laws lacks any semblance to Channing's personal and paternalistic God.[31]

Moreover, Emerson makes nature, not the human conscience, the supreme source of moral norms. Nature provides a painless form of spiritual discipline which makes possible that apotheosis of vision which constitutes redemption for Emerson. As he succinctly puts it, "Nature is made to conspire with spirit to emancipate us" (Wh, p. 43). Nevertheless, because Emerson's God respects people's freedom to reject this possibility, He uses no means to persuade them to accept it other than the lure of nature's beauty. Nature thus symbolizes in this early essay a just and beneficent deity whose relationship to the world and humankind poses no disturbing ethical question for Emerson.

In later essays, however, Emerson found it increasingly difficult to reconcile this vision of nature with the harsher realities of human experience. As he gradually realized the inadequacies of his world view, the world appeared arbitrary and inexplicable, so that the problem of evil gained increasing prominence in his maturing thought. He discussed and explored these difficulties with unflinching honesty. In attempting to resolve them, he redefined the process of redemption, reformulated his vision of God and nature, and, by means of this revisionary process, finally articulated a theodicy radically different from the one he presented in "Nature."

A REFOCUSING OF VISION

As early an essay as "The Method of Nature" (1841) is dotted with points that trouble his idealistic vision of nature;[32] his efforts to remove them engender a series of refocusing tactics. While elaborating his earlier idea that nature is an emanation of God's thought, he now adds the observation that nature appears to exemplify only a bumbling hit-and-miss method of achieving its end, namely, the creation of "holy or wise or beautiful men." Such people are rare; even when they do appear, "no one of them seen by himself . . . will justify the cost of that enormous apparatus of means by which this spotted and defective person was at last procured" (E, p. 62).

Rather than calling the chaotic energies of nature an amoral reality, Emerson describes them as a "redundancy of life which in conscious beings we call ecstasy"; it is a sheer overflow of creativity which "can only be conceived as existing to a universal and not to a particular end" (E, pp. 63, 62). In the earlier essay, nature represents a rational moral order through which God works in beneficent ways to help all people achieve redemption; in this essay, nature is a swirling mass of contrary forces which tyrannically shapes individual lives in ways that best facilitate the realization of its own impersonal ends. Emerson is not celebrating the profusion of

"ecstasy" in nature.[33] He is lamenting the fact that, in a world of uncontrollable randomness and tragic wastage of human lives, the individual's
quest for redemption cannot rely upon the rational processes defined in
"Nature." This quest must now hold its bearings as best it can, if indeed
it can at all, within the hurly-burly of a kind of universal raffle wheel;
perhaps its number will come up, perhaps not. People no longer choose
what they become; such possibilities are now randomly dictated by nature.

There is no explanation in this world view for our "essence" except that
it is mysteriously given to us. Emerson recognizes that in making this assertion he is essentially reaffirming the Puritan vision of God. "The 'royal'
reason, the Grace of God, seems the only description of our multiform but
ever identical fact. There is virtue, there is genius, there is success, or there
is not. There is the incoming or the receding of God: that is all we can
affirm; and we can show neither how nor why," but only posit that God
is thereby realizing His redemptive purposes (E, p. 63). The only appropriate response to such a world, Emerson asserts, is that people must relin-
quish the belief that they are their own masters. Sacrificing all personal
desires, they must fully submit themselves to God's treatment of them—
even when it requires their own suffering or damnation—rejoicing that
"the spirit's holy errand" is being carried out through them. In his effort
to recover this "sacred idea" (i.e., the doctrine of humiliation) from the
Puritan tradition, Emerson begins to develop a religious determinism which
initiates the refocusing of vision that characterizes such later essays as
"Compensation," "Spiritual Laws," "The Poet," "Experience," "Character," and "Fate" (E, p. 68).

Emerson's increasing acceptance of a deterministic stance is readily discernible in "Compensation" and "Spiritual Laws," two companion essays
in which he seeks to show why we must accept both what we are and
what happens to us as being both necessary and right. Such a deterministic
outlook, as he first articulates it in "Compensation," derives from his vision of human existence as being the outgrowth of "the law of Compensation" (ML, p. 172). According to this law, both the organic and inor-
ganic realms are inexorably shaped by a balancing process wherein every
gift is compensated by a defect and every defect by a gift. A lethal poison
can have curative powers, action is met with reaction, and the lion cannot
fly after faster running prey; the good is balanced by the evil, the affinity
by the repulsion, and the power by the limitation.

This physical law of compensation, Emerson asserts, has its analogue in
the spiritual realm. Our spiritual life, no less than our physical existence,
is inexorably shaped by its own forms of compensation. Those who suffer
from injustices and inequities in their conditions are recompensed with the
growth of character; those who suffer severe material limitations gain spiritual compensations. Emerson makes it clear that the law of compensation
does not provide material rewards for virtuous action or unmerited suffer-

ing. "Emerson's most constant moral objection is to that species of conventional morality which expects a material compensation for outwardly virtuous behaviour. Emerson wants to remind us that the wish for material advantages, or the power to enjoy them, engages only a portion of the Soul. Real virtue is not the possession of such things, he would say, but the action of faculties higher than those employed in such desiring and having, or in chaffering about things that may be desired or had."[34] Spiritual compensations help to expand these higher faculties and, as they are increasingly developed, the more the individual can benefit from the suffering, pain, losses, and injustices that are part of human existence.

But if misfortunes bring such desirable compensation, the pursuit of any value, goal, or ideal has its own liabilities. Amassing a large fortune corrupts the wealthy, commitment to scholarly values makes for solitude and alienation from others, the business career dulls the aesthetic, moral, and religious sensibilities. Even those human possibilities which, from a moral or religious perspective, are deemed most desirable can be realized only at great spiritual or physical cost to the individual. As Emerson dryly puts it, everything "has its price—and if that price is not paid, not that thing but something else is obtained, and . . . it is impossible to get anything without its price" (ML, p. 182).

Emerson further believes that the law of compensation establishes a rigorous system of moral justice. Every evil action, he maintains, is inevitably punished. It may be that neither the wrongdoer nor others can immediately discern the punishment, but eventually, perhaps over a period of years, at least the evildoer will come to understand "the retribution in the circumstance" (ML, p. 176). But the punishment has no redemptive connotation for Emerson. It is simply the inevitable price that must be paid for having committed the misdeed. By the same token, good actions are inevitably rewarded (but not with material rewards): nothing can prevent the law of compensation from benefiting the good person. Though the truly virtuous person's good action is, in Emerson's view, its own reward—and is enacted without seeking any benefit for himself—it nevertheless strengthens his character and increases his happiness (not smugness) in his own virtue. Even weaknesses and defects stand him in good stead by making him less self-assertive. Moreover, when such a person is unjustly maltreated for years without just reparation, he will ultimately be compensated not only for the injustice suffered but also for the length of time it is endured. The "order that so utilizes evil is moral because the evildoer, though ironically helpful, himself incurs harm."[35] According to this extremely rationalistic perspective, then, no one has any cause for complaint or personal sense of grievance. The onus of moral responsibility for evil falls directly on each individual, not on any impersonal processes set in motion by social or political structures.[36]

A universal system of moral necessity which maintains an exact balance between good and evil thus governs all aspects of human experience. Nothing in this world view is arbitrary or unpredictable. The moral life constitutes a kind of moral mathematics based on the predictable consequences of any particular action. In Emerson's words, "The world looks like a multiplication-table, or a mathematical equation, which, turn it how you will, balances itself" (ML, p. 175). Indeed, Emerson believed, as Stephen Whicher has observed, that the law of compensation made it "possible to construct a moral science, equally exact, equally unquestionable" as natural science.[37] By means of this "moral science" people could learn how this law works and how it could be used to foresee the predictable consequences of their actions, thereby enabling them to increase its positive effects in their lives.

In "Spiritual Laws," Emerson shows through his analysis of vocation how people can make the law of compensation work to their advantage. Like Natty in his notion of gifts, Emerson asserts that one's constitution can appropriately express itself in only a limited number of vocations. Through his natural talents each person receives a "call" to specific vocations; only by being true to this call can a person be successful. "There is one direction in which all space is open to him. . . . He is like a ship in a river; he runs against obstructions on every side but one, on that side all obstruction is taken away and he sweeps serenely over a deepening channel into an infinite sea. This talent and this call depend on his organization, or the mode in which the general soul incarnates itself in him" (ML, p. 195). This "general soul" rigidly determines the path of personal development it desires for each individual. A person who resists the dictates of his constitution by pursuing a vocation alien to it reaps only frustration, bitterness, and despair; the person who obeys the natural bent of his constitution will almost effortlessly attain a life of perfect contentment. For Emerson such relaxed conformity to "the nature of things" is true virtue because it empties a person of all egotistical self-regard while simultaneously increasing his spiritual force (ML, p. 206).

In these two essays, then, Emerson elaborated a determinism which he believed demonstrated the moral necessity and rightness of both what we are and what happens to us. In "Nature," the given order of things is said to conspire with nature to grant people the freedom of limitless possibilities; in "Compensation" and "Spiritual Laws" it is said to conspire with nature to severely restrict human choices. Nature in the earlier essay is a democratizing reality in that—through its woods, sunsets, and landscapes—it provides everyone the same painless means for achieving the redeemed consciousness. In the latter two essays, nature is not so evenhanded in the means or capacities it provides for this purpose, nor is it as amenable to people's desires for harmony with nature. Indeed the limitations it imposes upon people evoke their antagonism against nature. Not until such later essays as "Circles," "The Poet," "Experience," "Character," "Nature" (1844), and "Fate" did Emerson finally explore the moral and religious implications of thus modifying his earlier idealism along deterministic lines. This critical effort is an ambiguous one, however, since he also struggled, despite his emerging determinism, to reinstate the basic affirmations of his earlier idealistic vision of nature.

In "Circles" and "The Poet," for example, Emerson turned once again to an analysis of human consciousness in an effort to recover his belief that nothing can limit human spiritual possibilities. He envisions conventional modes of consciousness as mental jails which prevent further growth into the highest forms of spiritual consciousness. People's minds are entrapped within various customs and practices, or what he calls "village symbols." Though people look directly at nature, these village symbols blind them to the "universal signs" and "commandments of the Deity" that cover the "walls" of nature (ML, pp. 337, 327). Nevertheless, human consciousness has the capacity to outgrow such parochial symbols. But even the mode of perception achieved by this kind of self-transcendence is itself a form of spiritual imprisonment, though it provides the individual a more encompassing view of human experience. It too must be transcended, as must all succeeding forms of perception, until the human mind finally merges with the primordial thought process of God Himself. Emerson portrays human consciousness as a series of concentric circles continuously expanding toward the outermost ring of the redeemed vision.[38]

But this gradual expansion of human consciousness toward a final incorporation into the mind of God is not an inevitable process for every individual. The extent of such spiritual growth "depends [entirely] on the force or truth of the individual soul" (ML, pp. 280–81), and the strength of this "force or truth" is fully determined by the divine soul. Hence the divine soul, should it make this "force or truth" sufficiently weak, could be said thereby to debar many from attaining the redeemed consciousness.

Emerson tries to nullify this implication in two ways. His first ploy is to describe nature, in both "Circles" and "The Poet," as a series of hierarchical forms through which all people can gradually evolve until, upon reaching the highest form, they finally achieve redemption. People need only abandon themselves "to the nature of things"—to that "path or circuit of things through forms"—in order to emancipate themselves from "that jailyard of individual relations in which they are enclosed" (ML, pp. 332–33). So long as people trust "the divine animal who carries them through this world," they will experience further refinements of consciousness until it finally becomes one with the divine consciousness itself. Nevertheless, Emerson grudgingly admits that many who seek to attain the redeemed consciousness through nature do not achieve it.

Having failed in "Circles" to solve this problem of the seeming arbitrariness of the divine soul, he attempts another solution in "The Poet." In this essay Emerson humanizes nature by arguing that nature incarnates itself in the poet as a means of helping humankind attain salvation. The poet is the mouthpiece of nature. Through his artistic creations nature "shows us all things in their right series and procession" and discloses the spiritual laws shaping human existence, thereby facilitating "the passage of the soul into higher forms" until it achieves salvation (ML, pp. 329, 331). Furthermore, the redemptive effects of the poet's artistry are not restricted to his lifetime. In each of the poet's works, nature creates an indestructible "new self" which can help further generations achieve salvation (ML, p. 330). Emerson's poet, then, is said to be an expression of nature's tendency toward the universal realization of the redeemed consciousness.

This affirmation of nature's redemptive role becomes problematic at the end of the essay when Emerson laments: "I look in vain for the poet whom I describe" (ML, p. 338). By implication, this lament makes it questionable whether the kind of self-transcendence he attributes to the poet is actually the ultimate goal of nature. Interpretations of "The Poet" or of Emerson's aesthetics have typically emphasized Emerson's romantic view of the poet.[39] But in light of both this implication of the essay and Emerson's prolonged struggle to reformulate the idealism of "Nature," the fact that Emerson's savior-poet finally remains only a hypothetical being—or what Joel Porte calls "a universal and not a particular man"[40]—greatly diminishes the importance of his romantic theory and increases the importance of his growing conviction that life is structured in a way that seems to substantiate the Puritan notion of limited atonement.

"The Poet" finally remains a bleak portrayal of people who, though having within them "a force impelling [them] to ascend into a higher form," cannot do so because of some inbuilt defect or flaw of character (ML, p. 329). In this essay, Emerson no longer affirms as he did in "Compensation" that all defects and inequities of condition are necessarily compensated by a true soul. Personal defects are here presented as very real barriers to attaining the redeemed consciousness. Emerson describes, in both "Circles" and "The Poet," a universe which encourages self-transcendence in all people but which also makes the realization of this possibility impossible for many. This dilemma placed increasing pressure on Emerson's maturing thought in such later essays as "Experience," "Character," "Nature" (1844), and "Fate," essays in which he sought by means of his growing determinism to recover his earlier belief in people's unlimited possibilities.

He began this project in "Experience" with a reiteration of ideas which he had set forth in his previous essays. He reasserts that our constitution, temperament, and modes of perception inexorably shape our lives, that our moods and temperament create false modes of consciousness which deny us any genuine contact with the world and others, that we must conform our vocation to our given talents if we are to be successful and happy, and that the redeemed consciousness, because it is identical with the divine perspective, transcends all conventional moral and religious viewpoints.

But he further develops his view of human consciousness by exploring whether our powers of perception are trustworthy. The Christian idea of original sin as well as the idea of sin itself, he observes, compel us to distrust our powers of perception as inalterably "colored and distorting lenses" which force us to see evil or sin in events that are intrinsically neither evil nor sinful. People derive their ideas of sin and evil solely from those actions that issue in consequences which they experience as harmful to themselves or others, and they interpret such consequences this way only so long as they retain their parochial moral and religious values or their self-oriented sense of right and wrong. When these consequences are viewed from the perspective of "the eternal politics," however, they are seen to be the indifferent instruments which God uses to realize His own "external and beautiful" purposes (ML, pp. 362–63).

Furthermore, Emerson adds, the ideas of sin and evil are the kinds of lenses through which people see the misdeeds of others in judgmental terms which they do not apply to themselves. Exercising such moral leniency toward themselves—which he considers a universal tendency—exhibits to Emerson neither a process of self-justification nor a lack of self-critical powers but rather a spiritual force that has the potential for liberating people from their provincial morality. He calls it "the ill-concealed deity" in humankind. It proves that people are not, as Christianity teaches, helplessly afflicted with an inner "pravity or bad" (ML, pp. 360–61). It is not human nature but false modes of perception which account for the evil people see in the world or others. As Jeffrey Duncan puts it, "our perspective on life," what Emerson calls "our 'angle of vision,'" is of the utmost importance [W, XII, 10]. We must observe phenomena from the perspective of the absolute to see that they are the effects of self-executing laws, to see that these laws are moral, and to see that because of these laws all things, in their relation to the whole, are good and all goes well."[41]

Despite the optimistic view of human nature Emerson expresses in this essay, he had become, as can be seen in "Circles" and "The Poet," far less optimistic in the period between "Nature" and "Experience" about the process of spiritual liberation. In the earlier essay, he maintained that all people can easily liberate themselves in nature simply by submitting themselves to its spiritual discipline; he deemed gaining redemption a rational and humanly controllable process. In the latter essay, he asserts that our liberating moments occur quite unexpectedly in any circumstances within or outside nature; he now describes redemption as a chance occurrence beyond human control.

Emerson in fact portrays all human experience as a series of chance happenings, precisely because God is in all people as a "creative power"

(ML, p. 347). God unexpectedly bursts through their limited modes of perception to provide them a new way of seeing and therefore a new way of being. Circumstances, no matter how adverse, can surprise people quite by chance into self-transcendence. Of course, Emerson accentuates the positive aspect of this view by saying that God's beneficence touches people without their having to merit it or seek it out. Still, the arbitrariness with which God manifests Himself in human lives and the inequities He thereby creates can evoke a sense of injustice. As in "Circles" and "The Poet," the question of how Emerson can come to terms with the fact that many people do not, or cannot, achieve the redeemed consciousness remains unanswered.

A world governed by chance does not necessarily make life a random series of events. Like the Puritans, Emerson maintains that God is orchestrating all chance occurrences in ways that best enables Him to realize His own redemptive purposes. Chance therefore embodies for Emerson not sheer arbitrariness but a spiritual determinism dictated by God. But he never asserts in "Experience" that this determinism is moving humankind toward universal salvation. It remains a possibility that is neither precluded nor made necessary by the terms of the essay. He further intensifies this dilemma in two later essays, "Character" and "Nature." (The latter essay will be designated "Nature II"—no reference is intended to his poem of the same title—so as to distinguish it from its more famous namesake.)

In "Character," Emerson once again describes a world where chance dictates spiritual possibilities. He defines character as a natural force which nature quite arbitrarily and unevenly distributes among individuals. Character in some people is so great that they appear "to be an expression of the same laws which control the tides and the sun"; in others character is so feeble that they remain "a pendant to events" (ML, p. 366). Character is fated, and it in turn determines the kind of moral and spiritual possibilities the individual can realize; the individual cannot move beyond these established boundaries. Whereas in "Nature" Emerson had portrayed nature as a great spiritual equalizer that enables all people to acquire salvation, in "Character" he observes—more explicitly than in "Circles," "The Poet," and "Experience"—that the great inequities of character among people make it difficult, if not impossible, for many to achieve salvation. Nature does not support egalitarian values; "in democratic America," he observes, "[nature] will not be democratized" (ML, p. 374), an observation which he repeats in "Nature II."

In "Nature II," Emerson moves one step further in defining nature as being antagonistic to humankind by depicting it as a reality which lures people toward promised spiritual satisfactions it never grants.[42] Throughout nature "there is . . . something mocking, something that leads us on and on, but arrives nowhere; keeps no faith with us" (ML, p. 417). Emerson had proclaimed in "Nature" that the beauty of nature leads people toward redemption. Here he asserts that nature's beauty entices people to believe that it will bring them into contact with its underlying spiritual reality only to betray this "vast promise" (ML, p. 419). "This disappointment is felt in every landscape" (ML, p. 418). And he admits that this "balking of so many well-meaning creatures" could lead people to believe that they are the playthings of demonic forces (ML, p. 419).

Emerson rejects this view of the world, however, calling it a form of "insanity." It is a disease of the mind that can be cured only by viewing life from a universal perspective which enables people to see that their "innate universal laws" constitute "the soul of the Workman [streaming] through us" (ML, p. 420). From this perspective of the absolute—the realm of self-executing laws or external necessity—people can perceive that all their actions are being channeled by a beneficent God to realize better and greater purposes than their actions themselves were designed to achieve, that the thwarting of those advantages people seek for themselves is far more advantageous to their spiritual welfare than realizing them. Thus what appears to be chaotic, arbitrary, even demonic from a human perspective is, from the perspective of eternal law, the way everything must necessarily happen in order to make life conducive to people's spiritual benefit. Because an absolute necessity determined by God is shaping each individual's destiny, what happens is right. The law of compensation now reflects for Emerson a beneficent moral order which ensures not only that justice prevails in human affairs but also that what happens to people—even when it is painful, frustrates their schemes, or reorients their lives in tragic ways—ultimately benefits their spiritual welfare.

The period between "Nature" (1836) and "Fate" (1860) is one in which Emerson's gradually evolving determinism increasingly qualified the idealism of the earlier essay. There can be no doubt that during these years Emerson was greatly preoccupied with analyzing both the nature of human limitations and his growing vision of a world fraught with chance occurrences, a world which he experienced as being indifferent to all conventional moral and religious values. He was equally preoccupied with defining the moral implications of such a world in a way that would preclude any argument for moral indifference or amorality. This latter project gave rise to his efforts, in the essays briefly examined here, to demonstrate how chance happenings make self-transcendence possible. Not until "Fate," however, does Emerson fuse these elements into a unified world view which drastically differs from the one he portrayed in "Nature." In this sense, "Fate," more than "Nature," holds the key to Emerson's intellectual achievement.

"FATE": A REFORMULATED RATIONALISTIC THEODICY

"Fate" represents Emerson's attempt to reformulate the earlier idealism of "Nature" through a synthesis of freedom, determinism, and divine beneficence. The essay is basically divided into three sections: the first treats fate, the second freedom, and the third their synthesis. By first explaining human experience in terms of both concepts, Emerson hoped to achieve a balanced perspective which, in the third section, could give credence to a vision of life that gives neither concept normative status.

In the opening section on fate, Emerson forcefully articulates his vision of nature as a complex network of "immovable limitations" which "cannot be talked or voted away" (Wh, pp. 330–31). "The book of Nature is the book of Fate," "an irresistible dictation" that has no favorites (Wh, pp. 336, 330). One race of people lives at the expense of another race, one animal species at the expense of another, so that together humankind and nature create a vicious system of uncontrollable brutality in which people have no favored position. As Emerson puts it: nature "is no sentimentalist,—does not cosset or pamper us. We must see that the world is rough and surly, and will not mind drowning a man or a woman" (Wh, p. 332). Nature has become in this essay a predatory reality that randomly destroys life.

No less resistive to human expectations and desires are those natural biological laws which rigidly determine and severely curtail each person's possibilities. "When each comes forth from his mother's womb, the gate of gifts closes behind him. . . . So he has but one future, and that is already predetermined in his lobes and described in that little fatty face, pig-eye, and squat form. All the privilege and all the legislation of the world cannot meddle or help to make a poet or prince of him" (Wh, p. 334). Unalterable biological limitations thus often create unwanted destinies. Nevertheless, Emerson asserts, such a situation ultimately benefits both the individual and others, though no one may be able to discern its beneficial aspects. As in "Nature II," Emerson here portrays nature as antagonistic to humankind—as an impersonal reality which rides roughshod over human desires and ethical expectations. It symbolizes an ultimate reality which makes all human canons of justice, all human notions of right and wrong, not only parochial but seemingly irrelevant. True virtue, within this world view, constitutes a full acceptance of this impersonal realm of eternal necessity and a glad conformity to its dictates.

Emerson further states that people's moral possibilities are no less determined than their physical possibilities. "People are born with the moral or with the material bias" which constitutionally predisposes them to spiritual pursuits or to materialistic or sensuous pursuits, to moral or immoral behavior (Wh, p. 335). Emerson seeks to bypass the radical implications of this moral determinism by adding that, despite these inbuilt dispositions, everyone knows that his present condition has issued from his own choices. People are free to struggle against, and even have the capacity to transcend, unwanted dispositions that incline them to commit immoral or destructive actions.

But the struggle itself cannot be transcended. Overcoming one kind of limitation only leads people to experience other kinds of unwanted limitations. An antagonism exists between people and nature which not only predestines them to an unending struggle against it, but in each case predetermines the nature of the individual's struggle. "If we are brute and barbarous, the fate takes a brute and dreadful shape. . . . If we rise to spiritual culture, the antagonism takes a spiritual form. . . . The limitations refine as the soul purifies, but the ring of necessity is always perched at the top" (Wh, p. 338). Each individual's existence is the outgrowth of a universal will totally indifferent to all personal efforts to achieve a desired destiny. But as can be seen in his analysis of human freedom, Emerson believes that this situation is ultimately beneficial for humankind.

Emerson defines freedom in two different ways, each integral to the other. One might be called the "lower" freedom, the other the "higher" freedom. The "lower" freedom is the unfettered capacity to think and act in accordance with one's own desires and aspirations. Such "freedom is necessary," is itself "a part of Fate," since it makes possible that struggle against fate which fate itself provokes through imposing unwanted limitations. He rhetorically asserts that people can, as it were, hurl themselves against fate with a power equal to its own. But he warns that people who define freedom solely in these terms will exaggerate its possibilities and, in so doing, misuse their freedom in ways that dehumanize them. To overcome this tendency, people must give themselves over to the "higher" freedom.

This transition to the higher freedom is made possible only by the purified or redeemed consciousness. To achieve this possibility, people must initially use their lower freedom to resist fate as a means to expand their consciousness into higher levels of awareness. Each breakthrough is experienced as a new birth until they finally experience, as it were, the ultimate rebirth. "The day of days, the great day of the feast of life, is that in which the inward eye opens to the Unity in things, to the omnipresence of law;— sees that what is must be and ought to be, or is the best. This beatitude dips from on high down on us and we see. It is not in us so much as we are in it. . . . This insight throws us on the party and interest of the Universe, against all and sundry; against ourselves as much as others" (Wh, p. 341). This prosaic description of discerning the "universal ends" shaping human experience echoes the poetic image of the transparent eyeball, Emerson's image for the individual's immediate perception of how God's spiritual laws are determining every aspect of human affairs. But here, as in "Nature," the vision of divine law does not by itself constitute the redeemed consciousness. People must also will that the truth they perceive through the redeemed consciousness shall prevail; people are truly free only when they fully submit themselves to the necessities imposed upon them by universal law. Their struggle against a fate which uncontrollably works against their desires and aspirations must finally culminate in their becoming "its obedient members" (Wh, p. 339).

But Emerson cautions people against viewing such submission in fatalistic terms. This caveat is based on his contention that the adversary fate against which the individual struggles, as well as the struggle itself, are part of a larger organic system which he calls "Providence." He defines Providence as that impersonal "sphere of laws" which inexorably legislates all human limitations; by means of these unwanted limitations, it provokes people into an antagonistic relationship with fate, thereby assuring their failure, frustration, suffering, or despair (Wh, p. 341). Emerson's providence is not, as he puts it, "a pistareen Providence" which plays favorites; rather it is a neutral force which dooms every person to debilitating physical or spiritual defects, or both, and to diverse kinds of stultifying conditions in order to achieve its own ends (Wh, p. 332).

This understanding of divine providence inevitably led Emerson to question whether such a sovereign deity who transcends our conventional ethical categories can be conceived in ethical terms. In "Fate" Emerson ultimately says yes, there is a symbol of God which vindicates human ethical concerns in a universe which is experienced as indifferent to them. This symbol, as Emerson formulates it, is a beneficent providence which humanizes people through their limitations. People's inbuilt limitations create the conditions which make possible their gradual humanization. As he metaphorically puts it:

We can afford the limitation, if we know it is the meter of the growing man. We stand against Fate, as children stand up against the wall in their father's house and notch their height from year to year. But when the boy grows to man, and is master of the house, he pulls down that wall and builds a new and bigger. 'Tis only a question of time. . . . If Fate is ore and quarry, if evil is good in the making, if limitation is power that shall be, if calamities, oppositions, and weights are wings and means,—we are reconciled.

Fate involves the melioration. No statement of the Universe can have any soundness which does not admit its ascending effort. (Wh, pp. 343, 345)

Emerson's overarching system of providence thus uses people's limitations to nudge, push, and sometimes slam them into a redeemed consciousness. "Providence," he observes, "has a wild, rough, incalculable road to its end, and it is of no use to try to whitewash its huge, mixed instrumentalities" (Wh, p. 333).

Emerson had been struggling for years to resolve the conflict between the belief of his youthful idealism that nature can redeem all people and his growing conviction that character, temperament, and other limitations are deterrents, sometimes insurmountable barriers, to achieving redemption. The solution he finally sets forth in "Fate" is that an impersonal realm of self-executing laws establishes the human limitations which, in the suffering, pain, and tragedy they cause, evoke that continuous expansion of consciousness which is the condition for the individual's inevitable

growth into the redeemed consciousness. Emerson thus describes a beneficent moral order, but this beneficence has a harshness and ferocity which
defy all human notions of justice. Indeed, justice in this view has nothing
to do with conventional distinctions between right and wrong. Rather, it
constitutes the individual's capacity finally to see and accept the entirety
of his or her experience—its tragedies and pains, its ecstasies and delights—as having conspired to his or her benefit. Justice is the redeemed
consciousness joyfully accepting and conforming to its perceptions of the
true order of things.

In "Fate" Emerson develops his own version of the Puritan notion of a
sovereign God who uses what, from a human perspective, are unethical
means for achieving His redemptive purposes. Nature (i.e., the book of
fate) ultimately still conspires with universal being (i.e., providence) to
emancipate people. However, the process of emancipation, described in
"Nature" as being painless, is now defined as a painful one. Still, the pain
and tragedy involved make human transcendence not only possible but inevitable; and the individual once again is said to play an important role in
the process of redemption. The idealism of "Nature" therefore reappears
in "Fate" in revised form; it now includes determinism and painful growth.
People must still build their own "house" as in "Nature," but the building
material now includes not only consciousness but also experience and history.

"Fate" thus culminated the refocusing of vision which Emerson began
in "The Method of Nature." He not only reforged his earlier idealism in
the fires of such Puritan ideas as predestination (though Emerson emphasizes that such predestination provokes human antagonism against its rigid
limitations), divine sovereignty, and divine providence, but in the process
also transformed the Puritan affirmation of God's unresponsiveness to human ethical expectations into a principle that is ethically compatible with
his rationalistic concept of God in "Nature." In one sense this refocusing
of vision can be seen as a "strategic retreat" for Emerson, though this way
of describing Emerson's revisionary process overlooks its constructive dimensions.[43] When viewed against the background of the debate about the
Puritan and rationalistic theodicies, it can be defined as a creative and
tough-minded synthesis of these two religious interpretations of human
experience.[44]

On the one hand, the world view he presented in "Fate" could accommodate the Puritan affirmations of the limitations, precariousness, and arbitrariness of human existence, the necessity of divine grace for bringing
about people's redemption, a divine teleological suspension of the ethical,
predestination, and a superintending providence which is orchestrating
everything in ways best suited to achieve its redemptive purposes. On the
other hand, it could also accommodate the rationalistic affirmations that a
humane and humanizing moral order which compensates people for the

moral quality of their lives prevails in the universe, that all people can potentially achieve the redeemed consciousness, that God requires people to be co-workers with Him in shaping their destinies, and that God's treatment of people is ultimately conducive to their spiritual liberation, rough-hewn though it may be at times. But it repudiated the Puritan notions of innate depravity and limited atonement just as it rejected the rationalistic notions that the human conscience is the normative revelation of divine law and that God is a rational, paternalistic deity who refuses to act in ways which offend human ethical sensibilities.

It is a complicated compromise of these diametrically opposed world views, one which worked not because of any rational consistency but because it functioned in "Fate" more as a system of checks and balances. Emerson depicted a world of polarities wherein neither pole has normative status; each polarity plays its own role at different levels of human existence. When one level of polarities seemed to provide him an adequate explanation of human experience, he found that another level gave rise to a contrary explanation. It is as though a law of compensation were keeping an exact balance between various levels of human experience: a structural principle shaping particular areas of human affairs seems to require an opposite shaping principle in other areas.

The net effect of this compromise was a democratization of explanations. For example, Emerson explained biological and physical factors in terms of fate or predestination; the spiritual realm, though bound by a rigorous determinism, he explained in terms of human freedom within established boundaries. At both levels he described a divine teleological suspension of the ethical. But in the physical realm it is a principle of unpredictability while in the spiritual realm it is a purposeful principle which spiritually benefits each person. There is no equality between individuals in the physical realm; egalitarian values are morally irrelevant. In the spiritual realm, however, a democratization of spiritual possibilities exists which enables all people to achieve redemption. Emerson accorded the polarities of this world view equal importance and maintained that people must hold them in tension if they are to develop a comprehensive view of human experience.

This is the function of what Emerson calls the "double consciousness" (Wh, p. 351). Like the Puritan vision of God, Emerson's conception of providence embodies a dual focus on determinism and divine purpose. Unlike the Puritans, however, Emerson develops the logical implication of this dual concern for religious belief, namely, that it requires a complicated double vision. The believer must keep an equal eye on both fate and providence, fully accepting the dictates of each. "A man must ride alternately on the horses of his private and public nature, as the equestrians in the circus throw themselves nimbly from horse to horse, or plant one foot on the back of one and the other foot on the back of the other. So when a man is the victim of his fate . . . he is to take sides with the Diety who secures universal benefit by his pain" (Wh, p. 351). Viewing life simultaneously or "alternately" in terms of both his "private and public nature" requires that the individual live in the unresolved tension between the lower and higher freedom—between the struggle against fate (i.e., nature) and the acceptance of it (i.e., providence).[45]

But what is gained by living in this tension without resolving it? According to Emerson, the moral consequences of such a resolution would ultimately be dehumanizing. To view life only through one or the other of these modes of perception leads either to an enervating fatalism which absolves people of any responsibility for their life or actions, or to a grandiose sense of freedom which glorifies people's self-serving interests. To avoid these consequences, the individual must maintain a balanced perspective which affirms both freedom and determinism. Such a double consciousness constantly resynthesizes experience in terms of both, thereby making possible less self-oriented perceptions of one's self, others, and the world. This, in Emerson's view, is the only way consciousness can make truly virtuous action possible in a world where true virtue cannot be defined or evoked through one-sided affirmations of freedom or determinism.

Emerson in fact articulated the world view of "Fate" primarily to address an ethical rather than an epistemological concern. As he put it at the very outset of the essay: "To me . . . the question of the times resolved itself into a practical question of the conduct of life. How shall I live?" (Wh, p. 330). To analyze the human consciousness was for him to analyze moral possibilities. To be sure, he believed that the double consciousness enabled people to perceive the world correctly in all its complexity. But he also considered it the only appropriate ethical response to the world he depicted in "Fate." The double consciousness is simultaneously a mode of seeing and a mode of being.[46] It makes possible a way of living through which people can freely struggle both to overcome their limitations and to create the destiny they desire for themselves, while at the same time recognizing and accepting that their lives are being shaped in ways that are beyond their control and comprehension. But the individual must move beyond such recognition and acceptance to will that whatever happens is right and good, both for himself or herself and others, and to rejoice in this rightness and goodness. True virtue is the double consciousness when it evokes, to borrow Cotton Mather's phrase, "a sort of *holy Epicurism*" that is its own reward. In Emerson's words, truly virtuous persons live in joyful harmony with the "breath of will [which] blows eternally through the universe of souls in the direction of the Right and Necessary" (Wh, p. 342); they fully conform to "the Beautiful Necessity" which overrides the human will, "dissolves persons," and "solicits the pure in heart to draw on all its omnipotence" (Wh, p. 352).

Indeed, the redeemed consciousness as Emerson defines it in "Fate" no longer deifies people, as he had maintained in "Nature," but rather awakens and expands their awareness of their "impassable" limits. And yet, in heightening their awareness of human limits, the redeemed consciousness paradoxically discloses how these limitations make self-transcendence possible. Such a double consciousness, Emerson concluded, is the condition for the possibility of becoming fully human in a world which is said to be governed by a deity who transcends all conventional ethical categories. But the price people must pay for this humanization is a continuous antagonism against nature which Emerson never envisioned in "Nature." [47]

The essays examined here thus show Emerson, from the youthful idealism of "Nature" to the hard-nosed determinism of "Fate," enacting the metaphysical drama of the self implied in the debate regarding the rationalistic and Puritan theodicies. He continuously strove to construct a world view which, in its description of the ambiguous interrelationships of good and evil, would provide a rational and morally acceptable explanation for the existence of evil which celebrates those interrelationships. Emerson then used this world view to recommend an ethos—the double consciousness, finally—as the only response suitable to the world he portrayed. The world view makes the ethos seem necessary and right, while the ethos makes the world view seem correct and morally acceptable.

The result, whether intended or not, is that Emerson opened new horizons for re-examining and extending the discussion of the problem of theodicy in ways not previously considered by orthodox and liberal theologians. [48] Such a result certainly suggests that Emerson's long intellectual struggle to overcome the problems inherent in his idealistic vision of nature constitutes one of the most creative encounters in American letters between Puritan orthodoxy and American idealism.

10

Moby-Dick: An Unorthodox Theodicy

MELVILLE AND THE THEOLOGICAL DEBATE

The theological debate had become so vituperative by 1848, three years before the publication of *Moby-Dick*, that it provoked a strong response from the financier Stephen Girard when he donated six million dollars to establish Philadelphia's Girard College for white orphan boys. In his will Girard stipulated "that *no ecclesiastic, missionary, or minister of any sect whatsoever, shall ever hold or exercise any station or duty whatever in the said college; nor shall any such person ever be admitted for any purpose, or as a visitor, within the premises.*" Aside from providing a haven for homeless boys, Girard College was also to be a haven from the religious squabbles of the age—or, as Girard put it, he wanted "to keep the tender minds of the orphans free from the excitements which clashing doctrines and sectarian controversy are so apt to produce." [1]

Melville lived in an age when quarrels about religion rivaled popular discussion of politics, both in the press and in local establishments, quarrels which often evoked much resentment and scorn. His own response to the prevailing religious controversies was no less negative than Girard's. Critics have amply demonstrated, to the point that it is now an interpretive cliché, that for the most part Melville repudiated the orthodoxy he had learned during his upbringing within Dutch Calvinism. [2] Nineteenth-century orthodoxy had grown rigid and harsh. Its cardinal theological category, as Joseph Haroutunian notes, was God's punitive justice which theologians said expressed and glorified His sovereign right to determine human destinies. [3] As the highly respected Calvinistic theologian John Owen declared in 1862, God's "justice ought to be reduced" to His "*supreme, intrinsic, natural* right" to freely punish people in whatever mode or degree is "determined by the standard of the divine right and wisdom."[4] God's vindictive justice, according to this view, rightly exacted Christ's suffering and death as the necessary cost for humankind's innate depravity.[5] "It was for the display of [God's] justice," Owen asserts, "that he set forth Christ as a propitiation. . . . He spared him not, but laid the punishment of us all upon him."[6]

One year before the publication of *Moby-Dick*, R. S. Foster had described the Calvinistic view of the atonement as being

a mere commercial transaction—a thing of bargain and sale—so many souls given for so much blood—so many sins remitted at so much price. The Father agrees to give the Son so many tests at so much price. The Son agrees to suffer such a quantum for the forgiveness of so many sinners. . . . Upon this view of the atonement, it was once wittily and truthfully remarked: 'God must have loved the devil much more than his son, for he gave him the larger portion of the human race without any price, charging his Son full price for the meagre share he allotted to him.'[7]

Foster's analogy demonstrated that long after the Revolutionary era, orthodox theologians were still giving priority "to governmental or legalistic ways of conceiving traditional theological questions."[8] Melville rejected such orthodox formulations as well as their concomitant legalistic moralism which required strict obedience to the moral law as defined in the Old Testament. So stringent was contemporary orthodoxy in requiring such legalistic obedience, so stark were its descriptions of God's vindictive punishment of disobedience, that these emphases seemed to overshadow, if not obliterate, its portrayal of divine mercy and love.[9]

Still, Melville accepted the orthodox notion of innate depravity. The omnipresence of suffering and social injustice, he concluded in "The House-Top: A Night Piece" (1863), "corroborat[ed] Calvin's Creed" about human wickedness.[10] He even went so far as to suggest, in "Hawthorne and His Mosses," that a religious awareness of the pervasiveness and demonism of human depravity is necessary to the creation of enduring art. The "great Art of Telling the Truth," he asserted, emerges from a soul like Hawthorne's which is "shrouded in a blackness, ten times black. . . . Certain it is . . . that this great power of blackness in him derives its force from its appeals to that Calvinistic sense of Innate Depravity and Original Sin, from whose visitations, in some shape or other, no deeply thinking mind is always and wholly free. For, in certain moods, no man can weigh this world without throwing in something, somehow like Original Sin, to strike the uneven balance."[11]

Because he accepted the orthodox notion of innate depravity, he questioned the optimistic view of liberal theologians regarding humankind's capacity for realizing its best spiritual possibilities. Melville may have believed, as Ishmael puts it, that people have an "august dignity," a "democratic dignity which . . . radiates without end from God"; but he also repeatedly dramatized how quickly human experience can erode, corrupt, or ruin this innate dignity (Chapter 26, "Knights and Squires"). Critics have further demonstrated that Melville questioned the liberal belief in a rationally consistent and benevolent moral order that is said to provide a reliable foundation for a coherent moral life. He refused to gloss over the arbitrary inequities, sufferings, and injustices of human existence with theological niceties about a caring, parental God who fully conforms to the ethical dictates of the human conscience; and he pondered the negative implications, for both the liberal and orthodox views, of a world which philosophers and scientists were increasingly describing as being indifferent to traditional moral and religious values or, at best, as one which supported only their relative, not absolute, normative status in the scheme of things.[12] Moreover, his father's financial failures, consequent madness and death, the sudden reversal in his family's social status, his contact with the harsh realities of the sea during a five-year stint on merchant vessels, whalers, and men-of-war—all of these experiences called into question the basic assumptions of theological liberalism.[13] Such experiences suggested to the maturing Melville that the universe is demonic or, at best, indifferent to all moral and religious ideals.

It is clear that these experiences provoked a lifelong inner turmoil which posed for him the same ethical and religious questions which plagued the debate regarding the Puritan and rationalistic theodicies. From *Typee* and *Redburn* through *Moby-Dick* and *Pierre* to *Clarel* and *Billy Budd* he repeatedly worried these questions in ways that contemporary theologians never pursued. All of these works exemplify Melville's gropings toward a synthesis of world view and ethos that could simultaneously do justice to the Puritan notion of innate depravity, the liberal notion of a divine dignity bestowed upon the human personality by a beneficent, just, and democratic God, and the scientific notion that the universe is indifferent to moral and religious ideals. To accomplish this synthesis, Melville had to come to terms with both the Puritan and rationalistic theodicies. Either he could combine them in some symbiotic fashion, as Cooper, Hawthorne, and Emerson had tried to do, or else he could contrive a theodicy based upon different religious premises about the nature of the world. He developed the latter alternative in *Moby-Dick*, as will be argued later, by formulating a world view which is incompatible with a monotheistic framework.

However, it will be helpful to consider *Pierre* first. Although published nearly a year later than *Moby-Dick*, its treatment of the problem of theodicy from within a monotheistic perspective illuminates Melville's unorthodox approach to this problem in *Moby-Dick*. Then, too, there is something of a critical consensus that, in contrast to the all-embracing and synthesizing vision of human experience which characterizes the earlier novel, *Pierre* embodies a fragmenting, even nihilistic, vision.[14] One critic interprets this aspect of the novel as Melville's despairing recognition that the vision of human existence he had earlier articulated in *Moby-Dick* could not resynthesize the accepted cultural unities that were disintegrating as American society approached the brink of civil war.[15] Such a reading of the novel makes it an interesting propaedeutic study for clarifying and understanding how Melville used the debate between orthodox and liberal theologians as an important resource for evaluating his cultural heritage.

PIERRE: "CHRONOMETRICALS AND HOROLOGICALS"

The central theme of *Pierre* is ostensibly the common one of disillusioned idealism. The novel's protagonist, Pierre Glendinning, derives his Christian idealism and liberal rationalism from his upbringing in what appears to be an idyllic rural paradise, a virtual Garden of Eden in which Pierre is oblivious to human corruptness. Pierre believes that God has used the beauty of nature to evoke and sanction the moral impulses of his heart. Hence, when he discovers that his deceased father, a model of exemplary virtue in his family's eyes, had seduced a young French girl and then abandoned her with the child he fathered, Pierre believes that his natural impulse to reclaim Isabel as his sister discloses a divinely sanctioned way to right his father's wrong.[16] The loss of his idealized image of his father which had served as a moral surrogate for God, almost destroys his beliefs in human rectitude and in a benign universal moral order.[17] Despite his disillusionment, however, Pierre is certain that he can confirm the validity of these beliefs through reliance on natural instincts which he believes were implanted in him by God.[18]

Pierre affirms some of the assumptions basic to the rationalistic theodicy: namely, that a caring, benevolent, and paternalistic deity presides over the universe, that He refuses to violate the dictates of the human conscience which He Himself has ordained, that He enforces a reliable moral order in the universe, and that He is an egalitarian judge who equitably rewards human virtue and punishes the wicked. The dictates of his conscience and the intuitions derived from his youthful experience of nature lead him to believe that the world will ultimately answer his inbuilt sense of justice, that his choice of virtue will be rewarded, and that God will finally disclose the workings of justice.

To redeem his father's misdeed, Pierre breaks his engagement to his fiancée, Lucy Tartan, and plans to take Isabel (and Delly Ulver, an unwed mother repudiated by her family at his mother's behest) to New York where they are to live together under the pretense of being married while he pursues his career as a novelist. Upon learning of his pretended marriage to Isabel, his mother disowns him. He moves to New York believing that his cousin, Glendinning Stanly, will render them the much needed assistance Pierre has previously requested in a letter, but Glendinning, influenced by Pierre's mother, coldly denies him any help. Having no other recourse, Pierre rents three squalid rooms. From the outset, the three are reduced to poverty-ridden conditions in a city which becomes for Pierre a metaphor for a universe indifferent to his sense of justice and virtue.

Thoroughly disillusioned by his father's infidelity, his mother's vindictiveness, his cousin's betrayal, and his sudden reversal of fortune, Pierre wonders whether the struggle to uphold his moral ideals is worth the cost, whether these ideals are in fact only arbitrary human creations rather than trustworthy imperatives from God Himself. The narrator notes the danger inherent in such radical doubt about the reliability of any moral values.

In those Hyperborean regions, to which enthusiastic Truth, and earnestness, and independence, will invariably lead a mind fitted by nature for profound and fearless thought, all objects are seen in a dubious, uncertain, and refracting light. Viewed through that rarefied atmosphere the most immemorially admitted maxims of men begin to slide and fluctuate, and finally become wholly inverted; the very heavens themselves being not innocent of producing this confounding effect. . . . It is not for man to follow the trail of truth too far, since by so doing he entirely loses the directing compass of his mind; for arrived at the pole, to whose barrenness only it points, there, the needle indifferently respects all points of the horizon alike. (P. 195)

As Pierre discovers that his rationalistic assumptions cannot accommodate the web-like network of moral ambiguities which gradually encases his life, and as his effort to live in accordance with divine principles only brings misery, he concludes that God supports no distinctions between right and wrong. He therefore rejects all moral commitments outright. The direct consequence is that he and Isabel, who herself reinforces his nihilistic conclusions, consummate their incestuous relationship during their third night in New York.

His experiences prompt him to begin writing a nihilistic novel. And when he learns that his mother bequeathed his entire inheritance to Glendinning before her death, he openly flaunts conventional mores by permitting Lucy—despite the strong protests of her mother, brother, and Glendinning, her new suitor—to live with Isabel and himself as his secret lover. Such defiance of conventional moral values engenders his grandiose sense of being god-like. However, Pierre has a dream which transforms this defiant sense of grandeur into the "repulsively fateful and foreboding" figure of Enceladus, one of the hundred-armed Titans, who because of their unsuccessful rebellion against Zeus, was punished by having his arms cut off and his armless torso buried beneath Mt. Etna. Pierre dreams that he is at the base of the Mount of Titans where he sees an outcropping rock formation that bears a striking resemblance to Enceladus. This figure springs to life to

lead the host of Titans who are charging a precipitous mountain. As he
repeatedly and uselessly hurls his body against it, Pierre cries out the name
of Enceladus, and the figure turns to disclose Pierre's own face on the
Titan's armless trunk. The narrator, through a complicated analysis of in-
cest among the Greek gods, asserts that Pierre's dream dramatizes an inbuilt polarity in human beings between two opposing realms of truth, conventional morality and a divine order that encourages rebellion against
such morality, and suggests that people are to maintain a balanced tension
between the two.[19]

Pierre himself concludes that such a double vision could have a healing
effect on his spiritual malaise. After awakening from his dream, he tells
Lucy and Isabel that, before he can finish his "vile book . . . I must get
on some other element than earth. I have sat on earth's saddle till I am
weary; I must now vault over to the other saddle awhile. Oh, seems to
me, there should be two ceaseless steeds for a bold man to ride,—the Land
and the Sea; and like circus-men we should never dismount, but only be
steadied and rested by leaping from one to the other, while still, side by
side, they both race round the sun. I have been on the Land steed so long,
oh I am dizzy!" (p. 390). Like Emerson, Pierre describes a double consciousness in the image of a circus rider who continues a perpetual balancing act between two contrary perspectives. Such a double consciousness
can participate in both perspectives and accept the legitimate demands of
each, thereby creating a flexible moral stance which accommodates the
moral ambiguities of human experience without insisting that they form
any clear moral or rational pattern.

Pierre, however, is unable to adopt such a stance in the face of a world
which he believes is unjustly and malevolently persecuting him. Upon receiving two letters, one from his publisher denouncing his novel as atheistical and demanding repayment of the money advanced to him, the other
an insulting one from Glendinning and Lucy's brother, he kills his cousin
and is subsequently imprisoned. In jail, the unrepentant Pierre advocates
an inverted version of his earlier rationalistic world view. "Had I been
heartless now, disowned, and spurningly portioned off [Isabel] . . . then
had I been happy through a long eternity in heaven!" Thus settled in his
own mind that he has been victimized by an amoral universe, Pierre mel-
odramatically declares his irrevocable rebellion against it. "Well, be it hell.
I will mold a trumpet of the flames, and . . . breathe back my defiance!
. . . Pierre is neuter now" (p. 403). When Isabel and Lucy visit him, he
cruelly rejects them; after Lucy dies upon his telling her that Isabel is his
sister, Pierre kills himself by drinking poison from a vial concealed, signif-
icantly enough, in Isabel's bosom. Isabel follows suit.

To be sure, Pierre, as the narrator suggests, is the victim of a world that
is antagonistic to his undeniable generosity and genuine idealism. But he
is victimized no less by his misplaced sexual desires, his peculiar scheme

for affirming his responsibility for Isabel, and his desire for absolute moral certitude in a world which seemingly provides two irreconcilable sources of truth, namely, religious ideals and the apparent amoral structure of human experience. In Pierre's career, Melville dramatized what he saw to be the spiritual bankruptcy of the rationalistic theodicy which finally could not help those who accepted its underlying assumptions reconcile themselves to a world that disconfirms their moral expectations. The rationalistic theodicy, Melville concluded, lacked the capacity to synthesize, or hold in tension, the two incompatible realms of truth that are the ultimate principles shaping the fictional world of *Pierre.*

Melville underscores the importance of this tension in Plotinus Plinlimmon's pamphlet, "Chronometricals and Horologicals." This pamphlet sheds no new light on this problem; moreover, it is clotted with unnecessary contradictions. Yet it remains the philosophical heart of the novel. Plinlimmon's extreme conventionalism provides another perspective on the antagonism which Pierre experiences between a principled existence and expediency. The result, in contrast to Natty Bumppo's solution to this same problem, is a series of rationalizations for a self-serving practicality that dismisses commitment to religious or moral ideals as barriers to success in the world of mundane affairs.

Plinlimmon's description of opposing sources of truth is more moderate than Pierre's, since Plinlimmon only affirms the impracticality rather than the untruth of Christian ideals. The pamphlet in fact asserts that God is both the sovereign ruler over the universe and the indisputable source of ultimate values. He calls God "the great Greenwich hill and tower," and likens Christ to a chronometer which, because accurately adjusted to God, gives "Heaven's own truth" everywhere. The teachings of Christ reflect chronometrical time as established at Greenwich, whereas "the actual, practical relations between human beings, the working principles by which they really live, are compared to horological time—that shown by clocks and watches on any given part of the earth's surface, and observed and accepted there."[20] Such "a heavenly soul" has "an infallible instinct" which "knows, that the monitor [it has for intuiting right and wrong] can not be wrong in itself" (p. 247). Hence "the chronometric soul, if in this world true to its great Greenwich in the other, will always, in its so-called intuitions of right and wrong, be contradicting the mere local standards and watch-maker's brains of this earth" (p. 245); it must commit "a sort of suicide as to the practical things of this world" (p. 247). There is in Plinlimmon's view no acceptable middle ground between the requirements of God and those of the practical life.

Like Pierre, he resolves this dilemma by repudiating all commitments to divine principles, though for entirely different reasons. No one, he argues, can follow their dictates without finally violating them. Only Christ was able to live the life of "heavenly time upon the earth" because he was sinless. All other people are incurably wicked and their depravity inevitably corrupts their efforts to realize divine principles. The frequent result is "strange, *unique* follies and sins, unimagined before," though Plinlimmon fails to give examples (p. 246).[21] Legal and moral codes have been established in order to protect society against any such eruption of this potentially demonic character of the religious life. They assure people that, when religion threatens the status quo (and one suspects this is what Plinlimmon means by the demonism of religion), such threats can be rightfully contained, even stifled, through morally and legally justified means.

Plinlimmon concludes that the best precaution against this supposed dangerous tendency of religious values is to discard them and, instead, adopt a "virtuous expediency" which he maintains will curb the sinful impulses of human nature. Plinlimmon summarizes his solution in the contention that people can make "certain minor self-renunciations . . . but [they] must by no means make a complete unconditional sacrifice of [themselves] in behalf of any other being, or any cause, or any conceit. (For, does aught else completely and unconditionally sacrifice itself for [them]?)" The supreme rationalization for this gospel of moderation is Plinlimmon's belief that striving to live by chronometrical standards is "positively wrong" because realizing them would make the individual "an angel, a chronometer"—in short, a Christ—"whereas he is a man and a horologe" (p. 248). However, despite his viewing the practice of Christian ideals as an act of hubris, he never questions their truth.

Nor does he reject the Christian belief that a sovereign God beneficently controls the world. He observes that the felt discrepancy between the ways of the world and the ways of heaven give rise to the "infidel idea" that God "is not the Lord of this [world]" (p. 247)—or if He is, that such a contradictory world points not to a beneficent but to a demonic deity. Plinlimmon believes that his Greenwich analogy solves this problem. Discrepancies in time, he asserts, inevitably arise between meridians only because the earth rotates around a stationary sun. These differing times all correspond to Greenwich time in their common attempt to tell accurately when it is noon, sunset, or midnight within their respective meridians. Because these divergencies in time are analogous to conflicts of values, he envisions such conflicts as deriving solely from their "meridian correspondence" with God. Every meridian, though differing from the others, has its own correct expression of Greenwich time which reflects its particular circumstances. By "their very contradictions they are made to correspond" to "the central Greenwich" where God dwells (pp. 247, 246). Believing that he has demonstrated that no discrepancy exists between "God's truth" and "man's truth" (and ignoring the relativity of values implied in his analogy), Plinlimmon concludes that arguments for the existence of a demonic deity are untenable.

It is difficult to determine whether Plinlimmon is primarily arguing for the impracticality of religious values that remain valid for him, for the necessity to reject commitment to religious values because human sinfulness can pervert that commitment, for the ultimate "correspondence" between "God's truth" and "man's truth," or for the existence of a benevolent deity. The first and last arguments imply a contradiction between divine and human values that is denied in the third argument. The second argument is based upon an appeal to the Puritan notion of innate depravity that is not part of the other three arguments. Furthermore, he contradicts this emphasis upon an innate corruptness by maintaining that commitment to a self-serving "expediency" will somehow beneficently neutralize this depravity. The first argument rejects religious values because they are impractical while in the second argument Plinlimmon repudiates religious commitments because they can be put to perverse uses. And all four arguments maintain the validity of religious ideals without ever considering the question of why God would make them authoritative for humankind and yet, as Plinlimmon's solution suggests, make them so difficult to realize that rejecting them seems the only logical response.

Several other questions remain unanswered. If, in fact, as he asserts in his third argument, there is actually a correspondence between "God's truth" and "man's truth," then why even argue for a "virtuous expediency" in the first place? Adherence to "man's truth" would automatically be a realization of divine principles. Moreover, if all values correspond with "God's truth," why then are they so contradictory? Plinlimmon himself assumes in his last argument that differing value systems contravene each other, although he had earlier postulated their correspondence with "the central Greenwich." If God is beneficent, as Plinlimmon argues, why then does He create a world of diametrically opposed values which bring people into murderous conflict? Why would a beneficent God require people to realize divine principles if doing so constitutes an act of hubris? If, as he argues, God is the source of all ultimate values, how are we then to deal with the relativistic implications of his analogy for moral and religious belief? And finally, even if divine principles are valid for human existence, as all of his arguments assume, why even stress this validity (as he repeatedly does) when his notion of "virtuous expediency" already makes any concern for knowing these ideals superfluous?

These unanswered questions and contradictions point to the maze of dead ends created by a monotheistic approach to the problem of evil.[22] They at best make Plinlimmon's pamphlet a confused and confusing statement of Pierre's dilemma from the perspective of a conventional morality which can see nothing more important in human experience than providing for its own personal comfort, protection, and gain. As the narrator observes, the pamphlet "seems more the excellently illustrated re-statement of a problem, than the solution itself" (p. 243).

In *Pierre*, Melville explores many of the issues which remained a basic source of theological controversy during the first half of the nineteenth century. But these diverse issues are disconnected in *Pierre*, like abandoned threads torn loose from some designful fabric, thereby destroying any sense of rational and moral coherence.[23] This aspect of *Pierre* is even more noticeable when it is compared with its immediate predecessor, *Moby-Dick*, in which Melville's treatment of these issues conveys a sense of integration lacking in the later novel. One reason for this difference is that Melville explores the problems intrinsic to Plinlimmon's pamphlet through the narrative structure of the hunt or quest. This structuring device creates a context within which these problems attain the kind of living urgency that must come to terms with the moral and spiritual tensions they generate— tensions which Ishmael transforms into a unified mode of experiencing the world. The narrational difference between *Pierre* and *Moby-Dick* primarily lies in the Ishmaelean consciousness.

MOBY-DICK: THE PROBLEM OF THEODICY

Most major American writers of the nineteenth century understood American culture in terms of the Judeo-Christian tradition. Like their theological predecessors, such writers as James Fenimore Cooper, Henry David Thoreau, Ralph Waldo Emerson, Nathaniel Hawthorne, Mark Twain, Walt Whitman, and Emily Dickinson, for example, never questioned the assumption that the moral and religious implications of American democracy were to be formulated and evaluated in terms of Christian monotheism. Only one literary figure of the nineteenth century, Herman Melville, abandons this assumption. Or more accurately, it is Ishmael, the narrator of *Moby-Dick*, who explores how American democracy, with its growing diversity of cultural, moral, and religious values, gives rise to a pluralistic vision of the universe which redefines the problem of theodicy.

At one level this novel is a mediation on the problem of theodicy within a monotheistic framework. It is perhaps this dimension of the novel which led Conrad Aiken to describe it as "the final and perfect finial to the Puritan's desperate three-century-long struggle with the problem of evil."[24] But this way of viewing the novel is misleading since, within its complex fictional universe, a monotheistic theodicy, as Thomas Herbert has demonstrated, no longer provides Ishmael an adequate religious explanation for the disparate multiplicity of his experience.[25] Ishmael's whaling voyage gives rise to a vision of a world shaped by diverse and contrary forces which arbitrarily determine human destinies. Herbert, in defining this aspect of the novel, concludes that *Moby-Dick* represents Melville's complete dismantling of the inherited theocentric world view of Christianity.[26]

To describe the novel this way, however, overlooks its equally important constructive aspect, for Melville also formulated an alternative to the Puritan and rationalistic theodicies which is predicated on non-monotheistic assumptions.[27] Rather than dismantling a Christian theocentrism, he incorporated it into a larger pluralistic vision of the universe which reveals both the limitations and possibilities of a monotheistic outlook for humanizing people. In the Ishmaelean consciousness, Melville seeks to define the most humanizing response to a pluralistic universe and, having done this, to create a new synthesis of world view and ethos. Unorthodox as this synthesis is, Melville nevertheless wants to demonstrate through the quality of the Ishmaelean consciousness that a pluralistic vision of the universe is morally preferable to that advocated by the Puritan and rationalistic theodicies. Hence *Moby-Dick* is not the capstone of Puritan and rationalistic theodicy but rather the exploration of an unorthodox theodicy as a meaningful possibility for religious belief.

Melville thus moved beyond the established conventions of the theological debate regarding the Puritan and rationalistic theodicies. The stalemate in this controversy represented, in his view, the bankruptcy of monotheistic categories for incorporating, or at least adjusting to, the complexities of his contemporary world. It was an age of transition, both in Europe and America, from the inherited theocentric vision of Christianity to more secular and scientifically oriented frameworks.[28] Melville therefore set out in *Moby-Dick* to recast the theological debate into an appropriate aesthetic structure through which he could explore the kinds of dilemmas his age posed for monotheistic renderings of the world, the moral life, and the problem of theodicy. He used the opposing assumptions of the theological controversy—assumptions that were the basis of his own inner conflicts— to define the conflicts that formed the growing edge of his cultural heritage. By seeking to demonstrate that neither set of assumptions provided a reliable metaphysical outlook that could serve as the foundation for the moral life, that neither formulated a synthesis of world view and ethos which could make rational or moral sense of the ambiguities of human experience, and that such a situation issued in a sense of moral and religious incertitude, Melville plumbed the deepest spiritual problems of his age. In this sense, *Moby-Dick* dramatizes the religious dynamics of the split cultural mindset of his age, and Ishmael's narrative career provides a new way to think about and understand these dynamics that moves beyond the confines of the theological conventions established by the debate about the Puritan and rationalistic theodicies.

Two elements in Melville's treatment of the problem of theodicy in this novel deserve immediate consideration; namely, the nature of Moby Dick and Father Mapple's sermon. Both pose special difficulties for any interpretation of *Moby-Dick.* The immense body of critical literature on this novel represents a broad spectrum of response to Moby Dick. It ranges from the one extreme of viewing him as "a totality of meaningless impressions, a something that is nothing, a symbol of the void at the center of material reality"[29] to the other extreme of viewing him as representative of some sort of deity—the suffering God of the New Testament,[30] the retributive God of the Old Testament,[31] the Calvinist God,[32] a nature deity,[33] or a demonic god who exercises a "sovereign tyranny" of "infinite malice" over the universe.[34] Both kinds of responses are problematical, the former because Ishmael himself takes quite another view of the matter, the latter because it identifies one aspect of creation with God—an identification which Ishmael (and by implication Melville) refuses to make.

Several elements in Ishmael's narrative clearly indicate his explicit rejection of the notion that Moby Dick symbolizes some form of deity. His discussions of the habits which make the whale predictable and the split vision which accounts for its unpredictable behavior, his narrations of both the final three days of the chase and the Town-Ho's story to some priests in Lima several years later, his satirical treatment of Gabriel's conception of Moby Dick as the Shaker God, his own ambiguous responses to Moby Dick's seeming malice (even though he notes that the whale's assaults are provoked by human predators), and his recurring reminders that the whale itself, no less than the whalers, is at the mercy of "the masterless ocean [which] overruns the globe" (p. 363)[35]—all of these constitute Ishmael's deliberate efforts to demythologize any attempt to see in Moby Dick a symbol for deity, good or bad.[36] Moby Dick is, in Ishmael's view, a mammal—a gloriously beautiful and graceful mammal, a majestic force which evokes a plethora of meanings commensurate with the ambiguities of nature—but nevertheless a mammal for all that.[37]

The second element that complicates Ishmael's treatment of the problem of theodicy is Father Mapple's sermon. Its heroic admonitions of uncompromising loyalty to God, coming as they do just prior to Ishmael's sailing on the Pequod have been accepted by some as "the moral presuppositions by which we are to judge the speeches of Ahab and the rest."[38] However, others see in the sermon's "hyperbolic" style Melville's comical satire on values which have no socially redemptive import. This satire is said to be reinforced by the novel's land-sea dichotomy which contrasts the "pious" or "sentimental" Christianity of Father Mapple's sermon given on land with the "realism" of Fleece's "more pragmatic sermon" on sea.[39] Such a presentation of Father Mapple's sermon, according to this argument, implies that Melville never intended it to be a normative source of moral and religious values for evaluating the characters. At best it is only a sympathetic parody of the Puritan tradition. Neither of these views, however, seriously treats the most problematic aspect of Father Mapple's sermon, namely, his basic contention that obedience to God's dictates requires that people abandon their adherence to conventional moral norms of behavior—a contention that Plinlimmon believed gave religious commitment demonic potentialities.

To illustrate the radical nature of such obedience, Father Mapple turns to the story of Jonah. He imagines the inner struggle Jonah might have experienced upon fleeing from God when He commanded him to carry the message of salvation to the pagan Ninevites.[40] Jonah is caught between the dictates of his religious tradition—a tradition which maintained that God had made His covenant of salvation only with the Hebrew people—and the new dictates of God's command to share this covenant of salvation with pagans. To obey God's command requires that he repudiate his sense of self shaped by traditional Hebrew religious values. As Father Mapple succinctly puts it: "If we obey God, we must disobey ourselves; and it is this disobeying ourselves wherein the hardness of obeying God exists" (p. 72). The lesson which Father Mapple finally draws from Jonah's encounter with an implacable deity who denies Jonah any familiarity with Him is that obedience to such a God is incompatible with adherence to the religious and moral norms shaping one's society.[41] This is not Plinlimmon's "virtuous expediency," but rather a conception of moral integrity which, like that advocated by Natty Bumppo, is based upon a sovereign deity whose demands are to be unquestionably obeyed regardless of the consequences to one's self. In this sermon Father Mapple, unlike his Puritan predecessors, carries the Puritan notion of a divine teleological suspension of the ethical to its logical extreme by maintaining that God chooses people to carry out His redemptive purposes in ways that make conventional morality a temptation to disobey Him.

His list of seven woes must be seen in this light, for they give trenchant expression to the religious immoderation Father Mapple's God requires for full obedience to Him.[42] Among these is God's radical demand, one that Roger Williams had voiced for the early American Puritans, that people subsume their quest for salvation to their commitment to the truth. "Woe to him," says Father Mapple, "who would not be true, even though to be false were salvation" (p. 80). Such a radical demand expresses the kind of uncompromising religious heroism which, as the Puritan tradition exacted, demands that people accept eternal damnation if God requires it to realize His redemptive purposes. It is a double-edged principle, however, for the question arises—as it does in Plinlimmon's pamphlet—how such a religious hero avoids becoming demonic in the name of God. To put the matter another way, Father Mapple's definition of being "true" provides a religious justification for the unethical behavior of both the elect and those who believe that God has predestined them to eternal damnation. The latter possibility is clearly dramatized in Ahab's career. When viewed within the larger context of the novel's dramatic action, Father Mapple's sermon becomes a problematic statement of Puritan ideals, not because the ideals themselves are said to be false but because their requirements are fulfilled no less by Ahab than by Jonah, who faces the unrelenting pressure of God's command to preach to the Ninevites.

Ahab is a religious hero of those whose experience of the world disconfirms their ethical expectations. Such a universe, in Ahab's view, is demonic. He believes that God has maliciously singled him out to torture him with inexplicable and unbearable suffering. This belief ostensibly has its origins in the loss of his leg to Moby Dick and is further intensified when he falls one evening and his whalebone leg inflicts a painful groin injury. But his suppressed anger at being raised an orphan (his widowed mother having died when he was one year old) as well as his aggrieved sense of being old,[43] of having been remorselessly and unwillingly driven to hunt whales for forty years, "more a demon than a man" as he engages in the "strife of the chase," have already established a psychological history that contributes to that wracking sense of injustice and grievance against God which he expresses through his vindictive hatred of Moby Dick (pp. 683–84). "The White Whale swam before him as the monomaniac incarnation of all those malicious agencies which some deep men feel eating in them, till they are left living on with half a heart and half a lung. . . . all evil, to crazy Ahab, were visibly personified, and made practically assailable in Moby Dick. He piled upon the whale's white hump the sum of all the general rage and hate felt by his whole race from Adam down; and then, as if his chest had been a mortar, he burst his hot heart's shell upon it" (pp. 246–47). Ahab tersely expresses this obsessive sense of evil in his Hamlet-like soliloquy to a whale's decapitated head: "Thou saw'st the murdered mate when tossed by pirates from the midnight deck . . . and his murderers still sailed on unharmed. . . . O Head! thou has seen enough to make an infidel of Abraham, and not one syllable is thine" (p. 406). He voices this same sense of moral outrage when he proclaims "Were I the wind, I'd blow no more on such a wicked, miserable world. I'd crawl somewhere to a cave, and slink there" (p. 554).

Ahab rebels against such a universe by adopting what he considers its amoral standards. His self-destruction, rather than confirming the existence of a reliable universal moral order, reflects his rigid adherence to the logic of his vision of a demonic world.[44] It is a vision which greatly constructs his possibilities even as it encourages his belief that a heroic rebellion against human limitations makes life acceptable, or at least more tolerable than would any other response. Ahab's dilemma is that in accepting the logic of this vision he also wishes to repudiate it, but believes there is no other way to define or preserve his sense of human dignity.

Ahab is the democratic conscience *par excellence*—though certainly he is, in his tyranny over the crew, the antithesis of the ideal authority in a democratic society. In Job-like fashion, he accuses God of being indifferent, even hostile, to the democratic ideals of justice, equitableness, and human dignity. He demands that "the gods . . . honorably speak outright" to people and not "give an old wives' darkling hint" (p. 544). And, as soon as he boards the *Pequod* after being thrown into the water while chasing a whale, Ahab challenges the gods to be more equitable in their treatment of human beings. "I laugh and hoot at ye, ye cricket-players, ye pugilists, ye deaf Burkes and blinded Bendigoes! . . . ye've knocked me down, and I am up again; but ye have run and hidden. . . . Come, Ahab's compliments to ye; come and see if ye can swerve me. Swerve me? ye cannot swerve me, else ye swerve yourselves! Man has ye there" (p. 166). Ahab not only requires that God treat humankind in accordance with democratic ideals; he also seeks redress for the inequities of human existence. As Ishmael puts it, he forms the *Pequod*'s crew into an "Anacharsis Clootz deputation" which is "to lay [his and] the world's grievances" before God (p. 166).

Like Chauncy and Channing, Ahab asserts that the human self has been endowed with an inviolable dignity, and that it has the right to require an impeachable justice of the deity worshipped as well as to withhold submission to mere power which transgresses the ethical limits established by the democratic conscience. Ahab proclaims these rights during the storm scene as he addresses the flaming masts while holding the chains to the lightning rods: "In the midst of the personified impersonal, a personality stands here. Though but a point at best; whencesoe'er I came; wheresoe'er I go; yet while I earthly live, the queenly personality lives in me, and feels her royal rights." But these "royal rights," he continues, will give way to worshipful submission under stipulated conditions: "Come in thy lowest form of love, and I will kneel and kiss thee; but . . . come as mere supernal power; and . . . there's that in here that still remains indifferent" (pp. 641–42). Ahab thus affirms the basic assumptions of the rationalistic theodicy while acting out in destructive ways his disillusionment with a world that does not confirm them.

Ahab's defiance of what he considers a demonic deity is further complicated by his sense of damnation. When the lookout disrupts his soliloquy to the whale's head, announcing that an oncoming ship heralds wind, Ahab characteristically forms this situation into an analogy for his own inner struggles. "That lively cry upon this deadly calm might almost convert a better man. . . . Would now St. Paul would come along the way, and to my breezelessness bring his breeze. O Nature, and O soul of man! how far beyond all utterance are your linked analogies!" (p. 406). Ahab has a genuine desire for faith despite his belief that God has consigned him to damnation, a belief which he had earlier expressed after the diabolical ritual in which he bound the crew to his vindictive pursuit of Moby Dick: "Gifted with the high perception, I lack the low, enjoying power; damned, most subtly and most malignantly! damned in the midst of Paradise!" (p. 226). He later laments this sense of damnation as he meditates upon his obsessive pursuit of Moby Dick. "What is it, what nameless, inscrutable unearthly thing is it, what cozening, hidden lord and master, and cruel, remorseless emperor commands me; that against all natural lovings and longings, I so keep pushing, and crowding, and jamming myself on all the time; recklessly making me ready to do what in my own proper, natural heart, I durst not so much as dare? Is Ahab, Ahab? Is it I, God or who, that lifts this arm?" (p. 685). At just the critical moment when Ahab seems prepared for reasons of the "heart" to abandon his quest, he once again appeals to a life of acute suffering, obsessions, and mental anguish to reaffirm his vision of an amoral universe. After observing that preordained laws inexorably shape both inanimate matter and all forms of life, that even the sun and stars move according to God's established natural laws, Ahab concludes that his own inner necessities conform to preordained laws he must unquestioningly obey regardless of the consequences to himself. Because he believes the world is governed by mechanistic and impersonal natural laws and that God has predestined his demonic traits, his damnation, and his compulsive quest for Moby Dick, he finally declares himself to be "Fate's lieutenant."

But Ahab undermines the moral validity of his heroic rebellion. Even though he demands that God be just and humane in His dealings with humankind, Ahab exempts himself from such strictures. His deliberate insensitivity to the suffering of Pip and Captain Gardiner and to the crew's fate expresses the very cruelty and injustice he condemns in God. This callousness further reflects the kind of presumptuous arrogance that characterizes his belief that only he can forgive himself for rejecting Captain Gardiner's plea to join him in his quest for his son: "I will not do it. Even now I lose time. Good bye, good bye, God bless ye man, and may I forgive myself, but I must go" (p. 671). Ahab defies God in the name of those very ethical values which he himself must suspend in order to maintain his defiance. He justifies this inhumanity to others as the tragic price he must pay to preserve the integrity of his defiance. To be damned, according to Ahab's rendering of the Puritan doctrine of predestination, requires him to live out this damnation to the hilt as an act of obedience to the irrevocable will of God.[45] Like Pierre, he repudiates all moral distinctions when he declares that his "right worship is defiance" (p. 641). Whether or not the universe is actually demonic as Ahab envisions it, there evolves from Ahab's own monomaniacal commitment to this vision of the world an inexorably dehumanizing logic which generates a way of life that makes this vision believable to him.

Ahab's career thus demonstrates that the belief in one's damnation can evoke its own radical form of obedience to God which fulfills the demands of Father Mapple's sermon. Father Mapple's Puritan predecessors had sought to avoid this conclusion by emphasizing that living the moral life, though one had not yet experienced conversion, might nevertheless be the basis for such a conversion experience. However, Ahab, like Father Mapple, simply extends the Puritan doctrine of humiliation to its logical conclusion: that God not only requires the eternally damned to accept their fate unquestioningly but may also command them to act in ways that violate conventional moral and religious values.

Melville thus dramatizes the paradox in the theological controversy regarding what constitutes an appropriate ethos within the egalitarian context of American democracy. In the early 1800s, orthodox Calvinists still described this ethos in terms of the doctrine of humiliation; liberal theologians, viewing the Calvinistic doctrines of humiliation, predestination, and God's sovereignty as denying people all moral agency, described it in terms of human freedom and inalienable rights accorded them by God. In Ahab's self-assertion of the dignity and rights of his "queenly personality," Melville shows the demonic implications of the liberal ethos. No less demonic in its consequences is his rigid adherence to the impersonal logic dictated by the Calvinistic doctrine of predestination, a doctrine which he uses to support the scientific view of a mechanistic universe inexorably shaped by impersonal natural laws. His career gives credence to both Beecher's and Channing's fears that pursuing the rational and moral implications of God's justice from a human perspective leads to a disillusioned vision of a malevolent deity which evokes, or justifies, amoral behavior. It also suggests—as does Pierre's career—that in the face of such disillusionment the rationalistic theodicy provides no alternative for preserving its belief in the integrity and autonomy of the human personality other than Ahab's mad rebellion against such a universe or Starbuck's willful blindness to the existence of evil.

Through Ahab, then, Melville describes the basic cultural predicament facing Americans during the first half of the nineteenth century. If we take seriously the claims of Max Weber, Peter Berger, and Mary Douglas about the social implications of the problem of theodicy, *Moby-Dick* can be viewed as Melville's attempt to demonstrate that the two syntheses of world view and ethos which the Puritan and rationalistic theodicies articulated were losing their authoritative hold as representations of reality because they could neither accommodate the tensions of the contemporary social structure nor create a reliable foundation for the moral life from the newly emerging scientific world view. Whatever ultimate standard of virtue, if any, might emerge from this situation for creating a new synthesis of world view and ethos, Melville believed that it could not be defined in terms of the culturally prescribed modes of experience advocated by the Puritan and rationalistic theodicies.[46] Melville's basic insight is that when the modes of experiencing the world described by the inherited theological debate are the primary shapers of human consciousness, Ahab's dilemma must be recognized as expressing not only a cultural hiatus between competing world views, but also a logical resolution of that hiatus for which American culture had, as yet, provided no alternative solution.

Starbuck embodies this dilemma no less than Ahab. This spokesman for a moderate rationalistic pietism stands in stark contrast to Father Mapple's radical vision of Christian obedience. He is also the polar opposite of Ahab. Whereas Ahab seeks to understand himself in all his complexity,

Starbuck demonstrates little concern for gaining self-understanding, even denies his darker impulses. Ahab's obsession with the inequities of human existence relentlessly impels him to pursue disturbing questions about the moral structure of the universe to their logical conclusion, whereas Starbuck, when himself on the brink of broaching such questions, willfully represses them. Ahab is a domineering, self-willed, and strife-ridden person who acknowledges no limitations on his actions, while Starbuck, humane and self-controlled, refuses to commit any unethical action unless he clearly knows that God sanctions it. He embodies the liberal beliefs that God responds to the demands of the human conscience and that God will unambiguously disclose to him, through nature and his own religious insight, those dictates that are to govern his behavior. His God, like that of the rationalistic theodicy, mirrors the idealized image of a caring parent who will exact of his children nothing more than what is suitable to their limited understandings.

However, in spite of his humaneness and scrupulous piety, Starbuck is no match for the maddened Ahab. When Ahab announces that he is commandeering the *Pequod* for his vindictive pursuit of Moby Dick, Starbuck, as the ship's first mate, not only has the responsibility for thwarting Ahab's purpose but also the legal authority to organize the crew against Ahab and, if necessary, even to wrest command from him. But Ahab anticipates Starbuck's possible resistance. He performs a diabolical ritual in which the crew pledges to join his quest, thereby making it difficult, if not impossible, for Starbuck to unite the crew against him. Whether because he fears that opposing Ahab would provoke the crew's opposition to himself or because he fears Ahab—or both—Starbuck remains silent. Later, he admits that Ahab has successfully reduced him to obedience: "I plainly see my miserable office,—to obey, rebelling; and worse yet, to hate with touch of pity! For in his eyes I read some lurid woe would shrivel me up, had I it." He rationalizes his non-resistance through his belief that God will eventually "wedge aside" Ahab's "heaven-insulting purpose" and that under no circumstances should he violate his humanitarian impulses (p. 228). "O life! 'tis in an hour like this, with soul beat down and held to knowledge,—as wild, untutored things are forced to feed—Oh, life! 'tis not me! that horror's out of me! and with the soft feeling of the human in me, yet will I try to fight ye, ye grim, phantom futures! Stand by me, hold me, bind me, O ye blessed influences" (p. 229). Disturbed by this reminder of his own darker recesses, he pushes it aside.

He also pushes aside the troubling questions about God which assail him during his meditations on the nature of human existence. When Starbuck looks on the doubloon, for example, he articulates a religious vision in which Jesus Christ, "the son of Righteousness," offers his solace during the day, while at nighttime, when "we would fain snatch some sweet solace from him, we gaze for him in vain!" Though he accepts this vision of life, he rejects its negative inferences about the nature of God by quickly turning away from the coin "lest Truth shake [him] falsely" (p. 551–52). His repudiation of such inferences is even more explicit as he meditates on the same golden sea which evokes a quite different meditation from Ishmael as narrator:[47] "Loveliness unfathomable, as ever lover saw in his young bride's eye!—Tell me not of thy teeth-tiered sharks, and thy kidnapping cannibal ways. Let faith oust fact; let fancy oust memory; I look deep down and do believe" (p. 624). He refuses to face either the predatory aspects of nature or the memory of his father's "doom" and "the torn limbs of his brother," both of whom were lost "in the bottomless deeps" (p. 159).

It is precisely this kind of willfully blind faith, with its refusal to come to terms with the worst aspects of both nature and human nature, which makes Starbuck morally incapable of dealing with the "spiritual terrors" of Ahab's demonic madness (p. 159). It is not simply Ahab's probable maniacal resistance to any usurpation of his power that Starbuck fears. More terrifying to him is Ahab's probable response (as Starbuck imagines it) to being held captive for the remainder of the voyage. "Say he were pinioned even, knotted all over with ropes and hawsers; chained down to ring-bolts on this cabin floor; he would be more hideous than a caged tiger, then. I could not endure the sight; could not possibly fly his howlings; all comfort, sleep itself, inestimable reason would leave me on the long intolerable voyage" (p. 651). Facing this imagined prospect, Starbuck considers murdering Ahab, believing it to be his only means to stop him. It is "an evil thought," according to Ishmael, "but so blent with its neutral or good accompaniments that for the instant he hardly knew it for itself" (p. 650). While holding a musket just outside Ahab's door Starbuck, recalling that Ahab had previously threatened to shoot him, is convinced that Ahab will stop short of nothing, not even the crew's destruction, to gain revenge on Moby Dick. By killing Ahab he could save the crew from such a fate.

Starbuck questions his impulse to murder Ahab, wondering whether it is a demonic urge or the prompting of divine justice. Nor is Ishmael's description of Starbuck's decision any less ambiguous. "The yet levelled musket shook like a drunkard's arm against the panel; Starbuck seemed wrestling with an angel; but turning from the door," he replaces the musket and returns to the deck (p. 652). It is unclear whether Ishmael envisions the angel as trying to prevent or assist the murder. What is clear, however, is that Starbuck considers this alternative because he fears the spiritual extremes of Ahab's madness. Starbuck's dilemma is that, unable to find any rational means for convincing Ahab to abandon his pursuit of Moby Dick and perceiving no clear divine dictates for defining what he should do, he can find no ethical justification for confronting Ahab, no matter how urgent the situation, when such a confrontation might result in injury to himself, Ahab, or others. Starbuck demands absolute certitudes in a world that yields only moral ambiguities.

But even knowing that his impulse to kill Ahab came from God would not resolve Starbuck's dilemma. He questions whether killing Ahab, even at God's behest, would not make him a murderer who must face eternal damnation for his crime. Melville identifies in Starbuck's career a problem intrinsic to the rationalistic theodicy: namely, that it could not incorporate those morally ambiguous situations which contradicted its beliefs that God clearly manifested the ways of divine justice and that the human conscience provided clear intuitions of divine truth.

The liberal imagination refused to imagine a world—the world, say, of Father Mapple's sermon—wherein God would deliberately require people to act in ways that would violate conventional morality, entail their destruction or the destruction of others, or even jeopardize their salvation.[48] From the Puritan perspective, this was either sheer blindness to the nature of things or a failure of nerve; from Melville's perspective, it was a failure of imagination. This failure, in Starbuck's case, embodies the fear of seeking to imagine the tormented innerness of an Ahab, a failure which reinforces, if not gives rise to, his religious justifications for relying on God rather than himself to deter Ahab from his quest.

During the third day of the chase, when Ahab demonstrates that he will let nothing hinder his pursuit of Moby Dick, Starbuck's sense of doom moves him too late to acknowledge his personal responsibility: "I misdoubt me that I disobey my God in obeying Ahab" (p. 711). Rather than taking matters into his own hands, however, Starbuck once again appeals to God to turn Ahab away from his vindictive quest. When no such divine intervention occurs, Starbuck voices his deep sense of betrayal as Moby Dick bears down upon the *Pequod*: "Is this the end of my bursting prayers? all my life-long fidelities?" (p. 719). The question remains whether Starbuck should have put aside his religious and moral scruples and killed Ahab were it the only way to stop him. But certainly there is no question that Starbuck's unswerving adherence to his humanitarian values makes him an ineffectual opponent to Ahab's demonic tyranny. As Ishmael baldly puts it: "Here, then, was this grey-headed, ungodly man, chasing with curses a Job's whale round the world, at the head of a crew, too, chiefly made up of mongrel renegades, and castaways, and cannibals—morally enfeebled also, by the incompetence of mere unaided virtue or rightmindedness in Starbuck, the invulnerable jollity of indifference and recklessness in Stubb, and the pervading mediocrity in Flask" (p. 251). This description expresses Ishmael's clearest repudiation of any romanticized conception of either the *Pequod*'s crew or Ahab's quest.

But Ishmael is no less critical of his own participation in Ahab's scheme. Like the rest of the crew, he finds himself easily swayed and dominated by Ahab's forceful personality; like them, he too, at least for part of the voyage, joins Ahab's quest for Moby Dick. Yet this involvement in Ahab's career radically transforms Ishmael's moral and religious consciousness. *Moby-Dick* in part dramatizes Ishmael's self-critical journey from being a disillusioned rationalistic Christian (a disillusionment which destroys Pierre) through the virtual death of his old self to the creation of a new mode of consciousness commensurate with the moral complexities of his whaling experience. Indeed, the narrative itself is this new mode of consciousness imaginatively rendering the world as the older Ishmael now views it.

This metaphysical thrust of Ishmael's narrative has been explained in a variety of ways. David Minter, for example, argues that it stems from Ishmael's attempt to interpret a problematical world in terms of Ahab's heroic failure.[49] Like many other American novels, *Moby-Dick* embodies a narrative strategy which he roughly characterizes as that situation wherein a highly imaginative narrator seeks to understand why a heroic innocent fails to realize his idealized vision of life. He calls this narrative form "the interpreted design," and designates the heroic innocent in *The Blithedale Romance, The Great Gatsby,* and *Absalom, Absalom!* as "the man of action" and the narrator as "the man of interpretation."[50] This narrative strategy is based upon

the story of a man dedicated to realizing a grand design, a man of action who gives himself to erecting a magnificent edifice, establishing a new dynasty, or attaining a high office. By asserting himself, the man of design seeks to shape his world according to a vision or model; he seeks to make something that corresponds to his notion of what will suffice. His failure to do precisely what he intends to do provides the core of the interpreted design. . . . The man of interpretation seeks . . . to master a story that, in its outline, deeply threatens not simply faith in design, in careful planning and concerted devotion as means of assuring success, but even more faith in all intentional endeavors, including his own deliberate effort at understanding.[51]

Ishmael, in this view, is driven to speculate on the moral structure of the universe in order to explain Ahab's heroic failure.[52]

Paul Brodtkorb maintains through his phenomenological analysis of the Ishmaelean consciousness that *Moby-Dick* is Ishmael's attempt to prove, both to himself and to others, that the universe he experienced during the whaling voyage "is totally coherent, even if it occasionally seems not to be."[53] But this coherence is an aesthetic rather than a moral one. The novel, he contends, presents a morally incoherent universe from which Ishmael is unable to extract any basis for the ordering of his moral life. Hence Ishmael accepts artistic creation—the imaginative rendering of his experience—as the only appropriate response to such a world.[54] "One might summarize the self of the Ishmaelean narrator," Brodtkorb concludes, "as that of an artist who has constructed, as Melville's contemporary Flaubert hoped to, a highly personalized, stylized work: a something which creates

Ishmael's own ambivalent self for him and for us, and gives its peculiarly problematic existence to his world." Ishmael is here presented as a solipsist who, in a world of experienced pluralistic meanings, withdraws into himself "to create [through his narrative] his own world of meanings."[55]

A. D. Van Nostrand, whose interpretation of *Moby-Dick* prefigures the structural principle of the interpreted design formulated by David Minter, maintains that Ishmael, in meditating upon Ahab's tragic destruction of himself and his crew, must "generate a cosmos to explain it."[56] But Ishmael does "not re-create [his] given world"; he creates it.[57] Like Brodtkorb, Van Nostrand concludes that there is no adequate response to an ambivalent and contradictory world except the neutrality of artistic creation: "The truth, whatever it might be, is in the telling of it."[58] But for Van Nostrand this also involves Ishmael's creation of a cosmology which not only expresses and contains him but also extends and enriches both his personality and his perspective on life.

On the basis of these few interpretations, it can be said that Ishmael tries to make sense of Ahab's failure; that he interprets this failure in a way that explains his own participation in Ahab's scheme; that his artistic narrative constitutes a moral response to his past experience; and that he finally creates a "cosmology" which reproduces the ambiguities of the world he encounters during the *Pequod*'s voyage. These interpretations can be reconciled by saying that Ishmael not only creates a world view which seeks to explain life's inequities and injustices, but also dramatizes the mode of experiencing the world he depicts. Ultimately, he creates a synthesis of world view and ethos that articulates a theodicy which, for Ishmael, makes the existence of evil both rationally comprehensible and morally acceptable.

The younger Ishmael is a Presbyterian bitterly disillusioned by a Christian culture which, despite its self-proclaimed humanitarian ideals, perpetrates cruel injustice against the poor. Frustrated by his incapacity to alter such social injustices through his humanitarian and rationalistic goals as a schoolteacher, he quits his teaching post and leaves America by going whaling, a harbinger of the many expatriates to follow in American literature. His soured attitude toward his fellow Christians prompts him to befriend the cannibalistic harpooner, Queequeg, "since Christian kindness had proved but hollow courtesy" (p. 84). Their friendship is quickly cemented by Queequeg's acceptance of Ishmael and further strengthened by their mutual disillusionment with Christianity. Queequeg had left his country in order to learn from Christians how to improve the happiness and moral nature of his people, only to encounter many Christians who are more heathenish and miserable than his cannibalistic tribe. Believing himself contaminated by his contacts with such Christians, he refuses to return home to assume "the pure and undefiled throne of thirty pagan Kings" until he feels himself "baptized again" (p. 90).

Ishmael too goes whaling in quest of some such inner purgation, though a strong death wish also attracts him to life on the sea.[59] He asserts at the outset that his ocean voyages have functioned as a vicarious substitute for death. This suicidal attraction to the sea is most apparent in the ship's blacksmith, Perth, whose personal tragedies make him desire death but whose "interior compunctions against suicide" make him choose whaling instead. To such people, the older Ishmael observes, the ocean

alluringly spread[s] forth his whole plain of unimaginable, taking terrors, and wonderful, new-life adventures . . . the thousand mermaids sing . . . 'Come hither, broken-hearted; here is another life without the guilt of intermediate death; here are wonders supernatural, without dying for them. Come hither! bury thyself in a life which, to your now equally abhorred and abhorring, landed world, is more oblivious than death. Come hither! put up *thy* grave-stone, too, within the church-yard, and come hither, till we marry thee!' (Pp. 617–18).

According to Ishmael, this "ocean-perishing" has its analogue in the story of Narcissus "who because he could not grasp the tormenting, mild image he saw in the fountain, plunged into it and was drowned. But the same image we ourselves see in all rivers and oceans. It is the image of the ungraspable phantom of life; and this is the key to it all" (pp. 149, 26). It is difficult to determine whether Ishmael intends this analogy to illustrate a suicidal or self-destructive egotism in his fascination with water, an effort to grasp an elusive idealized image of man, or the futile attempt to find in nature his own human image. Ultimately, the older Ishmael uses the ocean to symbolize both the elusiveness and the contradictoriness of reality as well as a luring invitation to uproot one's spiritual bearings from conventional moral and religious norms in order to discover the ultimate nature of reality.

His famous hymn to the ocean in "The Lee Shore" clearly suggests that he considers his own suicidal attraction to the ocean an inbuilt impulse that is analogous to his metaphysical desire to seek truth. The occasion for the hymn is the *Pequod*'s departure on a stormy Christmas eve. The younger Ishmael, upon imagining that the restless seafarer, Bulkington, is at the *Pequod*'s helm, views him with "sympathetic awe and fearfulness." The older Ishmael compares Bulkington to a ship which a storm is blowing toward its nearby homeland. Though the land provides "safety" and "comfort," to be blown ashore could mean certain death (p. 148). The ship must therefore head into the seaward storm to avoid this peril, only to find that seeking such refuge can itself be fatal. This doubly jeopardizing situation, Ishmael asserts, is analogous to the quest for truth.

Glimpses do ye seem to see of that mortally intolerable truth; that all deep, earnest thinking is but the intrepid effort of the soul to keep the open independence of her sea; while the wildest winds of heaven and earth conspire to cast her on the treacherous, slavish shore?

But as in landlessness alone resides the highest truth, shoreless, indefinite as God— so, better is it to perish in that howling infinite, than be ingloriously dashed upon the lee, even if that were safety. (P. 149)

Ishmael's deification of the sea-seeking spirit defines his own quest for truth as being simultaneously an emotional analogue for Ahab's obsessive pursuit of Moby Dick and a secular analogue for Father Mapple's admonition: "Woe to him who would not be true, even though to be false were salvation!" Either comparison implies that his obsessive quest for truth may end with his destruction or damnation as the price he must pay to attain the truth.

The younger Ishmael's attraction to Ahab is so strong at the beginning of the voyage that he yields himself to Ahab's tyrannical influence. So sympathetic is he to Ahab's inner agony that during the ritual in which Ahab weds the crew to himself, Ishmael adopts his "quenchless feud" with Moby Dick as his own, though he can "see naught in that brute but the deadliest ill" (pp. 239, 252). However, this sympathetic sense of union with Ahab's purpose makes Ishmael a problematical figure to himself; eventually he adopts a more critical perspective. As early as the *Pequod*'s encounter with the first of nine ships, the *Albatross*, Ishmael perceives Ahab's monomaniacal indifference to everything but his desire to kill Moby Dick. Still later, other aspects of Ahab and whaling—Ahab's extreme isolation from others and his prideful disdain of them, his callous willingness to abandon one of his boat crews, and Ishmael's own realization that it is only natural for whales to defend themselves against human predators—further increase his awareness that Ahab's hatred of Moby Dick expresses an insane, even diabolical, obsession. Finally, while Ishmael is at the *Pequod*'s helm during the night the harpooners are boiling down the first whale caught on the voyage, he falls into a hypnotic trance as he stares into the flames of the tryworks (which make the harpooners appear to be demonic beings) and nearly capsizes the ship. After thus experiencing the potentially destructive consequences of a vision that focuses solely on the demonic aspects of human existence, Ishmael morally dissociates himself from Ahab's quest.[60]

Yet, no less than Starbuck, he accedes to Ahab's tyrannical command of the *Pequod*. Ishmael's own continuing complicity in Ahab's scheme is most clearly exemplified in his being chosen during the third day of the chase to replace the missing Fedallah as Ahab's bowman. Being in Ahab's boat makes him, as it were, an accessory to the *Pequod*'s destruction. As if admitting this to be the case, Ishmael obliquely suggests that he, like Coleridge's ancient mariner—the lone survivor of a ship's disaster precipitated by his own actions—also has an obsessive sense of guilt which compels him to tell his story.[61]

Like the ancient mariner, Ishmael is also the lone survivor of a ship-wreck. Prior to Moby Dick's attack on the *Pequod*, Ishmael is flung out of his boat when the white whale sideswipes it. Though he is caught in the whirlpool of the sinking ship, Ishmael miraculously escapes death when Queequeg's lifebuoy-coffin pops up from the center of the whirlpool and lands at his side. Grasping it, he floats for one day and one night on a "soft and dirgelike main," experiencing a longer and more horrifying abandonment than Pip, whose own abandonment cost him his sanity (p. 724). Ishmael's description of Pip's experience certainly derives from and probably explicitly renders his own experience.

The intense concentration of self in the middle of such a heartless immensity, my God! who can tell it? . . . The sea had jeeringly kept Pip's finite body up, but drowned the infinite of his soul. Not drowned entirely, though. Rather carried down alive to wondrous depths, where strange shapes of the unwarped primal world glided to and fro before his passive eyes; and the miser-merman, Wisdom, revealed his hoarded heaps; and among the joyous, heartless, ever-juvenile eterni-ties, Pip saw the multitudinous, God-omnipresent, coral insects, that out of the firmament of waters heaved the colossal orbs. He saw God's foot upon the treadle of the loom, and spoke it; and therefore his shipmates called him mad. So man's insanity is heaven's sense; and wandering from all mortal reason, man comes at last to that celestial thought, which, to reason, is absurd and frantic; and weal or woe, feels then uncompromised, indifferent as his God. (Pp. 529–30)

This vision of a deity who remains coldly indifferent to the pain and suf-fering He inflicts upon people as He weaves the fabric of life clearly echoes Ahab's vision of God. But this chilling vision is balanced by Ishmael's chance rescue the second day by the *Rachel*. For the ten days or so since Ahab refused Captain Gardiner's request to help him find his lost son, Gardiner has continued the search for the missing boy even though it is the height of the whaling season. His persistent but hopeless search for a lost son gives Ishmael a renewed lease on life.

Critics have basically explained Ishmael's survival in one of four ways, none of which corresponds with Ishmael's own explanation.[62] One of these, namely, the suggestion that Ishmael survives because, technically speaking, someone had to tell the story, sidesteps the issue.[63] Such an explanation not only overlooks Ishmael's own efforts to make sense of his survival, but also fails to consider the kinds of moral and religious questions it poses for Ishmael.[64] A second explanation is that Ishmael's aesthetic response to his experience—the careful rendering of his story—is itself sufficient to account for his survival. "His survival is therefore prior to all ethics, and the existentially sufficient reason for his survival is that what transcends death in time is art: art is what in fact does survive, often accidentally, and about its survival and Ishmael's as artist storyteller there is very little ethical that can . . . be convincingly posited."[65]

A third explanation states that his being saved by Queequeg's lifebuoy-coffin discloses the redemptive quality of Ishmael's relationship with Queequeg.[66] Three aspects of the novel make this a questionable interpretation. First, Ishmael himself, through his later critiques of his mystical tendencies, no longer endorses his own mystical experience of being redeemed by Queequeg's self-sufficient indifference. Second, despite their friendship, Ishmael never manages to enter Queequeg's consciousness in the way he does, say, that of Ahab. Rather than sharing a redemptive communion with Queequeg, the latter increasingly becomes an alien reality who puzzles him. Third, as Queequeg fully engages himself in Ahab's quest, the close relationship which he developed with Queequeg while ashore increasingly dwindles in importance for Ishmael. These factors suggest that Ishmael himself finally discards his initial interpretation of his relationship with Queequeg, though certainly he continues to admire the indomitable courage of Queequeg's death-defying feats.

A fourth explanation for Ishmael's survival accords redemptive status to the very nature of his consciousness.[67] According to this view, Ishmael merits his survival by virtue of his moral dissociation from Ahab's quest, his provisional acceptance of others which enables him to understand them, his compassion for all suffering life, and his highly developed imaginative capacity for tolerating ambiguity. This argument assumes, however, that a causal connection exists between the previous moral quality of Ishmael's life and his survival, that the universe in which he finds himself is shaped by ethical laws. But if there are such laws, they allow the innocent, like Pip, and the humane, like Starbuck, to be destroyed by Ahab's quest while sparing Ishmael. The universe of *Moby-Dick* exhibits a tragic lack of ethical consistency which this argument must ignore in order to make its case. As Paul Brodtkorb remarks, "whether the universe has any ethical character at all, lopsidedly tragic or otherwise, is a major part of what is in question [in *Moby-Dick*] in the first place; the argument assumes what it must demonstrate."[68] An equally important objection to this argument is that many of the Ishmaelean qualities which critics praise, particularly the Ishmaelean consciousness, characterize the older rather than the younger Ishmael. They are the consequence, not the cause, of his survival.

Ishmael himself clearly views his survival as one of those fortunate occurrences for which there is no rational explanation. Not only his rescue by the *Rachel* on the broad expanse of the Pacific, but even more his escape from nature's predators is for him nothing short of miraculous. "The unharming sharks, they glided by as if with padlocks on their mouths; the savage sea-hawks sailed with sheathed beaks" (p. 724). The various descriptions of sharks and sea-hawks throughout the novel dramatically support Ishmael's sense of the miraculous in his escaping what appears to be certain death. Nor does he tout his discovery by the *Rachel* as a joyful occasion; Captain Gardiner recovers not his son but, as Ishmael puts it in the novel's concluding words, only "another orphan." Ishmael does not idealize his sense of being saved, as he did in his earlier relationship with Queequeg, since his survival is made possible by the death, anguish, and suffering of others.

Moreover, he has no certitudes about why only he is saved. His survival could be the result of a divine plan administered by a God who is indifferent to individual merit, or else nothing more than a chance happening—a haphazard conjunction of events—in a godless, purposeless, and perhaps even demonic, universe. Or perhaps a beneficent deity may have either intervened on his behalf or predestined his survival—though Ishmael's attitude toward predestination as an explanation for human experience is ambiguous. On the one hand, he spoofs the idea that his whaling voyage was predetermined by God.

And, doubtless, my going on this whaling voyage, formed part of the grand programme of Providence that was drawn up a long time ago. It came in as a sort of brief interlude and solo between more extensive performances. I take it that this part of the bill must have run something like this:

> Grand Contested Election for the Presidency of the
> United States.
> "whaling voyage by one Ishmael"
> "BLOODY BATTLE IN AFGHANISTAN." (P. 29)

On the other hand, he also affirms, in one of the novel's most memorable images, that some people are mysteriously invested with spiritual capabilities that others lack. "And there is a Catskill eagle in some souls that can alike dive down into the blackest gorges, and soar out of them again and become invisible in the sunny spaces. And even if he for ever flies within the gorge, that gorge is in the mountains; so that even in his lowest swoop the mountain eagle is still higher than other birds upon the plain, even though they soar" (p. 421). Here, as when he later comments on his religious consciousness (see p. 480), Ishmael implies that such differences among people could feasibly reflect an incomprehensible divine scheme of predestination.

Ultimately, however, his experience provides Ishmael no unambiguous image of the kind of forces that shape human destinies. There simply is, in his view, no morally or rationally coherent explanation for the glaring inequities of human existence that make life comfortably secure for some and a torturous route of disease, poverty, suffering, and despair for others—for why some experience a stultifying and anguished damnation and others the heights of spiritual freedom and fulfillment.

Ishmael admits that he has a natural propensity to resolve this ambiguous metaphysical situation through an Ahab-like vision of a demonic spiritual world, a propensity which shapes his own response to Moby Dick.

What Ishmael finds most appalling about Moby Dick is his whiteness.[69] Many good things, Ishmael observes, are associated with the color white. It has variously signified "gladness," the innocence of brides, the benignity of age," "the majesty of Justice," and "the divine spotlessness and power." But "when divorced from these more kindly associations, and coupled with any object terrible in itself," whiteness heightens "that terror to the furthest bounds" (pp. 253–55). Whiteness has this power over the human imagination, Ishmael asserts, because its "indefiniteness . . . shadows forth" a terrifying apparition of a heartless, godless, blank void at the heart of existence (pp. 263–64). It is the power of whiteness to induce such an apparition which Ishmael compares to the muskiness of a western buffalo robe. When the robe is shaken behind a Vermont colt, he will exhibit violent symptoms of fright even though "the strange muskiness he smells cannot recall to him anything associated with the experience of former perils" among the western bison. In this colt's frightened response, Ishmael observes, "thou beholdest . . . the instinct of the knowledge of the demonism in the world" (pp. 262–63). His own response to the color white, especially the panoramic whiteness of milky seas, snow-covered prairies, and snow-capped mountains, parallels the colt's response to the buffalo robe; though neither can see the reality which each fears, neither doubts its existence. Ishmael thus asserts that he has an inbuilt instinct which senses the presence of unseen demonic forces in the world.

He further contends that everyone has this same instinct and that people respond to it in one of two basic ways. Many repress it through worship of a God whose purity and power are said to be analogous to an unspotted whiteness, thereby expressing the unconscious terror at the heart of their pietistic worship. Others, overwhelmed by this instinct, become atheists because they see themselves confronting an impersonal "palsied universe" that is enveloping them in its "monumental white shroud" (p. 264). This double response to a posited instinct that can sense unseen demonic forces shaping the universe poses a fundamental metaphysical problem for Ishmael. Should the religious vision prevail? the atheistical vision? or can both be integrated into a complex vision of reality which more fully reflects the ambiguities of human experience? Ishmael, as narrator, chooses this last option and, by effecting such a synthesis through his narrative, creates a double consciousness which he considers the only appropriate response to the morally ambiguous world he discovers during his whaling voyage.

ISHMAEL'S PLURALISTIC UNIVERSE: AN UNORTHODOX THEODICY

Indeed, the world as Ishmael experiences it is so kaleidoscopic, that, unable to explain it in monotheistic terms, he seeks an alternative explanation. *Moby-Dick* ultimately constitutes Ishmael's imaginative creation of a universe shaped by diverse kinds of forces which evoke diverse beliefs and values, a pluralistic universe wherein a theodicy based upon a monotheistic framework can no longer be used as the sole basis for reflection on the nature of deity. Ishmael's abandonment at sea, his chance rescue by the *Rachel*, and his instinctual knowledge of a demonic spiritual world give rise to and make credible three distinct visions of the universe which lie embedded in the narrative without comment. In each he posits a different kind of organizing principle shaping human existence. Since he attaches no disclaimer to any of these principles, each assumes the status of a separate existence in his imaginative vision of the world.

The younger Ishmael sets forth the first of these visions while he and Queequeg are dreamily weaving a sword mat during the day of their first lowering for a whale. Using his hands for a shuttle, Ishmael interweaves a marline woof though the long lines of the warp, while Queequeg, standing at Ishmael's side, "carelessly and unthinkingly" rams the woof with an oaken sword, sometimes strongly or weakly, sometimes slantingly or straight, thereby making corresponding contrasts in the overall design they are weaving into the fabric (p. 287). During this trancelike activity, Ishmael imagines time to be a loom in which he is the shuttle of free will weaving its own purposeful destiny into the inalterable warp of necessity as Queequeg, the element of chance, further shapes that destiny in haphazard ways. Ishmael here envisions a unified, coherent, and purposeful universe in which three separate, active, but mutually compatible forces—chance, free will, and necessity—are "all interweavingly working together. The straight warp of necessity, not to be swerved from its ultimate course—its every alternating vibration, indeed, only tending to that; free will still free to ply her shuttle between given threads; and chance, though restrained in its play within the right lines of necessity, and sideways in its motions directed by free will, though thus prescribed to by both, chance by turns rules either, and has the last featuring blow at events." His own determinative role in this scheme of things is quite limited and precarious, so precarious that "the ball of free will" drops from Ishmael's hand when the lookout shouts that whales are nearby (p. 288). But this view of life also encourages both a purposeful activity which is conscious of its limitations and inner compulsions and a willingness to conform to an overarching pattern of meaning which transcends the individual life. Nothing in this vision precludes the possibility that people can know this overall design or that this design might ultimately disclose a beneficent universal moral order presided over by a benevolent deity.[70]

Somewhat in contrast to this vision is the one which Ishmael later sets forth in "A Bower in the Arsacides." While celebrating part of the Arsacidean holidays with his friend Tranquo on the island of Tranque, Ishmael visits the vine-covered skeletal remains of a sperm whale which now serves as a temple for the islanders. He compares the entire scene—the trees, ferns, shrubs, grasses, and the skeleton covered by vines and flowers—to a loom with the sun working as a shuttle for weaving "the unwearied verdure" into an aesthetically pleasing design. The older Ishmael uses this analogy to question whether the design has any discernible purpose.

Oh, busy weaver! unseen weaver!—pause!—one word!—whither flows the fabric? what palace may it deck? wherefore all these ceaseless toilings? Speak, weaver!—stay thy hand!—but one single word with thee! Nay—the shuttle flies—the figures float from forth the loom; the freshet-rushing carpet for ever slides away. The weaver god, he weaves; and by that humming, we too, who look on the loom are deafened; and only when we escape it shall we hear the thousand voices that speak through it. For even so it is in all material factories. The spoken words that are inaudible among the flying spindles; those same words are plainly heard without the walls, bursting from the opened casements. (P. 573)

Ishmael here envisions the universe as a spiritual factory in which God's weaving of human experience—the divine creativity itself—deafens both God and people to the cries of human suffering. He weaves discernible patterns, but Ishmael leaves it an open question whether people can discover the ultimate meaning, if any, of this divine patterning of human experience. This God is so fully preoccupied with His creative activity that He neither discloses its purpose nor heeds its impact on human lives. Nothing about the analogy, however, warrants the conclusion that He is an indifferent, a demonic, or a benevolent deity. But the analogy does imply that any attempt to understand God through the generative and destructive forces of nature, as well as through its impersonal natural laws, could easily lead people to terrifying conclusions about His character.

Here, as elsewhere throughout the novel, Ishmael seeks to discredit a "natural theology" which uses nature as tangible evidence for demonstrating the existence of a benevolent deity.[71] There are some natural phenomena, Ishmael admits—such as the protective circle of male whales around the females who are nursing their young (itself a scene of idyllic peace and harmony) and those moments when the stillness and beauty of nature seem to confer upon people, even upon Ahab, the capacity to transcend their worst impulses—which reflect a beneficent design. But there are other natural phenomena—such as the shark's indiscriminate predatoriness, the necessity that all creatures in nature feed on each other in order to survive, and the immensely destructive capacity of the ocean itself—which are difficult to reconcile with the belief in a good and benevolent creator. Nature, in Ishmael's view, exhibits an ambiguous intertwining of idyllic beauty and demonism which, if taken as the normative revelation of the quintessence of reality, requires a redefinition of the moral life that radically differs from the Puritan and liberal conceptions of true virtue.

This conclusion is further reinforced by the third vision Ishmael articulates while describing a calm day on the Pacific when the ocean resembles a tranquil rolling prairie of grass which promises pleasure, rest, and the reinvigoration of life.[72] During such times, the older Ishmael says, people recover a lost sense of immortality. But he also adds the following commentary:

Would to God these blessed calms would last. But the mingled, mingling threads of life are woven by warp and woof: calms crossed by storms, a storm for every calm. There is no steady unretracing progress in this life; we do not advance through infancy's unconscious spell, boyhood's thoughtless faith, adolescence's doubt (the common doom), then scepticism, then disbelief, resting at last in manhood's pondering repose of If. But once gone through, we trace the round again; and are infants, boys, and men, and Ifs eternally. Where lies the final harbor, whence we unmoor no more? In what rapt ether sails the world, of which the weariest will never weary? Where is the foundling's father hidden? Our souls are like those orphans whose unwedded mothers die in bearing them: the secret of our paternity lies in their grave, and we must there to learn it. (Pp. 623–24)

Ishmael now envisions the universe as a loom which, using human life as its thread, randomly weaves a series of cyclical experiences that form no meaningful pattern. No transcendent weaver is controlling the process, or if there is it is an amoral or demonic deity who abandons people to recurring cycles of experience they can neither escape nor transcend. This vision of life's randomness implies the futility of pursuing any goals, or adhering to any values, and of seeking any kind of rational, moral, or religious meaning in human experience. All that remains is the bleak struggle to endure one's irremediable entrapment within endlessly repeated experiences that lead to no kind of progressive or purposive development for the human self. Were this vision of ultimate reality accepted as normative for Ishmael it could be concluded that he discovers no metaphysical basis for a coherent moral life and, lacking any such basis, that he provides no definition or model whatsoever of morality in such a world—that he himself in fact borders on moral disintegration.[73]

However, Ishmael's experience provides evidence for accepting all three visions. None of them emerges as a fully adequate explanation of human experience. Consequently, rather than seeking to explain his career in terms of only one of these visions, Ishmael presents his past experience as the makeshift result of the uncontrollable interactions between beneficent, indifferent, and demonic forces. Such a pluralistic perspective provides a new imaginative context for exploring the problem of theodicy, not only at the metaphysical level of ultimate reality but also at the ethical level of redefining the self. Indeed, it is the personal level which most interests Ishmael, since he searches for a conception of the self—or a way of being moral—which gives unity to the otherwise disparate forces shaping the pluralistic universe of *Moby-Dick.* Ultimately, his goal is to demonstrate that he can create a synthesis of world view and ethos which has humanizing possibilities excluded by the Puritan and liberal outlooks.

Ishmael defines his selfhood in two opposing ways that remain in tension throughout his narrative. The first relies on the novel's basic contrast between the land, which promises safety, comfort, and certitude, and the sea, which represents a precarious and ambiguous world, a realm of moral and religious incertitude. He suggests that just "as this appalling ocean surrounds the verdant land, so in the soul of man there lies one insular Tahiti, full of peace and joy, but encompassed by all the horrors of the half-known life. God keep thee! Push not off from that isle, thou canst never return" (p. 264). Ishmael describes an unbridgeable duality in the self which cannot tolerate moral ambiguities. The human self, according to this analogy, resolves these contradictions by adopting a one-sided view of human experience, either that of the land or that of the sea. Not only are these views mutually exclusive; the paradisaical outlook of the"insular Tahiti" can never be regained once it gives way to its opposite perspective on life.

In "The Grand Armada," however, Ishmael offers an alternative to this pessimistic sense regarding the self's capacity to incorporate moral ambiguity. The *Pequod*'s five whaleboats have been chasing a herd of whales for hours when the herd suddenly forms a series of concentric circles. The bulls swim in reverse directions in the outer circles while the females swim undisturbed with their young at the center. Queequeg harpoons a whale which drags their boat through the riotous outer rings into the center of calmness. Ishmael looks over the side of the boat and sees female whales suckling their newborn offspring. One of the young whales fearlessly sidles up to the boat like a playful puppy. Ishmael's sudden intrusion into a paradisaical garden of primordial innocence created and preserved by the bulls' protective outer ring of awesome violence suggests a new analogy for his selfhood. "But even so, amid the tornadoed Atlantic of my being, . . . while ponderous planets of unwaning woe revolve around me, deep down and deep inland there I still bathe me in eternal mildness of joy" (p. 499).[74] The duality of the self still remains; but he now views it as a reciprocating doubleness wherein the outer violence is necessary to preserve an inner peace. Ishmael now envisions the self as a fusion of peace and violence which ironically sustains its unity by means of this contradiction. From this perspective, spiritual joy, freedom, and peace—as well as a sense of unity and harmony with all sentient life—are renewable possibilities just as they are in his qualified vision of the ocean as a tranquil prairie of waving grass.

Ishmael incorporates both of these understandings of the self into his own response to what he considers a morally incoherent universe. The result is a synthesis which enables him to avoid the moral disintegration which Pierre and Ahab undergo as they confront the ambiguities and contradictoriness of human existence.

What finally emerges is the flexible Ishmaelean consciousness. Ishmael develops "a double vision of what is at once noble and vile, of all that is lovely and appalling" about people, society, nature, and the ultimate powers shaping human affairs.[75] He himself affirms this double vision when he discusses the conflict within himself between his instinctual belief in the existence of unseen demonic powers and his propensity to believe in a beneficent deity, and while describing the rainbow which can be seen in the misty vapor spouted by the whale, "as if Heaven itself had put its seal upon his thoughts. . . . And so, through all the thick mists of the dim doubts in my mind, divine intuitions now and then shoot, enkindling my fog with a heavenly ray. And for this I thank God; for all have doubts; many deny; but doubts or denials, few along with them, have intuitions. Doubts of all things earthly, and intuitions of some things heavenly; this combination makes neither believer nor infidel, but makes a man who regards them both with equal eye" (p. 480). Ishmael here resembles the Emersonian circus rider who performs the balancing act of standing atop two horses—infidelity and faith—one leg on each as he rides them around the ring.

This is, in fact, the kind of perspective he assumes throughout his narrative, for he continuously keeps his legs planted, as it were, on the two horses of various opposing stances: his ribald jokes and serious metaphysical speculations, his mysticism and hard-nosed realism, his irreverent iconoclasm and worshipful reverence, his benevolent and demonic attributes, his hope and despair, his cynical laughter and his sorrow for all suffering, his affirmations of free will and determinism, his sense of salvation and sense of damnation, his emphasis upon both the beauty and the cannibalism of nature, his contrary views of the self as an "insular Tahiti" and a "tornadoed Atlantic," and his paean-like tributes to both the sea-seeking spirit and the domestic life that is devoted to "the wife, the heart, the bed, the table, the saddle, the fire-side, the country" (p. 533). No one of these elements gains normative priority over the others. Rather, they function to establish an equilibrium of contraries. By maintaining this balancing act between contradictory perceptions, moods, beliefs, and values—a balancing act which Pierre thought would cure his own disillusionment—the Ishmaelean consciousness becomes a kind of floating perspective which anchors itself in no single possibility, viewpoint, or vision of the world as absolutely normative.

Ishmael's imaginative identification with Ahab and Starbuck perhaps most clearly exemplifies the ethical consequences of such a perspective. Ishmael is virtually one with both Ahab and Starbuck after "The Try-Works." Like Father Mapple, Ishmael uses his own experience at sea to imaginatively and sympathetically recreate the agonized spiritual struggles of an inner life not his own. He renders Ahab and Starbuck during private moments at which he could not have been present. He invents, for example, Fedallah's prophecies, which not only help explain Ahab's action but also make him a more sympathetic figure, and several times he imagines Ahab's thoughts while Ahab is alone in his cabin or on the deck. No less an imaginative creation is his rendering of Starbuck's inner struggle with Ahab. It is this imaginative identification with Ahab and Starbuck after "The Try-Works" which gives us our most intimate knowledge of them and, by implication, of Ishmael himself.[76] The two men represent polarities in Ishmael's own nature—his attraction to conventional and unconventional modes of life, his humanitarian and demonic impulses, his faith and infidelity, his beliefs in both a beneficent deity and demonic spiritual forces, his sense of salvation and his sense of damnation. As such, Ahab and Starbuck become imaginative projections of his own possible selves were he to resolve these polarities one way or the other. His refusal to resolve them seemingly enlarges Ishmael's imaginative capacity to render both Ahab and Starbuck so as to make each morally and spiritually comprehensible on his own terms.

True virtue, in Ishmael's view, is the imaginative capacity, based upon a double consciousness, to render sympathetically all possible human responses to a pluralistic world in a way that makes them less foreign, less strange, less irrational—in a way that makes us sympathize with the logic governing their behavior according to their perceptions of the world. He becomes a working democracy of diverse selves which, as one critic observes, virtually expresses the full spectrum of nineteenth-century American character.[77] Ishmael deems this protean existence to be the only appropriate response to the moral ambiguities he experiences in his world as well as the best way to make those ambiguities comprehensible to human reason. As William James put it later in his own affirmation of a pluralistic universe: "The only way in which to apprehend reality's thickness is either to experience it directly by being a part of reality one's self, or to evoke it in imagination by sympathetically divining some one's inner life."[78] Such an imaginative act, James declared, banishes "the foreignness from all that is human," or, at least in Ishmael's view (as for Natty Bumppo), creates the possibility for bridging the gaps between differing ways of experiencing the world.[79] Ishmael's double consciousness is a rich source of new experiences as it imagines the "otherness" of the people around him.[80] Because he has imaginative access to such an increased range of human experience, his imaginative capacity enables him to transcend both the modes of perception and the uses of the imagination shaping his Protestant culture.

Ishmael's narrative thus constitutes his transformation of the whaling voyage into a form of consciousness which finds its sanctions not in moral or religious traditions but in his accumulated experiences of the sea as a demonic, impersonal, and beneficent reality. He accepts the monotheistic Christian belief in a benevolent deity without expecting the world to conform to his ethical expectations; he believes in demonic spiritual forces without himself becoming amoral; and he accepts the scientific world view of impersonal natural law while simultaneously celebrating those experiences which suggest a beneficent deity. Each vision points to the necessity for the others. The result is a continuous circuit of belief which sustains both a doubleness of vision and a self-balancing system of world views within which none attains normative supremacy.

The Ishmaelean consciousness is in fact a working democracy of competing world views which mirrors a pluralistic approach to reality that expresses the religious essence of American democracy. William James articulated this religious implication of American democracy when he stated that a "pluralistic world is . . . more like a federal republic than like an empire or a kingdom. However much may be collected, however much may report itself as present at any effective centre of consciousness or action, something else is self-governed and absent and unreduced to unity."[81] Ishmael creates such "a federal republic" of world views in which each must prove its pragmatic worth. This mode of experiencing the world is, in Ishmael's view, more faithful to the moral complexities of human experience than those articulated by the Puritan and rationalistic theodicies. By dramatizing the humanizing consequences of his belief in a pluralistic universe, Ishmael seeks to demonstrate, in the same way William James did when he defined the "pragmatically different ethical appeals" of various ways of viewing the world, the moral desirability of believing in his vision of the world.[82]

Ishmael's narrative career thus embodies the metaphysical drama of the self implied in the debate regarding the Puritan and rationalistic theodicies. He tries to synthesize a world view and ethos into a theodicy which will make the existence of evil rationally comprehensible and morally acceptable. For Ishmael, as for James, the problem of theodicy is ultimately the philosophical problem of the one and the many.[83] And by finally resolving it, as James did, in terms of a "radical pluralism," Ishmael creates an unorthodox theodicy which articulates a mode of experiencing the world that fully conforms to the fundamental ethical ideals of American democracy.[84]

Through Ishmael, then, the stymied theological controversy regarding the Puritan and rationalistic theodicies becomes a rich resource for Melville's reflection on the moral and religious implications of American democracy. Melville transforms the basic religious tensions of early nineteenth-century America into a unified vision—the commodious Ishmaelean consciousness—which creates the possibility for a greatly expanded humanity. In so doing, Melville shows through Ishmael's career how the problematical conflicts of America's cultural heritage not only provided the basis for a redefinition of the moral life, but also made possible a form of self-transcendence which incorporates the kind of spiritual pluralism implied in the ethical ideals that form the foundation of American democracy. To the extent that we feel the logical tie between Ishmael's religious vision and the emergence of the Ishmaelean consciousness, to the extent that we accept Ishmael's synthesis of world view and ethos as having the most humanizing potential within a world that evokes a plurality of human possibilities, beliefs, and values, Melville thereby makes us experience Ishmael's formulation of an unorthodox theodicy based upon a pluralistic vision of the universe as a rationally coherent and morally acceptable possibility for religious belief.

Notes

INTRODUCTION

1. J. Coert Rylaarsdam, "The Two Covenants and the Dilemmas of Christology," University of Chicago Divinity School, Chicago. Photocopy. Although Rylaarsdam never employs the concept of theodicy, he treats this same dilemma in his analysis of the Jewish and Christian notions of the covenant.

2. This understanding of the Puritan dilemma differs from that which Edmund S. Morgan defines in *The Puritan Dilemma: The Story of John Winthrop*, ed. Oscar Handlin (Boston: Little, Brown and Co., 1958). He describes this dilemma as a tension between this world and the next, as the tension over remaining loyal to God or to society when they come into seemingly irreconcilable conflict.

3. These comments are based on two essays by Clifford Geertz, "Religion as a Cultural System" and "Ethos, World View, and the Analysis of Sacred Symbols," both of which are found in Clifford Geertz, *The Interpretation of Cultures* (New York: Basic Books, 1973).

4. Ibid., p. 124. See p. 141 for his comments on the imprecision of the concepts of "world view" and "ethos."

5. Donald R. Cutler, ed., *The Religious Situation: 1968* (Boston: Beacon Press, 1968), p. 665.

6. Geertz, *The Interpretation of Cultures*, p. 108.

7. Talcott Parsons provides an important critique of Geertz's essay "Religion as a Cultural System" in Cutler, *The Religious Situation: 1968*, pp. 688–94.

8. Robert G. Pope, *The Half-Way Covenant: Church Membership in Puritan New England* (Princeton: Princeton University Press, 1969), p. 9.

9. Joseph Haroutunian, *Piety Versus Moralism: The Passing of the New England Theology* (New York: Henry Holt and Company, 1932), has defined the evolution of the tension that emerged between orthodox and liberal theologians from 1750 to 1830. But whereas his intention, as his subtitle indicates, is to trace

the decline of Puritan orthodoxy and the rise of modern liberal Protestantism, the intention here is to demonstrate how a major dilemma endemic to Puritan ethics helped to create a larger theological debate about the religious meanings of American democracy, and how this debate was further expanded by several nineteenth-century authors.

10. This study thus supports not only the contention of Max Weber in *The Sociology of Religion* and Peter Berger in *The Social Reality of Religion* that theodicies, or religious explanations for evil, are the key loci for defining a culture's peculiar biases, but also the contention of Mary Douglas that theodicies "are closely related to the structure of social relations." Mary Douglas, "The Effects of Modernization on Religious Change," *Daedalus* 111 (Winter 1982): 8. She in fact proposes that a systematic study of the interactions between the "mapping structures" provided by ultimate explanations (or theodicies) and social structure can enhance our understanding of social and religious change in any society, thereby making such a study an important methodological tool for cross-cultural studies. See Mary Douglas, *Cultural Bias*, Occasional Paper no. 35, Anthropological Institute of Great Britain and Ireland 1978, and Mary Douglas, *Natural Symbols: Explorations in Cosmology* (New York: Vintage Books, 1973).

11. Richard Chase, *The American Novel and Its Tradition* (New York: Anchor Books, 1957); Lionel Trilling, "Manners, Morals, and the Novel," in *The Liberal Imagination: Essays on Literature and Society* (New York: Anchor Books, 1953), pp. 199–215; Richard Poirier, *A World Elsewhere: The Place of Style in American Literature* (New York: Oxford University Press, 1966); A. D. Van Nostrand, *Everyman His Own Poet: Romantic Gospels in American Literature* (New York: McGraw-Hill, 1968).

12. John Lynen has already provided an excellent model for such a study in *The Design of the Present: Essays on Time and Form in American Literature* (New Haven: Yale University Press, 1969).

1. A DILEMMA IN PURITAN ETHICS

1. Roger Williams, *The Complete Writings of Roger Williams*, Perry Miller, ed. (New York: Russell and Russell, 1963), 7:81.

2. Increase Mather, *Doctrine of Divine Providence* (Boston, 1684), p. 43. Microfilm.

3. Cotton Mather, *Bonifacius: An Essay upon the Good*, David Levin, ed. (Cambridge: Harvard University Press, 1966), p. 10.

4. See Henry Bamford Parkes, *The Pragmatic Test: Essays on the History of Ideas* (San Francisco: The Colt Press, 1941), pp. 10–38; Perry Miller and Thomas M. Johnson, eds., *The Puritans: A Sourcebook on Their Writings* (New York: Harper and Row, 1963), 1:37–63; and Samuel Eliot Morison, *The Intellectual Life of Colonial New England* (Ithaca: Cornell University Press, 1970), pp. 3–26.

5. John Calvin, *Institutes of the Christian Religion*, Henry Beveridge, trans. (Grand Rapids, Mich.: Wm. B. Eerdmans, 1953), 2:227.

6. Thomas Shepard, *God's Plot: The Paradoxes of Puritan Piety, Being the Autobiography and Journal of Thomas Shepard*, Michael McGiffert, ed. (Amherst: University of Massachusetts Press, 1972), pp. 61–62.

7. Ibid., pp. 69–70.

8. Miller and Johnson, *The Puritans*, 2:578–79.

9. This sense of the world's deceitfulness that characterized the Puritan outlook is forcefully expressed in Michael Wigglesworth's poem, "A Song of Emptiness" (Miller and Johnson, *The Puritans*, 2:608–11). This poem begins by describing man as "A Dream, a lifeless Picture finely drest," and "A Shadow of Something, but nought indeed." He extends this description of humankind to the world itself.

> Learn what deceitful Toyes, and empty things,
> This World, and all its best Enjoyments bee:
> Out of the Earth no true Contentment springs,
> But all things here are vexing Vanitee.

Beauty, pleasure, strength, wealth, social status, political power, honor, fame, and valor—all of these are "empty Shadows" which "deceive" people by luring them to believe that true satisfaction lies in achieving them. Even friendship has this deceitful quality.

> And what are Friends but mortal men, as we?
> Whom Death from us may quickly separate;
> Or else their hearts may quite estranged be,
> And all their love be turned into hate.

Wigglesworth thus presents history as the tragic record of humankind's endless betrayal by a deceptive world, and he endorses the conventional moral which the Puritan believed this view of history taught him: "That we might after better things aspire." He nevertheless ironically concludes:

> Go boast thy self of what thy heart enjoyes,
> Vain Man triumph in all thy worldly Bliss:
> Thy best enjoyments are but Trash and Toyes:
> Delight thy self in that which worthless is.

To trust the deceptive allurements of the world is, in Wigglesworth's eyes, to lose the only thing truly worth having, namely, eternal salvation.

Roger Williams memorably elaborates this radical mistrust of the world by comparing life to a journey on a ship.

> Gods children as travailers on the Land, as *Passengers* in a *ship*, must use this world, and all comforts of it, with *dead*, and *weaned*, and *mortified affections*, as if they used them not: If *Riches*, if *Children*, if *Cattel*, if *Friends*, if whatsoever increase, let us watch that the *Heart* fly not loose upon them: But as we use *salt* with raw and fresh meats, let us use no worldly comfort without a savoury Remembrance, that these worldly *Goods* and *comforts* are the common portion of the men of this perishing *world*, who must perish together with them. Let us muse upon their *insufficiency* to content, and fill our *Hearts*, upon their uncertain coming, and going with *Eagles wings*: upon their *anxiety*, and perplexedness full of *Thorns*, and *vexations*: upon their *certainty* of departing, how soon we know not. O let us therefore beg *grace* from *Heaven*, that we may use earthly *comforts* as a *stool* or *ladder* to help us upward to heavenly *comforts*, *profits*, *pleasures*, which are only *true*, and *lasting*, even *eternall* in *God* himself, when these *Heavens*, and *earth* are gone. *Complete Writings*, 7:103.

10. See Everett H. Emerson, "Calvin and Covenant Theology," *Church History* 25 (1956): 136–44; Anthony A. Hoekema, "The Covenant of Grace in Calvin's Teaching," *Calvin Theological Journal* 2 (1967): 133–61; Jens G. Møller, "The Beginnings of Puritan Covenant Theology," *Journal of Ecclesiastical History* 14

(1963): 46–67; and Leonard J. Trinterud, "The Origins of Puritanism," *Church History* 20 (1951): 37–57.

11. Møller, "Beginnings of Puritan Covenant Theology," pp. 46–67; Trinterud, "Origins of Puritanism," pp. 37–45; Hoekema, "Covenant of Grace," pp. 136–37; Emerson, "Calvin and Covenant Theology," pp. 136–42.

12. Trinterud, "Origins of Puritanism," p. 44.

13. Ibid., pp. 48–49.

14. Peter Bulkely, *The Gospel-Covenant; or, The Covenant of Grace Opened*, 2nd ed. (London: M. Simmons, 1651). Microfilm. Page citations refer to this work.

15. Bulkely devotes the fourth part of *The Gospel-Covenant* to this issue by seeking to refute the argument that the condition of faith implies that people control God (pp. 312–97).

16. Page citations refer to Williams, *The Complete Writings of Roger Williams*, vol. 7.

17. Roger Williams, *The Complete Writings of Roger Williams*, Samuel L. Caldwell, ed. (New York: Russell and Russell, 1963), 2:13.

18. Williams mistrusts the conscience as a too willing servant of the self's desires to gain merit, respect, and advantages for itself (7:61–66, 75, 78–79). Hence, Williams accepts neither good deeds nor an impeccable conscience as unquestionably genuine signs of the truly religious life. This mistrust of humankind's moral impulses further leads Williams to assert that no one can attain religious faith through "Moral wisdome," strong conviction of *conscience*," or good deeds (7:91, 88). Rather, he affirms the central contention of the covenant of grace that faith comes to people solely through the grace of God working within them.

19. Perry Miller, *Errand into the Wilderness* (New York: Harper and Row, 1956), pp. 1–15, and Perry Miller, *The New England Mind: From Colony to Province* (Boston: Beacon Press, 1966), pp. 1–39. For a more extensive treatment of the sacred-errand myth in early American Puritan writings, see the following studies: Alan E. Heimert, "Puritanism, the Wilderness, and the Frontier," *New England Quarterly* 26 (1953): 361–82; Kenneth B. Murdock, "Clio in the Wilderness: History and Biography in Puritan New England," *Early American Literature* 6 (1971): 201–19; Sacvan Bercovitch, "Horologicals to Chronometricals: The Rhetoric of the Jeremiad," *Literary Monographs* (Madison: University of Wisconsin Press, 1970), esp. pp. 3–26; and Peter N. Carroll, *Puritanism and the Wilderness: The Intellectual Significance of the New England Frontier, 1629–1700* (New York: Columbia University Press, 1969). For a study of the rhetorical strategies the errand myth gave rise to and the process whereby they were assimilated into American Romanticism, see Sacvan Bercovitch, *The Puritan Origins of the American Self* (New Haven: Yale University Press, 1975). For a critique of viewing early American Puritanism in terms of the errand myth, see Darrett B. Rutman, "The Mirror of Puritan Authority," found in Michael McGiffert, ed., *Puritanism and the American Experience* (Reading, Mass.: Addison-Wesley, 1969), pp. 65–79, and Darrett B. Rutman, *American Puritanism: Faith and Practice* (New York: J. B. Lippincott, 1970).

20. John Winthrop, et al., *Winthrop Papers* (Massachusetts Historical Society, Plimpton Press, 1931), 2:293. For an excellent analysis of Winthrop's sermon "A Modell of Christian Charity," see Darrett B. Rutman, *Winthrop's Boston: Portrait*

of a Puritan Town, 1630–1649 (Chapel Hill: University of North Carolina Press, 1965), pp. 1–22.

21. *Winthrop Papers*, 2:295. A detailed discussion of this image of the wilderness as a haven for completing the Reformation can be found in Carroll, *Puritanism and the Wilderness*, pp. 109–26, a work which carefully documents the diverse Puritan images of the wilderness.

22. This phrase is taken from the title of Conrad Cherry's book, *God's New Israel: Religious Interpretations of American Destiny* (Englewood Cliffs, N.J.: Prentice-Hall, 1971).

23. *Winthrop Papers*, 2:293.

24. As Ursula Brumm suggests, the Puritan notion of covenant is "basically a typological idea" which enabled the Puritans to transform the Old Testament into a sourcebook of types that prophesy the fulfillment of these types in New Testament—and also New World—antitypes. Within the typological framework of the covenant theology, the American wilderness became "the promised land" or a "second Jerusalem"; the attractions of a prospering commercial society were compared to the Canaanite deities that lured the ancient Israelites into idolatry; the Puritan leaders of the first generation were cast in the role of Moses and second-generation leaders in the role of Joshua; and biblical names like Abraham and Samuel were given to children in the hope that their careers would parallel the destinies of their namesakes. Ursula Brumm, *American Thought and Religious Typology* (New Brunswick: Rutgers University Press, 1970). Other important studies of Puritan typology include Bercovitch, "Horologicals"; Sacvan Bercovitch, "Typology in Puritan New England: The Williams-Cotton Controversy Reassessed," *American Quarterly* 19 (1967): 166–91; Sacvan Bercovitch, ed., *Typology and Early American Literature* (Amherst: University of Massachusetts Press, 1972); Charles Feidelson, Jr., *Symbolism in American Literature* (Chicago: University of Chicago Press, 1959); Mason I. Lowance, Jr., Introduction, *The Figures or Types of the Old Testament*, by Samuel Mather, Lowance, ed. (London, 1705; 2nd ed.; rpt. New York: Johnson Reprint, 1969); Allan I. Ludwig, *Graven Images: New England Stonecarving and Its Symbols, 1650–1815* (Middletown, Conn.: Wesleyan University Press, 1966); Perry Miller, Introduction, *Images or Shadows of Divine Things*, by Jonathan Edwards, Miller, ed. (New Haven: Yale University Press, 1948); Murdock, "Clio in the Wilderness"; and Bercovitch, *The Puritan Origins of the American Self*, pp. 109–35.

25. Perry Miller suggests that another possible explanation for this uncritical attitude toward the American wilderness is that the "covenant doctrine preached on the *Arbella* had been formulated in England, where land was not to be had for the taking; its adherents had been utterly oblivious of what the fact of a frontier would do for a European mentality" (Miller, *Errand*, p. 9). Moreover, these Puritans came mostly from England's lower classes and, for them, the wilderness—as Cotton Mather portrays it in the opening pages of his *Magnalia Christi Americana*—was a God-sent refuge from political tyranny and religious persecution.

26. See A. N. Kaul, *The American Vision: Actual and Ideal Society in Nineteenth-Century Fiction* (New Haven: Yale University Press, 1963), p. 14; John Lankford, ed., *Captain John Smith's America* (New York: Harper and Row, 1967), pp. 128–32, 138–43; and Sidney E. Mead, *The Lively Experiment: The Shaping*

of Christianity in America (New York: Harper and Row, 1963), pp. 1–15. For a more negative image of the American wilderness, see William Bradford, *Of Plymouth Plantation*, Harvey Wish, ed. (New York: Capricorn Books, 1962), pp. 40–42. For a fuller treatment of these contrasting images of the American wilderness, see Howard Mumford Jones, *O Strange New World; American Culture: The Formative Years* (New York: Viking Press, 1965), pp. 1–70, and Carroll, *Puritanism and the Wilderness*.

27. *Winthrop Papers* 2:295.

28. John Higginson, "The Cause of God and His People in New-England" (1633) found in *Elijah's Mantle* (Boston, 1722), p. 7. Microfilm.

29. Shepard, *God's Plot*, p. 9; John Winthrop, *Winthrop's Journal*, James Kendall Hosmer, ed. (New York: Scribner's, 1908), 1:322.

30. Edward Johnson, *Johnson's Wonder-Working Providence: 1628–1651*, John Franklin Jameson, ed. (New York: Scribner's, 1910), p. 272.

31. Miller and Johnson, *The Puritans*, 1:246.

32. Bradford, *Of Plymouth Plantation*, p. 214. For an analysis of how the Puritan effort to preserve an organic society necessarily resulted in such dispersion, see Stephen Foster, *Their Solitary Way* (New Haven: Yale University Press, 1971). See also Darrett B. Rutman, *American Puritanism: Faith and Practice*, pp. 71–88. For an analysis of Bradford's artistry as a historian see David Levin, "William Bradford: The Value of Puritan Historiography," in Everett Emerson, *Major Writers of Early American Literature* (Madison: University of Wisconsin Press, 1972), pp. 11–31. See also Edmund S. Morgan, *Visible Saints: The History of a Puritan Idea* (Ithaca: Cornell University Press, 1963).

33. Miller and Johnson, *The Puritans*, 1:121.

34. Ibid., p. 122; see also Murdock, "Clio in the Wilderness," pp. 210–11.

35. For a detailed analysis of the often striking images Puritan preachers used to express God's beneficent mercy, see Emory Elliott's excellent study, *Power and the Pulpit in Puritan New England* (Princeton: Princeton University Press, 1975). This study examines the shifting metaphors of God in the seventeenth-century sermons of American Puritans. Elliott gives particular attention to how these metaphors express and speak to the psychological needs of people coming into conflict over the extent to which the state should have control over the individual's destiny. See also Carroll, *Puritanism and the Wilderness*, pp. 67–72, 87–107, and Shepard, *God's Plot*, pp. 21–24.

36. Kaul, *The American Vision*, p. 12.

37. Foster, *Their Solitary Way*, p. 114. See also Miller, *The New England Mind: From Colony to Province*, pp. 40–52; Bernard Bailyn, *The New England Merchants in the Seventeenth Century* (Cambridge: Harvard University Press, 1955); and A. Whitney Griswold, "Three Puritans on Prosperity," *New England Quarterly* 7 (1934): 475–93. One of the best and most thorough treatments of the emergence of New England as a commercial society still remains Carl Bridenbough's *Cities in the Wilderness: The First Century of Urban Life in America, 1625–1742* (New York: The Ronald Press, 1938).

38. Robert G. Pope, "New England versus the New England Mind: The Myth of Declension," *Journal of Social History* 3 (Winter 1969/70): 95–108, and Robert G. Pope, *The Half-Way Covenant: Church Membership in Puritan New England* (Princeton: Princeton University Press, 1969), pp. 206–38, 279–86. Also see Ger-

ald Francis Moran, "The Puritan Saint: Religious Experience, Church Membership, and Piety in Connecticut, 1636–1776" (Ph.D. thesis, Rutgers University, 1973), and Daniel Walker Howe, "The Decline of Calvinism: An Approach to Its Study," *Comparative Studies in Society and History* 14 (1972): 306–27.

39. Pope, *The Half-Way Covenant*, p. 9.

40. Foster, for example, suggests that Pope's use of church membership statistics and his emphasis upon the increase of church members after 1676 are misleading. Foster contends that "the *absolute increase* in new admissions after 1676 is simply too small to offset the decline in the *proportion* of the adult male population in full communion, which fell steeply after 1650 because of the increase in total population and the death of the earlier church members." This view of the increase in church membership after 1676 leads Foster to conclude that "the revival of 1677–90 is really a *partial* arrest in the gradual relative decline in full church membership that took place throughout the latter half of the seventeenth century." *Their Solitary Way*, p. 178.

41. Alden T. Vaughan, *New England Frontier: Puritans and Indians, 1620–1675* (Boston: Little, Brown, 1965), p. 319.

42. Miller, *Errand*, pp. 7ff.; Miller, *Colony to Province*, pp. 19–39; David Minter, *The Interpreted Design as a Structural Principle in American Prose* (New Haven: Yale University Press, 1969), pp. 50–66; David Hall, *The Faithful Shepherd: A History of the New England Ministry in the Seventeenth Century* (Chapel Hill: University of North Carolina Press, 1972), pp. 227–48. See also Increase Mather, *Doctrine of Divine Providence*, pp. 78–79.

43. Miller and Johnson, *The Puritans*, 2:614. This trend continued into the early decades of the 1700s. See, for example, Cotton Mather, *Days of Humiliation, Times of Affliction and Disaster: Nine Sermons for Restoring Favor with an Angry God (1696–1727)*, George Harrison Orians, ed. (rpt. Gainesville, Fla.: Scholars Facsimiles and Reprints, 1970).

44. Miller and Johnson, *The Puritans*, 1:246.

45. Ibid., pp. 245, 244.

46. Quoted by Foster, *Their Solitary Way*, p. 59. See also William Hubbard, *The History of the Indian Wars in New England from the First Settlement to the Termination of the War with King Philip, in 1677*, Samuel G. Drake, ed. (Boston, 1677; rpt. New York: Burt Franklin, 1971), 1:9.

47. Williston Walker, *The Creeds and Platforms of Congregationalism* (Boston: Pilgrim Press, 1960), p. 427.

48. Ibid., p. 436.

49. Ibid.

50. Mather, *Doctrine of Divine Providence*, pp. 34–35.

51. Ibid., p. 58.

52. Elliott, *Power and the Pulpit*, pp. 60–62, 89–99, 149–55.

53. Miller and Johnson, *The Puritans*, 2:611.

54. Ibid., p. 612.

55. Alden T. Vaughan, ed., *The Puritan Tradition in America, 1620–1730* (New York: Harper and Row, 1972), p. 343.

56. Minter, *The Integrated Design*, p. 59; also see Kaul, *The American Vision*, p. 12.

57. Miller, *Errand*, pp. 1–15; also see Minter, *The Interpreted Design*, p. 59.

58. An interesting topic for research in the Puritans' typological use of the Old Testament is whether, during this period of uncertainty, Puritan sermons seek to understand this situation by appealing to the works of those later prophets who prophesied that God would soon create a new relationship—a new covenant—with the Israelites. Some sermons by Urian Oakes and Increase Mather give indications of such a tendency.

59. Sermons during this period, according to Elliott, express this element of uncertainty side by side with images of a wrathful God (*Power and the Pulpit*, pp. 13–14, 40, 88–135, 136, 201–2). However, in his excellent study, *The Design of the Present*, John Lynen views this doubt and uncertainty as a characteristic trait of the Puritan mind (pp. 74–75). See also Bercovitch, *Typology*, p. 3; Murdock, "Clio in the Wilderness," pp. 206–7; and Kai T. Erikson, *Wayward Puritans: A Study in the Sociology of Deviance* (New York: John Wiley, 1966), pp. 51–53.

60. Miller and Johnson, *The Puritans*, 1:153. Later Puritan preachers looked upon the vicissitudes of settling the wilderness as "a token of [God's] love," "a witness of [God's] Adoption" of the Puritans, and "a pledge of [their] future salvation" (Elliott, *Power and the Pulpit*, p. 176). See also Carroll, *Puritanism and the Wilderness*, pp. 28–29.

61. Roy Harvey Pearce, ed., *Colonial American Writing* (New York: Holt, Rinehart and Winston, 1966), p. 284.

62. Edward Taylor, *The Poetical Works of Edward Taylor*, Thomas H. Johnson, ed. (Princeton: Princeton University Press, 1966), p. 31. For a fuller statement of Taylor's poetical treatment of God, see pp. 19–28; also see Ursula Brumm, "Edward Taylor and the Poetic Use of Religious Imagery," found in Bercovitch, *Typology*, pp. 191–206, and Peter Nicolaisen's excellent monograph, *Die Bildlichkeit in der Dichtung Edward Taylors* (Neumünster, 1966).

63. Hubbard, *The History of the Indian Wars in New England*, 2:253–54.

64. Miller and Johnson, *The Puritans*, 2:656e.

65. Taylor, *The Poetical Works of Edward Taylor*, pp. 19–28.

66. Erikson, *Wayward Puritans*, pp. 135–41, 155–59.

67. See note 59 of this chapter and Elliott, *Power and the Pulpit*, pp. 99–135. "In addition to imagery of sickness and weakness," Elliott argues, "the ministers used symbolism of deprivation and loss to describe the condition of New England in the 1670's (p. 99). . . . Frequently, ministers made use of the imagery of loss by envisioning the covenant as a family contract between God the Father and his New England sons with inheritance of earthly as well as spiritual reward at stake (p. 101). . . . The figure most often repeated in the sermons of the 1670's was the departing of the father, usually symbolized by the abandonment of New England by God the Father" (p. 103).

68. The demonic aspects of human experience, as was typical of the age, were attributed to Satan—a notion which was used to explain the existence of witches and the supposed outburst of witchcraft that led to the infamous Salem witchcraft trials (1692), and which, in revised form, was also used to explain these trials. See Elliott, *Power and the Pulpit*, pp. 198–200; John Putnam Demos, *Entertaining Satan: Witchcraft and the Culture of Early New England* (New York: Oxford University Press, 1983); Chadwick Hansen, *Witchcraft at Salem* (New York: New American Library, 1970), chapter 13; Carroll, *Puritanism and the Wilderness*,

pp. 72–82; and Cotton Mather, *The Wonders of the Invisible World, Being an Account of the Tryals of Several Witches Lately Executed in New-England* (Boston, 1693; rpt. Cleveland: Bell and Howell Co.). Satan was, in fact, a central figure in the popular religious lore which presented him as the source of all problems that troubled the New England churches. See Richard M. Dorson, *America in Legend: Folklore from the Colonial Period to the Present* (New York: Pantheon Books, 1973), pp. 32–51. Increase Mather included many popular legends about Satan in his work, *Remarkable Providences Illustrative of the Earlier Days of American Colonisation* (1684), in order to help explain experiences of the demonic that were beyond human control. Even so, there were other kinds of experiences—such as premature deaths of children and adults, accidental deaths, the miseries and injustices suffered by exemplary Christians, the sudden reversals of personal fortunes, the wars between Indian tribes and the Puritans—which they attributed only to God. The notion that God was responsible for bringing about such events led people, at least in the last quarter of the 1600s, to raise disturbing questions about the justice and the goodness of a sovereign God. At least Increase Mather suggests this to be the case when he indicates that he had difficulties in proving the justice of God's ways to the relatives of those who were killed aboard a boat that exploded in Boston harbor. (See Elliott, *Power and the Pulpit*, pp. 115–16.) To accept God's sovereignty over human lives was one thing; to accept a sovereign God whose actions frequently were ethically repugnant and often contradictory in the lessons they taught—who even required the Puritans to obey a covenant which He Himself had seemingly abandoned—was quite another thing; and people apparently increasingly drove the point home.

69. For Perry Miller's treatment of this dilemma in the early Puritan federal theology, see *Errand*, pp. 48–98. However, George M. Marsden, in his article "Perry Miller's Rehabilitation of the Puritans: A Critique," *Church History* 39 (1970): 91–105, finds many loopholes in Miller's argument. More recent evaluations of Miller's interpretation of Puritanism can be found in Sacvan Bercovitch, ed., *The American Imagination: Essays in Revaluation* (New York: Cambridge University Press, 1974), p. 213, note 1; in *American Quarterly* 34 (Spring 1982): 3–94 (several authors); in Emil Oberholzer's review of the criticism of Miller's work in "Puritanism Revisited," found in Alden T. Vaughan and George Athan Billas, eds., *Perspectives on Early American History: Essays in Honor of Richard B. Morris* (New York: Harper and Row, 1973), pp. 193–207; and in John C. Crowell, "Perry Miller as Historian: A Bibliography of Evaluations," *Bulletin of Bibliography and Magazine Notes* 34 (April-June 1977): 77–85.

2. THE PURITAN THEODICY

1. Miller and Johnson, *The Puritans*, 1:358.

2. Ibid.

3. Ibid., p. 359.

4. Thirty years later, Increase Mather succinctly summarized this argument in the following way. "There are future things which happen necessarily, that a man may know them long before they come to pass: *God has appointed Lights in the Heaven to be for Signs and Seasons*. These move regularly and unfailably according to that Order which the Creator has established. Therefore a man may know

infallibly how many hours or minutes such a day or night will be long before the Time comes; He may know when there will be an *Eclipse* of the Sun or of the Moon, twenty, or an hundred years before it comes to pass: but for Contingent Things, which have no necessary dependance on the constituted Order of Nature, but upon the meer Pleasure and Providence of God, they are not known except unto God, or to them unto whom he shall reveal them." Ibid., pp. 343–44.

5. Ibid., p. 362.

6. Ibid., p. 366.

7. Ibid., p. 361.

8. Increase Mather, for example, uses this principle thirty years later to explain the accidental deaths of two Harvard undergraduates whose behavior, he says, had always been exemplary. Speaking to an assembly of Harvard students soon after the deaths of these two students, Mather descants on the redemptive possibilities of their deaths. "But Oh that the Lorde would sanctify what has hapned to awaken you unto serious thoughts about Death and Eternity. Who knows but that God may make these sudden Deaths, an occasion of promising the Salvation, and Eternal Life of some amongst you." Ibid., p. 348.

9. Ibid., p. 367.

10. See Mather's preface to *Remarkable Providences*.

11. Ibid., p. 27.

12. See Dorson, *America in Legend*, pp. 17–31, for an extended discussion of the Puritan view of divine providences. See also Samuel Adams Drake, ed., *A Book of New England Legends and Folk Lore* (Rutland, Vt.: Charles E. Tuttle, Co., 1975).

13. Cotton Mather, *Magnalia Christi Americana; or, The Ecclesiastical History of New-England; from Its First Planting, in the Year 1620, unto the Year of our Lord 1698* (1852; rpt. New York: Russell and Russell, 1967), 2:384.

14. Ibid., pp. 384–403.

15. Page citations refer to the 1684 edition of *Doctrine of Divine Providence*.

16. Cotton Mather develops this same point in the sixth book of *Magnalia Christi Americana*.

17. Miller and Johnson, *The Puritans*, 1:348.

18. Ibid., p. 335.

19. Ibid., p. 336.

20. Ibid., p. 335.

21. Ibid., pp. 337–38.

22. Mather here sides with those who argued for the doctrine of preparation. A history of the stormy emergence of this doctrine in Puritan thought can be found in Norman Pettit's excellent study, *The Heart Prepared: Grace and Conversion in Puritan Spiritual Life* (New Haven: Yale University Press, 1966).

23. Miller and Johnson, *The Puritans*, 1:340. Also, see Mather, *Doctrine of Divine Providence*, pp. 104-5.

24. Mather here exemplifies that renewed emphasis upon God's grace which Elliott traces in Puritan sermons written in the 1690s. See *Power and the Pulpit in Puritan New England*, pp. 13–14, 173–200. It is important to note here, however, that the early Puritans, always aware that people could easily counterfeit their morality, were unwilling to say that all moral behavior mirrors a genuine religious life (a point that Jonathan Edwards develops at length in *The Nature of True*

Virtue). See Larzer Ziff, *Puritanism in America: New Culture in a New World* (New York: Viking Press, 1973), p. 307. Of course, this emphasis upon appearances in the moral and religious spheres of life reinforced the problematic nature of their relationship.

25. Page citations refer to Cotton Mather, *Bonifacius*.

26. See also ibid., pp. 27–29, and Cotton Mather, *Days of Humiliation*, pp. 331–73.

27. Introduction to Cotton Mather, *Bonifacius*, p. xviii.

28. See also ibid., pp. 19, 150.

29. Sören Kierkegaard, *Fear and Trembling and the Sickness Unto Death*, Walter Lowrie, trans. (Princeton: Princeton University Press, 1969), pp. 30–37, 64–77.

30. Geoffrey Clive, *The Romantic Enlightenment* (Westport, Conn.: Greenwood Press, 1973), p. 150.

31. Such a view of the moral life implies that no person can credit or praise himself or herself for the good consequences of his or her actions, while the doctrine of innate depravity requires that people be blamed for the bad consequences of their behavior. For an excellent overview of Cotton Mather's work, see Sacvan Bercovitch, "Cotton Mather," found in Emerson, *Major Writers of Early American Literature*, pp. 93–149.

32. Jonathan Edwards, *The Works of Jonathan Edwards*, Edward Hickman, ed. (London: Henry G. Bohn, 1871), 2:513.

33. Cotton Mather, *Bonifacius*, p. xxviii.

34. Ernest Benson Lowrie, *The Shape of the Puritan Mind* (New Haven: Yale University Press, 1974), p. 2. See also James W. Jones, *The Shattered Synthesis: New England Puritanism before the Great Awakening* (New Haven: Yale University Press, 1973), pp. 54–75.

35. In chapter five of *The Real Christian* (1670), Giles Firmin elaborates his reasons for rejecting the notion of a sovereign God who uses His power in unethical and irrational ways. Page citations refer to this work (microfilm). Norman Pettit observes that "from the writings of Giles Firmin it is possible to date the beginnings of an era in which Puritanism finally degenerated into moralism and sentimentalism." Pettit, *The Heart Prepared*, p. 217.

36. Ibid., pp. 175–80.

37. Ibid., pp. 182–84.

38. Ibid., pp. 244–49.

39. "Preface" to "The Law Established by the Gospel or, A Brief Discourse, Asserted and Declared, the Great Honour which is put upon the Law of God, in the Gospel Way of Justification by Faith alone" (Boston: September 20, 1694, date preached), unnumbered page. Microfiche.

40. Samuel Willard, *A Compleat Body of Divinity*, Edward M. Griffin, ed. (1726; rpt. New York: Johnson Reprint Corporation, 1969), p. 148.

41. Ibid., pp. 133–45.

42. Quoted by Lowrie, *The Shape of the Puritan Mind*, p. 72. See Samuel Willard, *Useful Instruction for a Professing People in Time of Great Security and Degeneracy: Delivered in several sermons on solemn occasions* (Cambridge: Samuel Green, 1673), p. 24. Microfilm.

43. Willard, *A Compleat Body of Divinity*, p. 138.

44. Ibid., pp. 103–6, 134, 178–79, 186, 268–69, 309.

45. Quoted by Lowrie, *The Shape of the Puritan Mind*, p. 71.

46. Willard, *A Compleat Body of Divinity*, pp. 37–94.

47. Quoted by Lowrie, *The Shape of the Puritan Mind*, p. 162. See Samuel Willard, *The Doctrine of the Covenant of Redemption* (Boston: Benjamin Harris, 1693), p. 121. Microfilm.

48. Jones, *The Shattered Synthesis*, pp. 61ff.

49. Lowrie, *The Shape of the Puritan Mind*, pp. 169–70.

50. Samuel Willard, "Morality not to be Relied on for Life" (Boston: May 23, 1700, date preached), p. 12. Microfiche.

51. Ibid., pp. 20–28.

52. Ibid., p. 24.

53. Willard, "The Law Established by the Gospel," pp. 34–35, 37.

54. Ibid., p. 8.

55. Ibid., p. 24; see also pp. 14–15.

56. Ibid., p. 28.

57. Willard, "Morality not to be Relied on for Life," p. 22. Also see Willard, "The Law Established by the Gospel," pp. 32–33; *A Compleat Body of Divinity*, pp. 583–85; and *Brotherly Love Described and Directed* (especially pp. 229–30), published with *The Christian's Exercise by Satan's Temptation* (Boston: B. Green and J. Allen, 1701). Microfilm.

58. Willard, "Morality not to be Relied on for Life," p. 21.

59. Willard, *A Compleat Body of Divinity*, p. 580.

60. See Willard, *A Compleat Body of Divinity*, pp. 121, 137, 143, 508ff., 567, 573; "The Law Established by the Gospel," p. 24; and "The Truly Blessed Man: or The way to be happy here and for ever. Being the substance of divers sermons preached on Psalm 32" (Boston: B. Green and J. Allen, 1700), pp. 139–40, 149. Microfilm.

61. Willard, *A Compleat Body of Divinity*, p. 574.

3. JONATHAN EDWARDS: MORALITY AND A SOVEREIGN GOD

1. This chapter in no way attempts to analyze the complexities of Edwards' theology. Rather, the primary concern is to examine how his vision of God and the moral life expresses the synthesis of world view and ethos articulated by the Puritan theodicy.

2. Page citations, except those for *Treatise Concerning Religious Affections* and *The Nature of True Virtue*, refer to Jonathan Edwards, *The Works of Jonathan Edwards*, Edward Hickman, ed., 2 vols., 10th ed. (London: Henry G. Bohn, 1871). The abbreviation "W" will be used for page references in the text and notes.

3. Much has been made of this image in Edwards' sermon. Yet it was a stock image of the Puritan tradition. In *Pilgrims Progress*, for example, the Interpreter shows Christina and Mercy the best room in a house whose sole occupant is a spider on the ceiling. Christina responds that there is more than one spider in the room "whose venom is far more destructive than that which is in her." John Bunyan, *The Pilgrims Progress* (New York: The New American Library, 1964), p. 185.

4. There can be no doubt, as Perry Miller argues in *Jonathan Edwards* (New York: Dell Publishing Co., 1967), that Edwards rejected the Puritan covenant theology. But, as several students of Edwards have demonstrated, Miller drastically overstates this rejection. See, for example, Conrad Cherry, "The Puritan Notion of the Covenant in Jonathan Edwards' Doctrine of Faith," *Church History* 34 (September 1965): 328–41; Conrad Cherry, *The Theology of Jonathan Edwards: A Reappraisal* (Gloucester, Mass.: Peter Smith, 1974), pp. 113ff.; and John H. Gerstner, *Steps to Salvation: The Evangelistic Message of Jonathan Edwards* (Philadelphia: Westminster Press, 1959), pp. 173–88.

5. Certainly, on the one hand, Edwards' vision of human depravity and the human need for divine grace implies a strong leveling tendency which, in effect, supports a democratic ethic. On the other hand, Edwards undercuts such an ethic by denying people any rights in their relationship with God. Edwards expresses this denial of human rights as early as age nineteen, when he recounts his conversion experience. "I have been before God; and have given myself, and all that I am and have to God, so that I am not in any respect my own: I can challenge no right in myself, I can challenge no right in this understanding, this will, these affections that are in me; neither have I any right to this body, or any of its members. . . . I have given myself clear away, and have not retained any thing as my own. . . . I did take Him for my whole portion and felicity. . . . Now, henceforth I am not to act in any respect as my own." David Levin, ed., *Jonathan Edwards: A Profile* (New York: Hill and Wang, 1969), pp. 12–13. For Edwards, as for Puritanism in general, this means that people must fully rely upon God's merciful grace, itself an arbitrary reality. The common charge that "Sinners in the Hands of an Angry God" downplays this emphasis upon divine grace ignores the dramatic quality of this sermon and therefore misrepresents him. For when this sermon is viewed as an artistic rendering of people's plight before God, Edwards' emphasis upon divine grace can be seen to pervade, even shape, the nature of its execution. By clearly dramatizing the sinner's dilemma, from which only God can save him, Edwards dramatically renders the nature and efficacy of God's grace, and thereby heightens the felt necessity for relying solely on this grace. Hence, this sermon might be plausibly viewed as a celebration *via negativa* of God's glory and grace, a celebration designed to help his listeners affectionally as well as intellectually achieve a new spiritual sense of God's power and grace.

6. For more extensive treatments of Edwards' artistry and use of images in his sermons and writings, see Eugene White, *Puritan Rhetoric: The Issue of Emotion in Religion* (Carbondale: Southern Illinois Press, 1972), p. 67; Miller, *Jonathan Edwards*, pp. 154–63; Ziff, *Puritanism in America*, p. 309; Levin, *Jonathan Edwards*, pp. 220–30; Annette Kolodny, "Imagery in the Sermons of Jonathan Edwards," *Early American Literature* 7 (Spring 1972): 172–82; Edwin H. Cady, "The Artistry of Jonathan Edwards' Personal Narrative," *New England Quarterly* 22 (March 1949): 61–72; Daniel B. Shea, *Spiritual Autobiography in Early America* (Princeton: Princeton University Press, 1968), pp. 182–208; and Terrence Erdt, *Jonathan Edwards: Art and the Sense of the Heart* (Amherst: University of Massachusetts Press, 1980), pp. 63–82. For an analysis of Edwards' "idealist imagination," see Michael J. Colacurcio, "The Example of Edwards: Idealist Imagination and the Metaphysics of Sovereignty," in Emory Elliott, ed., *Puritan Influences in American Literature* (Urbana: University of Illinois Press, 1979), pp. 55–106;

and John Griffith, "Jonathan Edwards as a Literary Artist," *Criticism* 15 (Spring 1973): 156–73.

7. Edwards further adds that "it is more fit that all things be under the guidance of a perfect unerring wisdom, than that they should be left to themselves to fall in confusion, or be brought to pass by blind causes (W, 2:108)." The world is a far better place, he contends, under the arbitrary disposal of God's providential wisdom than it would be were it left to be arbitrarily shaped by random forces.

8. Roland Delattre, *Beauty and Sensibility in the Thought of Jonathan Edwards: An Essay in Aesthetics and Theological Ethics* (New Haven: Yale University Press, 1968), p. 78. For a fuller explication of Edwards' view of evil, see Douglas J. Elwood, *The Philosophical Theology of Jonathan Edwards* (New York: Columbia University Press, 1960), pp. 65–89.

9. Joseph Haroutunian's response to Edwards' view of divine justice is less than flattering. "Edwards' religion was divine republicanism, and his God a President of questionable wisdom and power. In a republic, prisons filled with convicts sentenced to life imprisonment are a reflection upon its rulers, or at best, unpleasant but unavoidable social necessities." *Piety Versus Moralism*, p. 152. However, Cedric B. Cowing adds the caveat that "in his revival sermons, Edwards, while driving home God's sovereignty, had sometimes made Him seem capricious, but later he insisted that the Almighty acted only by design, never hastily or accidentally." *The Great Awakening and the American Revolution: Colonial Thought in the Eighteenth Century* (Chicago: Rand McNally, 1971), p. 194.

10. See *The Works of Jonathan Edwards*, 2:511–15, for Edwards' full argument regarding why Christians, no matter what suffering and injustices they endure, must trust the reliability of God's moral government.

11. See C. A. Holbrook, "Edwards and the Ethical Question," *Harvard Theological Review* 60 (April 1967): 163–75; C. M. Newlin, *Philosophy and Religion in Colonial America* (New York: Philosophical Library, 1962), pp. 166–94; and Austin Warren, *The New England Conscience* (Ann Arbor: University of Michigan Press, 1966), pp. 88–101.

12. Edwin Scott Gaustad, *The Great Awakening in New England* (Gloucester, Mass.: Peter Smith, 1965); Alan Heimert and Perry Miller, eds., *The Great Awakening* (New York: Bobbs-Merrill Co., 1967), pp. xii–xxi; and Conrad Wright, *The Beginnings of Unitarianism in America* (Boston: Beacon Press, 1966), pp. 28–58.

13. For a detailed analysis of how children were raised in Puritan families to have conversion experiences in accordance with an established pattern, see Philip Greven, *The Protestant Temperament: Patterns of Child-Rearing, Religious Experience, and the Self in Early America* (New York: Alfred A. Knopf, 1977). William Perkins, a widely read theologian among American theologians, outlined the established pattern for a conversion experience in an intricately detailed map. See William Perkins, *The Works of William Perkins*, Ian Breward, ed. (Abingdon [Berks]: Sutton Courtenay Press, 1970), the foldout between pp. 167–71. For an analysis of role models in the process of conversion, see Margaret W. Masson, "The Typology of the Female as a Model for the Regenerate: Puritan Preaching, 1690–1730," *Signs: Journal of Women in Culture and Society* 2 (Winter 1976): 304–15, and Edmund Morgan, *The Puritan Family: Religion and Domestic Relations in Seventeenth-Century New England* (New York: Harper and Row, 1966), pp. 61, 161–62.

14. Heimert and Miller, *The Great Awakening*, p. 86; Rutman, *American Puritanism: Faith and Practice*, pp. 89–124.

15. Heimert and Miller, *The Great Awakening*, pp. 229–56. Charles Chauncy, *Seasonable Thoughts on the State of Religion in New England*, Richard Warch, ed. (Boston, 1743; rpt. Hicksville, N.Y.: Regina Press, 1975), pp. 264–74.

16. Wright, *Beginnings of Unitarianism in America*, pp. 22–58.

17. W, 2:600–601.

18. Jonathan Edwards, *Religious Affections*, John E. Smith, ed. (New Haven: Yale University Press, 1976), p. 17.

19. Edwards earlier defined these negative signs in his sermon "The Distinguishing Marks of a Work of the Spirit of God" first preached in the fall of 1741.

20. Heimert and Miller, *The Great Awakening*, pp. xvii–xxii, xxxix–xlii.

21. Page citations refer to Edwards, *Religious Affections*.

22. William A. Clebsch, *American Religious Thought: A History* (Chicago: University of Chicago Press, 1973), p. 40; and Perry Miller, "Jonathan Edwards on the Sense of the Heart," *Harvard Theological Review* 41 (April 1948): 123–45.

23. For extended discussions of the sixth sense and its relation to Lockean psychology, see Miller, *Errand into the Wilderness*, pp. 167–83; Miller, *Jonathan Edwards*, pp. 52–68; and Leon Howard, *The Mind of Jonathan Edwards: A Reconstructed Text* (Berkeley: University of California Press, 1963), pp. 120–35, who argues that Miller inaccurately understood Edwards' use of Lockean psychology. Other such critiques of Miller's thesis can be found in Edward Davidson, "From Locke to Edwards," *Journal of the History of Ideas* 24 (July 1963): 355–72; David Lyttle, "The Sixth Sense of Jonathan Edwards," *Church Quarterly Review* 167 (January 1966): 50–59; C. A. Smith, "Jonathan Edwards and 'The Way of Ideas,' " *Harvard Theological Review* 59 (April 1966): 153–73; and Delattre, *Beauty and Sensibility in the Thought of Jonathan Edwards*, p. 4, note 7.

24. This aesthetic element in Edwards' theology is thoroughly analyzed by Roland Delattre in his excellent study, *Beauty and Sensibility in the Thought of Jonathan Edwards*, and by Erdt in *Jonathan Edwards*.

25. Edwards never seeks to impose a standardized pattern upon the conversion experience. Rather, he argues that the authenticity of any purported conversion is to be determined not by its immediate physical manifestations, nor even by its inner certitude and assent to particular religious beliefs, but largely by the quality of life it generates. See Edwards, *Religious Affections*, pp. 20, 151–63, 416–18. See also Cherry, *The Theology of Jonathan Edwards*, pp. 56–70.

26. Edwards, *Religious Affections*, pp. 393–98. See also pp. 450–55 where Edwards answers the objection "that professors should judge of their state, chiefly by their inward experience that spiritual experiences are the main evidence of true grace" (p. 450). Edwards further reinforces the necessity for a balance between the public and private aspects of religion by giving equal importance to both the intention or "sincerity" of an act and the act itself. "Sincerity in religion," as Edwards defines it, "consists in setting God highest in the heart, in choosing him before other things, in having a heart to sell all for Christ," and the willingness to sacrifice one's self for the glory of God (p. 427). The believer himself can be inwardly convinced of his own sincerity, but unless it consistently gives rise to Christian deeds, neither his neighbors, nor God, nor the believer himself will have any external sign by which to detect his sincerity.

27. Ibid., pp. 455–59.

28. Page citations refer to Jonathan Edwards, *The Nature of True Virtue*, William K. Frankena, ed. (Ann Arbor: University of Michigan Press, 1969).

29. Moreover, "there is the agreement of justice to the will and command of God; and also something in the tendency and consequences of justice, agreeable to general benevolence, as the glory of God, and the general good." This means, for Edwards, that the benevolence toward being in general manifested by truly just affections and actions makes them pleasing and "beautiful to a truly virtuous mind" (p. 39). True virtue relishes this primary spiritual beauty which ultimately derives from the full conformity of virtuous justice "with the necessary nature of things" (p. 99). See Delattre, *Beauty and Sensibility in the Thought of Jonathan Edwards*, pp. 27, 78, 96–98, 191–96, 210–13.

30. W, 2:109, 7.

31. Perry Miller neglected Edwards' teachings on divine grace and, as some students of Edwards have noted, this is a serious flaw in his view of Edwards. See Cherry, *The Theology of Jonathan Edwards*, pp. 98ff. and Gerstner, *Steps to Salvation*, pp. 18–23, 71–149.

32. Jones, *The Shattered Synthesis*, p. 29.

4. THE RATIONALISTIC THEODICY

1. Sidney E. Mead, *The Lively Experiment*, pp. 16–37.

2. Alan Heimert, *Religion and the American Mind: From the Great Awakening to the Revolution* (Cambridge: Harvard University Press, 1969), p. 14. See also Alan Heimert, "Toward the Republic," in Darrett B. Rutman, ed., *The Great Awakening: Event and Exegesis* (New York: John Wiley and Sons, 1970), pp. 119–38.

3. See Perry Miller, "From the Covenant to the Revival," in James Ward Smith and A. Leland Jamison, eds., *The Shaping of American Religion* (Princeton: Princeton University Press, 1969), pp. 322–68.

4. See William G. McLoughlin, "The Role of Religion in the Revolution: Liberty of Conscience and Cultural Cohesion in the New Nation," in Stephen G. Kurtz and James H. Hudson, eds., *Essays on the American Revolution* (New York: W. W. Norton and Co., 1973), pp. 197–255.

5. Bernard Bailyn, *The Ideological Origins of the American Revolution* (Cambridge: Harvard University Press, 1976), pp. 230–319.

6. Martin E. Marty, *Righteous Empire: The Protestant Experience in America* (New York: Dial Press, 1970), p. 37, also see pp. 5–66. See also J. M. Bumsted, "The Stable Context of Americanization," in Rutman, *The Great Awakening*, pp. 181–97.

7. Edwin Scott Gaustad, *A Religious History of America* (New York: Harper and Row, 1966), p. 132.

8. Sydney E. Ahlstrom, *Religious History of the American People* (Garden City, N.Y.: Image Books, 1975), 2:442; see also pp. 433ff.

9. Catherine L. Albanese, *Sons of the Fathers: The Civil Religion of the American Revolution* (Philadelphia: Temple University Press, 1976), p. 8. See also Robert N. Bellah, *The Broken Covenant: American Civil Religion in Time of Trial*

(New York: Seabury Press, 1975), pp. 1–35, and Jerald C. Brauer, ed., *Religion and the American Revolution* (Philadelphia: Fortress Press, 1976), pp. 55–73.

10. Robert Bellah, *The Broken Covenant*, pp. 36–60; Conrad Cherry, *God's New Israel*, pp. 1–24. See also Robert Bellah, "Civil Religion in America," in Russell E. Richey and Donald G. Jones, eds., *American Civil Religion* (New York: Harper and Row, 1974), pp. 27–29; and Robert Bellah and Phillip E. Hammond, *Varieties of Civil Religion* (New York: Harper and Row, 1980), pp. 7–20.

11. Henry F. May, *The Enlightenment in America* (New York: Oxford University Press, 1976), pp. 181, xvii.

12. Ahlstrom, *A Religious History of the American People*, 1:442.

13. See, for example, Frederick Tolles, "The American Revolution Considered as a Social Movement: A Re-evaluation," *American Historical Review* 60 (1954): 1–12; Elisha P. Douglass, *Rebels and Democrats* (Chapel Hill: University of North Carolina Press, 1955); the last essay in Richard B. Morris, *The American Revolution Reconsidered* (New York: Harper and Row, 1967), pp. 127–67; Jesse Lemisch, "The American Revolution Seen from the Bottom Up," in Barton J. Bernstein, ed., *Towards a New Past: Dissenting Essays in American History* (New York: Vintage Books, 1969), pp. 3–45; Rowland Berthoff and John M. Murrin, "Feudalism, Communalism, and the Yeoman Freeholder: The American Revolution Considered as a Social Accident," in Kurtz and Hudson, *Essays on the American Revolution*, pp. 256–88; Jackson Turner Main, "Government by the People: The American Revolution and the Democratization of the Legislatures," *William and Mary Quarterly* 23 (July 1966): 391–407; Merrill Jensen, "The American People and the American Revolution," *Journal of American History* 57 (June 1970): 5–35; and Edmund S. Morgan, "The American Revolution: Revisions in Need of Revising," in Edmund S. Morgan, ed., *The American Revolution: Two Centuries of Interpretation* (Englewood Cliffs, N.J.: Prentice-Hall, 1968), pp. 166–79.

14. Peter Berger, *The Social Reality of Religion* (London: Faber and Faber, 1969); Douglas, *Natural Symbols*; Douglas, *Cultural Bias*; Clifford Geertz, "Blurred Genres: The Refiguration of Social Thought," *The American Scholar* 49 (Spring 1980): 165–79; Geertz, *The Interpretation of Cultures*; Victor Turner, *Dramas, Fields, and Metaphors: Symbolic Action in Human Society* (Ithaca: Cornell University Press, 1974); Victor Turner and Edith Turner, *Image and Pilgrimage in Christian Culture: Anthropological Perspectives* (New York: Columbia University Press, 1978); Victor Turner, *The Forest of Symbols: Aspects of Ndembu Ritual* (Ithaca: Cornell University Press, 1967). Also, see Introduction, note 10.

15. Edmund S. Morgan was the first historian to describe "Puritan tribalism" in *The Puritan Family*, pp. 161–86. See also Douglas, *Natural Symbols*, for an analysis of how different kinds of tribal groups generate cosmologies that reflect their social structure, and Peter L. Berger and Thomas Luckman, *The Social Construction of Reality: A Treatise in the Sociology of Knowledge* (Garden City, N.Y.: Doubleday, 1967).

16. Ahlstrom, *A Religious History of the American People*, 1:440–41.

17. See Douglas, *Natural Symbols*, for an analysis of how tribal groups redefine their boundaries and how this redefinition affects their cosmologies.

18. Accompanying this cultural and theological transition was also a corresponding intellectual change. See Edmund S. Morgan, "The American Revolution

Considered as an Intellectual Movement," in Arthur M. Schlesinger, Jr., and Morton White, eds., *Paths of American Thought* (Boston: Houghton Mifflin Co., 1970), pp. 11–33; May, *The Enlightenment in America*; Bailyn, *The Ideological Origins of the American Revolution*; Henry Steele Commager, *The Empire of Reason: How Europe Imagined and America Realized the Enlightenment* (Garden City, N.Y.: Anchor Press, 1977); Edmund S. Morgan, ed., *Puritan Political Ideas: 1558–1794* (Indianapolis: Bobbs-Merrill, 1978), pp. xiii–xlvii; Joseph Ellis, "The Puritan Mind in Transition: The Philosophy of Samuel Johnson," *William and Mary Quarterly* 28 (January 1971): 26–45; John Hope Franklin, "The North, the South, and the American Revolution," *Journal of American History* 62 (June 1975): 5–23; and Adrienne Koch, *The American Enlightenment* (New York: George Braziller, 1965), pp. 18–48.

19. "Mayhew's *Discourse*, as John Adams later recalled, was 'read by everybody, celebrated by friends, and abused by enemies.' It circulated widely in the colonies, and was reprinted within a few months of its initial appearance. It quickly became regarded as a classic formulation of the necessity and virtue of resistance to oppression. . . . It created for the extreme radical position on the subject of civil disobedience a more attentive public audience than it had had before in America. . . . In 1775, when the pamphlet was once again reprinted, it expressed what was then almost universally considered to be the simple common sense of the matter, and it was indistinguishable from dozens of other publications appearing everywhere in British North America." Bernard Bailyn, ed., *Pamphlets of the American Revolution: 1750–1776* (Cambridge: Harvard University Press, 1965), 1:209.

20. Bailyn, *The Ideological Origins of the American Revolution*, pp. 55–93.

21. Richard Buel, Jr., "Democracy and the American Revolution: A Frame of Reference," *William and Mary Quarterly* 21 (April 1964): 165–90.

22. Bailyn, *Pamphlets of the American Revolution*, p. 206.

23. Calvin, *Institutes of the Christian Religion*, p. 213; Morgan, *Puritan Political Ideas*, pp. xiii–xlvii; and Michael Walzer, *The Revolution of the Saints: A Study in the Origins of Radical Politics* (Cambridge: Harvard University Press, 1965), pp. 1–65.

24. Bailyn, *The Ideological Origins of the American Revolution* pp. 302–3.

25. Ibid., p. 303.

26. For example, see Edmund S. Morgan, "The Puritan Ethic and the American Revolution," in McGiffert, *Puritanism and the American Experience*, pp. 183–97; Jerald C. Brauer, "Puritanism, Revivalism, and the Revolution," in Brauer, *Religion and the American Revolution*, pp. 1-27; Winthrop S. Hudson, "Theological Convictions and Democratic Government," *Theology Today* 10 (July 1953): 230–39; Sacvan Bercovitch, "How the Puritans Won the American Revolution," *The Massachusetts Review* 17 (Winter 1976): 597–630; and Louis Hartz, "The Rise of the Democratic Idea," in John P. Roche, ed., *Origins of American Political Thought: Selected Readings* (New York: Harper and Row, 1967), pp. 59–77.

27. Gaustad, *The Great Awakening in New England*, pp. 102–40; Heimert and Miller, *The Great Awakening*, pp. xii–lxi; Wright, *Beginnings of Unitarianism in America*, pp. 28–58.

28. Bernard W. Sheehan, "Paradise and the Noble Savage in Jeffersonian

Thought," *William and Mary Quarterly* 26 (July 1969): 327–59. Daniel Boorstin argues in *The Lost World of Thomas Jefferson* (Boston: Beacon Press, 1948) that Jefferson's later concept of America's continental destiny finally led him to move beyond his earlier vision of America as a small agrarian Utopia.

29. Mead, *The Lively Experiment*, pp. 1–37.

30. Page citations refer to Bailyn, *Pamphlets of the American Revolution*.

31. Ibid., p. 211. Mayhew had earlier explicated some of the implications of his rationalistic vision of God in two sermons that advocate people's right to private judgment in religious matters. See Jonathan Mayhew, *Seven Sermons*, Edwin S. Gaustad, ed. (Boston, 1748; rpt. New York: Arno Press, 1969), pp. 42–90. See also Wright, *Beginnings of Unitarianism in America*, pp. 223–40.

32. E. Graham Waring, ed., *Deism and Natural Religion* (New York: Frederick Ungar Publishing Co., 1967), pp. x–xiii.

33. Haroutunian, *Piety Versus Moralism*, pp. 3–130.

34. Wright, *Beginnings of Unitarianism in America*, pp. 37, 39–43, 50–56, 185–99; Gaustad, *The Great Awakening in New England* pp. 80–101.

35. Page citations refer to Charles Chauncy, *The Mystery hid from Ages and Generations, made Manifest by the Gospel-Revelation: or The Salvation of all Men*, Edwin S. Gaustad, ed. (London, 1784; rpt. New York: Arno Press, 1969).

36. See Samuel Mather, *All Men will not be saved forever: Or, an Attempt to prove, That this is a Scriptural Doctrine; and To give a sufficient Answer to the Publisher of Extracts in Favor of the Salvation of all Men* (1782) in Charles Chauncy, *Salvation for All Men, Illustrated and Vindicated as a Scripture Doctrine in Numerous Abstracts from a Variety of Pious and Learned Men*, Conrad Wright, ed. (Boston, 1782; rpt. Hicksville, N.Y.: Regina Press, 1975), pp. 8–9.

37. Ibid., pp. 24–31.

38. The above summary of Chauncy's response to Mather's criticism is taken from Chauncy, *The Salvation of All Men*, pp. 323–26, 340–57. See also Wright, *Beginnings of Unitarianism in America*, pp. 196–99.

39. Jones, *The Shattered Synthesis*, p. 197.

40. William Clebsch, *From Sacred to Profane America: The Role of Religion in American History* (New York: Harper and Row, 1968), p. 18. For an insightful analysis of how Edwards' theology has made a deeper impact than Chauncy's upon American culture, see Ziff, *Puritanism in America*, pp. 303–12.

41. Giles Gunn, "F. Scott Fitzgerald's Gatsby and the Imagination of Wonder," *Journal of the American Academy of Religion* 41 (June 1973): 179. Also see Morton White, *The Philosophy of the American Revolution* (New York: Oxford University Press, 1978), especially pp. 185–228.

42. For further comment on this development in American Protestantism, see Sidney Ahlstrom, *A Religious History of the American People*, 1:418–42, and Haroutunian, *Piety Versus Moralism*, p. 145.

43. Haroutunian, *Piety Versus Moralism*, p. xxii; Gordon S. Wood, "The Democratization of Mind in the American Revolution," in Robert H. Horwitz, ed., *The Moral Foundations of the American Republic* (Charlottesville: University Press of Virginia, 1977), pp. 102–28.

44. See J. Hector St. John de Crèvecoeur, *Letters from an American Farmer*, Warren Barton Blake, ed. (New York: E. P. Dutton, 1957), p. xii; Ahlstrom, *A*

Religious History of the American People, 1:436; Koch, *The American Enlightenment*, p. 102; Mary E. Rucker, "Crèvecoeur's Letters and Enlightenment Doctrine," *Early American Literature* 13 (1978): 193–212. See also M. G. White and L. White, *The Intellectual Versus the City: From Thomas Jefferson to Frank Lloyd Wright* (Cambridge: Harvard University Press, 1962), pp. 6–20.

45. Page citations refer to Crèvecoeur, *Letters from an American Farmer*.

46. R. W. B. Lewis, *The American Adam: Innocence, Tragedy, and Tradition in the Nineteenth Century* (Chicago: University of Chicago Press, 1966), p. 5. Thomas Philbrick further argues that Crèvecoeur is himself an Adamic figure who tragically succumbs to corruption (represented by the figure of a snake in his *Letters*) and thereby brings upon himself his banishment from the Eden of his farm. See *St. John de Crèvecoeur* (New York: Twayne Publishers, 1970), pp. 88, 105–6.

47. For an analysis of how this Puritan emphasis upon sobriety, frugality, and industry helped to give rise to the American Revolution, see Morgan, "The Puritan Ethic and the American Revolution," and Michael Walzer, "Puritan Repression and Modernization," in Richard Reintz, comp., *Tensions in American Puritanism* (New York: Wiley Press, 1970), pp. 161–77. See also Karl J. Weintraub, "The Puritan Ethic and Benjamin Franklin," *Journal of Religion* 56 (July 1976): 223–37.

48. Jones, *O Strange New World*, p. 310.

49. David Noble contends that: "the concept of a Biblical commonwealth was replaced in the eighteenth century by the Enlightenment's belief that the society of the English colonies rested on natural principles and that the new republic that emerged from the American Revolution had a covenant with nature which freed it from the burdens of European history as long as its citizens avoided the creation of complexity." *Historians against History: The Frontier Thesis and the National Covenant in American Historical Writing Since 1830* (Minneapolis: University of Minnesota Press, 1965), p. 3. The *Letters* demonstrate that many understood the old colonial society as already based upon such a covenant with nature. For differing treatments of transformations in the Puritan idea of covenant during this period, see Morgan, *Puritan Political Ideas*, pp. xx–xlvii; Miller, "From the Covenant to the Revival"; and Bellah, *The Broken Covenant*, pp. 1–86.

50. See Philbrick, *St. John de Crèvecoeur*, for comments on how "Crèvecoeur is faithful to the doctrinaire environmentalism which Montesquieu had propounded in *The Spirit of the Laws* and which Raynal had echoed in his *Histoire*" (p. 51).

51. See A. W. Plumstead, "Crèvecoeur: A 'Man of Sorrows' and the American Revolution," *The Massachusetts Review* 17 (Summer 1976): 286–301; A. W. Plumstead, "St. John de Crèvecoeur," in Everett Emerson, ed., *American Literature, 1764–1789: The Revolutionary Years* (Madison: University of Wisconsin Press, 1977), pp. 213–31; and L. L. Hazard, "The Frontier and the Nester: Hector St. John Crèvecoeur," in L. L. Hazard, *The Frontier in American Literature* (New York: Thomas Y. Crowell Co., 1927), pp. 252–61.

52. For a contrary interpretation of Crèvecoeur's scheme, see Kaul, *The American Vision*, pp. 26–28, and M. Jehlen, "J. Hector St. John de Crèvecoeur: A Monarcho-Anarchist in Revolutionary America," *American Quarterly* 31 (Summer 1979): 204–22.

53. Ahlstrom, *A Religious History of the American People*, 1:442.

5. THEODICIES IN CONFLICT

1. May, *The Enlightenment in America*, pp. 354–55. Perry Miller, however, comments that "even in his most reckless moment, Channing was far from casting off his eighteenth-century inheritance." Perry Miller, ed., *The Transcendentalists: An Anthology* (Cambridge: Harvard University Press, 1971), p. 22. For a similar view, see Arthur W. Brown, *William Ellery Channing* (New York: Twayne Publishers, 1961), pp. 63–70. See also Robert E. Spiller, *The Oblique Light: Studies in Literary History and Biography* (New York: Macmillan Co., 1968), pp. 89–109.

2. Page citations refer to William E. Channing, *The Works of William E. Channing* (Boston: American Unitarian Association, 1901).

3. R. S. Foster, *Objections to Calvinism as It Is, in a Series of Letters* (Cincinnati: Hitchcock and Walden, 1849), p. 54.

4. Ibid., pp. 212–13.

5. Ahlstrom, *A Religious History of the American People*, 1:448–54; William E. Tucker and Lester G. McAllister, *Journey in Faith: A History of the Christian Church (Disciples of Christ)* (Saint Louis: Bethany Press, 1975), p. 129; H. Shelton Smith, Robert T. Handy, and Lefferts A. Loetscher, eds., *American Christianity: An Historical Interpretation with Representative Documents* (New York: Charles Scribner's Sons, 1960), 1:419–38.

6. May, *The Enlightenment in America*, pp. 308–9.

7. Channing similarly predicted the demise of Roman Catholicism. "The laws of our spiritual nature give still less chance of success to the system which would thwart or stay them. The progress of the individual and of society, which has shaken the throne of Rome, is not an accident, not an irregular spasmodic effort, but the natural movement of the soul. Catholicism must fall before it. In truth, it is very much fallen already." *Works*, p. 472.

8. Ahlstrom, *A Religious History of the American People*, 2:191–273; Cushing Strout, *The New Heavens and New Earth: Political Religion in America* (New York: Harper and Row, 1975), pp. 224–45; Ernest Lee Tuveson, *Redeemer Nation: The Idea of America's Millennial Role* (Chicago: University of Chicago Press, 1968); and Giles Gunn, ed., *Henry James, Sr.: A Selection of His Writings* (Chicago: American Library Association, 1974), pp. 3–29.

9. See *Radicalism in Religion, Philosophy, and Social Life: Four Papers from the Boston Courier for 1858* (Boston, 1858; rpt. Freeport, N.Y.: Books for Libraries Press, 1972), p. 10.

10. Quoted by Edward Beecher, *The Conflict of Ages; or The Great Debate on the Moral Relations of God and Man* (Boston: Phillips, Samson and Co., 1854), pp. 122–23.

11. Foster, *Objections to Calvinism*, p. 99; see also pp. 126ff.

12. Orthodox theologians also maintained that they were in harmony, but for different reasons. See, for example, John Owen, *The Works of John Owen*, William H. Goold, ed. (Edinburg: T. and T. Clark, 1862), 10:549–64, 569–74, 586–92. "Owen's works were a durable staple of Calvinist teaching. *The Magazine of the Dutch Reformed Church* 3 (April 1828-March 1829), 141, referred to him as the 'prince of theologians.' " Thomas Walter Herbert, Jr., *Moby-Dick and Calvinism: A World Dismantled* (New Brunswick: Rutgers University Press, 1977), p. 120, note 5.

13. Channing, *Works*, pp. 296–97, 376–77, 380–83.

14. *Radicalism in Religion, Philosophy, and Social Life*, pp. 41–57; Rosemary Radford Ruther and Rosemary Skinner Keller, eds., *Women and Religion in America* (New York: Harper and Row, 1981), 1:294–303.

15. *Radicalism in Religion, Philosophy, and Social Life*, p. 62.

16. May, *The Enlightenment in America*, p. 358.

17. Channing, *Works*, pp. 469–70.

18. Irving H. Bartlett, ed., *Unitarian Christianity and other Essays* (New York: The Liberal Arts Press, 1957), p. xxx.

19. Ahlstrom, *A Religious History of the American People*, 2:79–90; Timothy L. Smith, *Revivalism and Social Reform: American Protestantism on the Eve of the Civil War* (New York: Harper and Row, 1965), pp. 95–102.

20. Conrad Wright, however, argues that Channing is not to be so easily identified with Transcendentalism. Conrad Wright, *The Liberal Christians: Essays on American Unitarian History* (Boston: Beacon Press, 1970), pp. 37–40, especially p. 38. However, see Mary W. Edrich, "The Rhetoric of Apostasy," *Texas Studies in Language and Literature* 8 (1967): 547–60, who argues that the difference between Emerson's early position, as set forth in his "Divinity School Address," and Unitarianism was rhetorical rather than substantive.

21. Miller, *The Transcendentalists*, pp. 21–22. For a discussion of Channing's literary reputation and influence, see Spiller, *The Oblique Light*, pp. 89–109.

22. Miller, *The Transcendentalists*, p. 7.

23. Haroutunian, *Piety Versus Moralism*, pp. 266–80.

24. Sydney E. Ahlstrom, ed., *Theology in America: The Major Protestant Voices from Puritanism to Neo-orthodoxy* (New York: Bobbs-Merrill Co., 1967), pp. 212–13.

25. Ibid., p. 217. For further comment on the relationship of this sermon to the theological debates of the early 1800s, see Sidney E. Mead, *Nathaniel William Taylor, 1786–1858: A Connecticut Liberal* (Chicago: University of Chicago Press, 1942), pp. 220–26, and Elwyn A. Smith, "The Voluntary Establishment of Religion," in Elwyn A. Smith, ed., *The Religion of the Republic* (Philadelphia: Fortress Press, 1971), pp. 154–82.

26. Ahlstrom, *Theology in America*, pp. 222, 223.

27. Ibid., p. 215.

28. Ibid., p. 238.

29. Ibid., p. 246.

30. Ibid., p. 247.

31. Ibid., pp. 246, 248.

32. Ibid., pp. 246–47.

33. Ibid., p. 243; see also pp. 248–49.

34. Quoted by Herbert, *Moby-Dick and Calvinism*, p. 172. See Robert Merideth, *The Politics of the Universe, Edward Beecher, Abolition, and Orthodoxy* (Nashville: Vanderbilt University Press, 1968), p. 45.

35. Page citations refer to Beecher, *The Conflict of Ages* (1854).

36. Ibid., p. 122.

37. However, Beecher provides evidence which suggests that this idea arose in early church times but was repressed. See ibid., pp. 265–362.

38. Gordon S. Wood, "The Democratization of Mind in the American Revolution"; Smith, Handy and Loetscher, *American Christianity*, 2:8.

39. Beecher, *The Conflict of Ages*, p. 10.

40. Gordon D. Kaufman, "Nuclear Eschatology and the Study of Religion," *Journal of the American Academy of Religion* 51 (March 1983): 8.

41. Ibid., p. 9.

42. Ibid., pp. 8–9.

43. Loren Baritz, *City on a Hill: A History of Ideas and Myths in America* (New York: John Wiley and Sons, 1964), p. 209. Baritz overstates his case about the extent to which such writers repudiated the Puritan tradition when he states: "The Puritan synthesis was the primary threat to intellectual and artistic progress, according to those authors of America's renaissance. Step by step they said 'no' to most of the major Puritan affirmations, but in limiting themselves to the Puritan categories they gave to the creative writing of their time the peculiar metaphysical and theological flavor that only the particular intellectual enemy they shared could give. Their major intellectual task was to answer a series of questions with their contemporary voice: What is the nature of God and man? What is man's proper relation to society? What is the nature of good and evil?" (p. 208).

6. WILLIAM DUNLAP AND JAMES FENIMORE COOPER: A PROBLEMATICAL AMERICAN REVOLUTION

1. See, for example, A. D. Van Nostrand, *Everyman His Own Poet*.

2. Robert E. Spiller, *James Fenimore Cooper* (Minneapolis: University of Minnesota Press, 1965), p. 14. See also Spiller, *The Oblique Light*, pp. 71–87.

3. For descriptions of these changes, see May, *The Enlightenment in America*, pp. 307–9; Ahlstrom, *A Religious History of the American People*, 1:471–614; Irving H. Bartlett, *The American Mind in the Mid-Nineteenth Century* (New York: Thomas Y. Crowell Co., 1971); and George Dekker, *James Fenimore Cooper: The Novelist* (London: Routledge and Kegan Paul, 1967), pp. 254–59.

4. James Fenimore Cooper, *The Pilot: A Tale of the Sea* (Boston: Colonial Press Co., n.d.), p. 120.

5. Howard Mumford Jones, *Revolution and Romanticism* (Cambridge: Harvard University Press, 1974), pp. 188–227; Commager, *The Empire of Reason*, pp. 119–75; Albanese, *Sons of the Fathers*, pp. 81–111; Bercovitch, *The Puritan Origins of the American Self*, pp. 136–86; and William A. Clebsch, *From Sacred to Profane America*, pp. 56–59.

6. Commager, *The Empire of Reason*, p. 223.

7. May, *The Enlightenment in America*, pp. 180–81.

8. William Alfred Bryan, *George Washington in American Literature, 1775–1865* (Westport, Conn.: Greenwood Press, 1970), p. 179.

9. G. S. Argetsinger, "Dunlap's *André*: Beginning of American Tragedy," *Players Magazine* 49 (Spring 1974): 62–64.

10. See Norman Philbrick, "The Spy as Hero: An Examination of *André* by William Dunlap," in Oscar G. Brockett, ed., *Studies in Theatre and Drama: Essays in Honor of Hubert C. Heffner* (The Hague: Mouton, 1972), pp. 91–119, and

Fred Moramarco, "Early Drama Criticism of William Dunlap," *American Literature* 40 (March 1968): 9–14.

11. Philbrick wrongly criticizes *André* when he claims that "one of the chief weaknesses of [the play] lies in the choice of a spy as a hero, and Dunlap does not attempt to avoid this issue of the shocking nature of André's crime against a nation. He does mitigate it, however, and he obviously felt justified in doing so because of the character of the spy-hero and the romantic aura surrounding him." "The Spy as Hero," p. 98. The fact that Dunlap sympathetically portrays André's plight qualifies Ernest Leisy's observation that "All early treatments of the subject were of course highly romantic. The redcoats were made villains, while Washington and his men were heroized." *The American Historical Novel* (Norman: University of Oklahoma Press, 1950), pp. 68–69.

12. Page citations refer to the edition of *André* in Allan Gates Halline, ed., *American Plays* (New York: American Book Co., 1935), pp. 53–74.

13. For an analysis of the treatments of Washington in American writings from 1775 to 1800, see Bryan, *George Washington in American Literature*, pp. 3–180. Dunlap had composed an earlier play, *The Glory of Columbia* (1789), which is noted for its unabashedly laudatory references to Washington. Dunlap himself, in one of the few firsthand accounts we have of Washington attending a play, gives this account of Washington's response to a performance of *The Glory of Columbia*.

His countenance showed embarrassment from the expectation of one of those eulogiums which he had been obliged to hear on many public occasions, and which doubtless must have been a severe trial to his feelings, but Darby's answer that he had not seen him [Washington] because he had mistaken a man 'all lace and glitter, botherum and shine' for him until all the show had passed, relieved the hero from apprehension of further personality, and he indulged in that which was with him extremely rare, a hearty laugh.

Quoted by Richard Moody, ed., *Dramas from the American Theatre, 1762–1909* (New York: World Publishing Co., 1966), p. 90.

14. See Philbrick, "The Spy as Hero," pp. 107–8, 117–18.

15. It is interesting to note that in this early patriotic play about the American Revolution, no one, not even Washington, makes a single reference to God, though Washington might well have evoked the name of God in support of the American cause and also to justify his decision not to commute André's sentence.

16. See J. W. Pickering, "*Satanstoe*: Cooper's Debt to William Dunlap," *American Literature* 38 (January 1967): 468–77.

17. Mary E. Phillips, *James Fenimore Cooper* (New York: John Lane Co., 1913), pp. 332–34.

18. Stephen Railton, *Fenimore Cooper: A Study of His Life and Imagination* (Princeton: Princeton University Press, 1978), p. 240. For a fuller analysis of Cooper's treatment of the American Revolution in both his novels and nonfictional works, see John P. McWilliams, Jr., *Political Justice in a Republic: James Fenimore Cooper's America* (Berkeley: University of California Press, 1972), pp. 32–99; H. D. Peck, "Repossession of America: The Revolution in Cooper's Trilogy of Nautical Romances," *Studies in Romanticism* 15 (Fall 1976): 589–605; James Franklin Beard, "Cooper and the Revolutionary Mythos," *Early American Literature* 11 (Spring 1976): 84–104; Jeffrey Steinbrink, "Cooper's Romance of the Revolution: *Lionel*

Lincoln and the Lessons of Failure," *Early American Literature* 11 (Winter 1976/77): 336–43; and Mike Ewart, "Cooper and the American Revolution: The Non-Fiction," *Journal of American Studies* 11 (April 1977): 61–79.

19. Bryan, *Washington in American Literature*, p. 180.

20. James Fenimore Cooper, *The Spy* (Boston: Colonial Press Co., n.d.), p. 455.

21. Edwin Fussell, *Frontier: American Literature and the American West* (Princeton: Princeton University Press, 1970), p. 114. Spiller further notes that when Cooper "took the neutral ground around New York City for the scene of his Revolutionary War novel, *The Spy*, he probably had Scott's border country in mind." *James Fenimore Cooper*, p. 13.

22. Fussell, *Frontier*, p. 121.

23. *The Spy*, p. 13.

24. Railton, *Fenimore Cooper*, p. 8. See also Henry Nash Smith's introduction to Cooper's *The Prairie* (New York: Holt, Rinehart and Winston, 1963), p. xv, and Donald A. Ringe, *James Fenimore Cooper* (New York: Twayne Publishers, Inc., 1962), pp. 19–114.

25. Dekker makes this same claim about the Leatherstocking novels (excepting *The Pioneers*) in *James Fenimore Cooper*, p. 95.

26. Harry Levin, *The Power of Blackness: Hawthorne, Poe, Melville* (New York: Vintage Books, 1958), pp. 3–35.

27. Spiller, *James Fenimore Cooper*, p. 15.

28. See Louise K. Barnett, "Cooper's *Wyandotté*: The Indian as Split Personality," *Cimarron Review* 46 (January 1979): 25–31.

29. Edgar Allan Poe, "Review of *Wyandotté*," *Graham's Magazine* 23 (1843): 262.

30. Spiller observes that since about 1838 Cooper "had been growing more disillusioned with humanity and its ability to solve moral problems by reason alone. The themes of the ambiguity of right and wrong, the incapacity of man to live up to his ideals, and the vanishing line between reality and illusion, which began to appear in his novels after his return to fiction in 1838 and to dominate them after 1848, were rather the by-products of his own experience with the press and public than a positive religious awakening. The moral values he had always stressed must be sought in the next world if they cannot be realized in this." *James Fenimore Cooper*, p. 42.

31. Railton, *Fenimore Cooper*, p. 232.

32. Ibid., pp. 246–58.

33. Spiller, *James Fenimore Cooper*, p. 34; see also pp. 33–42 for an analysis of this stage.

34. Ibid., p. 43. James Grossman calls it "a remarkably unpleasant book." *James Fenimore Cooper* (Stanford: Stanford University Press, 1967), p. 178.

35. May, *The Enlightenment in America*, p. 308.

36. Stow Persons, *American Minds: A History of Ideas* (New York: Henry Holt and Co., 1958), p. 147. See pp. 147–213 for his full elaboration of these changes. See also Larzer Ziff, *Literary Democracy: The Declaration of Cultural Independence in America* (New York: Viking Press, 1981), pp. 297–302.

37. May, *The Enlightenment in America*, p. 309.

38. Spiller, *James Fenimore Cooper*, pp. 8, 9, 31.

39. May, *The Enlightenment in America*, p. 308.

40. For an excellent analysis of the expansion of American democracy and the changing structure of American politics from 1800 to 1815, see David Hackett Fischer, *The Revolution of American Conservatism: The Federalist Party in the Era of Jeffersonian Democracy* (New York: Harper and Row, 1965).

41. May, *The Enlightenment in America*, pp. 308–9.

42. See Mead, *The Lively Experiment*, pp. 103–33, and Sidney E. Mead, *The Nation with the Soul of a Church* (New York: Harper and Row, 1975), pp. 29–47.

43. Yvor Winters, *In Defense of Reason* (Denver: University of Denver Press, 1943), pp. 180ff. Henry Nash Smith, observing that Leatherstocking anticipates the character of Huck Finn, contends that Cooper's aristocratic leanings curtailed the truly innovative edge of his literary talent. As "a sensibility, and above all as a voice, Huck Finn represents the goal of Transcendence downward toward which Cooper was unwittingly moving when he conceived the character of Natty Bumppo. Cooper could not reach the goal because he was too deeply committed to his aristocratic ideal of social order." Henry Nash Smith, "Consciousness and Social Order: The Theme of Transcendence in the Leatherstocking Tales," *Western American Literature* 5 (Fall 1970): 194. Larzer Ziff, in *Literary Democracy*, pp. 265–67, argues that Cooper's treatment of Natty Bumppo as a democratic hero—whom, he says, Cooper patronizes from the viewpoint of a country squire—has many parallels with Melville's handling of the common seaman as the true democratic hero. "Such strong parallels," he adds, "do not so much suggest Cooper's influence upon Melville as they indicate the notable fact that the two American novelists who were most concerned with the character of the democratic man both traced this definitive quality to his exposure to nature and his avoidance of established society rather than to American political circumstances" (p. 267). See also L. J. Reynolds, "Kings and Commoners in *Moby-Dick*," *Studies in the Novel* 12 (Summer 1980): 101–13.

7. JAMES FENIMORE COOPER'S LEATHERSTOCKING NOVELS: A HYBRID THEODICY

1. *North American Review* 74 (1852): 147.

2. Ibid., p. 151.

3. Ibid., p. 155.

4. Yet, despite the racial biases that shape Parkman's various narratives of the westward migration, he did follow the Oregon trail in person to observe the land, the frontiersmen, and the Indians. And his classic account of the migration westward—*The Oregon Trail*—has Leisy observes, "served novelists as a valuable comment on the life and times of those who took the great overland route to the West." *The American Historical Novel*, p. 134.

5. Henry Nash Smith comments that Cooper treats the prairie in *The Prairie* "as if it were an Elizabethan stage, a neutral space where any character may be brought at a moment's notice without arousing in the audience a desire to have the entrance accounted for. Within this space Cooper maneuvers his characters into the situations he desires. Once his effect has been achieved he resorts to a quick and equally arbitrary manipulation of the plot for the sake of another effect." *The Prairie*, p. ix.

6. For a fuller analysis of this aspect of the Leatherstocking novels, see Harold Edward Clark, *Fenimore Cooper's Leatherstocking Tales: A Problem in Race* (Ann Arbor: University Microfilms, 1955).

7. Henry Nash Smith argues in *Virgin Land* that Natty's greatest profundity as a symbol is his expression of the tension between social order and individual freedom, a tension endemic to life on the frontier but one which Cooper did not satisfactorily resolve in his fiction. *Virgin Land: The American West as Symbol and Myth* (New York: Vintage Books, 1950), pp. 64–76.

8. Wayne Fields makes the following comment on Cooper's growing pessimism about human nature:

Having given us a hero who seems so like the new men Emerson and Thoreau celebrate, Cooper does not claim, as do the transcendentalists, that we are to become such heroes ourselves. He is never so optimistic about human nature as to suggest that we can live with such freedom or such responsibility. Our kinship with the novel's other whites is much stronger than our resemblance to Leatherstocking, and, like them, we require the ordering influence of an enlightened community. If, by comparison with grander claims for America and Americans, this seems unduly pessimistic, there is affirmation as well. . . . I mean that even though Leatherstocking does not vindicate the deepest myth of American individualism, still as an ideal, a figure so self-contained and true that out of his very humanity he orders the chaos around him, he provides us with a perspective from which to view both a new world and those of us who have come to inhabit it.

Wayne Fields, "Beyond Definition: A Reading of *The Prairie*," in Wayne Fields, ed., *James Fenimore Cooper: A Collection of Critical Essays* (Englewood Cliffs, N.J.: Prentice-Hall, 1979), p. 111. Unless otherwise specified, page citations refer to *The Works of James Fenimore Cooper*, 32 vols. (Boston: Colonial Press Company, n.d.). Throughout this chapter the titles of the individual Leatherstocking novels will be abbreviated as follows: *The Pioneers*—Pi; *The Last of the Mohicans*—LM; *The Prairie*—Pr; *The Pathfinder*—Pa; *The Deerslayer*—D.

9. Railton contends, for example, that not until 1848 did Cooper choose a religious theme for his novels. Railton, *Fenimore Cooper*, p. 248. Contrary to Railton's view, Ringe argues that such themes in his later fiction as "the conflict of appearance and reality, divided loyalties, and the importance of a religious view of life . . . were present in his earliest fiction." *James Fenimore Cooper*, p. 91.

10. In *The Pioneers*, Natty's life differs from that portrayed in the series as a whole. In this novel, he has not spent his early life among the Delawares, although he is fighting alongside the Delaware Indians with his friend Chingachgook. Instead, most of the time he has lived alone in his small ramshackle hut on the shore of Lake Ostego. This novel makes it appear that the Effingham family raised him from childhood through adolescence until he leaves to live the solitary life of the hunter.

11. R. W. B. Lewis, *The American Adam*, p. 104.

12. Robert E. Spiller, *Fenimore Cooper: Critic of His Times* (New York: Minton, Balch and Co., 1931), p. 7.

13. For a more comprehensive analysis of Cooper's use of landscape in the Leatherstocking novels, see Howard Mumford Jones, *The Frontier in American Fiction: Four Lectures on the Relation of Landscape to Literature* (Jerusalem: Magness Press, 1956), pp. 26–50, and Lynen, *The Design of the Present*, pp. 170–204.

14. David B. Davis, "The Deerslayer, A Democratic Knight of the Wilderness," in Charles Shapiro, ed., *Twelve Original Essays on Great American Novels* (Detroit: Wayne State University Press, 1958), p. 11.

15. James Fenimore Cooper, *The Prairie* (New York: Holt, Rinehart and Winston, 1963). All page citations from *The Prairie* refer to this edition.

16. Terence Martin, "Beginnings and Endings in the Leatherstocking Tales," *Nineteenth-Century Fiction* 33 (June 1978): 79.

17. *Pr*, p. 290.

18. Wayne Fields comments that "Natty's Jeremiad is not simply a conservationist's complaint. Just as the indefiniteness of the prairie judges the inadequacy of individuals, so it judges a society that promotes wantonness rather than restraint and panders to avarice rather than cultivates reason. This desert, Natty argues, is a moral as well as a natural phenomenon." Fields, "Beyond Definition: A Reading of *The Prairie*," pp. 107–8.

19. Cooper comments that "never did a day pass without his communing in spirit, and this, too, without the aid of forms of language, with the infinite Source of all he saw, felt, and beheld." *D*, p. 283. See also *Pr*, pp. 88–89, 246, 289–90; *D*, p. 508; and *Pi*, pp. 320–25.

20. For an analysis of this religious idea in Natty's thought, see Peter Valenti, " 'The Ordering of God's Providence': Law and Landscape in *The Pioneers*," *Studies in American Fiction* 7 (Autumn 1979): 191–207.

21. See also *Pr* p. 268.

22. *Pr*, pp. 63–64, 84–85; *Pi*, p. 175.

23. *Pi*, p. 320.

24. Ibid., p. 260.

25. *Pr*, pp. 402–3.

26. *Pi*, p. 320. It is interesting to note, in this regard, Cooper's own attitude toward the law in the many libel suits he brought against those who publicly criticized his works as "trashy," "worthless," "overrated," "balderdash," and a "disgrace to American Literature." "They have accused me—some, I do not say *all*—of ingratitude, by turning on the *power that made me*, because I have sued some of the fraternity for libels. In private, I am told, they boast they will let me feel the power of the press; and as *they made* me, so will *they destroy* me. In answer to all this, I have said, both in public and private, that I will make them feel the power of the law. In the end, we shall see which will prevail." James Franklin Beard, ed., *The Letters and Journals of James Fenimore Cooper* (Cambridge: Harvard University Press, 1964), 4:272.

27. In response to this passage, Henry Nash Smith asserts that "the depth and power of Cooper's characterization of Leatherstocking is due to his capacity to respond to this anarchic inference from the ideal of forest freedom despite his own commitment to the ideal of an ordered, stratified society based on the secure ownership of land by a leisure class." *Pr*, p. xviii.

28. *Pr*, p. 403.

29. Natty's primary fear about marriage is that it will evoke those acquisitive impulses which would destroy the sense of integrity he has developed in the wilderness. As he tells Jasper Western, "I once hunted for two summers during the last peace, and I collected so much peltry that I found my right feelings giving way to a craving for property; and if I have consarn in marrying Mabel, it is that I may

get to love such things too well, in order to make her comfortable" (*Pa*, p. 491). Though his love for Mabel could have led him to accept married life, no such threat ever exists to his Adamic integrity in *The Deerslayer*. When Judith proposes marriage to him, he considers her, without knowing about her sexual indiscretions, a woman corrupted by her fascination with society. Nevertheless, there is no danger that he will be tempted by her offer, since he has already refused to marry the squaw of a warrior whom he has slain, despite the torture he knows the Indians will inflict upon him for this refusal. Aside from the racial bigotry that might underlie this refusal (see notes 58 and 59 of this chapter), Natty also believes that God has ordained that he live a bachelor's life in the wilderness. For more extensive comments on his refusal to marry see Fussell, *Frontier*, pp. 57–58; Railton, *Fenimore Cooper*, pp. 196–98; Dekker, *James Fenimore Cooper*, pp. 161–69; Annette Kolodny, "Love and Sexuality in *The Pathfinder*," in Fields, *James Fenimore Cooper*, pp. 112–16; and Peter Vasile, "Cooper's *The Deerslayer*: The Apotheosis of Man and Nature," *Journal of the American Academy of Religion* 43 (September 1975): 503–6.

30. The beginning of the novel lauds the pioneering efforts, but halfway through the first chapter this mood is reversed. The novel then begins to pose the spectacle, in Natty and Cooper's view, of a second garden of Eden being gradually destroyed in the name of imposing law and order (*Pi*, p. 321). For Natty's laments regarding the changes in the wilderness that accompany the westward migration of the settlers, see *Pi*, pp. 39–40, 46, 147, 179, 227, 233, and 320–25; see also *Pr*, p. 290.

31. William Cooper, *A Guide in the Wilderness; or, The History of the First Settlement in the Western Counties of New York* (1810; rpt. Rochester, N.Y.: George P. Humphrey, 1897), pp. 11–12.

32. The same evening of Hiram's visit, Natty, knowing that the sheriff will return to arrest him and discover the major, burns his hut and moves the major, along with Chingachgook, to a secluded cave. The loss of his hut evokes two of Natty's most moving speeches in the Leatherstocking novels (*Pi*, pp. 394–95, 427). These speeches are rivaled only by his dirge-like hymn for a lost paradise (*Pi*, pp. 320–25).

33. See also *Pi*, p. 423.

34. For further analysis of the trial scene, see Robert Barton, "Natty's Trial, or the Triumph of Hiram Doolittle," *Cimarron Review* 36 (July 1976): 29–37.

35. Perry Miller attributes the popularity of *The Pioneers*, both in the country and in the city, to an "ingrained hostility to the law as a profession. . . . The majority of the people around 1800 simply hated the law as an artificial imposition on their native intelligence and judges as agents of constraint." *The Life of the Mind in America: From the Revolution to the Civil War* (New York: Harcourt, Brace and World, Inc., 1965), p. 103.

36. Spiller, *James Fenimore Cooper*, p. 17.

37. Railton, *Fenimore Cooper*, p. 111.

38. Cooper himself seemingly endorses this punishment when he comments on Ishmael's wife's acceptance of her husband's decision to execute her brother. "Satisfied now that the fate of her brother was sealed, and possibly conscious how well he merited the punishment that was meditated, she no longer thought of mediation" (*Pr*. p. 419).

39. See also *Pr*, p. 447; *LM*, p. 242.

40. *Pa*, pp. 351, 492; *D*, p. 134.

41. See also *LM*, p. 276.

42. Deerslayer laments, however, that nothing, not even friendship, can "alter the ways of Providence" (*D*, p. 499).

43. Fussell, *Frontier*, p. 31.

44. D. H. Lawrence, *Studies in Classic American Literature* (New York: Doubleday and Co., 1951), p. 64.

45. Vasile, "Cooper's *The Deerslayer*: The Apotheosis of Man and Nature," pp. 485, 487. See also Charles A. Brady, "James Fenimore Cooper, 1789–1851: Myth-Maker and Christian Romancer," in Harold C. Gardiner, ed., *American Classics Reconsidered: A Christian Appraisal* (New York: Charles Scribner's Sons, 1958), p. 84, and Thomas Philbrick, "Cooper's *The Pioneers*: Origin and Structure," *PMLA* 79 (December 1964): 579–93.

46. David B. Davis romanticizes this ritualistic episode when he observes that Natty's killing of the Indian is "America's gesture of apology for a vanquished foe. A sordid fact of American History was purified when the woodsman killed the noble savage in this idyll of death in the midst of unspoiled nature." "The Deerslayer, A Democratic Knight of the Wilderness," p. 17. Terence Martin is much closer to the mark when he says of the final chapter of *The Deerslayer* that "Natty Bumppo goes to war, not to heaven." "Beginnings and Endings in the Leatherstocking Tales," p. 87.

47. *D*, p. 499. However, unwilling to accept the implications of his religious determinism, Natty rejects the notion that God arbitrarily predetermines who will be saved and who will be damned (*LM*, pp. 146–47). See also *Pa*, pp. 29–30 and *LM*, pp. 249–50.

48. Martin Green writes that Natty is more religious in the last two novels because Cooper wanted to "stress the difference between him and Crockett. . . . The action is constantly interrupted while Natty explains away his behaviour as frontiersman, because it is incompatible with his principles as a Christian pilgrim." "Cooper, Nationalism and Imperialism," *Journal of American Studies* 12 (August 1978): 167. See also F. K. Bradsher, "Christian Morality and *The Deerslayer*," *Renascence* 31 (Autumn 1978): 15–24.

49. This religious conflict has not been treated in the criticism of Cooper's Leatherstocking novels.

50. See *Pr*, p. 289.

51. See *LM*, pp. 338–49, and *D*, p. 320.

52. Vasile, "Cooper's *The Deerslayer*: The Apotheosis of Man and Nature," p. 493.

53. Railton, *Fenimore Cooper*, p. 76.

54. Fussell, *Frontier*, pp. 56–57. For Cooper's own similar remarks about Natty, see *Pa*, p. 154.

55. James Fenimore Cooper, *Home as Found* (Boston: Colonial Press Co., n.d.) p. 215. By associating Natty and Washington in this way, Cooper perhaps suggests, consciously or unconsciously, how closely he identified Natty with those ideals he believed the Revolution had formulated for governing the individual's life within a democratic society.

56. Railton, *Fenimore Cooper*, p. 219. See pp. 209–20 for Railton's complete argument. James Grossman comes close to this same conclusion in *James Fenimore*

Cooper, p. 148. See also Terence Martin, "The Negative Character in American Fiction," in L. J. Budd, E. H. Cady, and C. L. Anderson, eds., *Toward a New American Literary History.* (Durham: Duke University Press, 1980), pp. 230–43. Such an argument ignores all the very real obligations and dangers Natty imposes on himself for the sake of others, regardless of the consequences to himself.

57. See, for example, *LM*, pp. 35, 147, 271.

58. See, for example, *LM*, pp. 36, 339.

59. *D*, p. 139; *LM*, p. 252. See also R. H. Pearce, "The Metaphysics of Indian-Hating: Leatherstocking Unmasked," in R. H. Pearce, *Historicism Once More: Problems and Occasions for the American Scholar* (Princeton: Princeton University Press, 1969), pp. 109–36.

60. *Pa*, p. 491.

61. *D*, p. 36.

62. Ibid., pp. 490–99.

63. *LM*, p. 264.

64. *Pa*, p. 193–95.

65. *Pr*, p. 128. In this regard, Cooper clarifies his own intentions in his creation of Natty Bumppo.

The idea of delineating a character that possessed little of civilization but its highest principles as they are exhibited in the uneducated, and all of savage life that is not incompatible with these great rules of conduct, is perhaps natural to the situation in which Natty was placed. He is too proud of his origin to sink into the condition of the wild Indian, and too much a man of the woods not to imbibe as much as was at all desirable from his friends and companions. In a moral point of view it was the intention to illustrate the effect of seed scattered by the wayside. To use his own language, his "gifts" were "white gifts," and he was not disposed to bring on them discredit. On the other hand, removed from nearly all the temptations of civilized life, placed in the best associations of that which is deemed savage, and favorably disposed by nature to improve such advantages, it appeared to the writer that his hero was a fit subject to represent the better qualities of both conditions, without pushing either to extremes. (*D*, p. 7)

66. Dekker, *James Fenimore Cooper*, pp. 92–97.

67. See Terence Martin, "Surviving on the Frontier: The Doubled Consciousness of Natty Bumppo," *South Atlantic Quarterly* 75 (Autumn 1976): 447–59.

68. *LM*, pp. 48, 261, 291.

69. Fussell, *Frontier*, p. 37.

70. For another approach to the theme of self-transcendence in the Leatherstocking novels, see Henry Nash Smith, "Consciousness and Social Order: The Theme of Transcendence in the Leatherstocking Tales," *Western American Literature* 5 (Fall 1970): 177–94. Smith argues that "Cooper had an inarticulate conviction that when white men moved out beyond the frontier they did indeed place themselves in contact with non-traditional sources of value, and underwent something like a cultural rebirth. The problem of criticism is to find the intimations of such experiences in the novels. If we can recognize them, we shall be on the track of the genuine as contrasted with the merely ideological and schematic representation of transcendence in Cooper's fiction" (p. 188). One form of this transcendence, according to Smith, is achieved through the skill required to survive in the wilderness. Such skills "become an emblem of the response of man's mind to challenges from a new environment. It escapes all traditional categories and involves a

harmony of senses, imagination, and reason that has nothing to do with social status or wealth or any other aspect of established institutions including conventional moral or esthetic principles. Such a release of the mind from predetermined patterns and constraints is a kind of transcendence growing directly out of the white man's Western experience" (p. 190). Another form of transcendence, though quite "rare" in the Leatherstocking novels, "is the direct, unmediated perception of the natural setting and activities related to it. It is not easy for Cooper to represent this kind of experience because when he deals with landscape he usually falls into well-worn ruts of moral and esthetic convention" (p. 190). Smith criticizes Deerslayer's first encounter with Lake Glimmerglass in this regard, though through Natty's vernacular speech, however ineptly rendered, Cooper seeks to make available to the uneducated "a kind of esthetic experience which literary convention restricted to members of the gentry" (p. 193). This leads Smith to conclude that "the transcendence Cooper was vaguely aware of in the white man's experience of the wilderness could be fully achieved only through the development of a vernacular perspective, which in turn demanded a revolution in the language of fiction" (p. 193)—a revolution successfully completed by Mark Twain in his creation of Huck Finn.

71. This is not to maintain, as Marius Bewley does, that "Leatherstocking represents an artistic resolution of that troubled experience" engendered by the new experiment in American democracy. *The Eccentric Design: Form in the Classic American Novel* (New York: Columbia University Press, 1963), p. 100. (See pp. 101–12 for his complete argument.) Rather, Cooper dramatizes the religious tensions of the new American experience and suggests a most tenuous resolution that can be defined in terms of the previous debate about the Puritan and rationalistic theodicies.

72. Cooper himself affirms the notion of an "inscrutable Providence which . . . uniformly and yet so mysteriously covers all events with its mantle" (*D*, p. 499).

73. Howard Mumford Jones perhaps saw this aspect of the Leatherstocking novels when he observed that "though the current of trinitarian Christianity, now hidden, now coming to the surface in particular novels, runs through most of Cooper's fiction, there is a parallel current equally important—a relief in natural theism." *Belief and Disbelief in American Literature* (Chicago: University of Chicago Press, 1967), p. 43.

74. This way of envisioning the religious outlook shaping Natty's behavior requires an important modification of that perspective on his career which maintains that his "conduct is regulated by principles of 'natural religion' which sound like an echo of eighteenth century Deism." Lucy Lockwood Hazard, *The Frontier in American Literature* (New York: Barnes and Noble, 1941), p. 107.

75. A full account of Cooper's religious thought is found in Spiller's *Fenimore Cooper: Critic of His Times*. See also William M. Hogue, "The Novel as a Religious Tract: James Fenimore Cooper—Apologist for the Episcopal Church," *Historical Magazine of the Protestant Episcopal Church* 40 (March 1971): 5–26, and Donald A. Ringe, "Religion and Ethics: Cooper's Last Novels, 1847–1850," *PMLA* 75 (December 1960): 583–90.

76. See Spiller, *James Fenimore Cooper*, pp. 34, 39–42 and Railton, *Fenimore Cooper*, pp. 246–58.

77. There is a tension in Cooper's thought at this point in the Leatherstocking

novels. For although nature is in some respects, in *The Deerslayer* as well as in the other four novels, the religious and ethical norm against which we judge the actions of the characters, it also discloses moral and religious norms that clearly contradict the teachings of the Scriptures, and is itself contradictory in what it discloses to be "lawful" or "right." It is John Lynen's view that

Cooper's morality, when one attempts to formulate it, proves to be inseparable from the natural setting of his novels. It becomes a matter of empty formulas whenever dissociated from the experience of landscape, which explains why value judgments evaporate on the lips of his upper-class characters. If Natty Bumppo's pronouncements seem somewhat more apposite, that is due less to their intrinsic truth than to their truth as things he might say, which, by characterizing his happy adjustment to the wilderness, point to a morality in the land itself. But even Leatherstocking's morals are an inadequate reflection of the setting, so that Cooper can occasionally risk a laugh at his protagonist. No one can state the moral truth successfully, for the morality of nature is different in kind from ethics in the usual sense. It subsists in the experience of nature, and therefore, despite his best efforts, Cooper is unable to make out a better mode of existence than Natty's life in the woods. *The Design of the Present*, p. 170.

8. NATHANIEL HAWTHORNE'S *THE SCARLET LETTER*: ANOTHER HYBRID THEODICY

1. *The Centenary Edition of the Works of Nathaniel Hawthorne* (Columbus: Ohio State University Press, 1974), 11:327–28.

2. Ibid., p. 327.

3. Millicent Bell, *Hawthorne's View of the Artist* (New York: State University of New York, 1962), pp. 136–50.

4. Cleanth Brooks, R. W. B. Lewis, and Robert Penn Warren, *American Literature: The Makers and the Making, Beginnings to 1861* (New York: St Martin's Press, 1973), 1:38.

5. Lewis, *The American Adam*, p. 113.

6. Nathaniel Hawthorne, *The House of the Seven Gables* (New York: Dell Publishing Co., 1967), p. 17. See also Pearce, *Historicism Once More*, p. 188.

7. Taylor Stoehr, in *Hawthorne's Mad Scientists: Pseudoscience and Social Science in Nineteenth-Century Life and Letters* (Hamden, Conn.: Archon Books, 1978), analyzes how Hawthorne's interest in science and his use of scientific materials helped to shape his habits of composition.

8. As Frederick Crews puts it: "The power of Hawthorne's best fiction comes largely from a sense that nothing in human behavior is as free or fortuitous as it appears. Even with characters much less fully observed than Hester, the emphasis falls on buried motives which are absolutely binding because they are unavailable to conscious criticism." *The Sins of the Fathers: Hawthorne's Psychological Themes* (New York: Oxford University Press, 1966), p. 17.

9. *The House of the Seven Gables*, p. 313.

10. Brooks, Lewis, and Warren, *American Literature*, 1:453.

11. Joseph Schwartz, "Nathaniel Hawthorne, 1804–1864: God and Man in New England," in Gardiner, *American Classics Reconsidered*, p. 140.

12. Richard Forrer, "*Oedipus at Colonus*: A Crisis in the Greek Notion of Deity," *Comparative Drama* 8 (Winter 1974/75): 328–46.

13. See Roy R. Male, *Hawthorne's Tragic Vision* (New York: W. W. Norton, 1957); Richard H. Fogle, *Hawthorne's Fiction: The Light and the Dark* (Norman: University of Oklahoma Press, 1969), pp. 132–49; Dan Vogel, *The Three Masks of American Tragedy* (Baton Rouge: Louisiana State University Press, 1974), pp. 116–28; F. O. Matthiessen, *American Renaissance: Art and Expression in the Age of Emerson and Whitman* (New York: Oxford University Press, 1968), pp. 179–91; John Frederick, *The Darkened Sky: Nineteenth-Century American Novelists and Religion* (Notre Dame: University of Notre Dame Press, 1969), pp. 27–78; Alfred S. Reid, "The Role of Transformation in Hawthorne's Tragic Vision," *Furman Studies* VI (Fall 1958): 9–20; and Peter L. Thorslev, Jr., "Hawthorne's Determinism: An Analysis," *Nineteenth-Century Fiction* 19 (September 1964): 141–58.

14. *The House of the Seven Gables*, p. 160.

15. Paul Ricoeur, *The Symbolism of Evil* (New York: Harper and Row, 1967), p. 221.

16. *The House of the Seven Gables*, p. 179.

17. See, for example, Leland Schubert, *Hawthorne, the Artist: Fine-Art Devices in Fiction* (New York: Russell and Russell, 1963), pp. 136–61; Marjorie J. Elder, *Nathaniel Hawthorne: Transcendental Symbolist* (Columbus: Ohio University Press, 1969), pp. 121–41; Charles Child Walcutt, "*The Scarlet Letter* and Its Modern Critics," *Nineteenth-Century Fiction* 7 (March 1953): 251–64; and Hyatt H. Waggoner, *Hawthorne: A Critical Study* (Cambridge: Harvard University Press, 1967), pp. 126–54. Waggoner, however, combines such an analysis with a concern for "the final questions of meaning and value" (p. 154). Waggoner's work on Hawthorne has been criticized by such critics as Edgar A. Dryden in *Nathaniel Hawthorne: The Poetics of Enchantment* (Ithaca: Cornell University Press, 1977), p. 10; Nina Baym, *The Shape of Hawthorne's Career* (Ithaca: Cornell University Press, 1976), p. 9; and Kenneth Dauber, *Rediscovering Hawthorne* (Princeton: Princeton University Press, 1977), p. 12. For Waggoner's spirited response to these critics, see *The Presence of Hawthorne* (Baton Rouge: Louisiana State University Press, 1979), pp. 118–30. A systematic analysis of the psychology and the aesthetics of the processes of Hawthorne's artistic creation is found in Jean Normand's *Nathaniel Hawthorne: An Approach to an Analysis of Artistic Creation*, Derek Coltman, trans. (Cleveland: Case Western Reserve University Press, 1970). Waggoner's last four essays in *The Presence of Hawthorne* also treat the creative process in Hawthorne's writings.

18. For a brief but insightful analysis of Hawthorne's experiments with various kinds of narrators, see Jac Tharpe, *Nathaniel Hawthorne: Identity and Knowledge* (Carbondale: Southern Illinois University Press, 1967), pp. 25–39.

19. Marius Bewley has argued that Hawthorne is not a psychologist—that his psychology is "often undistinguished, and sometimes crass." "Hawthorne and 'The Deeper Psychology,'" *Mandrake* 2 (Autumn and Winter 1955/56): 366. A good corrective to this view is Frederick Crews' fine study, *The Sins of the Fathers*, which takes its lead from Henry James' study of Hawthorne. See Henry James, *Hawthorne* (New York: Collier Books, 1966), p. 64, for James' estimate of Hawthorne as a psychologist.

20. This approach is to be distinguished from that, say, of Leonard J. Fick in *The Light Beyond: A Study of Hawthorne's Theology* (Folcroft, Penn.: The Fol-

croft Press, 1969) which seeks to establish "the initial dogmatic concepts which give coherence and meaning to Hawthorne's fictional representations of life" (p. vii). A more sensitive reading of Hawthorne's theological ideas and how they give coherence to his fiction can be found in Joseph Schwartz, "Nathaniel Hawthorne, 1804–1864: God and Man in New England," and Michael T. Gilmore, *The Middle Way: Puritanism and Ideology in American Romantic Fiction* (New Brunswick: Rutgers University Press, 1977), pp. 65–86, who treats Hawthorne's relationship to the Puritan tradition in the "Introductory" to *The Scarlet Letter*. Though the concern of this chapter is not with linking Hawthorne's biography or personal religious beliefs to that of the narrator, nor with Hawthorne's relation to his narrator, characters, or the reader, these kinds of concerns have been at the center of Hawthorne criticism over the last twenty-five years, during which time a number of ways to conceptualize these links have emerged. The symbolic readings of Richard Fogle, Roy Male, Hyatt Waggoner, Charles Feidelson, and others, the psycho-poetic approach of Jean Normand, the approach of Q. D. Leavis, Harry Levin, Daniel Hoffman, Lionel Trilling, Hugo McPherson and others which emphasizes the myth-making and poetic core of Hawthorne's vision, Frederick Crews' psycho-analytic approach, and Dauber's deconstructionist approach variously attempt to define Hawthorne's presence in his fictions.

21. However, Terence Martin has noted that as early as 1636, New Plymouth Colony enacted a law that required all persons convicted of adultery to be whipped and to wear "two Capitall letters viz. AD. cut out in cloth and sowed to theire upermost Garments on theire arme or backe." *Nathaniel Hawthorne* (New York: Twayne Publishers, 1965), p. 183, note 8.

22. Page citations refer to Nathaniel Hawthorne, *The Scarlet Letter and Other Tales of the Puritans*, Harry Levin, ed. (Boston: Houghton Mifflin Co., 1961).

23. It is not clear, however, whether Hester herself actually chooses or is required by the authorities to live in isolation from the community. Nothing is said about either her place of residence prior to Pearl's birth (though since the birth of the child both have been living in the prison for three months), or whether she has lost that residence or chosen not to return to it because of her adultery. But whether her isolated existence is self-imposed or required by the community, she clearly chooses this alternative over seeking to establish a new residence elsewhere.

24. John Caldwell Stubbs, *The Pursuit of Form: A Study of Hawthorne and the Romance* (Urbana: University of Illinois Press, 1970), p. 83.

25. Fussell, *Frontier*, pp. 98, 114.

26. The theme of isolation in Hawthorne's fiction has been the subject of much Hawthorne criticism over the last three decades. However, the most helpful distinctions regarding the kinds of isolation Hawthorne treats in his fiction are made by Arne Axelsson and David Levin. In his systematic treatment of the themes of isolation and interdependence in Hawthorne's fiction, *The Links in the Chain: Isolation and Interdependence in Nathaniel Hawthorne's Fictional Characters* (Uppsala: Uppsala University Press, 1974), Axelsson argues that "Contrary to what has often been assumed or tacitly understood, I argue that Hawthorne's famous chain of human brotherhood, to which the key of holy sympathy gives admittance, is not equivalent with society. Isolation from society does occur in Hawthorne, but that is another type of isolation which cannot be compared in importance to the inward alienation which an individual experiences when he is cut off from his

fellow man" (p. 12). Axelsson then distinguishes several types of inward isolation: "voluntary isolation: active withdrawal," "voluntary isolation: passive withdrawal," "involuntary isolation: 'chronic' wrongdoing," "involuntary isolation: 'acute' wrongdoing," "involuntary isolation: victims of other people," "involuntary isolation: victims of nature and circumstances," "involuntary isolation: detached observers," and "avoluntary isolation: preternatural creatures." (See also pp. 22–26 for his critique of how other critics have treated the problem of isolation in Hawthorne's works.) A variation on Axelsson's thesis is Edgar A. Dryden's *Nathaniel Hawthorne: The Poetics of Enchantment.* Earlier, in 1960, David Levin had distinguished three types of isolation in Hawthorne's fiction: that of "the publicly known, partially contrite sinner," that of "the secret sinner," and that of "the Unpardonable Sinner. The distinctions among them illustrate the conflict between head and heart, intellect and nature, that dominates most historical romances of the period. All three sinners are isolated from their fellows, but each in a different way that underlines the basic distinctions." *The House of the Seven Gables,* p. 11. For a sampling of the range of critical opinion regarding Hawthorne's solution for the conflict between the individual and society and the isolation that is part of this conflict, see Charles C. Walcutt, *"The Scarlet Letter* and Its Modern Critics." Also, see Glenn C. Altschuler, "The Puritan Dilemma in 'The Minister's Black Veil,' " *American Transcendental Quarterly: A Journal of New England Writers* 24 (Fall 1974): 25–27.

27. Two critical viewpoints have emerged regarding how Hester's isolation has affected her. Frederick I. Carpenter, in "Scarlet A Minus," *College English* 5 (January 1944): 173–80, maintains that Hester finds her true self through her independence. He criticizes Hawthorne for not identifying himself with Hester's antinomian views of a new order of society. Darrell Abel, expressing an opposing view in "Hawthorne's Hester," *College English* 13 (March 1952): 303–9, argues that Hester virtually loses all her physical and moral vitality in isolation. The point to be made here—which is really the narrator's point—is that Hester creates a self which has no roots in traditional moral values, while at the same time conforming in her external behavior to the punitive expectations of the Puritan community. For a broader sampling of the range of critical opinion on this issue, see Axelsson, *The Links in the Chain,* pp. 181–90.

28. *The Scarlet Letter,* pp. 158, 163, 164, and 198.

29. Ibid., pp. 115–16, 164–65.

30. Daniel G. Hoffman, *Form and Fable in American Fiction* (New York: Oxford University Press, 1961), pp. 177–78.

31. Waggoner, *The Presence of Hawthorne,* p. 121.

32. As Edward Wagenknecht rightly observes, "Hawthorne's physicians are not, in general, admiringly portrayed. When they are not malevolent, they are eccentric." *Nathaniel Hawthorne: Man and Writer* (New York: Oxford University Press, 1961), p. 29. For an analysis of Hawthorne's reliance on the Faust myth in his creation of Chillingworth, see William Bysshe Stein, *Hawthorne's Faust: A Study of the Devil Archetype* (Hamden, Conn.: Archon Books, 1968), pp. 104–22.

33. The issue here is not only the effect Chillingworth's curiosity has upon himself, but also its consequences for the reader who also desires to know the identity of the unnamed adulterer. Having learned his identity in this manner without having learned much more about him, the reader is led to view Dimmesdale as a

sexual miscreant, an attitude which, psychologically speaking, parallels that of the Puritan community toward Hester. It is difficult to detach this image of Dimmesdale from his voyeur-like discovery of his secret sin.

34. Crews, using his psychoanalytic perspective, suggests that Dimmesdale has repressed his sexual drive and, through reaction formation, has converted it into masochistic self-flagellation. *The Sins of the Fathers*, pp. 136–53.

35. Ibid., pp. 146ff. Also see Brooks, Lewis and Warren, *American Literature*, 1:449–50.

36. Stein, *Hawthorne's Faust*, p. 116.

37. Levin, *The Power of Blackness*, pp. 75–76.

38. Brooks, Lewis, and Warren, *American Literature* 1:451.

39. For a contrary reading of this episode, see Stubbs, *The Pursuit of Form*, p. 96. He concludes that "Dimmesdale is as triumphant as a human being can be." Earlier, he states that "the force of Dimmesdale's pride which Chillingworth's tortures itensify is absolutely essential to his final regeneration" (p. 92). Robert H. Fossum, in *Hawthorne's Inviolable Circle: The Problem of Time* (Deland, Fl.: Everett/Edwards, 1973), describes Dimmesdale as a Christ figure whose last day parallels the stations of the Cross (pp. 124–25). It is interesting to note that in this study on time in Hawthorne's fiction—especially the obsessive fixation on the past—Fossum, who contends that Dimmesdale has finally escaped the "demonic grip of the past" (p. 125), ignores Dimmesdale's advice to Hester to keep her attention riveted to their past sin, advice which, were she to follow it, would only sustain her punitive life style. Also, see Hugo McPherson, *Hawthorne as Myth-Maker: A Study in Imagination* (Toronto: University of Toronto Press, 1971), pp. 182–83.

40. This is one of the two times in the novel when the narrator suspends his use of what F. O. Matthiessen calls "the device of multiple choice" (*American Renaissance*, p. 276). He suspends this device one other time in order to make it clear that Dimmesdale acknowledges being Pearl's father.

41. Crews, *The Sins of the Fathers*, p. 151.

42. McPherson, however, sees a redemptive aspect to this tragic wastage of lives. Through the suffering and fortitude of Hester and Dimmesdale, he maintains, "Pearl . . . becomes a complete woman instead of a Puritan half-woman—the first representative of a new breed, the first *complete* American." *Hawthorne as Myth-Maker*, p. 183. Brooks, Lewis, and Warren set forth a contrary view. "As heiress to [Chillingworth's] fortune, [Pearl] goes to Europe, marries a nobleman, and as we are given to understand, fulfills the prediction that she would not 'do battle with the world, but be a woman in it.' This may be taken as a happy normality coming out of the distorted lives—but if so, then with what illogicality, and after what waste! Pearl's happiness can scarcely be taken to discount the grief of all the others." *American Literature*, 1:452.

43. Fick, in *The Light Beyond*, finds these ideas to be central to Hawthorne's own theological perspective (pp. 3–33). The narrator's use of such religious ideas throughout his narrative, as well as his own creation of a theodicy to explain the events he narrates, simply do not bear out Nina Baym's claims that *The Scarlet Letter* neither concerns itself with God nor presents adultery as a crime against divine law. *The Shape of Hawthorne's Career*, pp. 125–26.

44. Terence Martin in *Nathaniel Hawthorne* (pp. 112–13) overemphasizes the divine character of these intuitions, whereas the narrator himself is at pains to

balance this affirmation with his emphasis on the "despotic temper" of the multitude.

45. This way of viewing the novel demonstrates that, contrary to Yvor Winters' claim that Hawthorne was stuck on the horns of the dilemma of choosing "between [Puritan] abstractions inadequate or irrelevant to experience on the one hand, and experience on the other as far as practicable unilluminated by understanding," he met the dilemma head-on in the theodicy he created to explain the experiences he narrates. But surely Winters is correct in further claiming that this dilemma "is tragically characteristic of the history of this country and of its literature." *In Defense of Reason*, p. 174.

46. Along with what Matthiessen calls "the device of multiple choice," this attempt to synthesize such contrary beliefs partly accounts for why "some critics find inconsistency in Hawthorne" in *The Scarlet Letter*. Charles C. Walcutt, "*The Scarlet Letter* and Its Modern Critics," p. 74.

47. Waggoner, *Hawthorne*, p. 159. Many critics attribute the novel's bleakness to the fact that Hawthorne wrote *The Scarlet Letter* during a period of severe depression following his mother's death. Arline Turner provides a concise summary of the important biographical details pertinent to the writing and publication of *The Scarlet Letter* in *Hawthorne: A Biography* (New York: Oxford University Press, 1980), pp. 188–207.

48. The following remarks of Brooks, Lewis and Warren about "Ethan Brand" are equally applicable to the narrator's career in *The Scarlet Letter*. "Ethan Brand is, of course, no artist, but the way in which Hawthorne gives the diagnosis of his sin describes what Hawthorne took to be the moral danger that he feared in the practice of his art. 'He was no longer a brother, and opening the chambers or the dungeons of our common nature by the key of holy sympathy, which gave him a right to share in all of its secrets; he was now a cold observer . . . converting man and woman to be his puppets.' " *American Literature*, 1:445.

9. RALPH WALDO EMERSON: A REFOCUSING OF VISION

1. Stephen E. Whicher, *Freedom and Fate: An Inner Life of Ralph Waldo Emerson* (Philadelphia: University of Pennsylvania Press, 1953), p. vii.

2. Maurice Gonnaud, "Emerson and the Imperial Self: A European Critique," in David Levin, ed., *Emerson: Prophecy, Metamorphosis and Influence* (New York: Columbia University Press, 1975), p. 128. For a summary of critical response to Emerson the poet—not Emerson the prose stylist—see Hyatt H. Waggoner, *Emerson as Poet* (Princeton: Princeton University Press, 1974), pp. 3–52. Waggoner's own argument is threefold: that Emerson's poetry is to be studied not as compositions but as "illuminations," that his best verse is not deficient as composition, and that his best poetry is to be found in his prose writings. In contrast, David Porter, in *Emerson and Literary Change* (Cambridge: Harvard University Press, 1978), treats Emerson's poetry as aesthetic constructs. His essential thesis is that, in analyzing "the deep formal structures" of Emerson's poems, one can trace in Emerson's poetry the "passage Emerson made from closed poetic vision to a broad reconciliation of art and reality" (p. 5).

3. Sherman Paul, *Emerson's Angle of Vision: Man and Nature in American Experience* (Cambridge: Harvard University Press, 1952), pp. 5–26.

4. Mary Worden Edrich, "The Rhetoric of Apostasy," *Texas Studies in Language and Literature* 8 (1967): 553–54; Charles Feidelson, Jr., "Toward Melville: Some Versions of Emerson," in Milton R. Konvitz and Stephen F. Whicher, eds., *Emerson: A Collection of Critical Essays* (Englewood Cliffs: N.J.: Prentice-Hall, 1962), pp. 139ff.

5. For an elaboration of these roles or "persona," see Lawrence Buell's excellent study, *Literary Transcendentalism: Style and Vision in the American Renaissance* (Ithaca: Cornell University Press, 1973), pp. 265–330.

6. Levin, *Emerson: Prophecy, Metamorphosis, and Influence*, p. vi.

7. Quoted by Stephen E. Whicher, ed., *Selections from Ralph Waldo Emerson: An Organic Anthology* (Cambridge: Riverside Press, 1960), p. vi.

8. Ralph Waldo Emerson, "Natural History of Intellect," in *The Complete Writings of Ralph Waldo Emerson* (New York: William H. Wise, 1930), 2:1250. Emerson adds that anyone who constructs a system along these lines "does not interfere with its vast curves by prematurely forcing them into a circle or ellipse, but only draws that arc which he clearly sees, or perhaps at a later observation a remote curve of the same orbit, and waits for a new opportunity, well assured that these observed arcs will consist with each other." Also, see Josephine Miles, "Ralph Waldo Emerson," in Sherman Paul, ed., *Six Classic American Writers: An Introduction* (Minneapolis: University of Minnesota Press, 1970), pp. 86–121.

9. See, for example, Joel Porte, *Emerson and Thoreau: Transcendentalists in Conflict* (Middletown, Conn.: Wesleyan University Press, 1966), chapter 1; Carl Dennis, "Emerson's Poetry of Mind and Nature," *Emerson Society Quarterly* 58 (Part 3 1970): 90–97.

10. Whicher, *Freedom and Fate*.

11. Ibid., pp. 109–22.

12. A. D. Van Nostrand, *Everyman His Own Poet*, pp. 28–43.

13. Jonathan Bishop, *Emerson on the Soul* (Cambridge: Harvard University Press, 1964), pp. 215–27.

14. Quentin Anderson, *The Imperial Self: An Essay in American Literary and Cultural History* (New York: Alfred A. Knopf, 1971), pp. 88–93 passim and pp. 201–44.

15. Jeffrey L. Duncan, *The Power and Form of Emerson's Thought* (Charlottesville: University Press of Virginia, 1973), pp. xii–xiii.

16. Buell, *Literary Transcendentalism*, pp. 284–311.

17. Whicher, *Freedom and Fate*, pp. 109–22. Carl F. Strauch puts it quite succinctly: "The differences between *Nature* and 'Fate,' both in content and mood, are enormous." "Emerson's Sacred Science," *PMLA* 73 (June 1958): 243.

18. Paul, *Emerson's Angle of Vision* p. 207. For various evaluations of the impact of Darwin's theory of evolution on Emerson's thought, see Harry Hayden Clark, ed., *Transitions in American Literary History* (Durham, N.C.: Duke University Press, 1953), pp. 280–81; Stow Persons, ed., *Evolutionary Thought in America* (New York: George Braziller, 1956), p. 440; Bruce Wilshire, ed., *Romanticism and Evolution: The Nineteenth Century* (New York: G. P. Putnam's Sons, 1968), pp. 147–57; and Walter Benzanson's introduction to *Clarel, A Poem and Pilgrimage in the Holy Land* (New York: Hendricks House, 1960).

19. For good, brief overviews of Transcendentalism, see Alexander Kern, "The Rise of Transcendentalism, 1815–1860," in *Transitions in American Literary His-*

tory, pp. 245–314; Jones, *Belief and Disbelief in American Literature*, pp. 48–69; and Frederic I. Carpenter, *Emerson Handbook* (New York: Hendricks House, 1953), pp. 124–43. For its contemporary religious context, see Paul F. Boller, Jr., *American Transcendentalism, 1830–1860: An Intellectual Inquiry* (New York: G. P. Putnam's Sons, 1974); Miller, *The Life of the Mind in America: from the Revolution to the Civil War*, Book 1; Winthrop Hudson, *Religion in America* (New York: Scribner, 1965) pp. 158–203; Alice Felt Tyler, *Freedom's Ferment* (Minneapolis: University of Minnesota Press, 1944), Parts I and II; and Arnold Smithline, *Natural Religion in American Literature* (New Haven: College and University Press, 1966), pp. 93–126.

20. The following editions of Emerson's essays are used in this chapter: Stephen F. Whicher, ed., *Selections from Ralph Waldo Emerson*; Brooks Atkinson, ed., *The Selected Writings of Ralph Waldo Emerson* (New York: Modern Library, 1950); and *The Complete Writings of Ralph Waldo Emerson*. Page references are according to the following abbreviations:

> Wh Whicher, *Selections from Ralph Waldo Emerson*
> ML Atkinson, *The Selected Writings of Ralph Waldo Emerson*
> E *The Complete Writings of Ralph Waldo Emerson*

21. Sherman Paul provides a fuller discussion of the process of fusing reason and understanding in *Emerson's Angle of Vision*, pp. 27–102.

22. Joel Porte, "Emerson, Thoreau, and the Double Consciousness," *The New England Quarterly* 41 (March 1968): 42. Also see Paul, *Emerson's Angle of Vision*, pp. 51–60.

23. For a sampling of the range of critical opinion regarding Emerson's use of the image of the eyeball, see Paul, *Emerson's Angle of Vision*, p. 84; Bishop, *Emerson on the Soul*, pp. 9–15; Kenneth Burke, "I, Eye, Ay—Emerson's Early Essay 'Nature': Thoughts on the Machinery of Transcendence," in Myron Simon and Thorton H. Parsons, eds., *Transcendentalism and Its Legacy* (Ann Arbor: The University of Michigan Press, 1966), pp. 3–24; James M. Cox, "R. W. Emerson: The Circles of the Eye," in Levin, *Emerson: Prophecy, Metamorphosis, and Influence*, pp. 57–82; Albert Gelpi, *The Tenth Muse: The Psyche of the American Poet* (Cambridge: Harvard University Press, 1975), pp. 57–111; and Tony Tanner, *The Reign of Wonder: Naivety and Reality in American Literature* (New York: Harper and Row, 1967), pp. 26–45.

24. Regis Michaud, *Emerson, the Enraptured Yankee*, George Boas, trans. (New York: Harper and Brothers, 1930), p. 134.

25. Whicher, *Freedom and Fate*, p. 54. Whicher reminds us that, for Emerson, "to affirm the lack of a reality outside was only half the truth, unless reality were rediscovered inside; so Emerson moves from idealism to spiritualism."

26. Duncan, *The Power and Form of Emerson's Thought*, p. xii.

27. M. H. Abrams, *Natural Supernaturalism: Tradition and Revolution in Romantic Literature* (New York: W. W. Norton and Co., 1973), p. 117.

28. For an excellent study of the relationship between Carlyle and Emerson, see Kenneth Marc Harris, *Carlyle and Emerson: Their Long Debate* (Cambridge: Harvard University Press, 1978).

29. The sources of Emerson's thought have been thoroughly traced by David Lee Maulsby, Federic I. Carpenter, and most especially Kenneth Walter Cameron.

See David Lee Maulsby, *Emerson: His Contribution to Literature* (Tufts College, Mass.: Tufts College Press, 1911); Frederic I. Carpenter, *Emerson Handbook*; Kenneth Walter Cameron, *The Transcendentalists and Minerva: Cultural Backgrounds of the American Renaissance with Fresh Discoveries in the Intellectual Climate of Emerson, Alcott and Thoreau* (Hartford: Transcendental Books, 1963), 3 vols.; Kenneth Walter Cameron, *Transcendental Climate: New Resources for the Study of Emerson, Thoreau and Their Contemporaries* (Hartford: Transcendental Books, 1963), 3 vols.; Kenneth Walter Cameron, *Emerson's Transcendental Vision: An Exposition of His World View with an Analysis of the Structure, Backgrounds, and Meaning of Nature* (Hartford: Transcendental Books, 1971).

30. William H. Gilman, Alfred R. Ferguson, and Merrell R. Davis, eds., *The Journals and Miscellaneous Notebooks of Ralph Waldo Emerson* (Cambridge: Harvard University Press, 1961), 2:160, 238.

31. Wright, *Liberal Christians*, p. 38. Three excellent studies on the relationship between the religious views of Unitarians and the Transcendentalists are Harold C. Goddard, *Studies in New England Transcendentalism* (New York: Columbia University Press, 1908), especially pp. 1–5, 18–40; Clarence H. Faust, "The Background of the Unitarian Opposition to Transcendentalism," *Modern Philology* 35 (February 1938): 297–324; and William R. Hutchinson, *The Transcendentalist Ministers* (New Haven: Yale University Press, 1959).

32. Emerson criticism lacks any systematic treatment of this essay.

33. Joel Porte expresses a contrary view in *Representative Man: Ralph Waldo Emerson in His Time* (New York: Oxford University Press, 1979), pp. 163, 213.

34. Bishop, *Emerson on the Soul*, pp. 76–77.

35. Duncan, *The Power and Form of Emerson's Thought*, p. 91.

36. See Bishop, *Emerson on the Soul*, pp. 72–77, for his critique of the law of compensation.

37. Whicher, *Freedom and Fate*, p. 37.

38. Cox, "R. W. Emerson: The Circles of the Eye," in Levin, *Emerson: Prophecy, Metamorphosis, and Influence*, pp. 57–81.

39. See, for example, Vivian C. Hopkins, *Spires of Form: A Study of Emerson's Aesthetic Theory* (Cambridge: Harvard University Press, 1951), and R. A. Yoder, *Emerson and the Orphic Poet in America* (Berkeley: University of California Press, 1978).

40. Porte, *Emerson and Thoreau: Transcendentalists in Conflict*, p. 66.

41. Duncan, *The Power and Form of Emerson's Thought*, p. 89.

42. As with "The Method of Nature," there is, to my knowledge, no systematic treatment of "Nature II" (1844) despite its view of nature which is contrary to that in "Nature" (1836).

43. A. D. Van Nostrand, *Everyman His Own Poet*, p. 43.

44. As Carl Strauch puts it: "One is tempted to say that in ["Fate"] Emerson is escaping only by the skin of his teeth, for the reader is aware of a harsh undertone mingling with the strains of idealism that begin to dominate only toward the end. The mood throughout is not an exhilarating expansiveness, as in *Nature*, but rather a hard-won affirmation in the face of the 'odious facts' (Works, VI, 19)." "Emerson's Sacred Science," p. 243. In his discussion of "Fate," Daniel B. Shea asserts that this essay accomplishes "something more than the paper victory of dialectical opposition and synthesis," namely, Emerson's own metamorphosis into a new self

which can live in the world portrayed in this essay. He also claims that Emerson's "rediscovery of the relation between brokenness and grace makes him more the Puritan than when he first left the pulpit." "Emerson and the American Metamorphosis," in Levin, *Emerson: Prophecy, Metamorphosis, and Influence*, pp. 29–56.

45. Shea notes that "the double-consciousness, which is Intellect's version of the two-fold metamorphosis, sustains a creative antagonism in 'Fate' that converts any image—the steam locomotive, a piece of mosaic, 'reluctant granite'—to higher purpose." "Emerson and the American Metamorphosis," in Levin, *Emerson: Prophecy, Metamorphosis, and Influence*, pp. 47–48.

46. Joel Porte, in "Emerson, Thoreau, and the Double Consciousness," pp. 40–50, neglects this aspect of Emerson's understanding of the double consciousness.

47. "Fate" thus substantially qualifies the all-too-common assertion that Emerson either failed to confront the problem of evil or simply ignored the existence of evil. See, for example, Robert C. Pollock, "Ralph Waldo Emerson (1803–1882): The Single Vision," in Gardiner, *American Classics Reconsidered*, p. 28, and Henry James, *Partial Portraits* (London, 1919), who comments that Emerson's eyes were "thickly bandaged to the evil and sin of the world" (p. 31). It also qualifies that overemphasis upon Emerson's so-called "mystical" solution to the problem of evil which characterizes, for example, Frederic I. Carpenter's interpretation of Emerson's thought in *Emerson Handbook*.

48. Nor does Emerson's theodicy fit into any of the typologies for theodicies set forth in the works of Weber, Berger, and Douglas. See Introduction, note 10, and Chapter 4, note 14.

10. *MOBY-DICK*: AN UNORTHODOX THEODICY

1. Irving Wallace, David Wallechinsky, Amy Wallace, *Significa* (New York: E. P. Dutton, 1983), p. 272.

2. Yvor Winters, for example, in *Maule's Curse* (found in *Defense of Reason*) discusses how Melville's allegorical habit of mind is a legacy of Calvinism, though his interpretation of *Moby-Dick* neglects Melville's wide-ranging use of materials from the Calvinistic tradition. William H. Gilman stresses that, as Melville was growing up, he was exposed to both Calvinist theology and the theologically liberal views of his Unitarian father, and increasingly felt the tension between these two contrary theological viewpoints. See William Henry Gilman, *Melville's Early Life and Redburn* (New York: New York University Press, 1951), pp. 22–27, 79–82. Lawrance Thompson, in *Melville's Quarrel with God* (Princeton: Princeton University Press, 1952), treats the various religious themes in *Moby-Dick* in terms of their allegorical expression, but his analysis does not make the kinds of theological distinctions that were important to both conservative and liberal theologians of Melville's day. In *Melville's Religious Thought* (New York: Pageant Books, 1959), William Braswell discusses the religious faith of the Melville family but fails to describe in any detailed way the Calvinism that influenced Herman Melville, nor does he analyze how it influenced the themes and literary form of his fiction. And Thomas Walter Herbert, in *Moby-Dick and Calvinism*, discusses the tension between Calvinistic and liberal thought, both in Melville's life and in *Moby-Dick*, and makes the sweeping generalization that the novel "dismantles" western Christian monotheism altogether, a claim which overlooks the theologically constructive aspects of *Moby-Dick*.

3. Haroutunian, *Piety Versus Moralism*, pp. 157–76.
4. Owen, *The Works of John Owen* 10:508, 509; see also 10:595–607.
5. Haroutunian, *Piety Versus Moralism*, pp. 157–76.
6. Owen, *The Works of John Owen*, 10:547; see also 10:279–86.
7. Foster, *Objections to Calvinism*, p. 156.
8. Ahlstrom, *A Religious History of the American People* 1:442.
9. Haroutunian, *Piety Versus Moralism*, pp. 177–219.
10. Brooks, Lewis, and Warren, *American Literature* 1:922.
11. Ibid., 1:837.
12. Miller, *The Life of the Mind in America*, pp. 269–313; Merle Curti, *The Growth of American Thought* (New York: Harper and Row, 1964), pp. 517–39; Floyd Stovall, "The Decline of Romantic Idealism, 1855–1871," in Clark, *Transitions in American Literary History*, pp. 315–78; Bezanson's introduction to *Clarel*; Philip P. Wiener, *Evolution and the Founders of Pragmatism* (Cambridge: Harvard University Press, 1949), pp. 1–17; John Franzosa, "Darwin and Melville: Why a Tortoise?," *American Image: A Psychoanalytic Journal for Culture, Science and the Arts* (1976): 361–79. See also note 18 of Chapter 9.
13. Herbert, *Moby-Dick and Calvinism*, pp. 45–56.
14. See, for example, Brian Higgins and Hershel Parker, "The Flawed Grandeur of Melville's *Pierre*," in Faith Pullin, ed., *New Perspectives on Melville* (Kent, Ohio: Kent State University Press, 1978), pp. 162–96; Edgar A. Dryden, *Melville's Thematics of Form: The Great Art of Telling the Truth* (Baltimore: Johns Hopkins Press, 1968), pp. 115–48; Joyce Carol Oates, *The Edge of Impossibility: Tragic Forms in Literature* (New York: Vanguard Press, 1972), pp. 59–83; R. Milder, "Melville's Intentions in *Pierre*," *Studies in the Novel* 6 (Summer 1974): 186–99; C. C. Strictland, "Coherence and Ambivalence in Melville's *Pierre*," *American Literature* 48 (November 1976): 302–11; Karl F. Knight, "The Implied Author in Melville's *Pierre*," *Studies in American Fiction* 7 (Autumn 1979): 163–74; and Leon F. Seltzer, *The Vision of Melville and Conrad: A Comparative Study* (Athens: Ohio University Press, 1970), pp. 18–53.
15. Fussell, *Frontier*, pp. 280–94. Oates, who shares this view, denies Lewis Mumford's contention "that Melville 'conquered the white whale in his own consciousness' through the creation of *Moby-Dick*, [since] the appearance of *Pierre* in the following year would suggest that few problems had really been worked out, that even more had been discovered." *The Edge of Impossibility*, p. 66.
16. However, prior to this discovery, Pierre had already seen Isabel and greatly admired her beauty. The omniscient narrator sarcastically remarks that it is as much Pierre's sexual attraction to Isabel as any deep-seated ethical impulse which "invited him to champion the right." Herman Melville, *Pierre, or The Ambiguities*, Lawrance Thompson, ed. (New York: New American Library, 1964), p. 135. See Thompson's comments on the sexual relationship between Pierre and Isabel, pp. xvii–xix. (Page citations refer to this edition.) Contrary to those who, like Thompson, insist upon Pierre's incestuous desire for his sister, Oates argues that "the incest-motif might not be the concern or fear of the protagonist at all, but rather its opposite: he is really afraid of a healthy and normal love relationship." *The Edge of Impossibility*, p. 68.
17. Pierre's idealized image of his father, as the narrator tells us, "supported the entire one-pillared temple of his moral life. . . . Before this shrine, Pierre poured

out the fullness of all young life's most reverential thoughts and beliefs. Not to God had Pierre ever gone in his heart, unless by ascending the steps of that shrine, and so making it the vestibule of his abstractest religion" (p. 93). Pierre thus views God as the mirror image of his father.

18. As the narrator puts it, Pierre is "profoundly sensible that his whole previous moral being was overturned, and that for him the fair structure of the world must, in some then unknown way, be entirely rebuilded again, from the lowermost corner stone up. . . . He seemed to feel that in his deepest soul, lurked an indefinite but potential faith, which could rule in the interregnum of all hereditary beliefs, and circumstantial persuasions" (p. 113).

19. *Pierre*, pp. 388–89.

20. Frederick, *The Darkened Sky*, p. 100.

21. One can only wonder if Melville had in mind such comments as the following found in the *Boston Courier* when he composed Plinlimmon's pamphlet. The columnist describes an abolitionist as one who,

not having the guiding light of wisdom, either divine or human, ...is in that state of religious, moral, and intellectual confusion, which makes men mystics and fanatics, dreamers and schemers, always in conflict with practical truth, and rushing headlong after conclusions and aims, both moral and political, which neither religion nor natural reason do, or indeed can, possibly sanction. He has no settled principles which lead him to judge rightly and to act justly under all circumstances, and in the face of every question. His mind is crookedly warped; and he follows the tortuous windings of a perverse imagination from darkness to darkness, never coming to the light. He has broken clear of the restraints imposed by sovereign truth; and the region beyond it, in which he speculates and stumbles, is neither of heaven nor earth, but only that Fools' Paradise, in which unsettled minds roam through shadowy tracts of cloudland, and revel in places of dreams. (*Radicalism in Religion, Philosophy, and Social Life*, pp. 71–72.)

22. See Linwood Urban and Douglas N. Walton, eds., *The Power of God: Readings on Omnipotence and Evil* (New York: Oxford University Press, 1978), pp. 131–251.

23. This, in large part, derives not from Melville's portrayal of the gradual breakdown of Pierre's belief in the rationalistic theodicy and the destructive consequences of his acting in accordance with his vision of a demonic deity, but rather from a parallel dissolution in the narrator's own metaphysical outlook. At least the narrator expresses ideas no less nihilistic than Pierre's. Hence the narrative perspective itself further adds to the overall atmosphere of malaise and spiritual collapse which characterizes this novel. See note 14 of this chapter.

24. Howard P. Vincent, ed., *The Merrill Studies in Moby-Dick* (Columbus, Ohio: D. E. Merrill Publishing Co., 1969), p. 160.

25. Herbert, *Moby-Dick and Calvinism*, pp. 132, 162ff.

26. Ibid., pp. 159–78. See also Thomas Walter Herbert, Jr., "Calvinism and Cosmic Evil in *Moby-Dick*," *PMLA* 84 (October 1969): 1619.

27. For another critique of Herbert's argument, see Rowland A. Sherrill, *The Prophetic Melville: Experience, Transcendence, and Tragedy* (Athens: University of Georgia Press, 1979), p. 95, note 30.

28. See note 18 of Chapter 9 and note 12 of this chapter.

29. John Seelye, *Melville: The Ironic Diagram* (Evanston: Northwestern University Press, 1970), pp. 66–67.

30. Bewley, *The Eccentric Design*, pp. 197ff.

31. Vincent Buckley, *Poetry and the Sacred* (London: Chatto and Windus, 1968), pp. 160ff. John Frederick argues a variation of this position by contending that *Moby-Dick* has the theology of the Book of Job at its core. As such, he views *Moby-Dick* as a religious transition from what he calls the Christian perspective of *Mardi* to "the violently negative view" dramatized in *Pierre. The Darkened Sky*, pp. 87–104.

32. Herbert, *Moby-Dick and Calvinism*, pp. 125–26.

33. Newton Arvin, *Herman Melville* (New York: William Sloane Associates, 1950), pp. 188ff.

34. Thompson, *Melville's Quarrel with God*, pp. 192, 243. Thompson provides a "baldly stated summary" of his argument on pp. 242–43, but the argument proper begins on p. 188.

35. All page citations refer to Charles Feidelson, Jr., ed., *Moby-Dick or, The Whale* (New York: The Bobbs-Merrill Co., 1964).

36. For example, Ishmael's successive descriptions of Moby Dick during the three-day chase (pp. 537–39, 548, 559, 563) increasingly lose their imaginative quality as they become more realistic, as though Ishmael were demythologizing his original conception of the whale as a kind of grandiose god. Moreover, the older Ishmael describes Moby Dick in quite ordinary terms while narrating the Town-Ho's story (pp. 256, 259).

37. In this regard Daniel Hoffman writes that "Moby Dick is no more the God of *Moby-Dick* than Leviathan is the God of the Book of Job. The inscrutable Whale, titanic in power, lovely in motion, ubiquitous in space, immortal in time, is the ultimate demonstration and absolute convincement of all anarchic, individualistic, egotistical, human doubt that there is a God beyond the powers of man to plumb." *Form and Fable in American Fiction*, pp. 271–72.

38. W. H. Auden, *The Enchafèd Flood: or the Romantic Iconography of the Sea* (London: Faber and Faber, 1951), p. 103. Daniel Hoffman also argues this view when he asserts that Father Mapple's "sermon states the ethical standards against which the fates of Ahab, Ishmael, and the rest are subsequently measured." *Form and Fable in American Fiction* p. 236.

39. See, for example, Paul Brodtkorb, *Ishmael's White World: A Phenomenological Reading of Moby Dick* (New Haven: Yale University Press, 1965), pp. 56–57, and Hoffman, *Form and Fable in American Fiction*, p. 269.

40. Nathalia Wright, in *Melville's Use of the Bible* (Durham: Duke University Press, 1949), pp. 82–89, correctly notes that Father Mapple's sermon represents Jonah's career in a way that does not exactly correspond with the Book of Jonah. In accordance with her thesis that biblical "patterns of prophecy" shape the narrative of *Moby-Dick*, she contends that Father Mapple's sermon closely parallels the career of Jeremiah.

41. Father Mapple's portrait of a God who refuses humankind any familiarity with Him omits any reference to the last two chapters of the Book of Jonah, which describe a relenting, even familiar, God. In these last two chapters a paternal God seeks to persuade Jonah that, humanly speaking, His merciful forgiveness of the repentant Ninevites is both rational and morally appropriate. Omitting any consideration of this personal God enables Father Mapple to emphasize a God whose dealings with humankind transcend all rational and ethical notions of justice.

42. Hence these heroic admonitions which end Father Mapple's sermon are logically related to his narration of Jonah's story and are not, as Paul Brodtkorb contends, "a series of non sequiturs." *Ishmael's White World*, p. 57.

43. Indeed, seldom mentioned in the critical literature is Ahab's worrying sense of being old. His preoccupation with death crops up in various, often startling, ways. While secluded in the cabin with his groin injury, Ahab thinks about eternal life only to conclude that hell awaits the joyful and guilty alike. Ahab soon begins living more on deck than in his cabin because "It feels like going down into one's tomb" (p. 172); when the crew drinks to Ahab's quest, he remarks: "so brimming life is gulped and gone" (p. 223); he repeatedly dreams about hearses; the day prior to the three-day chase Ahab feels so old that he likens himself to "Adam, staggering beneath the piled centuries since Paradise" (p. 684); in a dying whale's movements he beholds an allegory confirming his belief that trust in God avails no man after death, and therefore he places his "prouder, if . . . darker faith" in the sea itself (p. 630). On his last day, however, Ahab allows himself one hopeful expression about an afterlife. He sees an analogy in a soft shower to leeward. "Such lovely leewardings! They must lead somewhere—to something else than common land, more palmy than the palms" (p. 711). Ahab's rapid-fire thoughts about his irrevocable oldness lead him to this brief meditation which closes his last exchange with Starbuck. "Some men die at ebb tide; some at low water; some at the full of the flood;— and I feel now like a billow that's all one crested comb, Starbuck. I am old;—shake hands with me, man" (p. 713). Starbuck weeps; Ahab tosses his arm aside and lowers for Moby Dick. Ahab's career, like that of Oedipus in *Oedipus at Colonus*, dramatizes an old man's sense that both his suffering and approaching death place him beyond all distinctions between good and bad.

44. Contrary arguments are set forth by Wright, *Melville's Use of the Bible*, p. 67; Howard P. Vincent, *The Trying Out of Moby-Dick* (Boston: Houghton Mifflin Co., 1949), pp. 72–75; and Newton Arvin, *Herman Melville*, pp. 179–80. Several other critics have also argued that Ahab's death is mandated by a divinely established moral order.

45. But in addition to this use of the Puritan doctrine of predestination to rationalize his quest to kill Moby Dick, Ahab—as Ishmael imagines him—also believes that Fedallah's three prophecies cannot be fulfilled, thereby assuring, in his mind, the success of his quest.

46. There is some truth in Herbert's assertion that Melville "uses Ahab to attack the notion that ethical insights may carry the authority of religious truth. To claim that the portrayal of Ahab's deterioration is meant to confirm a metaphysical standard of virtue is to miss the radicalism of Melville's explorations. As Matthiessen observes, Ahab's tragedy 'admits no adequate moral recognition'; we are given no cathartic moment of restoration to moral reality." But to further contend, as Herbert does, that no such "standard of virtue" emerges in the novel is to falsify the matter and to miss the novel's radical ethical implications. Herbert, *Moby-Dick and Calvinism*, p. 162.

47. *Moby-Dick*, pp. 623–24.

48. Lionel Trilling makes similar kinds of observations about the inadequacies of "the liberal imagination" in *The Liberal Imagination: Essays on Literature and Society* (Garden City, N.Y.: Anchor Books, 1953), pp. 1–19. See also Cushing

Strout, *The Veracious Imagination: Essays on American History, Literature, and Biography* (Middletown, Conn.: Wesleyan University Press, 1981), pp. 92–116.

49. David L. Minter, *The Interpreted Design*, pp. 140–44.

50. Ibid., pp. 17–35.

51. Ibid., pp. 18, 20. Minter's concern in elaborating this narrative device is chiefly the structural one of defining its evolution as a genre from its origins in seventeenth- and eighteenth-century Puritan writings through eighteenth- and nineteenth-century autobiographies to Nathaniel Hawthorne's *The Blithedale Romance*, F. Scott Fitzgerald's *The Great Gatsby*, and William Faulkner's *Absalom, Absalom!* Minter concludes that "the interpreted design as a prose form, at least in American literature, is archetypal" (p. 34). He adds, however, that "the interpreted design is significant, before and after all, because it has to do with man's existence and life and art" (p. 35).

52. Minter, however, does not provide a full-scale analysis of *Moby-Dick* in his book.

53. Brodtkorb, *Ishmael's White World* p. 102.

54. Ibid., pp. 102–39.

55. Ibid., p. 139.

56. A. D. Van Nostrand, *Everyman His Own Poet*, p. 113.

57. Ibid., p. 3.

58. Ibid., p. 140.

59. Many critics have recognized the centrality of the theme of rebirth in *Moby-Dick*, but the way in which Melville's pietistical leanings shaped the novel has largely been ignored. For a treatment of this subject, see William Rosenfeld, "Uncertain Faith: Queequeg's Coffin and Melville's Use of the Bible," *Texas Studies in Literature and Language* 7 (1966): 317–27.

60. Chronologically "The Try-Works" is out of sequence. The experience it records occurs while boiling down the first captured whale, and it is either the same or following day that Ahab soliloquizes to the whale's head (Ishmael's midnight meditation and Ahab's soliloquy share a common theme: overwhelming suffering and injustice). Ishmael's careful separation of these two meditations make his disengagement from Ahab's purpose appear slower than it is. It also emphasizes a far deeper sympathetic union with Ahab. For after Ishmael's crisis in "The Try-Works," he virtually disappears as a character in the novel and reappears (imaginatively) as Ahab, who now commands the center of attention, and as Starbuck.

61. *Moby-Dick*, p. 256. Also, see Hoffman, *Form and Fable in American Fiction*, p. 249. Brodtkorb contends that "Ishmael remains an habitual raconteur convivially telling tales . . . and because his tale of a whale is obsessively told—the product of almost total recall, invention, and what can best be termed extensively scholarly research—it may be suggested that the narrator is driven to tell it, as if he were a younger version of the ancient mariner, and his book the end result of many compulsive rehearsals. Ishmael is compelled to report and create meaning in what happened to him both despite, and because of, his sense of the uncertainty of meanings available to temporal man." *Ishmael's White World*, p. 138.

62. William Rosenfeld provides an excellent summary of various interpretations of Ishmael's survival and seeks to reconcile their differences in "Uncertain Faith: Queequeg's Coffin and Melville's Use of the Bible," pp. 317–27.

63. Alfred Kazin, "An Introduction to *Moby-Dick*," in *Discussions of Moby-Dick*, Milton R. Stern, ed. (Boston: D. C. Heath and Co., 1960), p. 57.

64. For example, see C. Hugh Holman, "The Reconciliation of Ishmael: *Moby-Dick* and the Book of Job," *South Atlantic Quarterly* 57 (1958): 477–90; Nathalia Wright, "*Moby-Dick:* Jonah's or Job's Whale?" *American Literature* 37 (1965): 190–95; and Janis Stout, "Melville's Use of the Book of Job," *Nineteenth-Century Fiction* 25 (June 1970): 69–83.

65. Brodtkorb, *Ishmael's White World*, p. 138. For a similar argument, see Dryden, *Melville's Thematics of Form*, pp. 83, 113.

66. See, for example, Bewley, *The Eccentric Design*, p. 156; M. O. Percival, *A Reading of Moby Dick* (Chicago: University of Chicago Press, 1950). pp. 121, 129; and Henry Nash Smith, "The Image of Society in *Moby-Dick*," in Tyrus Hillway and Luther S. Mansfield, eds., *Moby-Dick: Centennial Essays* (Dallas: Southern Methodist University Press, 1953), pp. 71–75. Daniel Hoffman offers a variation on this explanation. "Freed by his discovery in 'A Squeeze of the Hand,' of the organic unity of man with fellow-man, Ishmael wins his right to be the 'sole survivor' of the final catastrophe. Cast up by the sea, he is saved by the coffin prepared for his boon companion, Queequeg the cannibal, to whom the bonds of human love had bound him closest." *Form and Fable in American Fiction*, p. 235.

67. See, for example, R. E. Watters, "The Meanings of the White Whale," Stern, *Discussions of Moby-Dick*, pp. 84–85; Arvin, *Herman Melville*, p. 174; Minter, *The Interpreted Design*, p. 144; A. D. Van Nostrand, *Everyman His Own Poet*, p. 137; Sherrill, *The Prophetic Melville*, p. 169; and Leo Marx, *The Machine in the Garden: Technology and the Pastoral Ideal in America* (New York: Oxford University Press, 1968), p. 313. Gilmore presents a variation of this explanation when he argues that the Puritan covenant with God "forsaken by the nation at large survives in the person of Ishmael. . . . For Melville's objective in *Moby-Dick* is nothing less than to rewrite the covenant that God was to have made with the American people as the heirs of the biblical Hebrews. . . . By virtue of his redemption, in short, Ishmael figures as the saving remnant, a concept that the emigrant Puritans were wont to apply to themselves." *The Middle Way*, pp. 148, 149. See pages 143–51 for a fuller elaboration of this argument.

68. Brodtkorb, *Ishmael's White World*, p. 138.

69. For a broad sampling of the range of critical interpretation of Ishmael's response to Moby Dick's whiteness, see Watters, "The Meanings of the White Whale"; Edward Stone, "The Whiteness of 'The Whale,' " *College Language Association Journal* 18 (1975): 348–63; Khalil Husni, "The Whiteness of the Whale: a Survey of Interpretations, 1851–1970," *College Language Association Journal* 20 (1976): 210–21; Edward Stone, "More on the Whiteness of the Whale," *Melville Society Extracts* 41 (1980): 14–15; Claude Hunsberger, "Vectors in Recent *Moby-Dick* Criticism," *College Literature* 2 (1975): 230–45; and James Guetti, *The Limits of Metaphor: A Study of Melville, Conrad, and Faulkner* (Ithaca: Cornell University Press, 1967), pp. 22ff.

70. A. D. Van Nostrand contends that " 'The Mat-Maker' states what finally becomes Ishmael's theology." *Everyman His Own Poet*, p. 123.

71. Herbert provides a helpful analysis of Ishmael's critique of natural theology in *Moby-Dick and Calvinism*, pp. 136–40.

72. Fussell observes that, in *Moby-Dick*, there "are almost more allusions to the

West than to whaling; and the whales themselves, we quickly learn, are as often as not buffaloes." *Frontier*, p. 259.

73. This is Herbert's conclusion in *Moby-Dick and Calvinism*, pp. 161ff. Brodtkorb comes close to this same conclusion in *Ishmael's White World*, pp. 138–39, as does Dryden in *Melville's Thematics of Form*, pp. 83, 113.

74. Sherrill, *The Prophetic Melville*, pp. 143ff., takes this to be the normative image, both ethically and religiously, of *Moby-Dick*, or at least as revelatory of the kinds of moments that are normative for Ishmael.

75. Walter E. Bezanson, "*Moby-Dick*: Work of Art," Hillway and Mansfield, *Moby-Dick: Centennial Essays*, p. 40. See also Hoffman, *Form and Fable in American Fiction*, p. 277.

76. Brodtkorb, however, criticizes this aspect of Ishmael's narrative career. *Ishmael's White World*, pp. 138–39.

77. Hoffman, *Form and Fable in American Fiction*, pp. 236–40. See also John W. Young, "Ishmael's Development as Narrator: Melville's Synthesizing Process," *College Literature* 9 (Spring 1982): 97–111. As Robert E. Sayre notes, "finding new literary metaphors of the self required the greatest American audacity. . . . Melville, having fitted his earlier experiences into the formulas of captivity narratives and sea stories, eventually universalized his autobiography also. The self was at once a daring cosmic revolution and a pantheistical and calm solitary observer." Albert E. Stone, ed., *The American Autobiography* (Englewood Cliffs, N.J.: Prentice-Hall, 1981), pp. 23, 24.

78. William James, *Essays in Radical Empiricism and a Pluralistic Universe* (New York: Longmans, Green and Co., 1943), pp. 250–51.

79. Ibid., p. 318.

80. Giles Gunn proposes "that American writers have tended to imagine the experience of 'otherness' or the 'other' in three characteristic modes, which turn out on closer inspection to be distinctive of, but by no means confined to, three successive periods in the history of American culture. Having imagined the experience of 'otherness' in three different modes, I would contend that they have also proposed, respectively, three different ways of responding to it, have proposed, if you will, three very nearly generic definitions of what might be called 'the nature of true virtue.'" *The Interpretation of Otherness: Literature, Religion, and the American Imagination* (New York: Oxford University Press, 1979), pp. 202–3. The first is "the transcendental mode" which experiences "otherness" as "the expression of a God, Power, or Being" who is above or beyond human experience. The "appropriate form of response is some manifestation of 'the consent of being to Being'" (p. 203)—what Gunn calls "a kind of *transcendence upward*" (p. 204). "This is the mode of experience and resultant ethical orientation which typifies most American writing from the Puritan period through the first half of the nineteenth century" (p. 203). The second is "the social mode" in which "otherness" is experienced as the God who indwells people and is conceived in terms of human images. This mode redefines "virtue as a form of sympathy"—an "ethical ideal" which emphasizes the imaginative capacity "to feel with" others, "to project ourselves so completely into the interiority of their own distinctive inwardness that, as D. H. Lawrence once said, we 'feel with them as they feel with themselves.'" This Gunn calls "a kind of *transcendence outward*" (p. 204). This mode, he contends, typically characterizes much American writing from 1850 to 1925. He finds "the

immanental mode" emerging during the second quarter of the twentieth century (p. 206). This mode experiences "otherness" as "the astonishing numinousness of things as they are" (p. 205), and the appropriate response is "to become utterly transparent to the 'other,' " to become the other, and thereby achieve "a kind of . . . *transcendence downward*" (p. 207). Ishmael's notion of virtue clearly corresponds to that which Gunn describes in "the social mode" even though his experience of "otherness" must be characterized in radically different terms. Indeed, it is Ishmael's vision of a pluralistic universe which compels him to define virtue as a form of sympathetically imagining the "otherness" of others.

81. James, *Essays in Radical Empiricism and a Pluralistic Universe*, pp. 321–22.

82. Ibid., p. 327.

83. Ibid., pp. 124ff.

84. In *Literary Democracy*, pp. 260–79, Larzer Ziff discussed how Melville's portrayal of "the democratic hero" in his works, especially in *Moby-Dick*, articulates his concern about expressing and affirming democratic values through his artistry.

Selected Bibliography

Ahlstrom, Sydney, E. *A Religious History of the American People.* 2 Vols. Garden City, New York: Image Books, 1975.

Albanese, Catherine L. *Sons of the Fathers: The Civil Religion of the American Revolution.* Philadelphia: Temple University Press, 1976.

Anderson, Quentin. *The Imperial Self: An Essay in American Literary and Cultural History.* New York: Alfred A. Knopf, 1971.

Auden, W. H. *The Enchafèd Flood: or The Romantic Iconography of the Sea.* London: Faber and Faber, 1951.

Axelsson, Arne. *The Links in the Chain: Isolation and Interdependence in Nathaniel Hawthorne's Fictional Characters.* Uppsala: Uppsala University Press, 1974.

Bailyn, Bernard. *The Ideological Origins of the American Revolution.* Cambridge: Harvard University Press, 1976.

———. *The New England Merchants in the Seventeenth Century.* Cambridge: Harvard University Press, 1955.

Baym, Nina. *The Shape of Hawthorne's Career.* Ithaca: Cornell University Press, 1976.

Bellah, Robert N. *The Broken Covenant: American Civil Religion in Time of Trial.* New York: Seabury Press, 1975.

Bercovitch, Sacvan. *The Puritan Origins of the American Self.* New Haven: Yale University Press, 1975.

———, ed. *The American Imagination: Essays in Revaluation.* New York: Cambridge University Press, 1974.

———, ed. *Typology and Early American Literature.* Amherst: University of Massachusetts Press, 1972.

Bewley, Marius. *The Eccentric Design: Form in the Classic American Novel.* New York: Columbia University Press, 1963.

Bishop, Jonathan. *Emerson on the Soul*. Cambridge: Harvard University Press, 1964.

Braswell, William. *Melville's Religious Thought*. New York: Pageant Books, 1959.

Brauer, Jerald C., ed. *Religion and the American Revolution*. Philadelphia: Fortress Press, 1976.

Bridenbough, Carl. *Cities in the Wilderness: The First Century of Urban Life in America, 1625–1742*. New York: The Ronald Press, 1938.

Brodtkorb, Paul. *Ishmael's White World: A Phenomenological Reading of Moby Dick*. New Haven: Yale University Press, 1965.

Brooks, Cleanth; Lewis, R. W. B.; and Warren, Robert Penn. *American Literature: The Makers and the Making, Beginnings to 1861*. Vol. 1. New York: St. Martin's Press, 1973.

Brown, Arthur W. *William Ellery Channing*. New York: Twayne Publishers, 1961.

Brumm, Ursula. *American Thought and Religious Typology*. New Brunswick: Rutgers University Press, 1970.

Buckley, Vincent. *Poetry and the Sacred*. London: Chatto and Windus, 1968.

Buell, Lawrence. *Literary Transcendentalism: Style and Vision in the American Renaissance*. Ithaca: Cornell University Press, 1973.

Carpenter, Frederick I. *Emerson Handbook*. New York: Hendricks House, 1953.

Carroll, Peter N. *Puritanism and the Wilderness: The Intellectual Significance of the New England Frontier, 1629–1700*. New York: Columbia University Press, 1969.

Chase, Robert. *The American Novel and Its Tradition*. New York: Anchor Books, 1957.

Cherry, Conrad. *God's New Israel: Religious Interpretations of American Destiny*. Englewood Cliffs, New Jersey: Prentice-Hall, 1971.

———. *The Theology of Jonathan Edwards: A Reappraisal*. Gloucester, Massachusetts: Peter Smith, 1974.

Clebsch, William A. *American Religious Thought: A History*. Chicago: University of Chicago Press, 1973.

———. *From Sacred to Profane America: The Role of Religion in American History*. New York: Harper and Row, 1968.

Commager, Henry Steele. *The Empire of Reason: How Europe Imagined and America Realized the Enlightenment*. Garden City, New York: Anchor Press, 1977.

Cowing, Cedric B. *The Great Awakening and the American Revolution: Colonial Thought in the Eighteenth Century*. Chicago: Rand McNally, 1971.

Crews, Frederick. *The Sins of the Fathers: Hawthorne's Psychological Themes*. New York: Oxford University Press, 1966.

Cutler, Donald R., ed. *The Religious Situation: 1968*. Boston: Beacon Press, 1968.

Dauber, Kenneth. *Rediscovering Hawthorne*. Princeton: Princeton University Press, 1977.

Dekker, George. *James Fenimore Cooper: The Novelist*. London: Routledge and Kegan Paul, 1967.

DeLattre, Roland. *Beauty and Sensibility in the Thought of Jonathan Edwards: An Essay in Aesthetics and Theological Ethics*. New Haven: Yale University Press, 1968.

Demos, John Putnam. *Entertaining Satan: Witchcraft and the Culture of Early New England*. New York: Oxford University Press, 1983.

Dryden, Edgar A. *Melville's Thematics of Form: The Great Art of Telling the Truth*. Baltimore: Johns Hopkins Press, 1968.

————. *Nathaniel Hawthorne: The Poetics of Enchantment*. Ithaca: Cornell University Press, 1977.

Duncan, Jeffrey L. *The Power and Form of Emerson's Thought*. Charlottesville: University Press of Virginia, 1973.

Elder, Marjorie J. *Nathaniel Hawthorne: Transcendental Symbolist*. Columbus: Ohio University Press, 1969.

Elliott, Emory. *Power and the Pulpit in Puritan New England*. Princeton: Princeton University Press, 1975.

————, ed. *Puritan Influences in American Literature*. Urbana: University of Illinois Press, 1979.

Elwood, Douglas, J. *The Philosophical Theology of Jonathan Edwards*. New York: Columbia University Press, 1960.

Emerson, Everett H. *Major Writers of Early American Literature*. Madison: University of Wisconsin Press, 1972.

————, ed. *American Literature, 1764–1789: The Revolutionary Years*. Madison: University of Wisconsin Press, 1977.

Erdt, Terrence. *Jonathan Edwards: Art and the Sense of the Heart*. Amherst: University of Massachusetts Press, 1980.

Erikson, Kai T. *Wayward Puritans: A Study in the Sociology of Deviance*. New York: John Wiley, 1966.

Feidelson, Charles, Jr. *Symbolism in American Literature*. Chicago: University of Chicago Press, 1959.

Fields, Wayne, ed. *James Fenimore Cooper: A Collection of Critical Essays*. Englewood Cliffs, New Jersey: Prentice-Hall, 1979.

Fogle, Richard H. *Hawthorne's Fiction: The Light and the Dark*. Norman: University of Oklahoma Press, 1969.

Fossum, Robert H. *Hawthorne's Inviolable Circle: The Problem of Time*. Deland, Florida: Everett/Edwards, 1973.

Foster, Stephen. *Their Solitary Way*. New Haven: Yale University Press, 1971.

Frederick, John. *The Darkened Sky: Nineteenth-Century American Novelists and Religion*. Notre Dame: University of Notre Dame Press, 1969.

Fussell, Edwin. *Frontier: American Literature and the American West*. Princeton: Princeton University Press, 1970.

Geertz, Clifford. *The Interpretation of Cultures*. New York: Basic Books, 1973.

Gelpi, Albert. *The Tenth Muse: The Psyche of the American Poet*. Cambridge: Harvard University Press, 1975.

Gilmore, Michael T. *The Middle Way: Puritanism and Ideology in American Romantic Fiction*. New Brunswick: Rutgers University Press, 1977.

Grossman, James. *James Fenimore Cooper*. Stanford: Stanford University Press, 1967.

Guetti, James. *The Limits of Metaphor: A Study of Melville, Conrad, and Faulkner*. Ithaca: Cornell University Press, 1967.

Gunn, Giles. *The Interpretation of Otherness: Literature, Religion, and the American Imagination*. New York: Oxford University Press, 1979.

Hall, David. *The Faithful Shepherd: A History of the New England Ministry in the Seventeenth Century*. Chapel Hill: University of North Carolina Press, 1972.

Haroutunian, Joseph. *Piety Versus Moralism: The Passing of the New England Theology.* New York: Henry Holt and Company, 1932.

Heimert, Alan. *Religion and the American Mind: From the Great Awakening to the Revolution.* Cambridge: Harvard University Press, 1969.

Herbert, Thomas Walter, Jr. *Moby-Dick and Calvinism: A World Dismantled.* New Brunswick: Rutgers University Press, 1977.

Hillway, Tyrus, and Mansfield, Luther S., eds. *Moby-Dick: Centennial Essays.* Dallas: Southern Methodist University Press, 1953.

Hoffman, Daniel G. *Form and Fable in American Fiction.* New York: Oxford University Press, 1961.

Hopkins, Vivian C. *Spires of Form: A Study of Emerson's Aesthetic Theory.* Cambridge: Harvard University Press, 1951.

Horwitz, Robert H., ed. *The Moral Foundations of the American Republic.* Charlottesville: University Press of Virginia, 1977.

James, Henry. *Hawthorne.* New York: Collier Books, 1966.

Jones, Howard Mumford. *O Strange New World; American Culture: The Formative Years.* New York: Viking Press, 1965.

Jones, James W. *The Shattered Synthesis: New England Puritanism Before the Great Awakening.* New Haven: Yale University Press, 1973.

Kaul, A. N. *The American Vision: Actual and Ideal Society in Nineteenth-Century Fiction.* New Haven: Yale University Press, 1963.

Koch, Adrienne. *The American Enlightenment.* New York: George Braziller, 1965.

Konvitz, Milton R., and Whicher, Stephen E., eds. *Emerson: A Collection of Critical Essays.* Englewood Cliffs, New Jersey: Prentice-Hall, 1962.

Kurtz, Stephen G., and Hudson, James H., eds. *Essays on the American Revolution.* New York: W. W. Norton and Co., 1973.

Lawrence, D. H. *Studies in Classic American Literature.* New York: Doubleday and Co., 1951.

Levin, David, ed. *Emerson: Prophecy, Metamorphosis and Influence.* New York: Columbia University Press, 1975.

Levin, Harry. *The Power of Blackness: Hawthorne, Poe, Melville.* New York: Vintage Books, 1958.

Lewis, R. W. B. *The American Adam: Innocence, Tragedy, and Tradition in the Nineteenth Century.* Chicago: University of Chicago Press, 1966.

Lowrie, Ernest Benson. *The Shape of the Puritan Mind.* New Haven: Yale University Press, 1974.

Ludwig, Allan I. *Graven Images: New England Stonecarving and its Symbols, 1650–1815.* Middletown, Connecticut: Wesleyan University Press, 1966.

Lynen, John. *The Design of the Present: Essays on Time and Form in American Literature.* New Haven: Yale University Press, 1969.

McPherson, Hugo. *Hawthorne as Myth-Maker: A Study in Imagination.* Toronto: University of Toronto Press, 1971.

Male, Roy R. *Hawthorne's Tragic Vision.* New York: W. W. Norton, 1957.

Martin, Terence. *Nathaniel Hawthorne.* New York: Twayne Publishers, 1965.

Marx, Leo. *The Machine in the Garden: Technology and the Pastoral Ideal in America.* New York: Oxford University Press, 1968.

Matthiessen, F. O. *American Renaissance: Art and Expression in the Age of Emerson and Whitman.* New York: Oxford University Press, 1968.

May, Henry F. *The Enlightenment in America.* New York: Oxford University Press, 1976.

Mead, Sidney E. *The Lively Experiment: The Shaping of Christianity in America.* New York: Harper and Row, 1963.

Michaud, Regis. *Emerson, the Enraptured Yankee.* Translated by George Boas. New York: Harper and Brothers, 1930.

Miller, Perry. *Errand into the Wilderness.* New York: Harper and Row, 1956.

———. *The Life of the Mind in America: From the Revolution to the Civil War.* New York: Harcourt, Brace and World, Inc., 1965.

———. *The New England Mind: From Colony to Province.* Boston: Beacon Press, 1966.

Minter, David. *The Interpreted Design as a Structural Principle in American Prose.* New Haven: Yale University Press, 1969.

Morgan, Edmund S. *The Puritan Family: Religion and Domestic Relations in Seventeenth-Century New England.* New York: Harper and Row, 1966.

———. *Visible Saints: The History of a Puritan Idea.* Ithaca: Cornell University Press, 1963.

———, ed. *The American Revolution: Two Centuries of Interpretation.* Englewood Cliffs, New Jersey: Prentice-Hall, 1968.

———, ed. *Puritan Political Ideas: 1558–1794.* Indianapolis: Bobbs-Merrill, 1978.

Morison, Samuel Eliot. *The Intellectual Life of Colonial New England.* Ithaca: Cornell University Press, 1970.

Morris, Richard B. *The American Revolution Reconsidered.* New York: Harper and Row, 1967.

Normand, Jean. *Nathaniel Hawthorne: An Approach to an Analysis of Artistic Creation.* Translated by Derek Coltman. Cleveland: Case Western Reserve University Press, 1970.

Oates, Joyce Carol. *The Edge of Impossibility: Tragic Forms in Literature.* New York: Vanguard Press, 1972.

Paul, Sherman. *Emerson's Angle of Vision: Man and Nature in American Experience.* Cambridge: Harvard University Press, 1952.

———, ed. *Six Classic American Writers: An Introduction.* Minneapolis: University of Minnesota Press, 1970.

Percival, M. O. *A Reading of Moby Dick.* Chicago: University of Chicago Press, 1950.

Pettit, Norman. *The Heart Prepared: Grace and Conversion in Puritan Spiritual Life.* New Haven: Yale University Press, 1966.

Phillips, Mary E. *James Fenimore Cooper.* New York: John Lane Co., 1913.

Poirier, Richard. *A World Elsewhere: The Place of Style in American Literature.* New York: Oxford University Press, 1966.

Pope, Robert G. *The Half-Way Covenant: Church Membership in Puritan New England.* Princeton: Princeton University Press, 1969.

Porte, Joel. *Emerson and Thoreau: Transcendentalists in Conflict.* Middletown, Connecticut: Wesleyan University Press, 1966.

———. *Representative Man: Ralph Waldo Emerson in His Time.* New York: Oxford University Press, 1979.

Porter, David. *Emerson and Literary Change.* Cambridge: Harvard University Press, 1978.

Pullin, Faith, ed. *New Perspectives on Melville*. Kent, Ohio: Kent State University Press, 1978.

Railton, Stephen. *Fenimore Cooper: A Study of His Life and Imagination*. Princeton: Princeton University Press, 1978.

Reintz, Richard, comp. *Tensions in American Puritanism*. New York: Wiley Press, 1970.

Ringe, Donald A. *James Fenimore Cooper*. New York: Twayne Publishers, 1962.

Rutman, Darrett A. *American Puritanism: Faith and Practice*. New York: J. B. Lippincott, 1970.

Schubert, Leland. *Hawthorne, the Artist: Fine-Art Devices in Fiction*. New York: Russell and Russell, 1963.

Seelye, John. *Melville: The Ironic Diagram*. Evanston: Northwestern University Press, 1970.

Seltzer, Leon F. *The Vision of Melville and Conrad: A Comparative Study*. Athens: Ohio University Press, 1970.

Shapiro, Charles, ed. *Twelve Original Essays on Great American Novels*. Detroit: Wayne State University Press, 1958.

Shea, Daniel B. *Spiritual Autobiography in Early America*. Princeton: Princeton University Press, 1968.

Sherrill, Rowland A. *The Prophetic Melville: Experience, Transcendence, and Tragedy*. Athens: University of Georgia Press, 1979.

Smith, Elwyn A., ed. *The Religion of the Republic*. Philadelphia: Fortress Press, 1971.

Smith, Henry Nash. *Virgin Land: The American West as Symbol and Myth*. New York: Vintage Books, 1950.

Smith, James Ward, and Jamison, A. Leland, eds. *The Shaping of American Religion*. Princeton: Princeton University Press, 1969.

Spiller, Robert E. *Fenimore Cooper: Critic of His Times*. New York: Minton, Balch and Co., 1931.

———. *James Fenimore Cooper*. Minneapolis: University of Minnesota Press, 1965.

———. *The Oblique Light: Studies in Literary History and Biography*. New York: Macmillan Co., 1968.

Stein, William Bysshe. *Hawthorne's Faust: A Study of the Devil Archetype*. Hamden, Connecticut: Archon Books, 1968.

Stern, Milton R., ed. *Discussions of Moby-Dick*. Boston: D. C. Heath and Co., 1960.

Stoehr, Taylor. *Hawthorne's Mad Scientists: Pseudoscience and Social Science in Nineteenth-Century Life and Letters*. Hamden, Connecticut: Archon Books, 1978.

Stubbs, John Caldwell. *The Pursuit of Form: A Study of Hawthorne and the Romance*. Urbana: University of Illinois Press, 1970.

Tanner, Tony. *The Reign of Wonder: Naivety and Reality in American Literature*. New York: Harper and Row, 1967.

Tharpe, Jac. *Nathaniel Hawthorne: Identity and Knowledge*. Carbondale: Southern Illinois University Press, 1967.

Thompson, Lawrance. *Melville's Quarrel with God*. Princeton: Princeton University Press, 1952.

Turner, Arline. *Hawthorne: A Biography*. New York: Oxford University Press, 1980.

Van Nostrand, A. D. *Everyman His Own Poet: Romantic Gospels in American Literature*. New York: McGraw-Hill, 1968.

Vaughan, Alden, T. *New England Frontier: Puritans and Indians, 1620–1675*. Boston: Little, Brown, 1965.

Vaughan, Alden T., and Billas, George Athan, eds. *Perspectives on Early American History: Essays in Honor of Richard B. Morris*. New York: Harper and Row, 1973.

Vincent, Howard P., *The Trying Out of Moby-Dick*. Boston: Houghton Mifflin Co., 1949.

————, ed. *The Merrill Studies in Moby-Dick*. Columbus, Ohio: D. E. Merrill Publishing Co., 1969.

Wagenknecht, Edward. *Nathaniel Hawthorne: Man and Writer*. New York: Oxford University Press, 1961.

Waggoner, Hyatt H. *Emerson as Poet*. Princeton: Princeton University Press, 1974.

————. *Hawthorne: A Critical Study*. Cambridge: Harvard University Press, 1967.

————. *The Presence of Hawthorne*. Baton Rouge: Louisiana State University Press, 1979.

Warren, Austin. *The New England Conscience*. Ann Arbor: University of Michigan Press, 1966.

Whicher, Stephen E. *Freedom and Fate: An Inner Life of Ralph Waldo Emerson*. Philadelphia: University of Pennsylvania Press, 1975.

White, Eugene. *Puritan Rhetoric: The Issue of Emotion in Religion*. Carbondale: Southern Illinois University Press, 1972.

Wright, Conrad. *The Beginnings of Unitarianism in America*. Boston: Beacon Press, 1966.

————. *The Liberal Christians: Essays on American Unitarian History*. Boston: Beacon Press, 1970.

Yoder, R. A. *Emerson and the Orphic Poet in America*. Berkeley: University of California Press, 1978.

Ziff, Larzer. *Literary Democracy: The Declaration of Cultural Independence in America*. New York: Viking Press, 1981.

————. *Puritanism in America: New Culture in a New World*. New York: Viking Press, 1973.

Index

About the Author

RICHARD FORRER is Associate Professor of Religion at Texas Christian University. His articles have appeared in such journals as *Comparative Drama, Journal of the American Academy of Religion, The Southern Literary Journal,* and *Journal of the American Studies Association of Texas.*